Life and Teachings of Sri Ma Anandamayi

A Bird on the Wing

Sri Garib Das Oriental Series No. 243

Life and Teachings of Sri Ma Anandamayi

A Bird on the Wing

Bithika Mukerji

Sri Satguru Publications
A Division of
Indian Books Centre
Delhi, India

Published by
Sri Satguru Publications,
Indological and Oriental Publishers
A Division of
Indian Books Centre
40/5, Shakti Nagar,
Delhi-110007
India

Email: ibcindia@vsnl.com
Website: http://www.indianbookscentre.com

First Edition : Delhi : 1998
Paperback Edition : Delhi, 2005

ISBN 81-7030-810-0

Phototypeset by Dhirendra K. Sahoo B/1/159 Assi Sagam ; Varanasi 221005

Printed at Chawla Offset Printers, Delhi 110 052

Verily I am one with everyone, after all, there is the One Supreme Being alone, isn't it so?

Sri Ma Anadamayi
(S.S. Vol. II, p. 1)

eṣa ha devaḥ pradiśonu sarvāḥ
pūrvo hi jātaḥ sa u garbhe antaḥ:
sa eva jātaḥ sa janiṣyamānaḥ –
pratyanjanaṁs
tiṣṭhati sarvatomukhaḥ.

Śvetāśvataropanīṣad II.16

This God, in soothe, in all the quarters is long, long ago indeed, he had his birth, he verily (is now) within the germ. He has been born, he will be born, behind all who have birth he stands, with face on every side.

Preface

It is often said, and with some truth, that India is a land of saints and god-men. A list of spiritual teachers who have attained world renown in the last decades of this century would indeed be a long one. It will not be right, however, to situate Sri Ma Anandamayi amid this company. It is true that she occupied a position of great authority as an upholder of the traditions of India, but this she did by virtue of her way of being in the world, rather than anything else. She professed no philosophy of her own, nor formulated any messages for humanity, except the one *vāṇi* (utterance): *hari kathai katha ārsab vṛthā vyathā* (to talk of God alone is worthwhile, all else is verily pain and in vain), and its many variations. She promised nothing and unless asked specifically, had nothing to say. In spite of this, her aura of spiritual eminence attracted people to her wherever she happened to be. Her incomparable charming smile and her gentle enquiries regarding the welfare of the visitors, kept them enthralled. This happened invariably, in big towns, villages, wayside inns, temple verandas or in the houses of devotees. Sometimes people who passed her on roads or on mountain paths, would stop to glance back and then they would retrace their steps to her as if they had encountered a long-lost friend. Sri Ma greeted all such chance-met strangers in her own inimitable style of familiarity which at once overcame all barriers of language, creed or social status.

On leaving Dhaka in 1932 Sri Ma Anandamayi came to Dehra Dun in the northern part of India, a distance of more than a thousand miles. Within a very short time she became the focal point of the gatherings of a large number of people who did not speak her language. I once asked Mahalakshmiji, a very prominent member of this group. 'Tell me, how was it that you, your family, your friends, your entire community became so attached to Sri Ma? You, after all, saw only a young married woman, accompanied by an attendant (Bhaiji) as you thought him in the beginning, staying simply on the open veranda of a Temple in the manner of poor pilgrims. She did not speak your language so you could not have communicated with her directly. She showed you no miracles or divine powers. So what was the secret which brought the rather sophisticated large Kashmiri community of this big town to her feet?'

Mahalaksmiji showed her impatience with such a nonsensical question. 'Don't be stupid', she said, 'what miracle should she show us? She herself was the greatest miracle! To look upon her, to sit near her was fulfilment itself.' If Mahalaksmiji had been familiar with scriptural texts she may have cited the following one:

bhidyate hṛdayagranthiśn *chidyante sarvasaṁśayāḥ;*
kṣīyante cāsya karmāṇi tasmin dṛṣṭe parāvare.

Muṇḍakopanisad II.2.9

The knot of the heart is penetrated, all doubts are dissolved, all bondage destroyed on beholding Him who is here and beyond.

This experience was repeated many times. In Gujrat, South India, or the Punjab, people had no difficulty in establishing immediate contact. These new devotees, to begin with, knew nothing of her early life, her years of house keeping or of *sādhanā* or what she would have to say to them had she been able to speak their languages. For them also her presence was fulfilment itself.

In Dhaka where she first gained public renown, she was hailed as '*Mānuṣ Kālī* that is Kālī in human form because the Goddess Kālī is especially dear to the heart of the people of Bengal. When she travelled to South India, she would be surrounded by crowds wherever she stopped for a while. One of Sri Ma's attendants was interested enough to ask a few of them in Madurai their reason for showing such devotion to a person who apart from giving them her inimitable smile and singing *kīrtan* ('*he bhagavāna*') did nothing for them ? The answer was simple. For them she was the visible form of their Goddess Mīnākṣī who was inside the Temple and that Sri Ma's '*darśana*' (audience, seeing) was enough. ('Sri Ma Herself is Devī Mīnākṣī' The

Executive officer of the Temple, 17th November 1952 DD. Vol. XI p. 54). In the Punjab, in Hoshiarpur, she was given the same place of honour as the Holy Granth Sahab by her Sikh devotees. ('We do not distinguish between Sri Ma and He who we call the Akala Puruṣa' Bhai Lakṣman at Jallandhar to Dhirendra M. Datta A.V. 1991 no. 1, p. 34).

Instead of multiplying such instances, perhaps it will not be out of place to recall here, the background of the Indian religious consciousness which lends itself easily to such phenomena: The Names and Forms of God are many, in fact, infinite would be a better word. The generic term which is most commonly used in sacred literature for God is, *saccidānanda*. Without going into the exegesis of the word it may be said that it is the personalized form of the Upaniṣadic statement about the Supreme Reality or Brahman. People of India embrace the idea that the presence of God is not only all-pervasive and ever-abiding but also responsive to invocatory prayers. The intermingling of the dimensions of transcendence and immanence is emphasized repeatedly in all forms of religious literature. He, who in essence is without Form assumes countless ones in order that a devotee may find refuge at His feet. He is not apart from His creation but ever with it. The spiritual longings of humankind in quest of God coalesce and give shape to various Images which an artist may concretise in a variety of media: clay, wood, metal, stone, paper or canvas. The many Images are thus not many gods but are different Forms of the same ultimate reality *saccidānanda*. This accounts for the proliferation of Images in our own age. The ancient Temples, however, hold true to their own traditions, faithfully adhering to relevant sacred texts.

This way of relating to God is peculiar to Hinduism. Sri Ma Anandamayi, at times likened it to the various roles a man is required to assume in the world. The same man is father, son, friend, husband, superior or junior officer etc. to different people. A son knows about his father's many commitments but his own attachment flows along the singular relationship of son to father. This dimension of a personal attachment to God as Father, Mother, Friend, Child, Beloved or Master explains the meaning of the phrase '*iṣṭa-devatā*'. *Iṣṭa* means 'most desirable' and '*devatā*' indicates the particular Image of God that inspires the devotee to his greatest effort toward spiritual emancipation. The God-Image (*Iṣṭa-devatā*) most dear to the heart of a man is his personal key to the mystery of the divine cosmic panorama that he seeks to unravel. All who worship the same *Iṣṭa-devatā* become a brotherhood, a *sampradāya*. We thus have *Vaiṣṇava-sampradāya* or *Śaiva-sampradāya* or *Śāktas, Gāṇapatyas* and so on. These are distinctive ways of worship but they are not contradictory to each other. A poet gives expression to this sentiment:

Maheśware va jagatāmadhīśvare
Janardane va jagadāntarātmani
dvayorna bheda pratipattırasti me
tathāpi bhaktistaruṇendūśekhare.

(From Bhartṛhari's *Vairāgya Sataka*)

My faith is that there is no difference between Śiva, the Lord of the Universe and Nārāyaṇa, the Indwelling spirit of creation, yet my devotion goes to Him who (supports) the young moon on his crest (that is Śiva).

The variety in the ways of relating to God, is therefore, pleasing to the Hindu. They look upon it as an enrichment. Even declared enemies of God are not excluded from the tally of grest devotees because by the sheer power of one-pointed concentration, they may arrive sooner than the friends of the Lord. Religious literature is replete with the ramifications of this theme.

A book about Sri Ma Anandamayi, therefore, is required to deal with the whole panorama of the Hindu vision of reality and then to go beyond it because no parametres of religious convictions can be placed to delimit her freedom to be herself. One must keep in mind her oft-repeated words, 'I am what *you* think I am.' By these words, she seemed to have installed herself in every heart which was aware of her, irrespective of religion, country, sex or age.

This book then, is in the nature of an invitation to a *satsang*. A *satsang* is a gathering of like-minded people who meet occasionally to listen to the *lilā-kathā* of the Person they cherish in their hearts. A *lilā-kathā* is a descriptive tale, a recounting of the delightful ways of the Person who holds the centre of attention in a *satsang*. Since all paths are viable, the raconteur is not aiming at any conversions, but the narrative could be so interesting as to command the attentions of even passers by. A *satsang* is for a strengthening of the devout way of life; a sharing of the delight of conviction that God is ever near and sometimes, perhaps the touching of an erstwhile indifferent heart.

In this connection, the memory of a particular *satsang* comes to mind. This was in Varanasi, many years ago. A mammoth crowd had gathered to listen to the enchanting *līlā-kathā* of the Child Krishna. The speaker was the great scholar and ascetic, Swami Akhandanandaji of Vrindaban. The crowd would sit in pin-drop silence for two to three hours every day. At the conclusion of each session, it is customary for the audience to loudly pronounce *jayadhvanis*, that is, 'victory to Sri Krishna' and other similar cheers. This crowd after enthusiastically shouting all the regular *jayas* (cheers), ended up as one man with the sonorous and resounding '*Hara Hara Mahādeva, namaḥ Pārvatīpataye*' (Śiva, Śiva, Śiva, salutation to the consort of Parvati) which seemed hardly apposite till one remembered that the town being Varanasi, the crowd must have consisted mostly of Śaivaites. After listening devoutly to *Krishna-kathā*, they reiterated their allegiance to Śiva by the age-old salutation which is peculiar to Varanasi and a common mode of public acclaim.

There is all the strength of an ancient tradition in this behavioural pattern. The profundity of religious consciousness which allows one to be loyal to one's own *Iṣṭa* while paying homage to another can be gauged by those only who are used to looking upon the many Images as identical with the One Reality who alone is. This is true dialogue; listening 'to the other' is ingrained in the Indian ethos. Moreover it is possible in India that an ascetic who is a Vedantist, should give a discourse on *Krishna-kathā*.

This book then is not a biography. Indeed it is neither necessary nor possible to write a biography of Sri Ma Anandamayi, because she did not 'grow up' or 'develop' into what she was not at birth. It is true that her body was small and she became aged as time passed but as far as the indwelling spirit is concerned, nothing happened which left its influence on it. It was always free and sufficient unto itself. We shall then, recall, the different facets of her behaviour as they were seen by her own people in the villages where she grew up, by other devotees and admirers who came in contact with her in later years. Sri Ma sometimes referred to herself as a *uḍā pākhi*, that is, a bird on the wing; a bird which is free to alight on random perches and then fly off again. The title of the book is Sri Ma's description of herself.

We shall try to keep to a semblance of chronological order although strictly speaking in the case of this *līlā-kathā*, if could only be superfluous. After all has been said and written no doubt I shall remain as far away from gauging the enigmatic personality of Sri Ma Anandamayi as on the first day of encounter almost sixty years ago.

May Sri Ma's *kheyala* prevail. Jai Ma.

Mahāśivarātri, 1997
31, George Town
Allàhabad - 211002

I had boasted among men that I had known you. They see your picture in all works of mine. They come and ask me, 'Who is he?' I know not how to answer them. I say, 'Indeed I cannot tell.' They blame me and go away in scorn. And you sit there smiling.

I put my tales of you into lasting songs. The secret gushes out from my heart. They come and ask me, 'Tell me all your meanings.' I know not how to answer them. I say, 'Ah, who knows what they mean!' They smile and go away in utter scorn. And you sit there smiling.

Rabinaranath Tagore
Gītānjali No. 102

Acknowledgements

This biography was written in commemoration of Sri Ma Anandamayi's centenary year 1995-96. For various reasons this book could not be published in 1996. The fact that it is being published at all, is due to the constant encouragements from my friends Dr. Bettina Baümer, Dr. Premlata Srivastava and my sister Renudi who had made it possible for me to work undisturbed for almost two years.

I take this opportunity to thank Sri S.K. Datta and Brahmacharini Guneeta Marwa for providing me with suitable photographs. I gratefully acknowledge the hard work put in by Dhirendra K. Sahoo in transforming my manuscripts into workable typescripts. I received many constructive suggestions from Nicholas Bradbury such as including a map of India. Last but not least, the coincidence of my visit to my brother Prabhash Kumar and his wife Meera, in New Delhi, facilitated the meeting with my Publishers. My thanks are due to the Publishers also, who have been most courteous and helpful so that it has been a pleasure to work with them.

Contents

CHAPTER ONE

The Places where Sri Ma Anandamayi lived as a Child

Once in a long while Humanity puts forth a rare flower of exquisite Beauty and Fragrance. It cannot be said to teach, to have a message, it lives for only one purpose, to demonstrate the existence of a Power, that is ever at work creating by the transforming influence, Beauty out of ugliness, Love out of strife. Such a Power is Sri Anandamayi. May she bring peace and harmony into this world of strife.

B. Sanjiva Rao[1]

Question : Ma, why this birth? Are people born to fulfill the desires of previous births?

Sri Ma : Yes.

Question : What desires made you take this birth?

Sri Ma, with a smile: Your desire to come to me!

* The villages of Bengal at the turn of the century
* Sultanpur
* Vidyakut
* Kheora in District Tripura now in Bangla Desh

The Places where Sri Ma Anandamayi lived as a Child

The Villages of Bengal at the turn of the Century

Seen from the perspective of the closing years of the twentieth century, the villages of undivided Bengal at the turn of it, seem to have been enjoying a lull before the storm which was soon to overtake them. Political upheavals were in the offing. The storm when it broke was devastating in its effects. Tradition-oriented ways of life were wiped out and a new era of bewildering changes in military rules, left the masses terrified and insecure. All this and much more became part of the experiences of Sri Ma's families and also the families of her early devotees. At the time of her birth, however, all was peace and harmony in the countryside.

The rural scene was beautiful with fields of golden crops, green meadows profusely decorated by bright coloured seasonal flowers of many varieties; plantain groves, mango and other fruit trees provided of their plenty at different times of the year. The meandering waterways reflected the deep blue of the skies. People were used to unlimited space, bounteous nature and friendly neighbours.

Sri Ma Anandamayi was born and reared in that part of rural Bengal which is now Bangla Desh. Her early years were spent in Kheora (District Tripura), where she was born, Sultanpur, her maternal grandfather's village, and Vidyakut, her father's village. Sultanpur and Vidyakut were big prosperous villages. While Sri Ma was growing up in Kheora she had occasion to visit both these villages very often. Her two families were related like this:

Sultanpur (District Agartala)	Vidyakut (District Tripura)
Sri Ramakanta Bhattacharya = Srimati Harasundari Devi	Sri Trilochana Bhattacharya = Srimati Tripurasundari Devi of Kheora
|	|
Srimati Mokshada Sundari Devi (daughter) also known as Bidhumukhi Devi	Sri Bipin Bihari Bhattacharya (son)

|

Srimati Nirmala Sundari Devi
(later known as Sri Ma Anandamayi)

Sultanpur: The House of Sri Ramakanta Bhattacharya

All Brahmin families of those times were universally looked up to by virtue of their saintly ways of living. Sri Ramakanta Bhattacharya, his brothers and sons were specially respected for their scholarship and other–worldliness. The heads of this family were recognised as *sabhā-paṇḍits* (court priests) of the Raja of Agartala. Their cottage was the focal point for neighbourly gatherings irrespective of caste or religion. The outer reception-room was nearly always full of visitors who came for various purposes; some seeking advice, some with questions regarding religious rites, others with major or minor problems needing resolutions and lastly just friends.

The big cottage was surrounded by cultivated gardens and hedges. There were two ponds beyond the gardens and plenty of fruit trees. Whatever came in from the fields, gardens or orchards was first dedicated to God. The daily worship of the family deities was the main business of the day. Throughout the year many festivals were celebrated with great care and circumspection. The most important was the annual Durgā Pūjā in Āśvin (September/October). With Bengalis, it is the yearly renewal of a deep-seated belief in the legend that the Goddess comes to visit her erstwhile earthly home for three days. The whole of Bengal prepares for this advent with music, flowers, incense, sweets, each household doing whatever lies in its power to add to the festivities.

At Sultanpur preparations got underway much ahead of the date. Large quantities of grains were stocked. The women made marvellous sweets from coconuts and sugar. The incense-laden air and the sweet strains of invocatory songs (*āgamanī*) would proclaim that Durgā Pūjā was at hand.

For the three days of the *pūjā* the cottage of Sri Rama Kanta Bhattacharya became a temple of worship for the entire neighbourhood. Everybody was welcome to partake of the *prasāda* (consecrated food) which would be available in large quantities. No invitations were necessary; all were equally welcome to come and join in.

The children of the family would be given new clothes. Those who were old enough would be engaged in stringing garlands of flowers gathered from the gardens. Paste was made from red and white sandalwood. The emerald green grass was carefully plucked and arranged in neat bundles. There were hundred and one things to be done and everyone could be busy in the service of the Goddess. All this Sri Ma[2] saw in her childhood when she visited Sultanpur on these occasions. Every festival has a religious overtone in India; but in some places and at certain times it acquires a special quality of solemnity which raises it above the ordinary. Sri Ma has said that the Durgā Pūjā at her grandfather's always did assume an extra-mundane aura, as if the prayerful invocations were truly answered.

Not only the Durgā Pūjā but other religious festivals were also solemnised: Mahāśivarātri, Sri Krishna Janmāṣtamī, Kālī Pūjā, Saraswati Pūjā, Sri Rama Navami and so on. We can be reasonably sure that such a way of life was not peculiar to Bengal. In other parts of this ancient land, there must have been such villages which resembled the hermitages of Upanisadic times, where people lived in obedience to the precept of:

Īśavāsyamidam sarvam yatkincya jagatyām jagat:
tena tyaktena bhunjithā māgṛdhah kasyasvitdhanam.

Īśavasyopaniṣad I

All this - Whatsoever moves on the earth - should be covered by the Lord. Protect (Your Self) through that detachment. Do not covet, for whose is wealth? - Tr. by Swamī Gambhīrānanda.

To enjoy the good things of life, only as *prasāda* (heavenly gift) created that milieu of self-sufficiency and contentment which is the hall mark of inner peace. Such life styles do seem to forge a link with the age of the *ṛṣis* (seers) thereby making it a living tradition even in modern times.

A joint family owes its inner harmony to the judicious management of the mistress of the house. Sri Ma's grandmother Srimati Harasundari Devi was an ideal chatelaine. She exercised a benign influence on the entire household. She diffused all conflict situations; tale-telling was not countenanced. In fact if somebody made a mistake, she would expect another to render help and not seek to be praised for it. There was, thus, an overall feeling of friendliness and mutuality in this household. Sri Ma's mother Srimati Mokshada Sundari Devi a daughter of this house was a living example of the ideals inculcated in such a family. Born in 1877 in the month of May, she lost her mother when She was little more than a child. It is reported that Srimati Harasundari had predicted that her end was near. Her daughter, thereupon asked her, 'I hear that you are going away?' The mother reassured her saying, 'My eldest daughter-in-law will take my place.'

Srimati Mokshada Devi, thereafter, enjoyed a privileged position with her brothers and sisters-in-law as a special protégé bequeathed to them by their mother. In the fullness of time she was married to Sri Bipin Bihari Bhattacharya of Vidyakut. The quietly affluent atmosphere of her brother's household was not matched by her new home. Not that the circumstances were so very different - in fact they were not but Sri Bipin Bihari turned out to be a householder who would have been better suited to the calling of a wandering minstrel.

Vidyakut

It may be a fanciful thought but it cannot but come to the mind that the transition from Sultanpur to Vidyakut is comparable to a going toward asceticism, a moving away from the hermitages to penetrate deeper into the forest for a life of renunciation and austerities, because Sri Bipin Bihari was at heart an ascetic. A strong streak of otherworldliness in his mental make-up made it difficult for him to settle down to the business of steadily providing for his family. He had no talents for managing his household and very soon his considerable inheritance began to show signs of his neglect. He spent his time in the usual pursuits of a devout Brahmin of his day. His mornings were given over to the performance of *pūjā* at the family Shrine. His was a family of spiritual preceptors (*guru*). Sometimes members of such families as were under their religious guidance came to receive initiations. If asked by his elder brothers, he would perform this rite for them.

Along with his religious training, he had received secular schooling also. At one time after his marriage he had been persuaded by one of his affluent nephews to work on his Estates as an accountant. The nephew wanted an honest man, he could rely upon. This arrangement, however, was short-lived. Sri Bipin Bihari was too independent to take kindly to a form of service under another, albeit a respectful junior.

Sri Bipin Bihari's mother Srimati Tripurasundari had inherited some property in the village of Kheora in the same district. After a few years of his marriage, he came to Kheora with his wife to assume charge of this small inheritance. In due course a girl was born to this couple. His mother was living in Kheora also. We do not know if he considered that he had provided for his wife and mother by settling them in Kheora, because he now left home for an unknown destination in order to become an ascetic.

Srimati Mokshada Devi was a true daughter of the house of Sri Ramakanta Bhattacharya. She accepted her husband's way of life not only without demur, but with complete understanding. She was one of those rare personalities who exemplify all the gentler human virtues. Her utterly undemanding nature was tried to the utmost by her circumstances but she never lost the serenity of her spirit or the dignity of her behaviour. There was a bond of love and regard between the two women left on their own. Unfortunately for both of them the little girl passed away before long, leaving them sad and lonely. Srimati Tripura Sundari got into the habit of walking to the well-known temple of Kali at nearby Kasba, to pray for her son's return. Some members of her family look it upon themselves to locate Sri Bipin Bihari in his place of retreat. They also persuaded him to return to Kheora. So after almost three years he returned home, once more to take up the position of a householder. Now his mother again trekked to Kasba to pray for a grandson. Strangely, at the time of uttering the prayer, she found herself saying 'a daughter' instead of 'a son'. In any case, she thought, a child would help to anchor her son's restless spirit to his hearth and home.

A second daughter was born to Srimati Mokshada Devi and Sri Bipin Bihari on April 30, 1896, who later became well-known as Sri Ma Anandamayi.

Brahmacharini Chandan, a third generation daughter of the house of Sri Ramakanta Bhattacharya of Sultanpur had the privilege of listening to Sri Ma when she was answering some questions regarding the manner of her presence on earth and was moved to think in terms of the *triveṇī sangam*,[3] the holy confluence of the three rivers Ganga, Yamuna and Saraswati. The simile came to her mind specially because the third river Saraswati is said to symbolize *brahmavidyā* the Highest Knowledge; moreover the faithful believe that Saraswati is a mysterious trans-natural presence at the *sangam* because this river is not visible to the pilgrims now.

Sri Ma Anandamayi's given name was Nirmala Sundari, which in English would mean 'the taintlessly beautiful one.' By all accounts this name was appropriate. She was a very winsome little baby. Everyone who came to see her was immediately enamoured of her and could only leave her presence with some difficulty. Her mother got used to the sight of even strangers stopping over to admire the baby or play with her for a while. One occasion especially lived in her memory for all time. They were visiting Vidyakut at the time. One day Mokshada Devi saw an extra-ordinary looking person, with an air of luminosity about him, approach the playful infant, who was about ten months old at this time, and squat in front of her as if paying homage. Glancing at the mother, he said, 'You have a very special child. You will not make an ordinary housewife of her. She is the Mother. She belongs to the world.'

Mokshada Devi thought he was an eccentric but his words lingered in her memory.

Kheora - The playground for the līlā of childhood

Kheora was a small village. The west-side consisted of just two Brahmin households, surrounded on three sides by Muslim neighbours. There were other Hindu families on the east-side. The two sides were separated by big fields and forests. There was a short cut through the habitation of the Muslim families. As soon as Nirmala was old enough to walk by herself, she could be seen skipping and dancing along this path ever so often and also stopping at all doors which were opened to her. According to Indian custom all elders are given family epithets by the children. The Muslim elders also were known to her variously as *Nānā* (grandfather), *Cācā* (uncle), *Dādā* (brother) *Buā* (aunt) and so on. The entire village, no matter how far flung the cottages became one big home to the little girl.

Nirmala was a very friendly child. She would readily render whatever service she was capable of to whomsoever was in need of it. She fetched and carried for all neighbours as well as her own family. She was uniformly good-tempered, never gave any trouble to anybody; in fact her mother does not recall that she ever threw temper tantrums or cried in distress. Yet two incidents are recalled which were exceptions to this rule. It so happened that after the birth of Nirmala three sons were born to her parents in due course of time. Unfortunately the eldest Kaliprasanna died at the age of seven and the other two in childhood and infancy. Mokshada Devi at all times the personification of courageous fortitude, at odd moments would succumb to grief and shed quiet tears. If Nirmala happened to see her at such times, she would set up such a wailing that her mother was obliged to hasten to her comfort, her own tears forgotten.

The other instance of crying took place when Nirmala was yet an infant. A young girl called Ekabbar from one of the neighbouring Muslim houses was specially fond of Nirmala and came to play with her every day. One day Ekabbar started a new game by beckoning the child from a little distance. When the baby eagerly and smilingly started to crawl forward, she would step further back and beckon again. After four or five times of this tantalising manoeuvre, the baby sat back and started to cry loudly. Ekabbar then quickly picked Nirmala up and sought to quieten her. The sobs and wails increased to such a degree that Ekabbar was frightened into giving the baby back to her grandmother. She never played such a teasing game again. When both girls had grown up, Ekabbar would sometimes recall this incident, 'What a baby you were! How you cried! It was an extraordinary experience for me. My hair still moves on my scalp whenever I think of it!'

There were others who could recall strange experiences with the baby. Kheora was inhabited by many of her grandmother's contemporaries, who were all Dadas (grandfathers) and Didis (grandmothers) to her. One Dada, (Krishna Sundar Bhattacharya) was in the habit of tossing up the baby and catching her again in his arms. The child expressed her delight in gurgling laughter. Once as he held her up she placed one foot on his shoulder and stretched out the other as if to place it on his uplifted arm. Suddenly he cried out, 'Catch! Catch!' and almost fell down to his knees. It was not quite clear whether he wanted people to catch the infant or support him! He put the child down, ejaculating in great wonder 'What a strange girl!' It was conjectured by the onlookers that the weight of the baby had suddenly become unbearable. The family noticed that when playing with the child he never again attempted to toss her aloft.

As Nirmala grew up, her family and neighbours found her a joyous elfin creature ever at hand, making herself useful to everyone in the village, irrespective of caste, religion or social position.

The little girl found anything and everything a source of delight. One night a portion of the thatched roof blew away in a sudden storm. The inmates took shelter under what remained of the roof. Nirmala clapped her hands and laughed aloud, 'Ma, Ma, we can see the stars from here! The outside and inside have become one - what fun!' Nirmala was not very much affected by the heat of summer, the cold climate or the monsoons. She would dance around in a heavy downpour or play on a sand-hill in the scorching sun quite unmindful of the heat. She was not a prey to childish ailments. Her sunny disposition earned her many nicknames in the village, such as Hashi (Smiles), Khushir Ma (the Happy One) and so on.

Nirmala had a disconcerting trait of almost literally obeying the bidding of elders. Her family came to a full realization of this after many an aggravating incident. One day her mother asked her to go and wash an agate cup at the pond. Wishing to draw the child's attention to the fragility of the cup she said, 'See if you can break it also.' Nirmala returned after a while holding carefully the broken pieces of the cup in her small hands. She said that the cup had just dropped. Her mother trying hard not to laugh, asked why she had brought the pieces back. Nirmala said she had seen the shards being used for treating burns, so perhaps they were still useful. At such incidents Nirmala never got a reprimand because her innocence was so palpable.

One favourite story is about the 'full stop.' While teaching her to read, her father had pointed out that she should pause at the full-stop before beginning another sentence. Sometimes later he was amused and rather appalled to see how Nirmala was following his instructions. If the sentence happened to be a long one, she would twist and contort her little body to arrive at the full-stop in one gasping breath.

As a matter of fact, this trait of abiding by the spoken words or wishes of the people around her was a constant feature of her behavioural pattern. It was a veil drawn over her true *kheyāla*. Even people who were supposed to be close to her, never penetrated this veil.

The word '*kheyāla*' needs to be explained because it is going to be used very often in this narrative. Sri Ma used this word when others would have said, 'I wish,' or 'I will' or 'it is my desire.' She had no wish, or will or desires but sometimes a towardness for a certain course of action, perhaps dictated by the needs of the people around her; a spontaneous thought which took shape out of the circumstances rather than any spring to action from within. It took considerable time for her family and early devotees to figure out what she meant by this word, that is, if ever at all it has been understood.

When Sri Ma Anandamayi was a child her total egolessness which led to her ready acquiescence in all things suggested by her elders was construed to mean a docility and even a little simplicity of the mind. She was sometimes considered to be a little below par because no normal child could be so uniformly joyous and good. Even if people doubted her intelligence, she met with no dearth of love and indulgence. Moreover,her undeviating truthfulness also had to be taken into account. In time the elders came to rely on her implicitly for her version of any controversial situation because it was noted that she never could be pursuaded to undertake anything remotely untoward or unseemly. Perhaps Nirmala herself enjoyed all these puzzlements about her. One day she happened to be carrying a pitcher of water on her hip and watched her shadow on the ground. When she stood in front of her mother she said, 'You say I am straight, (*sojā*, meaning also a simpleton) am I not crooked (*bāṅkā*, meaning also clever) now?'

There was a private school for children near the village. Nirmala attended this school for a while. She could not go everyday because some days she would be helping her mother with the children and sometimes her mother could not find a suitable escort for her. Even so, the teacher always found her keeping up easily with the class. So much so that after a visit by the Inspector of schools she and two other regular bright girls of the class were promoted to the Lower Primary School.

This school had a young Headmistress. Once, when the Inspector called, she became nervous when her girls could not answer one of the questions. From outside the window of the classroom she held up a slate on which she had written the answer. It was Nirmala's turn; she could see the slate plainly but took no advantage of this manoeuvre. Such deceptions were quite foreign to her nature. This Headmistress visited Sri Ma in later years in Varanasi, where we heard this ancecdote from her and various other incidents of Nirmala's very short school career. She never learnt to read or write fluently, although at times her handwriting seemed quite set and mature.

Nirmala was always very keenly interested in all kinds of religious rites, even in other religions. While they were visiting in Sultanpur, she and her cousin met two Christian nuns who were selling some tracts. Nirmala ran back to her mother for the small coins needed for buying this booklet. In the evening she was as if irresistably drawn to their camp outside the village. She stood outside the tent listening to their prayers and then ran back home before she could be missed.[3]

Nirmala had many playgrounds in Kheora. There was a big sand-heap near their cottage. She could be seen constructing many shapes with the sand. One day she made a big round ball. When asked by her mother as to what it was, she said, 'It is Narayana, Lakshmi, Siva, Parvati, Radha, Krishna and many other Gods as well. Didn't you tell me that all is contained within one and the one is everything?'

Mokshada Devī was taken aback a little but said mildly, 'All right, but come away now, or you'll get sunstroke.' Nirmala immediately broke the carefully constructed mound and followed her mother without a backward glance.

The forest provided her with flowers of many colours, which she would gather and arrange in intricate designs. The mother could not but notice that the child's absorption was tinged with a kind of aloofness - she would suddenly abandon everything and walk away with an withdrawn expression on her face. This was true as regards her friends also. She would play with them or by herself without seeming to miss their company.

What was really extra-ordinary about little Nirmala was a sudden change from the ordinary playful child into an extra-ordinary ethereal being. In the midst of some mundane activity she would suddenly seem not to be with her playmates or with her elders. Her expression, always serene and beautiful, would be as if shot with an inner luminosity. The best description that people could think of was to say that it was like a play of lightning in the skies. How did they behave with the child after they had seen her as an ethereal being with the spark of divinity in her? The same people hastened to recall her, as it were, to their stratum of life; they would seek to draw her attention toward play and make her talk and laugh in her usual way.

When later in life, Sri Ma was questioned on these recollections of her family and neighbours she said, 'You are using the words 'ordinary', 'extra-ordinary.' To me there is no difference; it is like the blinking of the eye.'

References

1. 'Sri Anandamayee', *Mother as Seen by Her Devotees*, Varanasi, 1956, p. 17.
2. Sri Ma Anandamayi's name is shortened to Sri Ma in subsequent pages.
3. S.S. Vol. I, p. 7.
4. This incident has a sequel. In 1974 Sri Ma spent some time in Pune during May and June. She was one day invited to a Christian Ashram where the Sisters welcomed her with *ārati* and *pujā*. Sri Ma remarked to one of her Christian devotees (Melita Maschmann) that her *kheyāla* of attending the evening sesion of prayers in Sultanpur was now being fulfilled. Melita got the impression that Sri Ma had had the *kheyāla* to go to the tent in answer to their prayers.

CHAPTER TWO

From Childhood to Maturity

So the humble parents selected an equally humble husband for their girl as soon as she stepped into her twelfth year; and she went to live with the husband's family in Dacca district, hiding her angelic face under a cubit long veil, as village girls of those days invariably did for years after their marriage. Something unusual was noticed in the girl even in her childhood. She was often absentminded, seeing or dreaming of one knew not what, but nothing connected with play or work in hand. The trait developed after marriage into frequent fits of apparent insensibility to external surroundings - although at other times she was perfectly natural doing all that she was required to do to the satisfaction of every person concerned.

- Raisahab Sri Akshay K. Datta Gupta[1]

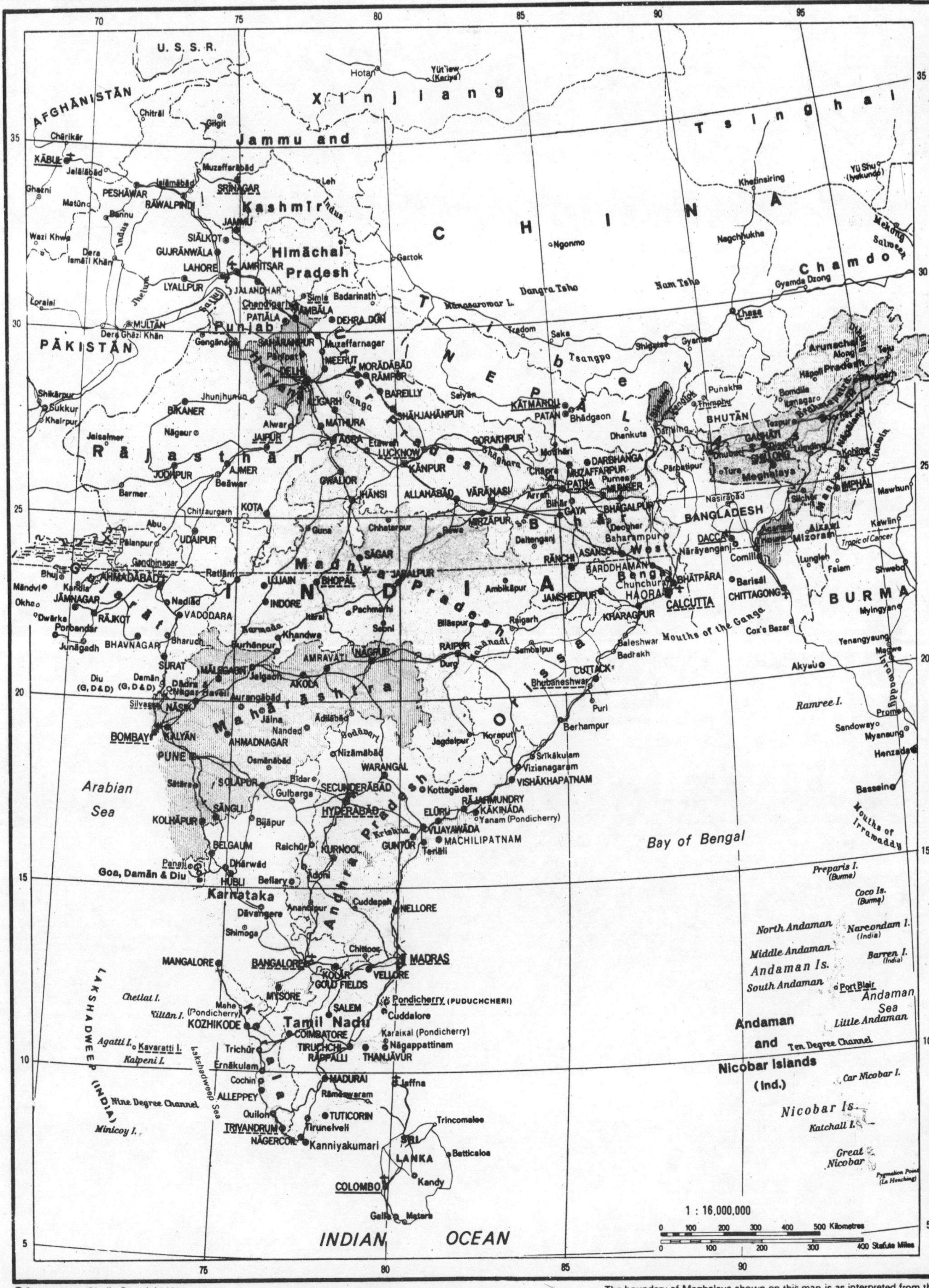

Based upon Survey of India Map with the permission of the Surveyor General of India.
The territorial waters of India extend into the sea to a distance of twelve nautical miles

The boundary of Meghalaya shown on this map is as interpreted from the North Eastern Areas (Reorganisation) Act 1971, but has yet to be verified.
The administrative headquarters of Haryana and Punjab are at Chandigarh

The Image of the Goddess Durga as it is constructed for annual festivals.

The Siddhasanā.

Sri Ma at Shahbagh.

Sri Ma and her parents Dīdima and Dadamashaī.

Sri Ma and Bholanath.

Ramna Ashram in Dhaka. The Ashram was razed to the ground at the time of the partition of Bengal.

Sri Ma with the teachers and students of Kanyapeeth.

Sri Ma and Mahatmas.

Nāmayajña. (Abhya with Harmonium.)

I have not had the sort of [illegible] which you understand by the term in its ordinary sense. For [illegible] with father, mother, husband and other relatives [illegible] served the husband, so you may call it a [illegible] dishes for all, so you may call it a cook [illegible] of scrubbing and menial work, so you may call it [illegible] if you look at the thing from another standpoint [illegible] that [illegible]
[illegible]

I have not had the sort of renunciation which you understand by the term in its ordinary sense. For this body has lived with father, mother, husband and other relatives. This body has served the husband, so you may call it a wife. It has prepared dishes for all, so you may call it a cook. It has done all sorts of scrubbing and menial work, so you may call it a servant. But if you look at the thing from another standpoint you will realize that this body has served none but God. For ... I simply considered (everyone) as different manifestation of the Almighty.

Sri Ma Anandamayi[2]

* The Playmates.
* The Child Bride.
* The meeting of opposites: house-keeping and *mahābhāva*.
* Bholanath (Ramani Mohan) and Sri Ma.
* Vidyakut.
* Atpara

From Childhood to Maturity

The Playmates

The playmates of Sri Ma Anandamayi were many. Firstly her little brothers; she played with them, took care of them, tended them when they were ill. They would be trailing round with her wherever she went. Their attachment to their little sister was quite touching. Once Nirmala was invited to Sultanpur for some festival or other. Her brother Kaliprasanna said to her 'Sister, don't go or I shall never see you again.' In fact he did become seriously ill and passed away shortly after. Nirmala stayed with him till he breathed his last. So it was with the other little ones who were mere infants when they died.

Nobody doubted that she had been very attached to her brothers, but she was not seen to cry or mourn their loss. People were puzzled by this insensitivity and it was another reason for thinking her simple-minded. This conjunction of total commitment and aloof detachment remained with her all along causing surprise to newcomers. In fact it was a paradox integral to her personality and was never resolved by anyone.

Two sisters were born after the brothers, Surabala, who died at the age of sixteen, shortly after her marriage, and Hemlata, who lived to see middle age. Lastly, a brother nicknamed Makhan (Sri Yadunath Bhattacharya) who alone survived Sri Ma, as well as their parents. Sri Ma had said once that after the untimely death of her brothers she was left alone; she then had a *kheyāla* for one or two playmates. Surabala was about 14 years younger than her and a very lovely baby. Hemlata was born soon after. Both little girls were quite inseparable from Nirmala.

Another favourite playmate was her own grandmother, whom she called Thakurma. Thakurma had numerous relations living in Kheora as this was her own village. Nirmala frequently accompanied her Thakurma on her visits to her friends and family and also on the expeditions for gathering herbs and edible greenaries from the forests. Kheora was not a fertile village and nothing much grew out of the soil, at least not on the land belonging to them. Thakurma managed to provide the household with some little thing or other.

Once while Sri Ma was talking about her Thakurma in this strain, her first biographer Gurupriya Didi was provoked into saying, 'Marvellous! Your compassion and grace on your parents seem to have been boundless! They did not even have sufficient to eat!'[3] Sri Ma smiled and disclaimed, 'Not at all, we always had plenty. You are reckoning without the ingenuity of my Thakurma, and whatever she cooked, even if it were just edible green leaves and rice, was like divine food. I have hardly tasted food which is better than what Thakurma used to prepare for us!'

The neighbours always asked Thakurma to take whatever was growing in their fields but this she never did, neither did she allow the children to trespass onto others' lands. Nirmala was so obedient to the behest of not touching anything belonging to others that she would make a detour to avoid a fruit-laden branch hanging in front on the path.

Nirmala's Thakurma Tripura Sundari Devi had been married into a prestigious family of spiritual-preceptors and scholars. She could have exercised the right of accepting gifts from families of disciples who accorded them the greatest respect. This however was not her way at all. Abstinence and self-sufficiency came naturally to her. She should have been dressed in ochre robes because at heart she was a recluse. From morning till night, her one pointed attention was directed toward an inner journey. One day Nirmala asked her, 'Thakurma what is this 'word' that you keep repeating all the time under your breath?' Thakurma was surprised at the child's question. 'Hush', she said, 'Children are not supposed to pronounce these 'words'. When you are older you will know about them.' Nirmala meekly acknowledging reproof, hung her head a little. Who knows if she at that early age did not begin her ministration of 'giving *dikṣā*' (which became such a surprising phenomenon of the last years of her life) with her own Thakurma.

One of the cousins of Thakurma had taken formal initiation from their own family guru. She being quite untutored, used to forget the instructions for the *sandhyā-pujā*. This ritual is to be gone through mornings and evenings with accompanying movements of fingers and breathing exercises (*prāṇāyāma*). This grandmother spoke to Nirmala once, saying, 'Look, I feel embarrassed to ask your mother to show me these *kriyās* (gestures) again and again. Can't you show them to me?' So she learnt them from her little granddaughter, not at all struck by the fact that the small girl should know about such matters in the first place.

When other odd expectations were fulfilled, the recipients were gratified but not so amazed as to think her a child-prodigy. Nirmala had a way of doing marvellous things in the most ordinary way possible. The same grandmother to whom she had shown the *pūjā*-rites had acquired a pair of conch-shell bangles, but alas, neither she nor anyone else could slide them over her rather prominent knuckles on to her arms. Such bangles are fragile and rather expensive. She then brought them to Nirmala and was very pleased when she found them gliding over easily. She did express her surprise by saying 'How could such small hands manage to squeeze my hard knuckles! Didi (grand daughter!) you are a clever girl!' Another 'grandmother' who was a friend of her Thakurma and who was known to her as Chikkandidi, gave her the first certificate of being the best cook ever, while she was yet a very small girl. Nirmala used to cook for her sometimes and elicit such responses, as 'Didi, whatever you cook, tastes out of this world!'

Nirmala was not required to cook at home, so nobody really knew how and whence she had acquired this adult art. She did however watch her mother and Thakurma and also help in other ways in the kitchen. She would accompany her Thakurma when she went out to gather broken dry twigs and leaves for their daily cooking. She saw that her mother carefully stored bundles of firewood against the possibility of a sudden influx of guests. When guests came, a proper fire was kindled on which a good meal could be cooked. Her mother was a careful housewife and she never allowed anyone to guess how straitened her means were. It was out of question for her to ask for anything from her neighbours who were family as well; the children were strictly forbidden to ask for anything and unless specifically invited to do so, not to eat or accept sweets from anyone. Mokshada Devi had a very nice sense of humour quite free from malice, which enabled her to play all the roles required of her by Providence with quiet dignity and complete self-assurance. She often used to recite a limerick to us in later years as the secret of a trouble-free life:

Come and go; do not stay,
Observe and listen; comment not
Eat and accept; ask not (for anything)
(Then) no troubles will come your way!

Mokshada Devi had a natural talent toward writing poetry. The songs that she has composed, express a poignancy, a yearning toward the fulfilment of the religious aspirations of a devout heart. The child Nirmala was almost constantly with her, helping, running errands or just talking. It may be said that after her little brothers and sisters and her Thakurma, Nirmala's closest companions were her own parents. She would sit near them and chat away, sometimes asking them questions such as these:

'Ma, people speak of heaven. Is it possible to go to heaven?'

'Yes certainly. Whoever is keenly desirous of going to heaven can do so.'

'Do you know the way? Tell me!'

'Whoever has the yearning, is shown the way.'

'What is so special about heaven?'

'People say heaven when they mean God. God knows everything and He does everything for us. He is everywhere but remains untouched. We do not know this because we belong to this earth only. To go to heaven means to know about all such things.'

It seems that Sri Ma elicited many a religious conviction by such dialogues with her elders. The times were such that people had a natural bent toward the devout way of life. It was a common village custom for wandering minstrels (*vairāgis*) to go around from door to door at dawn singing *uṣā-kirtan* (morning-hymns). The burden of their songs would be 'a new dawn is breaking, arise, it is time to engage in the worship of God. Do not waste time in sleep,' and so on.

Nirmala's father very often joined them and sometimes even wandered off to neighbouring villages in their company but always returned home sooner or later. The singing of *kirtan* was the mainspring of his life. He may have been an indifferent householder but he was rich in the possession of a vast repertoire of devotional music; indeed, his knowledge of music was matched by his deep and melodious voice. It is said that his voice was so arresting that even if he were humming a tune, people would stop to listen to him. He could play on all the instruments which were used in his time. He counted many Muslim Ustads among his friends. These names, Ustad Gulmahmood, Ustad Aftabuddin, heard in her childhood, Sri Ma was able to repeat to Ustad Ali Akbar Khan when he told her that his forefathers had lived near Vidyakut. He confirmed that Ustad Aftabuddin was Ustad Alauddin Khan's brother.

Sometimes there were gatherings for a musical evening. If Sri Bipin Bihari were given the first turn, then other performers would complain, 'Now, who will stay to listen to us, after they've heard you!' He was often compared to the saint-bard of Bengal, Ramprasad who, it is firmly believed, could invoke Divine presence by his inspired singing. Bipin Bihari also was quite capable of losing himself entirely when singing *Hari-kirtan. Kirtan* is a repetitive form of melody, composed of the Names and words describing the auspicious qualities of the Divine Person. Generally there is a leading voice followed by a chorus, but a really gifted singer can perform it solo.

Once there was a storm and the thatched cottages as always came to grief. When the storm had abated Mokshada Devi repaired to the hut where her husband sat engrossed in singing *kirtan*. He was quite unaware that there was no roof over his head and that he and his instrument were getting drenched. He now responded to his wife's shakings and said mildly, 'Yes, I see it is all getting wet - I shall come away.' His wife tried to hide her grin by pulling her sari over her face.

Nirmala asked her father one day, 'You are always singing about Hari. Who is Hari?'

'Hari is one of the Names of God. He has many names.'

'Why should one sing His names?'

'If you sing His names, He will come to you - just as when we call out to you, you come and do whatever we ask you to do for us. So He also does as much for us because He is everywhere and He hears when we call out to Him.'

'Is He then very big?'

'Yes, Indeed!'

'As big as this field here?'

'Much bigger. He is not to be measured. When He appears, you will see how great, how magnificent Hs is. And He will appear if you call upon Him to do so.'

Bipin Bihari, it seems, gave expression to his own sentiments regarding his personal *Iṣṭa-devatā* as if sharing them with a friend. Nirmala thereupon joined her sweet young voice to his rich and melodious one. *Hari-kirtan* must have reached new heights on such occasions and these were quite frequent because father and daughter sang together whenever possible.

Nirmala had some cousins to play with when she visited Sultanpur. One such cousin, Sushila, later came to the Ashram and became a permanent inmate. She used to narrate that even animals were attracted to Nirmala. Cows returning from the pasture would stop near her and nudge her gently. Sushila also said that sometimes they would find Nirmala as if talking to trees and plants; this used to scare the other children because they could almost imagine that it was a conversation and that the plants were bending forth a little.[4] Before they could really think anything more of it, Nirmala would run along and join them and they would forget about her odd behaviour with the trees.

All these traits which were noticed by one or the other of her relations and playmates remained with Sri Ma all her life. She was seen often not to differentiate between animate or inanimate objects. Didi Gurupriya had noticed that when Sri Ma was about to leave a habitation for good, she would sometimes, go round touching the walls, almost as if she were bidding farewell to old friends. That she easily communicated with plants and animals was witnessed by many people and in due course ceased to strike them as anything unusual in her. Her magnetic attraction, even for complete strangers, similarly, was taken for granted and not wondered at later. While still a child, Sri Ma was seen in many such situations. Once her father took her along to his sister's village to attend the function of the Annual Durgā Pūjā.

Father and daughter set out for the river bank where they would board the steamer for going across. At midday Bipin Bihari stopped at a market place to buy some food for themselves.

Nirmala was a little way off from the shop. One woman, probably a street-walker, approached her, asked her name and destination. Nirmala gave her name and said she was going on a visit to her aunt for the Durgā Pūjā. The woman then asked if she would like to come to her house and eat something to which Nirmala replied in the negative. After more questions and answers it was time to go as her father had finished and was beckoning her to follow him. They arrived at the pier, the woman following at a little distance. When they had boarded the steamer, the woman was seen to stand on the shore looking at the little girl for as long as she remained visible.[5]

The aunt's village Tantar was a considerable distance and they had to stay overnight at a friend's house. These friends had not seen Nirmala before. The women seemed besides themselves with joy. They looked upon her visit at this auspicious time, as that of the Goddess herself. They gave her new clothes, presents, made much of her and were reluctant to say good-bye the next morning.

The Child Bride in the house of Sri Revati Mohan

The carefree days of childhood for Nirmala drew to a close when she was barely thirteen years old. A marriage was arranged between Nirmala and Ramani Mohan Chakravarty of Atpara. Ramani Mohan's father was old and not in good health. His eldest son-in-law Seetanath Kushari on his behalf, came to see Nirmala in Kheora and to finalize the arrangements. He also headed the bride-groom's party when they arrived for the ceremony on February 7, 1909. They were received at Kasba and were taken in a festive procession to the bride's village. In the Hindu system of arranged marriages it is a family affair on both sides. Not only the families but the neighbours also are involved. Nirmala's uncles and aunts came from Sultanpur, as well as Vidyakut. Her Sonamama (the youngest uncle from Sultanpur) who was specially fond of her, brought costly gifts for the occasion.

The entire village of Kheora participated in the festivities. At the time of the ceremony Lakshmi Charan Bhattacharya one of the elders, said to the bridegroom, 'Son, you don't know what a treasure you are taking home today!'[6]

When the bridal-party was returning to Atpara after the marriage-ceremony, one of those incidents occurred which was such a recurrent feature of Sri Ma's life. At Kasba Railway Station the bride was escorted to a compartment in the train. She sat quietly almost surrounded by a mountain of luggage. All of a sudden it transpired that the compartment had to be changed and quickly because the train was about to leave. Seetanath Kushari asked Nirmala to come down, and started to move the luggage. He found unexpected help from the slim little girl dressed in bridal clothes. In a trice the heavy loads were shifted and rearranged in the new compartment. This was Nirmala's first train journey. Although she had not previously seen a train she grasped the situation instantly and moved with the speed of lightning or so it appeared to Seetanath Kushari. He used to relate this incident in later years as the first occasion on which he was impressed by his young sister-in-law as an unusual girl. All his life he remained devoted to her and came to look upon her as a manifestation of Divine Sakti. His granddaughter Maroni grew up in Sri Ma's household and was adopted by Sri Ramani Mohan as his daughter. Maroni's brother; Dashu needs no introduction to the family of Sri Ma's devotees and admirers. People may not know, however, that he is Seetanath Kushari's grandson.

It is customary for the child-bride to remain with her parents after all the marriage ceremonies are concluded. So after her reception at Atpara, where the whole village assembled to celebrate the coming of a bride to her new house, Nirmala came back to Kheora. She stayed with her parents for another year and a half. Ramani Mohan had been told that his bride was a pupil at the Lower Primary School. So he wrote her a letter. This was a sensational event in the village. Mokshada Devi put the letter in a prominent place so that Nirmala could see it and take it to read by herself without any self-consciousness. Nirmala, however, was not concerned, and since she had not been told to do so, did not take the letter. Eventually, Mokshada Devi sought help of Nirmala's friends, who very enthusiastically took the letter and not only had it opened and read but made a joint effort to compile a reply. This respectful and polite epistle was copied out by Nirmala in her handwriting and sent off.

Ramani Mohan was working in the Police Department in his village at the time of his marriage. Right after, he lost this job. Many years later, while talking about the different professions for men Sri Ma had said that there were some which easily added to the burden of karma. The policing of other fellow creatures was difficult without giving way to the harsher qualities of human nature. Doctors and lawyers also earned their wages out of the misery of people. She did not minimize the important side of rendering help to those who need it most endemic to these professions; she meant to say that the pitfalls loomed larger for these men than say, those who were in the teaching profession.

So, perhaps, after being married to Nirmala, Ramani Mohan could not have continued in his job. He remained without one for some time. He left his village and went to **Dhaka** to look for work. In Dhaka he stayed with his sister and her husband Rajendra Kushari doing something or other till he found a permanent job as Law Clerk in the Settlement Department of the Estates of the Nawab of Dhaka, at Ashtagram (1913) after almost four years of his marriage.

His next brother a little older to him Surendra Mohan was also married at about the same time. His bride Nirmala and Surendra Mohan's bride Prafulla were nearly the same age. The time drew near for both these girls to be received in their new household. Ramani Mohan's eldest brother Revati Mohan was now the head of the house because their father had passed away sometime after the brothers' marriages. Their mother was already no more.

Revati Mohan had two other brothers Kamini Kumar and Jamini Kumar. Kamini Kumar had gone away from his village and nobody knew where he was. It was rumoured that he had converted to Christianity. Jamini Kumar was a small boy at this time. He had three more sisters apart from the two already mentioned. We mention all these names because this large family, scattered all over the country, was brought together again by Sri Ma in later years in Dhaka; she even invited the youngest sister whom the others had not seen for nineteen years. The brother who had become a Christian and a clergyman, the Rev. K.K. Chakravarty also came with his non-Bengali wife to meet his other brothers and sisters and their families. His brother and Sri Ma stayed at his Calcutta residence many times.

All this happened when Sri Ma had emerged as the focal point of not only this large family but the larger one of ever increasing throngs of devotees. For the time being she and Prafulla came to stay with Revati Mohan and his wife Pramoda Devi at Sripur where he was posted as the Station Master on the Dhaka-Jagannathganj Railway Line.

Pramoda Devi was pleased with her young sisters-in-law. Prafulla became Mezdi (second sister) to Nirmala because she was the wife of the second brother but a little younger than her. Nirmala now was Sezdi (third sister) to Prafulla. This is how Pramoda Devi solved the problem of age and protocol. Mokshada Devi, Sri Ma's mother, had been a little nervous about her daughter's ability to cope with the new situation into which she was being pitchforked almost overnight, when she came to Sripur from Kheora escorted by her father in 1910. She, need not have worried. Nirmala proved to be much more than adequate. Just as she was an obedient, happy child so was she a well-behaved, hardworking and sunny-tempered young girl. The working hours were long and arduous. Here also she displayed all the qualities which are the ingredients of a happy joint family. She assumed charge of the cooking because everyone preferred hers to Prafulla's or even Pramoda Devi's. There were no misunderstandings about sharing the work or the responsibilities. In any case the children of the house, Kalipada to begin with and later Labanya and Ashu, were so attached to her that their entire nursing and care-taking devolved on Nirmala automatically.

Many stories are extant about her way of life with Revati Mohan and his wife. It is the custom in conservative households for a young woman to keep her face veiled with the border of her sari pulled down over the head in the presence of elders of the new household. Sri Ma, had been instructed to do this by her mother before going to Atpara or later to Sripur. Ordinarily young women follow this rule in spirit only and raise the veil whenever inconvenienced by it. The elders, however, had reckoned without Sri Ma's way of scrupulous obedience to instructions about deportment. When veiled, Sri Ma could only see a few inches of the ground near her feet; in consequence her movements were severely restricted. Moreover, such injunctions as 'fetch that,' or 'take it away', etc. had to be explained by description because she didn't see the indicative gestures. As earlier in her childhood, this quality of obedience tended to exasperate the elders a little. Their irritation turned to indulgence as soon as they realized that the young bride was consistent and sincere in her obedient attitude and that it was not any kind of passive resistance to authority.

Those who have seen Sri Ma work around the house have testified to the neatness and quickness of her movements. She seemed to get a lot of things accomplished within a short while. She left no mess after she had finished cooking or serving a meal. She did not hesitate to undertake the jobs of the servant Antu whenever he was absent for some reason or other. Nothing seemed to be a chore to her. As a matter of fact she was overworked by any standard of housekeeping at this time, but perhaps her sister-in-law should not be found fault with because Sri Ma never lost her tranquil look and there were no murmurs of complaints from her.

In time Revati Mohan and Pramoda Devi came to love her as their own daughter. Sri Ma's compassionate concern for all those who came near her may be gauged by odd incidents such as these: Pramoda Devi at one time suffered from some kind of skin disease. She would sometimes ask Nirmala to rub the sore spots with her soft and delicate fingers. Prafulla noted that she did not wash her hands immediately afterwards but much later, as one generally does before starting some housework. Prafulla asked her, 'Don't you mind at all?' Nirmala answered, 'Well in this way she does not feel bad about asking me to do the rubbing for her. If she saw that I was squeamish, she wouldn't ask again.'

One of Ramani Mohan's sisters, Matori came to stay with them for a while. She was about the same age as Nirmala and the two girls formed a friendship which lasted till the death of Matori Pishima (aunt Matori) in Varanasi almost forty years later. Matori Pishima was a jolly little person with twinkling eyes. She would suggest some mild mischief like sampling the store of pickles and chutneys while their sister-in-law enjoyed her siesta in the afternoon. Even this harmless prank was foreign to Sri Ma's nature. Although, being the taller of the two, she lifted the jars down for her friend, she never partook of the condiments.

We had all heard stories about Sri Ma's phenomenal stint of housekeeping after her marriage. We once had the opportunity of listening to an account of it straight from the chief person concerned. In 1948 Sri Ma was in Calcutta on the occasion of the annual Durgā Pūjā. The Ashram on Ekdalia Road was full to overflowing. Sri Ma was busy with a hundred and one things. We barely caught glimpses of her from afar. Some of us were billeted in the great hall, one corner of which was reserved for a very old lady, who got some V.I.P. treatment from the Ashram people. We did not know who she was.

One late night, after the visitors had all departed and the Ashram had settled down to rest, Sri Ma quietly emerged from her room. Followed by one or two people she came to the bedside of the old lady in the hall and gently woke her up. Sitting down close to her, Sri Ma clasped her hands in her own and talked to her gaily in a village dialect, hardly understood by those of us who happened to be awake. We were told that the old lady was Pramoda Devi, Sri Ma's eldest sister-in-law with whom she had stayed for four years after leaving Kheora. Circumstances had changed beyond Pramoda Devi's wildest imagination. She so far had had no opportunity to come close to Sri Ma who was all the time surrounded by a mammoth cluster of devotees. Although taken aback a little at first, Pramoda Devi quickly gained confidence and began to look happy. Earlier she must have despaired of ever being able to exchange a few words with her young sister-in-law. She seemed now to recognize in the august personality of these days the well-beloved girl who had served her so faithfully in the past. She was particularly pleased to see how well Sri Ma remembered the old days, some funny incidents and many long lost friends. Sri Ma's rendering of the village dialect was extremely entertaining. The hilarious laughter of those who were awake quickly roused those who were still sleeping, and the room became crowded with women. Sri Ma turned to her sister-in-law and said 'Look, all these women think that they are good housewives and experts at their work. Tell them whether or not I too looked after your household satisfactorily?' Pramoda Devi seemed to consider this question seriously and then ungrudgingly made this answer 'You cannot imagine how sweet and good she was. She not only did my entire work but I will acknowledge that she never gave me the slightest cause for any dissatisfaction throughout the years she was with me. Truly such a spirit of service (*sevā-bhāva*) is rare.'

To me (the author), what appeared to be more wonderful than this ready testimony was Sri Ma's look of gratification. She indeed was pleased to have her services recognised and appreciated. She had not taken anything for granted, neither had she been enacting the role of a young bride in her in-law's house. She truly was what she was expected to be. This characteristic, in fact, was the leitmotif of her life; just as she was a *sādhaka* for a short period of her life and so on. There was no pretence, so it could be called a *līlā* only.

To return to our narrative: Ramani Mohan visited them once in a while, bringing a few simple gifts for his nephews, niece and wife. Sri Ma in one of her moods of recollection, related this charming anecdote which is quite in keeping with her piquant sense of humour: 'Bholanath[7] use to bring me one or two simple books. Once he asked me to read aloud to him. After I had read a couple of passages in my usual gasping style (she still had problems with the full-stop!) he said, 'That will do'; then turning aside he muttered to himself 'Lower Primary indeed!'

Sri Ma's relationships with all the people around her was as if a song of endearment. The neighbours were always delighted to welcome her whenever she had a little leisure. During these pleasant visits Sri Ma learned many handicrafts, like coir-work, the spinning of fine thread etc. One of the Assistant Station Masters was a Muslim Officer. His sister became a friend. Sri Ma recalls that she and this girl used to converse amicably together about religious convictions without coming to any areas of conflict. Indeed, it did not seem that they belonged to different faiths.[8]

Sri Ma visited Kheora once during these years. She went round all the houses in the village accompanied by her sisters and brother. At one of the neighbouring Muslim houses, an elder of the family asked to see her new gold bracelet. She took it off immediately and gave it to him - He did not give it back for a long while. It was time to go. Sri Ma got up to leave without mentioning the bracelet; then the bracelet was brought back to her. The neighbour said, 'You truly are a strangely forgetful girl - supposing I had not given it back to you?' Sri Ma smiled and seemed not to have noticed anything untoward. This gentleman was not to know that this aloof attitude toward her so-called possessions was typical; in later years she distributed costly ornaments which were given to her by those possessed of worldly goods as openhandedly as flowers, fruits and sweets.

As written earlier Bholanath obtained a suitable job in Ashtagram in the year 1913 and now he was in a position to bring Sri Ma to keep house for him for the first time.

In the meantime many changes had taken place in both households. Sri Ma's parents had sold their property in Kheora and gone back to their own village Vidyakut with their last born son, Makhan. The other two sisters were married. Revati Mohan had been ailing for some time; Bholanath took him to Dhaka for medical aid and treatment. He recovered for a while and after resting at Atpara had returned to his post at Narundi. But he suffered a relapse and passed away in 1913. The bereaved family returned to Atpara. Sri Ma went with them and after about six months went to stay with her parents at Vidyakut where she stayed for about one year. Bholanath now visited Vidyakut for the first time after his marriage. He himself brought Sri Ma to their new rented suite of rooms in Ashtagram.

The Meeting of Opposites - Housekeeping and Mahābhāva

Sri Ma and Bholanath came to Ashtagram in the month of May (or early June) 1914 from Vidyakut. They occupied rooms in the big house of Jaishankar Sen. His wife, an elderly lady was the mother-figure for young women of the neighbourhood, and automatically became *mashima* (aunt) for Sri Ma. Bholanath's fellow-worker Madhu Babu and a friend Ksetramohan also had rooms in the same house where they lived with their wives. All these people were eye-witnesses of the beginnings of the display of the *sātvic bhāvas* which manifested themselves on Sri Ma's body. Ksetramohan's wife was not in Ashtagram at this time. Her husband wrote to her 'Ramani Babu has brought his wife back with him. There is an aura of luminousity around her which is extra-ordinary - she is like a glowing flame inside a lantern!'[9]

To begin with, Sri Ma enchanted all neighbours by her radiant smile and happy deportment. Jaishankar Sen's wife used to call her Khushir Ma (the Happy One), which was one of her childhood names. Sri Ma came to be known by this name in Ashtagram. Very soon all the neighbouring women developed an admiration for her neat and clean rooms, a high standard of cooking skill and her exemplary spirit of service toward Bholanath. She scrupulously observed all rules of behaviour extant in villages. Her childlike simplicity and openness was endearing and worked against any kind of gossip or idle chatter.

Khushir Ma used to keep aside one measure of the rice from the ration used for daily cooking. When the rice saved in this way came up to ten seers or so (approximately 20 pounds) she would take its cost from Bholanath. This money she kept aside for religious purposes, like fruits and sweets for temples or alms giving. She planted a *tulasi* in her side of the courtyard and tended it carefully.

Sri Ma's propensity toward identifying with the elements became more marked, but as before, the eye-witnesses mistook the states for a sudden onslaught of sleep or just absentmindedness. There was a large lake in Ashtagram. During the rainy season it seemed almost like the ocean because the other shore became invisible. One day Bholanath and some of his friends and their wives went out on a boating expedition. Sri Ma recalls, 'I had never before seen the ocean. The huge expanse of water seemed my own self. I felt a *kheyāla* towards integrating with it. Sometimes these sudden spurts of movement toward a boundlessness became visible to onlookers like flashes of light. Lest people should see me in this state now, I covered myself with my wrapper and lay down in the bottom of the boat. Madhu Babu, who had noted this, said '*Ṭhākrun* (madam) is sleepy!' Someone from the audience asked, 'Why did such transnatural things happen ?' Sri Ma answered with a smile, 'For this body[10] there is no distinction between what you call natural and that which would be considered trans-natural.'

Sri Ma also recalled that in spite of her tendency toward concealment many people came to notice her absorbed demeanour in front of Images in Temples, or other places of religious worship. But all these sparks from a latent immeasurable source of *sakti,* as it were, did not quite disturb her friends because Sri Ma's over-all deportment remained normal and friendly as usual.

The inhabitants of Ashtagram had to contend with sudden cyclones. During one such onslaught Bholanath and his wife had to remove to a safer place. They returned home after some days. Bholanath undertook such repairs to his rooms as were necessary. During the cyclone, the cane-work matting used for fencing had been blown off. A few of these sheets lay on the ground nearby. When Sri Ma picked these up, she was interested to find the ground underneath free of the dreaded weed which was the bane of life of the people of Ashtagram. This quick growing grass defied control and was forever encroaching onto paths and courtyards. Sri Ma now collected all the discarded matting and spread them around her courtyard. This worked like magic. The clean surroundings evoked admiration from neighbours. This led to other events. It was the custom in Ashtagram to hold *kirtans* in all houses from time to time. All neighbours would gather to sing *kirtan*, perhaps augmented by organised groups who could be invited to participate in these functions.

Bholanath also took his turn and a *kirtan* was arranged in this courtyard. Sri Ma sat with the wife of Madhu Babu who was ill at the time. Sri Ma recalled, 'I was sitting on her cot and watching the *kirtan*-party through the gaps in the fencing. Suddenly I saw the whole house illuminated by a bright light and this body at the centre of the kirtan mingling in with the effulgence and the joyousness. At that moment the body slipped down from the cot on to the floor. It rolled a little and then became still and inert. I was not unconscious. I heard the invalid cry out in alarm; Bholanath was fetched. He was told that Khusir Ma is in a fit. They sprinkled water on my face and raised the body to a sitting position. Bholanath helped me to walk back to my room. On being asked by him, I explained to him a little of the true state of my experience. This was the first time that I saw how it was that a person may be affected by the strains of devotional music.'

This phenomenon was repeated in a more powerful form when a well-known singer Gagan Rai came to Ashtagram to sing *kirtan* for them. He was a well-known minstrel, a sadhu, respected by everyone. Bholanath had invited him and his companions to have food at his place at the conclusion of the *kirtan*. Sri Ma, after cooking the meal, went out to sit with the other women who had gathered to listen to the singing. The *kirtan* started in the evening; soon it was dark. At its conclusion, the women left one by one, and since there was no light in the place, without noticing that Sri Ma's inert body was lying on the ground in a *samādhi*. Only one elderly lady whose little grandson had fallen asleep was left sitting by. When Bholanath found her absent from their room, he started looking around for her; the elderly woman then called out to him and the others that Khusir Ma was lying on the ground near her. This time Sri Ma could not be roused at all. So Bholanath with some help carried her to their room and laid her down in a corner of it. In the meantime, dogs had entered the room and spoiled all the cooked food. Bholanath was distracted, but first he had to make alternative arrangements for providing a proper meal for his guests. By the time everybody had been fed and bidden farewell to, it was almost dawn. Sri Ma was lying as she was, no changes of returning animation were visible in her. There was an effulgence surrounding her body. Nobody could mistake this state for a hysteric fit or unconsciousness or even death. There was an atmosphere of the sublime all around her. Even the site of the *kirtan* was pulsating with it. All those who had helped to carry her inert body were experiencing an ineffable joy and seemed transported to a different world. Bholanath however, was at his wits' end, not knowing how to recall Sri Ma to her normal state. Sri Ma's normal appearance after all was the best and most endearing sight. The majesty or glory of Divine Presence cannot be borne in comfort by human beings for long. Perhaps it will not be out of place to state here that no matter how exalted the *samādhi*-like states were, Sri Ma's companions always sighed in relief when her inimitable smile dawned to dispel the awesomeness and confirm the restoration of the norm. Someone had the happy idea of performing *kirtan* again. Gagan Rai was fetched from a neighbouring village. He was overwhelmed to see that Sri Ma had entered into a *samādhi* which had apparently been induced by his singing. He regretted that he had not been told about it the previous night. Now with a full heart, he sang again the songs with which he had started the evening before. To him it was the fulfilment of his efforts toward the evoking of the presence of the Princes of *saṃkirtana*, Sri Gaur, and Sri Nitai. He recognised in Sri Ma the *lakṣaṇas* (symptoms, indications) of the *mahābhāvas*[11] described in Vaisnava literature. He made his obeisance to her when she roused out of her *samādhi* after almost 19 hours. It was again evening when the *kirtan* was concluded.

The entire village was affected by the atmosphere of spiritual influence, but Sri Ma herself diffused, as always, any attempt to raise her above the ordinary. She was again the same friendly young girl not claiming any special recognition for her state of *samadhi*. On other occasions when she felt the stirrings of *mahābhāva*, she would quickly return to her room and shut herself in. Nevertheless, a rumour spread that Khushir Ma was prone to fits and this reached her parents in Vidyakut. They wrote to Bholanath making anxious enquiries. Even in those early days, Bholanath proved himself worthy of the very crucial position he was destined to occupy. He wrote back to say that their daughter was perfectly well and that there was no need to worry about her. From the very first days of their life together, his faith in her integrity and a kind of ethereal divinity remained unwavering and steadfast despite the many vicissitudes which threatened to engulf them at times.

There was another person in Ashtagram who had the distinction of penetrating the veil of anonymity with which Sri Ma surrounded herself. This was Harakumar, the brother of Srimati Sen, then living at his sister's. He was educated and well employed, but at times would be carried away by religious fervour and during these spells it became impossible for him to work normally. Hara Kumara's mother had died in the room which was given to Bholanath and Sri Ma when they came to Ashtagram. Either because of this or for some other reason best known to himself, he prostrated himself before Sri Ma and addressed her as 'Mother'. He would look for opportunities to render her some little service and was transported with joy when he received any hint of recognition from her. Village customs prevailed in Ashtagram. Ordinarily Sri Ma would not speak to menfolk who were not members of her family or very close friends of Bholanath. But Bholanath himself developed a kindness for Harakumar and allowed him the privileges of belonging to the family. Harakumar used to declare, 'Now it is only I who call you Mother. The day will come when the world will recognise you and call you so.' In this context it will be remembered that Harakumar's prophecy was the second one. The first had been spoken when Sri Ma was still an infant.

Sri Ma became slightly indisposed for some time at Ashtagram. Bholanath did his own cooking and took care of Sri Ma as best as he could. She recovered very soon and resumed her happy way of life.

Sri Ma used to be alone in her room for many hours when she had nothing to do. She sometimes sat quietly and watched herself repeating '*harībol*' the word which is used in the refrains of a *kirtan* or sung as a chorus at the end. Sri Ma found it came to her as a resonance, a *dhvani.* Soon it passed from her lips and tongue to become one with the breath of life passing in and out, in and out, in ever widening circles to an immeasurable horizon.

One night after the days work was done and Bholanath had lain down to his rest, Sri Ma said 'Shall I sit up for a while? You go to sleep.' Bholanath acquiesced. Sri Ma sat quietly repeating the sacred word. She watched her limbs arrange themselves in a yogic posture which much later she found was called the *siddhasana.* There was a feeling of joyousness within. Everyday she had new experiences. Her body would undergo other transformation, sometimes it become heavy and inert; at other times very light as if it had no contact with the earth. Once while she felt she was extraordinarily powerful, her hand happened to fall on Bholanath who was sleeping at her side. He woke up with a start and in the dark mistook it for a man's hand; he grasped it strongly shouting 'Thief, thief!' When he realized his mistake he was puzzled, but Sri Ma persuaded him to go back to sleep again.

One day she saw herself assume the *padmāsana.* Her back straightened; she felt a tremor near the base of the spine and to the accompaniment of a slight rhythmic sound the spinal column seemed to get locked in an upright position block by block. It came to her *kheyāla* that it was almost like what she had seen in Narundi when a derailed train had been hoisted up on the rails piece by piece making a rhythmic noise. She described it by using another image, that of the placing of smaller and smaller pots on the firm base of a big pot like the topmost spire of a temple. She envisioned a cluster of nerves at each centre which looked like lotus flowers in bloom. At this time she said she had a feeling of utter ease and freedom. The body was itself a help rather than an obstacle to meditation and *nāmajapa.* She felt a tremendous power inside her. Then suddenly she would think that it was very late and she should sleep so at once the whole phenomenon seemed as if switched off. She lay down and went to sleep.

Sri Ma from time to time has described many such experiences which in their range and variety defy an exhaustive compilation. Moreover she has said that she has not disclosed even one hundredth of the entirety of her spiritual adventures. It is however clear from the description that she was aware of what was taking place and she was also not helplessly given over to the surging tides of this spiritual *līlā* of *śakti.*

Bholanath (Ramani Mohan) and Sri Ma

Bholanath knew Sri Ma to be a friendly cheerful girl, scrupulously truthful and unquestioningly obedient to her elders. Her mother had told her that she should respect and obey Bholanath just as she did her parents. This was the key-note of her deportment toward Bholanath. Throughout his life, she never did anything without his permission or prior acquiescence. He for his part learned very soon to respect her *kheyālas* and rarely went against them, or at least not for very long.

When Sri Ma came to Ashtagram to keep house for him he one day asked her in some curiosity if she had never felt the slightest desire to get news of him? He was moved to ask because although all his letters were scrupulously answered by her, he had guessed correctly that they were dictated by her parents, if she were in Kheora or Pramoda Devi if she were in Narundi or Sripur. Sri Ma answered no, it had never crossed her *kheyāla* to think about him. Bholanath persisted, saying, 'If I go away, or am taken ill, or even if I were to die, will you not mind at all?' Sri Ma answered, 'What is there to mind? Will it be any different?'

Bholanath was not offended or saddened by this equable attitude. He said in some wonderment, 'You are innocent like a child - It will be all right when you grow up.' Sri Ma, recalling this incident, added with a smile, 'But it seems that I never grew up!'[12]

In a more serious mood of recollecting her early life with Bholanath, Sri Ma has said, 'After all, this body was given unto his care, it was for him to do as he wished; but he saw that even a trace of worldly thought was repelled by it. Even a slight change in his demeanour toward it used to produce death-like symptoms; he would be scared and immediately engage in *nāma-japa* in order to restore it to its normal state. His behaviour was always exemplary; he was wholly concerned about my well-being'.

Bholanath's continued proximity to such a presence of luminous purity, must have metamorphosed his total being; perhaps it is not entirely right to say this because no one but he could have so occupied the position of a guardian, a bulwark, for Sri Ma, while she went through the years of house-keeping as well as her *līlā* of *sādhanā*. He evidently was the person-elect for this onerous post which he graced easily and competently till the time of his *samadhi* in 1938.

To the question as to why Sri Ma had rejected the legitimate scope of enjoyment for a married couple, she once made this very crucial answer:

'For this body there is no question of enjoyment or rejection. Whatever happens to it is necessary for all of you - perhaps this aspect is not so necessary (for human beings).'

Can we read in these words a new interpretation of what it means to be a human being? All her other *vāṇis* derive straitly from this supreme elevation of dispassion in life, as for example:

'The one and only duty for man is to engage in God-remembrance.'

After a stay of almost four years at Ashtagram, Bholanath was transferred to Bajitpur. Before joining his service there, they decided to pay a short visit to Vidyakut. Madhu Babu and his wife were very friendly with Bholanath and Sri Ma. They were invited to come with them on a visit. The journey was undertaken by boat. In midstream they were hailed by another big boat, who wanted a little fire from them. Bholanath and Madhu Babu had been warned against river-dacoits on this stretch of the river. They asked their own boatmen to quicken their pace to outstrip the boat which was following them. Their own boat was loaded with baggage as both families were changing house. The women were wearing lots of ornaments as was usual in those days. Evening was upon them and it started to drizzle. Soon it was quite dark but the big boat seemed to be pursuing them swiftly. Sri Ma signalled to Bholanath to ask the boatmen to enter a narrow channel of water which was just discernible in the dark. This was done, and rowing carefully they came to a village of fishermen. The big boat obviously had missed this manoeuvre. The villagers told them that they had escaped in the nick of time because no doubt they were being followed by dacoits. They spent the night in this village and next morning arrived at Vidyakut.

Vidyakut

There were scenes of rejoicing at this homecoming! Madhu Babu and his family were entertained to a feast and then bidden an affectionate farewell by Bholanath and Sri Ma. They continued on their journey to their own village. Sri Ma resumed her playful activities with her little cousins who became her playmates and also she would visit the host of aunts, uncles, grandmothers and grandfathers who abounded in the village; also the neighbours who would eagerly await her coming. The elderly people would marvel at her playing with the children, 'It doesn't seem that she is a grown-up young woman - she is so childlike.' Sri Ma did not practice her *nama-japa* or meditation in Vidyakut, so up to this time Bholanath only knew about the *yogic kriyas.*

The whole village of Vidyakut assumed a festive look with the coming of their beloved Nirmala. She unexpectedly met Harish, the postman in Vidyakut who had previously been in Sultanpur while Sri Ma was a child. He had been very fond of her; now he met her with affection. Sri Ma recalled that when she looked at him it was as if a torch light was shone on his face - it looked so lighted up. This man later became an ascetic and spent his life in *sādhanā.*

Bholanath's joining-time leave came to an end. It was decided that while Bholanath would proceed to Bajitpur to find suitable quarters etc, Sri Ma would go to Atpara to stay with his family for some time. Farewells were difficult. The whole village was plunged in gloom. The girls from Muslim households walked with the family to see the ferry-steamer off. Sri Ma also looked sad and her smile was misty when she tried to answer everybody's repeated question 'When will you come again?'

Bholanath went separately to Bajitpur. Sri Ma's father escorted her to Atpara. Disembarking at the pier, a *palki* (a palanquin, borne by 4 bearers) was engaged for Sri Ma by Bipin Bihari while he planned to accompany her on foot with a coolie carrying the baggage.

The palanquin bearers soon outstripped Bipin Bihari and the coolie. They wouldn't listen to Sri Ma's appeals to go slow. Soon they arrived at a junction of lanes and did not know which to take. Belatedly obeying Sri Ma they advanced along one lane but soon lowered the palanquin and sat down at the roadside because they felt they were just lost. Sri Ma then asked them to fetch any passer by they could find. So after a while she heard an educated voice ask, 'Where do you wish to go?' Now this being her husband's village, she could not show herself or talk to him. She would be expected to behave like a bride. She put out her right hand through the curtains and wrote Revati Mohan's name in the dust of the road with her finger. The gentleman then escorted her to her home. Bipin Bihari arrived much later.

Atpara

Sri Ma was already well-known in Atpara. She had stayed at the village for 6 months with Pramoda Devi and her family after the passing away of Revati Mohan. There was a settlement of poor low-caste people nearby. The girls from this settlement had become very attached to Sri Ma. They used to help her with household work when they saw how hard-pressed she was with the responsibility of cooking and cleaning for a large family. Sri Ma on her part gave them whatever she could spare from the storeroom or her own share of fruits or sweets. They sometimes brushed out her hair or washed her clothes. Sri Ma herself sometimes arranged the hair of these young girls in a variety of styles.

An interesting incident had occured while Sri Ma was staying in Atpara previously. One day a bell-metal plate slipped and broke while she was returning from the pond with a stack of them in her hands. The girls saw the accident; they immediately approached Bholanath who was visiting Atpara at the time and prevailed upon him to assume the blame, knowing Pramoda Devi would not scold her brother-in-law as she definitely would Sri Ma. Bholanath got carried away by their concern for Sri Ma, although he himself was not prone to deviousness of any kind. He pretended that it was he who had broken the plate and so saved Sri Ma from a reprimand. It was lucky that nobody asked Sri Ma, otherwise the truth would have come out to the consternation of the conspirators! It was a small incident but it demonstated the love and concern of the poor people for their 'friend'. As far as he was concerned, Bholanath never found fault with her either then or in later life.

Now Sri Ma met these friends again. She also became involved in household activities because she would not allow her elder sister-in-law Pramoda Devi to do anything while she was at hand. After a few weeks there was a theft in the house which upset Pramoda Devi, already suffering from bereavement. Bholanath came from Bajitpur and took all of them back with him. After a few months Pramoda Devi her two sons and daughter Kalipada, Labanya and Ashu returned back to Atpara. She was a little bit more relaxed and able to cope with her depleted family.

References

1. Raisahab Sri Akshay K. Datta Gupta, Kaviratna, M.A., 'God as Love' in *Mother as seen by Her Devotees*, Varanasi, 1956 pp. 33-34.
2. Amulya Kumar Datta Gupta 'A page from my Diary' *Mother as Seen by Her Devotees*, 1956, p. 13.
3. S.S. Vol. II, p. 19.

4. S.S. Vol. II, p. 37.
5. S.S. Vol. II, p. 37.
6. S.S. Vol II, p. 63.
7. This name was given to Ramani Mohan by Sri Ma in later years. It will be convenient to use it for these accounts, as he came to be known by it in Dhaka.
8. S.S. Vol. II, p. 82.
9. S.S. Vol. III, p.133.
10. Sri Ma always used the words 'this body' when referring to herself. We have substituted the pronoun 'I' in many places.
11. The transformations induced by a high spiritual state of awareness of the divine play of Sakti, possible only in bodies unsullied, and of pristine purity such as those of Lord Gauranga and Prabhu Nityananda.

    The romantic heart of Bengal believes that the Incarnation of Lord Gauranga was in the nature of a fulfilment of a debt - a *ṛṇmukti.* As Krishna he had had no occasion to respond to or acknowledge the utterly undemanding, selfless and one-pointed love of Sri Radha; He had said, He would be reborn to spend one life time doing this. The Bengal Vaiṣṇavas believe that Krishna came as Sri Gauranga to uphold the love of the Gopi as an exemplary way of relating to God - to add *prema* (undemanding love) as the fifth *puruṣārtha* (aim in life) to the traditional four of *dharma, artha, kāma* and *mokṣa.*
12. S.S. Vol. II, p. 75.

CHAPTER THREE

The Manifestation of Śakti as Sādhanā

It is beyond our ordinary intelligence to understand what Mother really is. Though she is constantly saying, 'I am but a wayward crazy daughter of yours', yet underlying all Her movements and behind Her ever-enchanting Līlā amongst us, is to be discerned the manifestation in bodily form of the Supreme Divine Sakti.

- Bhaiji

Matṛdarśana, p. 159

If somebody has an experience about any occurence, then he feels it as the greatest truth vouchsafed to him. If somebody feels awe and reverence for a person, then, of course, he will automatically believe in the words of that person. But until such an authority is found, one in general remains bound up within his system of beliefs. I have told you so often that even within a group which, say, worship Kṛṣṇa there are differences. Not all of them adore the same Kṛṣṇa. The aim of all spiritual endeavour is to realize that the Kṛṣṇa that you adore is the same Kṛṣṇa being worshipped by others, that is, to discover the unity of all ways of understanding the Lord (the *Iṣṭa*). To see yourself in everyone and to realize that everyone is in you, is the supreme aim of spiritual knowledge.

- Sri Ma Anandamayi

* The manifestation of Śakti as Sādhanā
* Bholanath's Initiation

The Manifestation of Śakti as Sādhanā

As far as spiritual exercises for a religious life are concerned we have to consider that a full command of such knowledge was absolutely spontaneous with Sri Ma Anandamayi. She had received no training or instructions from anybody. She had never withdrawn from her family to lead the solitary life of a recluse in quest of religious felicity. She had not studied books or listened to discourses. Whatever she said or did, came from within like the response of a bell when sounded. Sri Ma Anandamayi, sometimes used this simile to account for her way of talking to people who came for spiritual guidance. To some she returned simple answers, others she answered at length; the variety and range of her answers, defies any simplified account of them. Sri Ma has said, 'This body is like an instrument, you will hear the tune you can strike on it'

Yet, at one period of her life she did go through the motions of a committed pilgrim (*sādhaka*) in quest of Truth. She has related how this happened to come about: 'One day in Bajitpur I had gone as usual to a pond nearby for my daily bath. While I was pouring the water over my head, the *kheyāla* came to me, 'How would it be to engage in a *līlā* of *sādhanā*?' and so it began.'

Bajitpur has acquired some significance for those, who seek to look beyond their given worldly conditions to a region of Grace which is spoken of by the scriptures of all the religions of the world. During the short period of just six years or so, Sri Ma lived out the reality of the promise of fulfilment to all pilgrims who dare to step out onto the razor's edge path of the quest for Truth. In retrospect we realize that during this time Sri Ma quietly and unobtrusively allowed her body to become the playground of that Śakti which engenders, sustains and withdraws into itself, all that there is in this world and beyond. There was no fan-fare, no awed audience (other than Bholanath) or any indication that a very remarkable phenomenon was revealing itself which would later amaze the great scholars and renowned ascetics of our country and hold them in thrall for hours together just listening to her exposition of the innermost experiences of a *sādhaka* in quest of Supreme Knowledge on gaining which everything is attained at once.[1]

The beginning of this pilgrimage was simple enough. Sri Ma has said repeatedly, 'The Name alone is sufficient (wherewithal for *sādhanā*)', and we see that she demonstrated this truth for us in Bajitpur.

She had the *kheyāla* for performing *sādhanā*. She made a beginning by doing what she had seen her mother and grandmother perform at the time of their evening rituals. She swept and cleaned the already spotless room in which she lived. She enkindled incense and walked around the cottage with the burner in her hand. The evening air became suffused with the pure scent of sandalwood. When Bholanath returned from his work and had rested for a while, she served him his evening meal; she also prepared for him the indigenous smoking gadget known as a *hookāh* for his after-dinner smoke! Then she asked his permission to sit in *nāma-japa* for a while. He readily consented, being in the habit of indulging her rarely-expressed *kheyāla*.

Sri Ma, after obtaining his permission, seated herself in one corner of the room and in a soft voice, orally commenced to repeat the name, 'Hari, Hari', for no other reason than that she had learnt to sing this Name with her father in her childhood. Very soon Bholanath saw her assume a yogic-posture, sitting up straight with eyes closed and an expression of inwardness. Every day she seemed to go deeper inside in concentration; after many hours of this meditative posture she would gradually rouse out of it. She would get up slowly and sometimes eat a little of her evening meal and then lie down on her bed. For many months this light meal at midnight or even later was her only intake of food during a twenty-four hour period. Throughout the day, she remained in a sort of other-worldly rapture, going about her housework like an automaton.

Bholanath after a few days of this routine, said to her in some anxiety, 'Why do you pronounce the name of Hari ? We are not Vaishnavas. We are Shaktas.'

'Should I then say, Śiva, Śiva?'

'Yes, that is allright.'

Sri Ma changed over to the name, Siva. This small incident foreshadows the entire gamut of *sādhanā* as practiced by her and later the panoramic vision she seemed to have when talking about the One and only Reality. She has said that when she pronounced Hari', it was just the sound of the word she meditated upon. She did not visualize a Form and so with Śiva. The resonance of these sacred sounds led to the revelation of the unity of all such sound-forms and to their significance as indicators to the One Reality underlying all Names and Forms.

For some months, afterwards Sri Ma continued to practice her *sādhanā*. Her body became as if an instrument for the play of this profound music. With the sounds of the letters her limbs, her entire body moved as if in vibrant dance-forms, trembling and responding to an exhilarating choreography of inner *Śakti*. Her body assumed a variety of yogic postures while she sat in meditation, the hands and fingers assuming appropriate positions. Bholanath watched her, amazed and awed. Some of the *āsanas* he recognised for what they were, but many were beyond his comprehension. Sometimes he watched her, fascinated by the beautiful spectacle, and sometimes overcome by tiredness after the day's work, he fell asleep while Sri Ma sat in her corner absorbed in an universe not of this world. He knew that Sri Ma had no previous knowledge of yogic *āsanas*. Moreover it was obvious to him that these motions were being gone through automatically, as if her limbs were being arranged in these postures. Sri Ma has said that she was merely an onlooker to these proceedings.

This *līlā* however, did not pass unnoticed. Some curious people peered through the fences during the day because although her *sādhanā* was performed at night, the mornings found her in exalted states which made her seem aloof and unapproachable. The erstwhile well-beloved girl of the neighbourhood began to be shunned by her friends. They felt scared of her, thinking she had become possessed of spirits. The educated among them thought that she was suffering from some kind of hysteria. Sri Ma, for her part welcomed the sudden quietude; it was the right thing to happen at the time because a *sādhaka* needs to be alone. Two friends only stayed the course, as it were. One was the servant-girl who noticing that her young mistress was not able to perform the housework in her usual efficient style, did considerably more than her own share of the chores. If she saw Sri Ma lying in a state of *samādhi*, she would quietly finish whatever needed to be done. The other friend was a dog called Toma. Bholanath had brought him as a puppy. Sri Ma had reared him with her usual loving care for animals. He used to be on guard, all the while that she was alone in the house. He would sit or lie near her; he never touched any of the foodstuff which Sri Ma had cooked and had not been able to put away or cover properly. Sometimes in the midst of cooking, she would be overtaken by a beatific state and roll over on the ground in deep *samadhi.* Toma kept guard till Bholanath returned from the Kutchery.

Bholanath, although completely convinced that whatever was happening to Sri Ma was of great spiritual significance and not a travesty of it, occasionally felt some misgivings because he believed in the tradition which said that nothing can be achieved in this trans-natural sphere without help from one's Guru. Perhaps in response to this perplexity in him Sri Ma had the *kheyāla* for a Spiritual Initiation which was fulfilled on August 3, 1922.

Nothing happened outwardly. On this night Sri Ma, as usual cooked and served the evening meal to Bholanath, his nephew Ashu and her own cousin Nishikanta who were staying with them. Earlier that evening her neighbours had come to invite her to go with them to see the special decorations in the Temples as it was the night of *Rakhi-Purnima.* She had declined the invitation. Years later when she related those incidents, the date was calculated from these reminiscences. In 1922, *Rakhi Purnima* happened to fall on August 3. When her family had retired to rest, she sat in her corner for her daily worship. After sometime, she watched her finger draw a mystic design (*yantra*) on the floor. She herself became the Guru; a *bīja-mantra* (a mystic syllable) came from within her; she saw herself write this mantra inside the mystic diagram already drawn in front of her. She now became the *śiṣya* (disciple) and received the *mantra,* as it were, from herself as the Guru. The unity of *Guru, Śiṣya* and *mantra* was self-evident but remained as if in abeyance, while she began the *japa-sādhanā* of the *mantra* instead of the Names which she had been repeating earlier.

Sri Ma has described the importance of Initiation in these words: 'Supposing you wish to attract the attention of a person who is far away from you. You use any words to call out to him like, hey!, or you there! He says, You wish to speak to me? My name is such and such! Then you learn how exactly to call out to him. So the *dikṣā* (initiation). It is God alone who is the Guru always!'

For the next five months her *sādhanā* assumed a more concrete form. After the *līlā* of *dikṣā* (spiritual initiation) hymn-like compositions in Sanskrit would at times flow from her lips, generally preceded by the single syllable OM. The spontaneity of these utterances was all too obvious because she had no previous knowledge of Sanskrit let alone the ancient form of it used in the Vedas. During this time the normal functions of her body were suspended for hours and even days. She did not feel hungry or in need of rest. Her days were not divided into mornings, evenings or nights - there was only one prolonged period of indescribable bliss. She has said that her mouth would have the flavour of a honey-like substance which came from within and which became so profuse at times that she would swallow it down. But it left no bad after taste in her mouth as is usual with sweet things. Sometimes she felt that her body had become as light as a feather and had risen from the floor or again that it had become as heavy and immovable as a rock. At this time Sri Ma was not able to do her housework properly. Bholanath had to cook for the family sometimes, and also look after her as best as he could.

Sri Ma's cousin Nishikanta Bhattacharya had come on a visit. He was taken aback to see her state of preoccupation with religious exercises and what he deemed Bholanath's indulgence of this state of affairs. Bholanath on his part was glad to talk over this matter with his brother-in-law, who was considerably older and a learned man. They were in the habit of playing a game of chess after their midday meal. After the game Bholanath used to return to his Kutchery. One day (probably the fourth day after the *līlā* of *dikṣā*) instead of their usual game, they came into Sri Ma's room, where she was sitting rapt in her own aura of inner light. Her cousin had evidently decided upon remonstrating with her. He now said to Bholanath in a rough sort of voice, 'Why don't you ask her what she is doing?'

In general Sri Ma accorded him the respect due to an elder brother but this day she met his look head-on, as it were, and spoke sharply in a manner quite unlike her own, 'What is it you want to know?' Nishikanta was taken aback and was moved to fold his hands in an unwonted gesture of humility. Then Sri Ma said in a milder tone, 'Don't be afraid, what is it?'

'Why do you practice all these *kriyās* (exercises). Have you been initiated into spiritual life?'

'Yes'

'Has Ramani (Bholanath) also been initiated?'

'No, but he will be after five months. (Sri Ma named the exact day, and date with its presiding star.)'

'I do not understand what you mean by the star.'

'Go and ask Janaki Sen, He is fishing at the pond.'

'Why do you speak in such an unnatural manner to us?'

'It seems so to you. I am same, as always.'

Bholanath and Nishikanta were thoroughly upset. Janaki Sen was fetched from the pond. Nobody had time to wonder as to how Sri Ma could know his whereabouts, especially as he should have been in his office at the time. Janaki Sen had never before seen Sri Ma without her veil pulled decorously over her face. He also was astonished at her aura of a powerful and divine personality. After some questions and quick rejoinders from Sri Ma, Janaki Sen said, 'Who are you?' To this question which had been put to her by her cousin earlier, she returned the same answer, Purṇa Brahma Nārāyaṇa (the Supreme Being). Janaki Sen said, 'You are the devil, the devil, the devil!' Sri Ma seemed amused and said, 'You wish to test me isn't it?'

'Yes! If you have any spiritual powers, give us a demonstration.'

Sri Ma beckoned to Bholanath to seat himself. She then lightly touched his head. Immediately he seemed to go into a deep state of meditation. He became utterly still and his face was calm and serene. His friends were non-plussed. Most probably they had expected some miracles from her; they did not have the calibre to understand that a gift of *samādhi* by a mere touch of the hand is possible only in the dimension of Divine Grace. *Samādhi*, a state coveted by the *sādhakas* of all ages; life-times are spent in rigorous spiritual exercises in the hope that they will culminate in *samādhi*, and here Bholanath received the bliss of attainment as a gift.

They did not understand that Sri Ma had done what was asked of her.

All this was conjectured by scholars later on; at the time everything was confusion. Both Nishikanta and Janaki Sen were frightened. Ashu, Bholanath's nephew, on his return from school was bewildered to see his aunt looking somehow different and his uncle sitting immovable as if lost to the world. He began to cry. Both men now requested Sri Ma to restore Bholanath to normalcy. Sri Ma more in response to Ashu's distress than their request, again gently touched Bholanath. He gradually roused out of his *samādhi.* Questioned about his experience, he said with some difficulty that he had never known such bliss, that he had been indescribably joyous and at peace. The time for revelation was not yet, so this interlude was allowed to sink down in the memories of the people concerned. It is true that Sri Ma was not doubted any more. Neighbours and friends thought that she was extra-ordinarily gifted and seized with the religious way of life. The main reason that she did not cause any stir in the neighbourhood was her own quiet, unassuming deportment of normal behaviour, not the least remarkable feature of which was her charming smile which seemed at once to dispel doubt and inculcate an irresistable attraction. Thus no radical changes took place in Sri Ma's vicinity after her display of a little of the wealth which as far as she was concerned always lay well-hidden. She continued with her *sādhanā* and in due course Bholanath was initiated by her on the day and date specified by her.

Bholanath's Initiation

Although Sri Ma had not mentioned the matter again, Bholanath remembered the date of his promised Initiation. With a vague idea of avoiding anything that might happen he hurried off to his office without his breakfast. The disciple is expected to keep complete fast until the rite is over. Unintentionally Bholanath fulfilled this condition. At the appropriate hour Sri Ma sent word to him to come home. Bholanath replied that he was busy and could not leave the office. Sri Ma then had the message conveyed to him that if he did not come immediately, she would herself come to the office. Not daring to risk this, Bholanath reluctantly came home. Sri Ma gave him a change of clothes and told him to bathe and put them on. She had set an *āsana* for him. Bholanath seated himself and composedly awaited further developments. Sri Ma was walking up and down the room. He saw that she was in one of her states of *bhāva*; beautiful *mantras* issued from her lips, their sound and cadence exquisite and awe-inspiring. After a while she came and sat near him. He heard her repeating just one *mantra* softly to herself. By leaning forward and bringing his ear close to her lips he heard this *mantra* clearly. He concluded correctly that this was meant for him.

When the exalted mood had passed, Sri Ma gave him detailed instructions how to use the *mantra* he had heard. He did not doubt her teachings, because from his own knowledge of ritualism, he saw the perfection with which each detail of the Initiation was explained by her.

This incident marked a new turn in their relationship, every phase of which was exemplary and beautiful: as a guardian and young ward, as friends, as Guru and *śiṣya*, and as just companions who understood each other with perfection on one side and unquestioning dependence on the other. This was an unique relationship because we cannot call to mind any parallels. In later years Bholanath was automatically expected to adopt the role of the priest who could offer ritualistic worship to Sri Ma Anandamayi when the devotees began to celebrate the time of advent of their adored Ma. No one else was considered suitable for this rare service.

Sri Ma herself remained unchanged in her attitude toward him. She would ask his permission for all suggestions regarding her movements, render him service if he so required it of her, like rubbing his feet when he was tired; she treated him like a close friend, with humour and understanding, coaxing him back into good humour if he were annoyed with anything. She herself never said or did anything to diminish his position as the head of the ever expanding family which began to collect round her as soon as she emerged into the limelight of public acclaim.

The time of emergence was approaching fast but in Bajitpur all was quiet and serene. After Sri Ma's own Initiation she followed an intensive course of one-pointed, relentless, all-encompassing *sādhanā* for approximately five and a half months. It culminated in an experience of fulfilment which is described in the Upanishads as: 'On gaining which everything is attained.' (*Taittirīya* II.1)

Sri Ma has said that the *sādhanā* by which man endeavours to attain self-realization are of endless variety, and each has innumerable aspects. All these became a living experience to her when she became a *sādhaka*.[2] During this period she went through countless forms of worship, not only the various Hindu forms, but other non-Hindu ways of relating to the Supreme Being. When scholars expressed their wonder and amazement at the depth and range of her knowledge regarding the religious way of life, she said that not even one-hundredth part of the totality of that which happened in the six-year period at Bajitpur has been disclosed by her. The Infinite has infinite ways of manifesting itself; each spark is a whole in Itself. It is for man to become a wayfarer, a pilgrim, to feel a thirst for knowledge. A true quest is sure to bring about fulfilment.

The end of Sri Ma's period of *sādhanā* coincided with Bholanath's *dikṣā* as well as the beginning of her own period of *maunam* for almost three years. She became silent as if the inner blessedness had found expression in outer stillness. The period of this *maunam* most probably lasted from December 1922 to December 1925. It so happened that Bholanath's youngest brother Jamini Kumar came on a visit to Bajitpur around this time. He was very depressed to find his sister-in-law observing silence. He would follow her about disconsolately pleading with her to talk to him. Sri Ma was always kindness itself toward her young relatives. One day she sat on the floor in the posture of *siddhāsana*. With the tips of her thumb and forefinger joined, she drew an imaginary circle on the ground all around her body forming a *kuṇḍalī* (ring) by twisting at 180^0 angle on either side. It was a very quick and graceful movement. After a while some *mantras* emerged from her lips. Thereafter she spoke in a soft voice which gradually became stronger and normal. In this manner she responded to her young brother-in-law's desire to hold a conversation with her. He was very happy. She, then, wiped away the imaginary circle in the same manner and resumed her *maunam*. When occasion demanded, she, once or twice spoke to Bholanath from inside the circle during the entire period of her silence.

In later years many scholars of distinction became interested in this *līlā* of *sādhanā*. Speculations and theories were mooted but as Pandit Gopinath Kavirajji has stated clearly it could not be classified under any rubric mentioned in the Śāstras.[3] Sri Ma has, on occasions, spoken about this *līlā* in her own inimitable style, which is simple but profound:

'The yogic *kriyas* were just like the playfulness of earlier years – for me there was no difference or necessity either for the one or the other. (D.D. Vol. V, p. 143).'

Again, in answer to the question that, if a physical body is assumed then it becomes obligatory to practice *sādhanā* to neutralize this bondage, Sri Ma said:

'Whatever anybody judges this body to be is how he looks at it. Some others say that if *sādhanā* has been performed in previous lives, then the last life sees a culmination of it. But here, when we speak of '*sādhanā*', wherefrom did this body learn the way of it? There was no outsider who came to teach this body anything! Have I not said many times that *sādhanā* is just playfulness. Don't I say sometimes 'Let us visit such and such a place' although the place is already known to me. In truth it was just a *kheyāla* and nothing else.'[4]

Referring to authenticity, Sri Ma has said,

'*Sādhanā* must conform to scriptural injunctions. If you do not find it in one place, you will find it in another. How much can be written after all? In a Railway Time-Table you can see the names of big cities. If you keep on travelling you will see much of what is not mentioned in a travelogue. The indications are all given in the Scriptures. If you come across some exceptions as far as *sādhanā* by this body is concerned then you will know it as other than the orthodox way. At least you will find them mentioned as unorthodox procedures! So after all, you have found them mentioned, isn't it?

'Here there was no question of a gradual advancement. Some later stages happened earlier or in the usual way - there was no distinction between upper and lower or later and earlier or simpler and advanced.

'It all came from within. Sometimes I used to hear distinctly, Repeat this *mantra*'. It was again I who asked 'whose mantra is this?' At once the answer came 'Gaṇeśa or Viṣṇu or some other Form'. A query rose in me again, 'How does he look?' A Form seemed to take shape out of my body and then vanish within. Do not think that I encountered the Forms of your ways of worship only; what you would say alien Forms, were also manifested in a similar way and worshipped by me. This is why you find me so conversant with the details of ritualistic procedures of countless ways of relating to God.

'Then it would come from within me 'What do you need to worship? You are everything!' At once - the Realization - partial knowledge submerging into an integral knowledge - I was the One that appears as many.

'This body, therefore, responds to the state of understanding of the interlocuter. What limits can be set to the opinions of this body? But if you go along a traditional line of approach, you can reach the goal and again beyond that remains the unattained. But where the distinction between the attainable and the unattained does not arise is That Itself. What you hear depends upon how you play the instrument. For this body difference of opinions remains a non-issue.'

Pandit Gopinath Kaviraj summarises Sri Ma's *līlā* of *sādhanā* in these words:

'In this play she started with ignorance and proceeded through various austerities, observing silence, regulating diet, practicing *japa* and yogic excercises and performing *pūja* and other similar rites. Dawn of knowledge formed also a part of this play. A sense of agony and dryness of the soul followed by the bliss of union had their own places in this self-enacted drama .... One should not take it as an illustration of divided self and of its activities - it is rather the outcome of an eternally vigilant and self-conscious Will playing the double part of impersonation of a *sādhikā* passing through the shadows and lights of a disciplined life and of the still Witness behind observing and directing its own play on the stage.'

Pandit Gopinath Kavirajji's words were read out to Sri Ma. Sri Ma's response was:

'Acting? What is not, is to be presented as real? At a set time, for the pleasure of onlookers, isn't it? Then a rehearsal is required for bringing about in the imagination a well-ordered sequence.

'Where One alone is, how to distinguish between player and witness? Consider, whatever can be burnt down by a big fire can be accomplished by a spark as well - The conflagaration and the little burning cinder are one - If you say the whole and its part, it is still the same. Oneness - if there is no other than the One only then what should be drama and what real?'

The quiet days in the backwaters of the villages of Bengal were soon to become a memory only for the people close to Nirmala. The time was approaching when Sri Ma would make her public appearance as a person of great spiritual eminence. The people who formed the nucleus of her entourage were almost ready to receive her in their midst as the fulfilment of inarticulated but nevertheless deeply felt yearning for the other life which finding the fragmented joys of this world unsatisfying aims at nothing less than the plenum of Delight which the tradition extols as Self-Realization, or God-Realization.

For the sake of convenience we mark out a period of transition in a life which knew no change overs from one stage to another. Apparently after a life of *sādhanā*, Sri Ma started to speak on the religious quest for God-realization to an audience which was competent and worthy of receiving this teaching. In this context we quote here from a letter written by Sri Ma herself in answer to the questions of one such person who was quick to recognize her extra-ordinary air of transcendence.

'I am writing a little about the first stage of my *sādhanā* (which you wished to know about). The sound of *kīrtan* used to generate an attraction, fill me with bliss.. as if I were being carried away on waves of joy. An outside power (*Śakti*) would make this body move in exultation. I was fully aware of myself at the time... When this plenum of joy started to evaporate, I would yearn for a renewal of this supreme bliss. I would feel like sharing it with the whole world - I would think, let all beings experience this inexpressible joy... (Letter to Sri Pran Gopal Mukhopadhyaya)'[5]

So, the 'giving' out of a boundless compassion for humanity and the seeking for Grace (*kṛpā*) came together in Dhaka in rather a spectacular way and established a way of life for Sri Ma's entourage for the future also.

References

1. Taittiriyopaniṣad II.1.
2. Sri Ma always used the mascutive gender when speaking about herself, so we have written *sādhaka* instead of *śādhīkā*.
3. 'Introduction' *Mother as Seen by Her Devotees*, Banaras 1956, pp i-xxxviii.
4. Amulya Kumar Dattagupta, *Anandavarta*, Vol. XV, no. 2, 1967.
5. S.S. - Vol. II, pp. 79-80.
6. Letter published by Prof. Govinda Gopal Mukhopadhyaya in *Adbhut Katha* (in Bengali) Calcutta, 1993 pp. 109-110 (Tr. by author).

CHAPTER FOUR

The Ma of Dhaka

All of us children were studying upstairs. Somebody called out from below, 'Come down, the Ma of Shahbagh has come.' We were struck dumb; 'the Ma of Shahbagh?' 'the *manuṣ-kālī* (Kālī in human form) in our house?' We descended slowly trembling with fear. When we entered the room we saw a beautiful lady with a radiant smile. We approached her eagerly. We did *praṇāms*, one by one. To me she said, 'You are a good boy!'

These words have been like a bridle-rein in my life. Whenever I have been tempted to go astray, and I have been so tempted, the memory of these words have saved me. Jai Ma!

From Shakti Kumar Ghosh
(Second son of Sri Manmohan
Ghosh of Dhaka)

A question : Ma, your *līlā* in Dhaka was fascinating but it was of a very short duration. I wish we could hear more about those days.

Sri Ma : Dhaka? (lit. a covering) Dhaka will remain *dhaka* (covered, hidden) forever.

- **Gathering of the devotees**
- **Life at Shahbagh. The *kirtan* on January 26, 1926.**
- **The atomsphere of the miraculous.**
- **Sri Ma and a Muslim devotee**

The Ma of Dhaka

Gathering of the Devotees

Bholanath lost his post of Law Clerk in April 1924. His employers, for reasons of economy, were winding up their business in Bajitpur. Hoping for better employment in a bigger town, he came to Dhaka with his wife on April 10, 1924. In spite of his best efforts he was unable to find work immediately. He decided to send Sri Ma to his village home and stay on alone. Sri Ma was still observing silence. She indicated to him that he should wait for three more days. Bholanath, thankfully, found work on the third day. On April 17, he was appointed Manager of the extensive Shahbagh Gardens belonging to the daughter of the Nawab of Dhaka, Nawabzadi Pyari Bano. He was engaged by Jogesh Chandra Ghosh, the Trustee of the Nawabzadi's Estates in Dhaka. Jogesh Chandra Ghosh had heard about Bholanath and Sri Ma from his son-in-law, Bhudeb Basu, who had known them in Bajitpur.

The Gardens covered a lot of area. Much of it had remained unkempt and overgrown with wild shrubbery and creepers. Only a portion of it was well laid out with seasonal flowers. There were many fruit trees and green grassy areas also. The Manager's quarters adjoined a swimming pool and a dance-hall for the recreational purposes of the owners. The entire property was enclosed by a high wall, because ladies from the Nawab's family sometimes came to visit the garden and bathe in the swimming pool. It was Bholanath's job to supervise the work of a gang of labourers and look after the property in general. After they had settled in, Bholanath's nephew Ashu came to stay with them.

Sri Ma was not only observing silence, but the states of *bhāva* also continued to occur any time during the day or night. Bholanath had to be away from home for long hours. He began to worry about her physical well-being. He invited his widowed sister Matori and her son Amulya to come and make their home with him. Sri Ma and Matori Pishima (aunt Matori) were already friends from their days at Narundi; so Sri Ma now had a companion who lightened her work considerably and Ashu had a friend to play and go to school with everyday.

Janaki Sen and Bhudeb Basu had also come to Dhaka. From them and other chance visitors, people began to hear about Sri Ma. There was talk in the town about a young housewife who evidently radiated an unusual aura of spiritual power. Shahbagh was private property not easily accessible to all. Even so the townspeople trickled in, in twos or threes, introduced by those already known to Bholanath. Once Bholanath himself invited in a gentleman who was sheltering under a tree in a sudden shower, near the gates of Shahbagh. This was Professor Nani Gopal Banerjee who became a devotee and brought in some of his friends. Perhaps the names of these early devotees should be recorded here because they have to be mentioned repeatedly from now on.

The first amongst the galaxy of pioneering names, must always be that of **Jyotish Chandra Rai**, I.S.O. Assistant Director in the Ministry of Agriculture. The story of his surrender at Sri Ma's feet, his sustained allegiance, his ascetism and final renunciation will always inspire all pilgrims on the path of God-realization. He had to face many problems in his life to which he did not find easy solutions. Since he occupied a high position in society his behaviour was noticeable and a matter of general interest. For quite some time he and others like him, were criticised adversely for running after 'a woman saint' who was young and beautiful. His own family, that is, his elder brother and his wife were not in sympathy with his dedication toward the spiritual quest. Jyotish Chandra Rai was in the habit of maintaining a diary. He wrote in this journal[1] about his search for a suitable Guru all over the country. Nowhere had he found what he was seeking and also that he was not clear in his mind as to what he was looking for! In this state of an inner yearning, he came to meet Sri Ma at Shahbagh. He writes in his diary that, the first glimpse of that veiled figure had been an experience of fulfilment. He knew he had arrived at the end of his quest, but he wrote also that since the Guru had adopted the guise of a retiring young housewife, he would not approach her again till she chose to discard her veils. He did not go to Shahbagh for almost a year. During this time a lot of changes occurred near Sri Ma. She became more approachable. She talked more freely with her visitors. Jyotish Chandra Rai on the occasion of his first audience asked her:

'Is there any chance of success in my spiritual journey?'

Sri Ma answered, 'So far, there is no hunger in you for it!'

During the years 1924 - 1932, Jyotish Chandra Rai became very prominent among the early devotees. He was seen to understand Sri Ma's spoken or unspoken *kheyāla* better than anyone else. He assumed charge of many responsibilities. He and his friend Niranjan Rai did the initial work toward putting up the first Ashram for Sri Ma in Dhaka. In time he came to be known as Bhaiji (respected brother) amongst the group of early devotees in Dehra Dun, Simla and other new places. We shall use this title for him in our subsequent account of the *līlā* of Sri Ma.

Shashanka Mohan Mukherjee : When he met Sri Ma he was 66 years old. He was a very well-respected Doctor in Dhaka; his demeanour of grave self-sufficiency easily marked him out as a person of some consequence. He was head of a very large household. In time all his children and their families became devoted to Sri Ma. His eldest son Birendra Chandra Mukherjee was Professor of English in Agra College, Agra. He became one of the group of interlocuters for the daily *satsanga* at Shahbagh whenever he was in Dhaka. Sri Ma generally had the *kheyāla* to speak at length when he was among the audience. Birendra Chandra was one of those who had the distinction of being initiated by Bholanath. Shashanka Mohan's adoption of the ascetic way of life in his old age, his subsequent life of one-pointed *tapasyā* (austerities), his total obedience to the *kheyāla* of Sri Ma are ideals which can be emulated by many a younger person. He was the first person for whom Sri Ma had the *kheyāla* that he should formally adopt the ochre robes of a *sannyāsi* (renunciate), so he became Swami Akhandananda Giri. An anecdote may be related here which gives some idea of the profound but light and easy atmosphere prevailing near Sri Ma at all times. Sri Shashanka Mohan's increasing detachment from his family was rather resented by his youngest son Nandu. He would at times remonstrate with Sri Ma that she was taking him away from home and reducing him to the ways of mendicants. After Shashanka Mohan had adopted *sannyāsa*, Nandu took a photograph of his father with the minimal accrouments of an ascetic - in just a loin cloth, a staff in his hand and a *kamaṇḍalu* (the water vessel) at his side. He had these words printed within the photograph: 'Ma, have you not done enough even now?' (In Bengali: *aikhano ki hayni Ma*?) He sent this photograph to Sri Ma. It hangs on a wall of the Vindhyachala Ashram.

Gurupriya Devi: Gurupriya Devi was the third child and second daughter of Shashanka Mohan. Her family name was Adorini Devi. She was a studious girl, not given over to the general forms of amusements indulged in by young girls. She would tell her parents not to arrange a marriage for her, but they mistook her disinclination for shyness and at the appointed time a suitable ceremony did take place. When she was old enough to be sent to her husband's home, she made it very clear that she was not interested. In fact she wrote a letter to her husband, apologising for her disinclination for a family life and begging him to get married again to a more suitable girl. (Her husband Upendra Nath Banerjee of Calcutta, did marry a second time. This lady Amala Devi, along with her sons and daughters, became devoted to Sri Ma in later years. They were quite attached to Gurupriya Devi as well).

The name Gurupriya was given by Sri Ma. In the Ashram she was generally known as Didi (sister). Her diaries are to-day invaluable as source material for the early days in Dhaka and also Sri Ma's incessant travels all over India.

Didi's one-pointed undeviating aim in life was to render service to Sri Ma. She was not interested in *tapasyā* (austerities) but she scrupulously obeyed Sri Ma whenever this was demanded of her. Because she had suffered some inconvenience in the beginning regarding her way of life, she was very keen to establish an ashram for young girls. She used to say that there are many young girls who do not wish to get married and also do not wish to follow a career of money-making professions. In her time, there was no suitable places or ashrams where such girls could follow their inclinations toward *sādhanā* and the other-worldly way of life. These ideas gave shape to the Mahilā Ashram established by her in 1938. Nearly all the Ashrams in Sri Ma's name owe their existence to her efforts and constant surveillance for many years.

Niranjan **Rai** and his wife **Vinodini Devi**: A devout couple, well-beloved of the entire community of devotees in Dhaka. It so happened that Vinodini Devi died after suffering a short illness. Sri Ma used to visit her everyday. The invalid waited anxiously for this daily visit. If there were clouds in the sky, her anxiety lest it rain would know no bounds, but without fail, Sri Ma came and sat with her for a while. Vinodini Devi's untimely death had a very tragic sequel. Niranjan Rai, unmindful of all advice from his friends took to going away to the cremation *ghats* and sit for hours at the site of his wife's funeral pyre. Bhaiji spoke to Sri Ma about him. Sri Ma herself one day accompanied Niranjan to the *ghat* and spoke at length about the undesirability of such a vigil. He could not make the turning around inspite of all such efforts. He died very soon after. In the last year of his life, his only efforts in the world were directed toward the construction of the Ashram at Ramna for Sri Ma and Bholanath. It may be of interest to many to know that the gold bangle seen on Sri Ma's left wrist was a gift from Vinodini Devi.

Nishikanta Mitra: was another of the elders among the early devotees of Dhaka. He was the Zamindar of Samsiddhi. In his old age, he lived for many years in the Ashram at Varanasi as an ascetic.

Nani Gopal Banerjee was a Professor in Dhaka. He was one day taking shelter from a sudden shower under a tree near the gates of Shahbagh. Bholanath happened to see him and invited him to his quarters, where he had the fortune to see Sri Ma. The first encounter was a decisive one. He felt profoundly impressed. He then pursuaded his friend Pran Gopal Mukhopadhyaya (Assistant Post-Master General) to visit Shahbagh also. Pran Gopal was a man of great ability and intelligence. His understanding of a spiritual journey was profound. Because of Pran Gopal Mukhopadhyaya many others came to Shahbagh at this time. **Atal Bihari Bhattacharya** (Professor at Rajshahi College), **Girija Shankar Bhattacharya** (originally from Ashtagram and Professor in Calcutta); and his successor to the post of Assistant Post-Master General, **Pramatha Nath Basu**. All these men and their families remained close to Sri Ma and Bholanath throughout the subsequent years. Atal Bihari had a merry sense of humour. He had his own way of causing untoward incidents when Sri Ma was close at hand to enjoy and appreciate them. His correspondence with Sri Ma was always productive of great wit and humour on both sides, although the subject always remained of profound spiritual import.

Pran Gopal Mukhopadhyaya was instrumental in spreading the good news about Sri Ma's advent in their midst. He immediately recognised her as a Teacher of men and would often ask her, 'When are you going to reveal yourself?' Sri Ma would just smile in response. It is possible that he brought about the *kheyala* of making a public statement of the very nerve of her teaching at Siddheswari on August 6, 1926 (in the book infra p. 82).

Baaul Chandra Basaak: Bholanath's boyhood friend and subsequent devotee of both Sri Ma and Bholanath. He was a constant support and a reliable worker ever at hand at Shahbagh, Siddheshwari and later at Ramna.

Amulya Kumar Dattagupta: Professor, Law College at Dhaka. Amulya Kumar's diaries can be compared easily with the *kathamṛta* of Master Mahashaya. He was a very sober-mannered man, with a keen interest in the theological and philosophical themes which were discussed in Sri Ma's presence. His memory was phenomenal. He could reproduce almost verbatim the lengthy discussions in their dialogical forms. These writings are being published now by his daughter Sati, as continuation of the first two volumes of *Sri Ma Anandamayi Prasanga*.

After the partition of Bengal in 1947, he was obliged to leave East Pakistan almost at a moment's notice. Leaving his family in Calcutta he came on to Varanasi to meet Sri Ma in order to consult her about his future. She said, he could stay near his brother in Calcutta and visit Varanasi from time to time, knowing that the extreme climate of U.P. would not be agreeable for people coming from the Eastern Provinces. Amulya Kumar said in a slightly exasperated tone:

'You have already reduced me to destitution - now you wish that I spend the little that I have, on railway fares?'

'Have I reduced you to destitution?'

'What else! I had to leave behind all my possessions. I have nothing but a little cash with me.'

'Fine! you have become a *sannyāsi*!'

He chose to settle down in Varanasi, thinking he would have greater opportunities of her *darśana*. It is possible that Sri Ma's frequent visits to Varanasi during and after 1948 were mainly rehabilitation-oriented. This could have been a major reason for the splendid *satsangs* which were held in the newly constructed hall. The philosophical discussion in Sri Ma's presence was food and drink for Amulya Kumar and more than enough recompense for all his deprivations. His daughter Sati confirms this impression. She said (to the author) 'In 1972 when Sri Ma left Varanasi after my father's death, she turned to me and said 'the era of such *satsangs* is over'.'

Man Mohan Ghosh : was an Engineer and the Steward of Dhaka University and a close friend of Amulya Kumar. He also elected to settle down in Varanasi after the partition of Bengal. Coincidentally there was work also for him in Varanasi. For many years he was fully engaged in constructing the new Ashram. The very beautiful Annapurna Mandir remains a memorial to his expertise. The people of Dhaka were especially attached to the Image of Annapurna. The Hall and terrace, while they lasted witnessed innumerable functions and festivities. Sri Ma's association with this family remained deep and all-encompassing. On the sudden death of his eldest son, Sri Ma came from Ananda Kashi to Varanasi. It was she who went to his house to break the news to the old man because nobody else wanted to do so. Inspite of her pressing engagements elsewhere she stayed in Varanasi for ten days, visiting Man Mohan Ghosh every day. Innumerable, are the ways in which Sri Ma looked to the needs of her devotees.

Other names which should be mentioned are those of Dinesh Chandra Rai, Ashwini Kumara, Mathur Babu, Nagen Babu, Anadi Babu, Jotu Bhai and many more – some of them not less in any way than those we have written about. Moreover we have written in some detail about people who came to our part of the world. There were dozens of families who were rehabilitated in other parts of India. Sri Ma's extensive travels, not only attracted new devotees but gave the solace of her *darśana* to older ones as well.

Life at Shahbagh and Siddheshwari

The city of Dhaka was a big metropolis. The visitors to Shahbagh were well-placed in life and enjoyed such felicities as wealth can command. At this time Indians could rise only to the posts of Deputies or Assistants in Government Offices. Top positions were held by British Officers. The cultural atmosphere was an admixture of the Hindu orthodox, Islamic good manners and the western influence of modern times.

In the early twenties of this century, all social customs were conservative in the extreme. Bholanath would receive the men-folk and sit with them in the outer room. Sri Ma sat quietly near the door of the inner room. If the men asked questions and if Bholanath requested her to speak in answer, she would do so.

Women, however found free access to her. Sri Ma herself would make them welcome, putting down mats for them to sit upon and giving them betel leaf as was the custom of those days. One of her earlier visitors was Hiranbala Ghosh from the house of Rai Bahadur Jogesh Chandra Ghosh. It became Hiranbala's daily practice to visit the young housewife (*Shahbager badhu*) at Shahbagh. She had no religious aspirations as such but was tremendously attracted to Sri Ma. She later related her first impressions to new comers, 'She looked so beautiful and was so charming in her behaviour. Her smile alone held me spell-bound. I used to feel sad that she was dumb!'

On coming to Dhaka, Sri Ma had once enquired of Bholanath if he had heard anybody mention a 'Siddheshwari Tree'. He had replied in the negative, offering to make enquiries. Sri Ma had told him it was not necessary.

The Shahbagh Gardens adjoined the huge race course and polo grounds of Ramnā. Sri Ma frequently walked across this sea of green to the Kālī Temple on the opposite side. She and her companions would sit for many hours on the temple veranda. One such companion was Bholanath's school friend Baaul Chandra Basaak. When the rest of the party returned to Shahbagh, Baaul Chandra quite often went off by himself on a side road. These places were very lonely and unfrequented in those times. One day Bholanath asked him curiously 'Where do you go, at such a late hour?'. Baaul Chandra said, 'There is a Kālī Temple at Siddheshwari. It is a very beautiful site. I would like to take you both there, some time.'

Sri Ma signalled to Bholanath not to say anything about her vision of the Siddheshwari Tree, and so he kept quiet. A few days later they went to Siddheshwari with Baaul Chandra. There was a rough track only and not a proper road. The path was almost smothered by overhanging creepers and lush undergrowth. Big trees made the place look like a forest. In the midst of this wilderness, they came to a very ancient Temple of Kālī. In front of the Temple they saw a huge fallen *pipal* tree. Sri Ma recognised it as the tree of her vision. She put her hand caressingly on it . Baaul Chandra told them a little of the history of the place. It was a *siddhapiṭha*, that is, a place where ascetics had performed *sādhanā* and attained *siddhi* (success) or Self-Realization. It was a place of great sanctity. According to local tradition it had some association with the Adi Śamkarācārya also. Hundreds of years ago, there were three big trees, to which the place owed its other name, Tintiri. Now there was this one fallen tree only. A story was related that when this tree fell, a light had emerged from it and was seen to enter the Image inside the Temple. The Temple itself was built by an ascetic named Saṃvarvan.

Listening to all these legends they walked around the precincts a little. It had become dark. They returned to Shahbagh carrying lanterns which Baaul Chandra had provided himself with beforehand.

Siddheshwari played an important role in the life of the devotees of Dhaka. In retrospect it can be seen as the place where almost all of Sri Ma's early followers became transformed into ascetics of a high order. It became for them, as if, a forest hermitage of ancient times. It was the place where Bholanath passed the most difficult period of his life and also the place where he realized a long cherished dream of arranging for a magnificent Pūjā Festival. At the time, however, all was normal. In any case, it was never Sri Ma's way to disturb the susceptibilities of the people around her. On the contrary, even startling things were easily made acceptable as not being so very extraordinary after all.

Bipin Bihari and Mokṣada Devi[2] came to Shabbagh in late August 1924 at the invitation of Bholanath. Earlier in the month Sri Ma's second sister Surabala had died at Jaidevapura at the young age of sixteen. Sri Ma and Bholanath had gone to see her. Sri Ma's parents had also came from Vidyakut. Bholanath had thought that it would be a change for the parents to stay with their eldest daughter and that it would be an occupation for Sri Ma also. He himself had felt the tragic death of the young girl very keenly. He surmised that Sri Ma would be grief-stricken because she was so fond of her sister. He as yet had much to learn about Sri Ma, namely that her care and concern were not related to the outcome of her ministrations. She was never seen in grief when persons who were very close to her died.

Sometime in the beginning of September 1924 Sri Ma and Bholanath one day came on a visit to Siddheshwari. After a while Ṣri Ma expressed her *kheyāla* of staying in the Temple itself, for a few days instead of returning to Shahbagh. Bholanath demurred a little, not liking the idea of leaving Sri Ma alone by herself in such a lonely desolate place. He was prevailed upon to leave her for a short time while he went back to Shahbagh and requested Bipin Bihari to go to Siddheshwari to be with Sri Ma the whole day. After his day's work Bholanath returned to Siddheshwari enabling Bipin Bihari to come back to the City for the night.

Thus in this most natural way both Sri Ma's father and husband came to be staying in a temple veranda for a few days in the manner of homeless ascetics. Unknowingly, Bholanath had started on a new career. Sri Ma took up her abode in a small room at the back of the temple. She was not seen throughout the day. Late in the evening she emerged and sat awhile with Bholanath and his friend Baaul Chandra who came every evening with some fruits and sweets. There was no question of cooking or partaking of regular meals. Bholanath stayed in the main temple room. Baaul Chandra posted himself at the main entrance of the temple. He had a feeling that something miraculous was going to take place, and in order not to miss it, he would keep awake the whole night. In this manner they spent a week at Siddheshwari.

The following incident may best be related in Sri Ma's own words: 'On the eighth day, it was drizzling at dawn. Beckoning

Bholanath, who was awake, to follow me, I walked out of the temple. We had almost to step over Baaul Babu but he did not awake. Tired out by his night-long vigil, he had fallen asleep at the break of day.

'Although we were not familiar with the surroundings I unhesitatingly advanced in a northern direction from the temple. Walking a little through the wilderness, we came to a small clearing. I seemed to have arrived at my destination and walked round that particular plot of ground thrice in the manner of a *pradakṣiṇā* (circumambulation). Then, drawing a circle, with my finger (*kuṇḍali*), I sat down where I was standing facing south. What you call *mantras* were then pronounced. In the meantime, I had placed my right hand on the ground and was leaning on it. The ground had looked solid enough but my hand went down into the earth unresisted. It felt as if layer after layer of the solid-looking earth was sliding off, like the removal of curtains, and my arm went down right up to the shoulder. Bholanath took fright and pulled me up, saying 'Let us go away from here.' At the same time, warm reddish water spouted forth from the hole thus made in the ground. The water was so red that my white conch bangle had become red. This colour lasted for many days.

'I then asked Bholanath to insert his arm in the hole. At first he was reluctant. I told him not to be afraid and that it was necessary for him to do so. Thereupon Bholanath also put in his arm. When he withdrew it the warm reddish water again welled forth from the hole. We stood there for sometime watching the water trickling away on the ground. Then after stopping up the mouth of the hole, we came away.'[3]

Baaul Chandra was very sad when he realized that he had after all missed witnessing this strange incident, but he took it upon himself to clear a space all around the spot and later thoughtfully planted a few flowering shrubs and a *tulasi* to mark it. Pran Gopal, on hearing of this incident contributed toward the upkeep of the place. With this money a platform (*vedi*)[4] about twenty-two and half inches square was constructed over the hole. A light bamboo fence marked off a piece of ground five yards square with the *vedi* in the centre.

Sri Ma paid frequent visits to Siddheshwari. She would sit on the *vedi,* surrounded by her companions. Sometime entire nights would pass in this way. It was an atmosphere of unimaginable peace and tranquillity. They would return at dawn to Shahbagh and to Dhaka. Pran Gopal said that a few months earlier he would not have been able to stand such exposure and sleepless nights. His son writes, 'Whenever my father spoke of Sri Ma, there was a thrill of awe and reverence in his voice which remained undimmed over the years. He knew her to be a teacher who had come to show the way. He would ask her very often, 'When are you going to reveal yourself?' Sri Ma would just smile.'[5]

Sri Ma kept her *maunam* for about one year and nine months in Shahbagh and then she started to speak at first, very softly. Gradually her voice gained in strength and words were spoken in her normal tone of voice. Didi (Gurupriya Devi) writes in her Diary, her first impressions:

'I did not feel shy before Ma. I approached her confidently and stood near her as if I had always known her. It is beyond my power to describe the personality I saw. One look at that radiant form, and my head, of its own accord bowed down in adoration.'[6]

Sri Ma smiled a welcome. Her *maunam* had come to an end (December 1925), she spoke softly to Didi, 'Where have you been all this time?' Thus began a lifetime of dedicated association and devotion on Didi's part and unfailing *kṛpā* on Sri Ma's. Other new-comers began to collect at Shahbagh and mingle with old friends. Bhudeb Basu from Bajitpur once expressed his nostalgia for the earlier days when Sri Ma would cook gourmet meals of chops and cutlets for them. He remarked a little ruefully, 'Your exalted states are indeed a loss for us.' Sri Ma smiled and with Didi's inexpert help she one day prepared a dinner to please all the old acquaintances, as well as the new devotees. Bholanath being a generous host, such meals became the norm at Shahbagh. Sri Ma's personality was such that opposites were held together in great harmony. Devotees accepted good food from her as naturally as advice regarding their *sādhanā.*

Among other regular visitors was Didi's father, Shashanka Mohan Mukherjee, retired Civil Surgeon of Dhaka. He was at this time Director of the Medical School. Didi used to accompany her father every day to Shahbagh. She would eagerly wait for her father's return from the Medical School in the evening. If he were delayed she would be in an agony of suspense till she saw his carriage. Gradually she began to assist Sri Ma in looking after the ever-expanding household. She would help with cooking, serving food or in guarding the person of Sri Ma when in a state of *bhāva*. Didi recalls that she had no real interest in cooking. In Sri Ma's company she learnt to look upon this art as something more than a means of keeping body and soul together.

Thus many families in Dhaka became very attached to Sri Ma. Whoever came first wanted friends and relations to share in the same joy. Sri Ma and Bholanath became the nucleus of an ever expanding clan of devotees. By and by Bholanath came to be known as Baba (father). A large cross-section of society was involved; people would repair to Shahbagh as if attracted by a magnet, whenever they had time. They would bring fish, vegetables, and fruits with them. It was Sri Ma's practice to utilise daily the offerings to the last pieces of ginger or green chilli. Nothing at all was stored for another time. She devised all-round meals with the ingredients at hand, to the great admiration of the women folk who surrounded her almost at all times. Not the least remarkable feature about these impromptu meals was that invariably the food would be just sufficient for the guests. Nothing would be wasted and nobody would go away disappointed. This sort of coincidence or concurrence of incidents and timings has been a regular feature of Sri Ma's life. Anybody who stayed around for a few days would be sure to see one or more instances of it.

All Hindus are familiar with the routine of *nāma-japa* or the singing of *bhajans* and *kirtans*. In Sri Ma's vicinity, personal ways of worship received new impetus. A new exhilarating spirit was abroad which welded large groups together in the performance of joint acts of worship. Many times big crowds, irrespective of caste and position sat out in the open to share the food after a special festive occasion. The break down of norms of erstwhile staid behaviour gave a new feeling of freedom to everyone. Women specially came into their own near Sri Ma.

The *kirtan* on January 26, 1926

Sri Ma began to be more widely known after the day of the solar eclipse on January 26 in 1926. The devotees had wanted to arrange for a *kirtan* on a large scale. Bholanath welcomed the suggestion and enthusiastically set about making arrangements with the help of Baaul, Atal Bihari and others. The dance-hall was made available to them for this purpose. A large number of people were invited. Everyone who came to the *kirtan* would partake of the *prasāda* (meal) at night.

The *kirtan* started at about 10 a.m. Sri Ma, with her women companions, sat in a room nearby from where they could watch and hear the *kirtan*. Didi at that time was a new comer. She wrote in her diary a description of this day, 'At one moment Sri Ma was sitting like one of us. The next moment she had changed completely. Her body started swaying rhythmically. Her sari fell back from her head. Her eyes were closed and the entire body swayed to the rhythm of the *kirtan*. With her body still swaying she stood up or rather was, as if drawn upwards on her toes. It looked as if Sri Ma had left her body which had become an instrument in the hands of an invisible power. It was obvious to all of us that there was no will motivating her actions. Sri Ma did not seem aware of her surroundings. She circled round the room as if wafted along by the wind. Occasionally, her body would be as if falling to the ground - but before it completed the movement it would regain its upright position, just like a wind-blown leaf which flutters to the ground and then is uplifted and blown forward by a fresh gust of wind. It seemed her body had no weight or substance. Moving in this manner Sri Ma crossed the veranda and entered the hall, her gaze unblinkingly fixed in an upward direction, her face glowing with a wonderful light. Before the crowd had time to realize that she was in their midst, she fell to the ground from an upright position but did not seem hurt. Like a dry leaf in a whirlwind, her body rolled at tremendous speed over the floor. Some of the women tried to hold her, but they were thrown off. Even a little of that swift movement could not be checked.

After a few seconds, her body, of its own accord became still; Sri Ma sat up. The utter quiescence of her form was as wondrous as had been the tempestuous movement. Her face was radiant; there was an effulgence all around her.'

Didi records that the whole day passed in an atmosphere of sublime joyousness. The men singing *kirtan* were inspired to their best efforts. When evening drew near Sri Ma again had beautiful *bhāvas* the like of which people had read in books about Sri Gauranga Mahaprabhu and Sri Ramkrishna Paramhamsa. This was also the first occasion when an entire congregation was fortunate enough to hear the *mantras*[7] which issued from her lips spoken in some beautiful language which sounded like Sanskrit. Everyone listened in spell-bound silence with folded hands and bowed heads.

Still later in the evening when it was time for the meal Sri Ma was a different, yet the same person. She, accompanied by Didi, served the food to the rows upon rows of guests. She was efficient and quick. One could hardly imagine that this was the same person who had been lying in an ecstatic state earlier in the evening.

In the next two years or so, the devotees of Dhaka had many more opportunities to see the states of *bhāva* which manifested themselves on Sri Ma's body. The external stimulus of *kirtan* was not always necessary, although they generally occurred during one. The eye witnesses say that Sri Ma's *bhāvas* cannot be described in words. The shape and substance of her body, the colour of her skin, the expressions on her face underwent incredible changes. Actions, gestures and facial expressions would change so rapidly as to defy observation. Her movements were like swift flashes of lightning. It was well-nigh impossible for anyone to keep track of her progress through the crowd. Even one glimpse of the matchless beauty of this display of the ecstatic mood held all onlookers enthralled.

At times her body seemed to be in tune with the motions in her environment. The rippling waves in the wake of a boat drew her to them so that her body seemed to flow towards the water. The climbing of stairs would give her body a buoyancy which seemed to be soaring upward. If caught in a sudden storm, her body seemed like a wind-blown cloth. Storms were exhilarating. Sometimes her ringing peal of laughter (*aṭṭahāsa*) mingled with the sounds of the elements to orchestrate a wild symphony of nature.

After a *bhāva*, Sri Mā would sometimes lie in a heap for hours together. People conjectured that this was a yogic state of *samādhi*. Not only after a *bhāva* but in the midst of conversation or work, her gaze would become fixed, and her body rigid and statue-like. Or her eyes would close and the body sink down on the floor. Like the slowly setting sun in the west, all bodily functions would gradually disappear as if withdrawing inwards. Breathing would slow down and finally stop altogether. Her limbs occasionally became rigid like wooden appendages and then again limp like cloth. After ten, twelve, or twenty-four hours of a state of this kind, people would try to rouse her but mostly to no effect. An eyewitness says, 'I myself rubbed her hands and feet and sometimes struck sharply against them, but elicited no response. Many doctors tried to feel her pulse or locate signs of respiration, but apparently both functions were absent for hours together.'[8]

Sri Ma would rouse of her own accord - her breath coming back faintly and then more vigorously. There would be some slight movement of the muscles of her limbs. But after a while she would again sink back into immobility. At this stage she would respond if people called her or spoke to her. Didi writes that the difference between Sri Ma's normal state and the state of *samādhi* was one of degree only. Even in the midst of ordinary housework, she seemed in a beatific state of joy. If not spoken to for any length of time or made to answer questions, her speech tended to become indistinct and lisping as if she had to make an effort to use her vocal chords. Didi writes, 'It amazed me that Sri Ma should be so naturally in a permanent state of God-intoxication, a state which is coveted by *sādhakas* of all times. No, not God-intoxication - The state could not be called that. I have no language to describe a state which was sublime and yet normal.'[9]

The Atmosphere of the Miraculous

At about this time, the manifestation of many yogic powers became the norm in Sri Ma's life. She did not become different from what she was, but there was an accentuation and proliferation of what is called the miraculous. People came from far and near to Shahbagh to beg her to cure physical ailments. Cures would be effected by a glance, a touch, the gift of a flower, or in a dozen different ways. Sri Ma did not set out to do any cures. In general she would say, 'Pray to God. He will do what is best for the patient. The only thing for you to do is to look after the patient and get the best medical aid available. For the rest you must put your trust in God.'

Sometimes people insisted on her visiting the patient in the belief that he would recover if she did so. In such cases Sri Ma had her own way of prophesying the future. She would look about her and ask her companions, 'What do you say? He is asking me to go because he thinks the patient will pull through. Will it be so?' The companions, in general, would answer emphatically in the affirmative. Sri Ma made them repeat this three times. Then she would say, 'Who knows, since all of you say so, may be it will be so.' It was the experience of the people of Shahbagh, as well as Sri Ma's later companions that although everyone had come to know about this ritual, at times they would fail to return the answer emphatically in the affirmative. Unaccountably they would hesitate, stammer and make weak rejoinders. Sri Ma then would say, 'Why do you hesitate? Then perhaps the patient won't recover.' And so it happened always.

One day, the wife of Atul Datta, a devotee, came to Shahbagh to request Sri Ma to visit her son who was bed-ridden with a serious illness. Sri Ma went about unheeding, or so it seemed to the lady. She then appealed to Bholanath, to speak on her behalf to Sri Ma. From Sri Ma's manner and words her companions knew that the boy would not survive his illness. Bholanath, who had a very kind heart, went to their house with Sri Ma. Sri Ma, in answer to their plea said, 'Even if I tell you what to do, you will not be able to carry it out.' For the parents this was unthinkable; they promised eagerly to do as she bid them. They were told not to let the boy out of his bed for a specific number of days, probably 18. Immediately after this visit the boy started improving slowly, but all of a sudden he took a turn for the worse and died. Sri Ma said to the inconsolable mother, 'You see, he was allowed to get up on Monday.' The mother would not believe this and lost her faith in Sri Ma. After quite some time she came to know from other members of the family that the boy had been seen standing on the balcony on the Monday specified by Sri Ma, watching a passing wedding procession. Full of remorse, the bereaved mother came again to Shahbagh. Sri Ma comforted her in her double sorrow.

On occasions Sri Ma would herself go out to visit people. One day as she was strolling about near the gates of Shahbagh, a cab drove by. She signalled to the driver; when he drew near she climbed in. The cabman said 'Where will you go?' Sri Ma said, 'To your house.' The cabman, a Mohammedan, without another word drove home. On arrival, they found an old man lying on his death bed. His relations were weeping. Sri Ma asked Bhaiji (who had accompanied her) to fetch some sweets. These were distributed amongst the family and neighbours. Sri Ma then came away. Bhaiji[10] later on was interested enough to find out the outcome of this visit. The old man did recover from what had appeared to be his last illness.

At times Sri Ma would take upon herself the illness of others. Didi, one day came to Shahbagh to find Sri Ma suffering from a sudden cold and cough. On enquiry she discovered that Pratul (Pramatha Nath's young son) who was due to appear at an examination, had felt a severe cold coming on and had prayed to Sri Ma to prevent this. Sri Ma recovered after a while.

Such incidents taught Bholanath and others not to ask Sri Ma to cure sick people. They found that to her, life and death were same. She would say, 'Don't ask me to cure anybody. Everybody must work out his destiny. If obstructions are deliberately placed in his path, the results may be anything but beneficial.'

There were other untoward results when Sri Ma was made to use her yogic powers. On one occasion Bholanath and Sri Ma had been invited to the Trustee's house. At this time the owner of the property Nawabzadi Pyari Bano was in Calcutta. She had not come to Dhaka for many years due to personal reasons. Sri Ma and Bholanath came to the house of the Trustee Jogesh Chandra Ghosh to find that they were under some stress because the civil case which the Nawabzadi was fighting in the Calcutta High Court would be decided that day. The family wished to know from Sri Ma what was happening in Calcutta. Not quite daring to speak to Sri Ma directly they asked Bholanath to intercede on their behalf. Sri Ma always did her best to obey him, so now at his insistence, she described the events taking place and said they would win the case. Before answering their question, Sri Ma, had unknown to others, placed a live coal on the back of her hand. Much later, she explained the reasons for this deliberate infliction of a wound in the following words, 'Well, it is possible that a certain action (*kriyā*) may be performed which will have some concrete effect in some other sphere. Or again, it is also said that if yogic powers are used deliberately, then the *sādhaka* has to perform penance (*prāyaścitta*) for it. This body sometimes has the attitude of *sādhaka*[11]. These and other explanations also are possible.'

After one or two such occasions Bholanath ceased to intercede on people's behalf and left Sri Ma to her *kheyāla*.

Incidentally Nawabzadi Pyari Bano became so devoted to Sri Ma that she prayed for her presence at a family gathering where long standing disputes were going to be tabled. The Nawabzadi believed that due to Sri Ma's presence all differences of opinion were settled amicably. Pyari Bano later invited Bholanath and Sri Ma to the weddings of her son and daughter. In her turn at times she would attend the *kirtans* at Shahbagh. The entire family was as close to Sri Ma as any other family in Dhaka.

Since the time of the *līlā* of *sādhanā* at Bajitpur, Sri Ma hardly ever ate a full meal. When she came to Dhaka in April 1924 she was taking three mouthfuls of food inclusive of water, twice a day. When Didi first met Sri Ma she was eating even less. On Mondays and Thursdays she would take the 3 mouthfuls and on the other five days nothing but nine grains of rice. These rules were not rigid. She broke them now and then without any adverse effects. At about this time it was noticed that Sri Ma could not raise her hand to her mouth. The hand would stop midway, and she would bend her head down to take the food from her own hand. None knew better than Bholanath that all phases in Sri Ma's life came about naturally and spontaneously. It would be as futile to remonstrate with her as with any other onlooker. Also the savouring of food was an anomaly in her case, so he took upon himself the duty of feeding her like a child. Didi was pleased to be given the opportunity of rendering this service to Śri Ma when she came to stay with them at Shahbagh.

In later years when she was questioned by scholars regarding all these phases she spoke like this, 'Once this body lived on 3 grains of rice daily for four or five months. Nobody can live for so long a time on such a meagre diet. It looks like a miracle. But it has been so with this body. It has been so, because it can be so. The reason for this is that what we eat is not at all necessary for us. The body takes in only the quintessence of the food, the rest is thrown out. As a result of *sādhanā* the body becomes so constituted that, though no food is taken physically it can imbibe from the surroundings whatever is necessary for its maintenance. In three ways, the body can be maintained without food: one way has just been referred to, namely, that the body can take from the environment the necessary nourishment. Secondly it can live on air alone, for I have just said that everything exists in all things, so that the properties of all things are in the air in some measure. Therefore, by taking in air alone we get the essence of other things. Again, it may so happen that the body is not taking anything at all, yet it is being maintained unimpaired as in a state of *samādhi*. Thus you find that as a consequence of *sādhanā* it is quite possible to live without what we call food.'[12]

Sri Ma abstained from drinking also sometimes, once for as long as 10 days and another time for 23 days. On the 24th day she asked for a sip of water saying, 'I wanted to see what it would be like without drinking but the very necessity for water is becoming extinct. This will not do. As a matter of convention, a semblance of normal behaviour must be kept up.'

On odd occasions Sri Ma could consume large quantities of food also. Didi relates that once acceding to a request that she should eat more, she began to swallow the food given to her at double her normal rate. She remarked to Didi 'You are not quick enough, call somebody else to help you.' But even two people could not keep pace with her speed of eating. The man who had made the request was now thoroughly frightened; he now prayed to her to desist. Sri Ma spoke plaintively, 'First you ask me to eat, but no sooner do I start than you tell me to stop. Now, what am I to do?'

Sri Ma and a Muslim devotee

Bhaiji had a devout Muslim friend, Maulavi Ziauddin Hussain. One evening, Bhaiji, Niranjan Rai and the Maulavi went to Shahbagh. They found that *kirtan* was in progress in the hall. They stood outside watching the performers. After a while Sri Ma came out of the hall followed by a few of the people. Somebody brought a lantern. Sri Ma seemed to be in an exalted state of *bhāva*. She walked straight to where the three friends were standing in the dark. She lightly touched the Muslim gentleman with her right hand and walked on ahead without pausing. The three friends followed. Sri Ma went to the small mausoleum of two Arab fakirs which was situated in one corner of the Gardens. An Arab fakir, Shah Sahab and his disciple had come to Dhaka many years ago. The Nawab of those times had asked them to take up their residence on his property. On the fakir's death he had built a mausoleum which housed his and his disciple's graves. The Shahbagh Gardens were named after the fakir.

On this evening, to every one's amazement Sri Ma began to perform the *namaz* at the grave side. After a few seconds the Maulavi overcoming his surprise, stepped forward and joined in the prayer. He later said to Bhaiji that the execution of the namaz was perfect in every detail. Sri Ma at that time was a Muslim of as devout a demeanour as perhaps the fakir Shah Sahab. After completing the *namaz* Sri Ma returned to the kirtan hall. The Maulavi also entered the hall with her. By a coincidence the man who was supposed to offer a light and a few *batāsās* (sugar puffs) at the mausoleum had not come that day. Sri Ma entrusted the duty to the Maulavi. He was given a plate of the sugar puffs for this purpose. After offering the sweets at the grave-side he had a strong desire to give a few to Sri Ma. When he reached the hall Sri Ma of her own accord took one of the sweets. The Maulavi from that day became as attached and devoted to Sri Ma as any of her Hindu devotees.

Bhaiji and Niranjan Rai went to Shahbagh one day to find that Sri Ma had just finished drawing some diagrams on the floor with a piece of coal. Bholanath remarked with a smile, 'Your mother has been drawing the *ṣaṭcakras*'. Sri Ma said 'This afternoon I sat in an *āsana* and measured with my fingers the distances from the centre of the head to the middle of the eye-brows, then to the neck and heart and then down to the end of the spine. I have a *kheyāla* that there are centres at these specific spots in the human body. From the lowest to the highest they range from gross to refined. I have not drawn these diagrams deliberately, but they have drawn themselves as it were. These centres are formations of nerves only. The aptitudes and propensities of the human being, determined by the experiences of his sense-organs, are located in these centres. The stream of vitality flows through them slowly or fast, determining the emotions and actions of the individual. Just as the world has different strata, such as earth, air, water, the void and so on, the human body also has different levels. The vital force lies as if somnolent at the base of the spine. By perseverance and faith, thought and action are purified. The vibrations engendered by the actions of inner and outer purity shake this sleeping power into motion. When the power moves upwards, penetrating level after level, the *sādhaka* feels freed of many ties.'[13] Sri Ma went on describing the various *cakras*, their inner significance and some of the experiences that may come to a *sādhaka* who treads this path. Bhaiji had read of these matters in books but he now realized that Sri Ma was describing the Yogic progression of *sādhanā* from her own direct experience.

These were happy days for the people of Dhaka. Shahbagh for some time was the centre of a large family of devotees.

References

1. *Mātṛdarśana*, p. 3. Jyotish Chandra Rai's diary was published posthumously by his uncle Ganga Charan Dasgupta entitled *Mātṛdarśana*.
2. Bipin Bihari and Mokshada Devi - Sri Ma's parents came to be addressed by the devotees as grandfather and grandmother that is, Dadamashai and Didima. At his time the people of Dhaka heard about Sri Ma's childhood days from Didime.

3. When Bholanath had pulled Sri Ma's arm up, he had seen something clasped in her hand. He disliked the look of it and taking it from her hand threw it in a nearby pond. It may be recorded here that nobody was able to evoke Sri Ma's *kheyāla* toward explaining any of these mysterious events. Richard Lannoy has written a scholarly and convincing exegesis of this incident in his recently published book *Anandamayi* (England, Element Books Inc. 1997).
4. The forearm of the devotee is the unit of measurement for all ritualistic calculations. The platform measured Bholanath's *sawā-hāth*, that is one and a quarter forearm.
5. Gour Gopal Mukhopadhyaya, *Ma Anandamayi*, Varanasi 1946, p. 200.
6. D.D. Vol. 1, p. 2.
7. Pandit Gopinath Kaviraj wrote about these spoken *mantras* when he heard them in Varanasi, about a year later, 'The pronounciation was so perfect that even a conjunct sound, made up of several consonants without any intervocative linking, was distinctly audible.' *Ma Anandamayi*, 1946, p. 11.
8. Jyotish Chandra Rai: *Māṭṛdarśana*, p. 70.
9. D.D. Vol. pp. 14-15.
10. Jyotish Chandra Rai, ibid, p. 84
11. Sri Ma always used the word '*sādhaka*' when referring to herself and not the feminine form *sādhikā*. When speaking in Hindi she would use the masculine gender with 'this body'. In Bengali, the verb ending does not change with the gender of the subject as in Hindi.
12. A.K. Dattagupta, *Mother As Seen by Her Devotees*, 2nd Ed. 1967, p. 117-118.
13. Jyotish Chandra Rai, *Māṭṛdarśana*, p. 55.

CHAPTER FIVE

The Beginning of the Ceaseless Wanderings

It is seldom that Rishis in this country go about to preach their gospels and inspire and uplift the people by their example and inner experience. Usually they are sedentary and, by the power of their mighty tapas and Supreme Realization, automatically act as giant spiritual magnets and attract to their abodes seekers from many levels and climes. Yet, there are illustrious names in history, e.g. Lord Buddha, Sri Shankaracharya, Lord Gauranga and others, who travelled the length and breadth of the land and showed the way to infinite peace and happiness by their teachings and devotional songs. To this category belongs Sri Anandamayee Mata, the famous saint of Bengal, whose name is known in every household in North India.

- S.S. Cohen (Sri Ramanashrama, Tiruvannamalai)[1]

... It is you who see me travelling from place to place. In reality I do not move at all. When you are in your own house, do you sit still in one corner? No, you freely walk about in the whole of it and yet remain in your house. Similarly I also wander round in my house - I don't go anywhere - I am always at rest in my own home.'

Sri Ma Anandamayi

* The first journey out of East Bengal
* Siddheswari
* The first ascetics
* Farewell to Shahbagh
* Bholanath's Sādhanā

The Beginning of the Ceaseless Wanderings

The first journey out of East Bengal

Pran Gopal Mukhopadhyaya after his retirement had planned to settle in Deoghar to be near the Ashram of his Guru Sri Balananda Brahmachari Maharaj. In answer to his repeated invitations Sri Ma undertook a journey to Deoghar sometime in May 1926. Sri Ma and Bholanath, accompanied by Shashanka Mohan, Didi, Atal Bihari and his wife and a few others, set out for Deoghar via Calcutta. This was Sri Ma's first visit to the Capital of undivided Bengal. They had been invited to stay with Pramatha Nath who was now posted in Calcutta after Dhaka. It was a festive gathering. Many new people came to have her *darśana*. At Deoghar also, the atmosphere of Shahbagh was recreated especially because Sri Ma had *bhāvas* in the *kirtan* organised in the Ashram. This event was a little out of the ordinary. Brahmachari Maharaj himself was a saint of great repute and his recognition of her as a person of the highest achievement was comparable to a jeweller's assessment of a flawless gem. He and Sri Ma had a little conversation regarding the Supreme Being. He posited a duality saying Brahman and Maya but Sri Ma would not be shaken out of her position of the One alone who is Everything. The saint after a while smilingly accepted her statement.

On their return to Calcutta they put up at Surendra Mohan Mukherjee's place. He had not seen Sri Ma before but had agreed to receive the party as guests. This was the beginning of a long association and also a pattern of coming together which was repeated many times in the future. Another type of event took place which can be called almost normal with Sri Ma because it happened with such regularity. On the day of her departure she went to visit Pramatha Nath. He could not bring himself to bid farewell to her. Sri Ma missed the train. Many people had come to see her off, bringing sweets and fruits for the journey. There was a sudden downpour drenching the assembled people outside the house. They started to sing *kirtan* and were content just to be able to see Sri Ma. Bholanath joined in the *kirtan*. Strangers became friends. When the rain stopped Sri Ma somehow devised adequate meals for everybody out of the available eatables brought for her and her party. A festive air of rejoicing reigned supreme. The discomfort of wet clothes was forgotten; they had another day of Sri Ma's company before she returned to Dhaka. Such impromptu meals under adverse conditions were made most enjoyable by Sri Ma's presence who seemed to take delight in creating order out of chaos. Most devotees will have many memories of such events.

Shahbagh again became the centre of activities for the people of Dhaka. It so happened that on August 6, 1926, Sri Ma, accompanied by a crowd of people went to Siddheswari. As usual, she sat on the little platform, her normal seat. The people stood around her. One of the eye-witnesses wrote: 'Mother sat upon the platform that *ambuvaci* day and the change that came over her person was simply astounding. Her whole body seemed afire - but it was a fire that emitted the sweetest, the most comfortably cool rays that you could imagine. She shone gloriously but did not cause any pain to our vision. To this day I have a vivid recollection of this transfiguration... she had, I should say here, not yet 'come out' and very few people had any knowledge about her.' The eye-witness Professor Girija Shankar Bhattacharya goes on to write that Sri Ma spoke to a few of them individually. To him she said 'I know but One' (*āmi jāni aik*). After this declaration, she was heard to pronounce *slokas* in Sanskrit. The Professor writes, 'It was not possible to follow her in it, so rapid was the stream of words welling forth, but it was clearly understood that she was speaking of the Unity of things and I seem to remember the word *ābrahmastaṃbaparyantam* occuring in it. Thus even at the beginning of my acquaintance with her, Mother spoke of the Unity in Diversity - The truth, which has been so forcibly borne upon me by her utterances and conduct subsequently.'[2]

Didi Gurupriya also made a note of this incident in her Diary. 'Sri Ma looked at her people and spoke in a firm voice. Her face was no longer covered. The sari was left drawn up on top of the head only. Her manner was august. In her ordinary dress she looked resplendent. All of us stood overwhelmed.' This may be considered Sri Ma's first public address as a Teacher of Spiritual Knowledge. She gave definitive advice concluding with these words: 'All those who have come here must be ready to engage in spiritual endeavour. So far a beginning only has been made, a mere turning of the soil.'[3]

Sri Ma's emphasis on inner and outer renunciation was not grasped immediately by her entourage. They continued to celebrate all festivities with great enthusiasm specially because Sri Ma's presence leant a magnificence to all such occasions. The prevailing atmosphere was that of joyous merriment rather than the quietude of austerities.

Siddheshwari

The mystery of the *Siddheshwari-āsana* that is, the original mud-stoppered hole and then the platform covering it, was never made clear by Sri Ma. That it was in some way connected with Bholanath, further that it was a very holy site where generations of ascetics had achieved Self-realization down the centuries, was understood by everyone. Could Bholanath himself, in a previous life, have practised austerities invoking the presence of Divine Śakti in human form was a question which rose in every mind because Sri Ma was seen and heard to declare herself in this spot. Sri Ma's *kheyāla* nearly always arose out of the wishes and desires of people around her. It is possible that her clear appearance as a Teacher was the result of Pran Gopal's prayers, just as the festival of Vasanti-pūjā came to be performed at Siddheshwari (in April 1926) due to Bholanath's once-expressed desire for this ritual. Another important event took place at the same holy site, namely, the naming of Sri Ma.

One day, when Bhaiji was working in his office, his assistant Bhupen brought a message from Shahbagh that Sri Ma wanted to see him. Bhupen had told her, 'The Director is expected back from leave to day and will take over charge from Bhaiji', but she wanted the message conveyed all the same. Bhaiji left his files and papers as they were and came to Shahbagh. Sri Ma said, 'Let us go to Siddheshwari.' Arriving there she sat on her usual seat, the platform. Her countenance was joyous and radiant. Bhaiji on an inner impulse turned to Bholanath and said, 'We will call her Sri Sri Ma Anandamayī from today!' Bholanath smilingly acquiesced.

On their way back, Sri Ma said to him, 'You were cheerful enough up to now. Are you in a worry about something?' Bhaiji answered that the Director, no doubt, would consider him irresponsible for leaving the Office without a word to anybody. As a matter of fact nothing happened at all. The Director himself had been delayed for unavoidable reasons and sought to give an explanation of these when he met Bhaiji.

Later, Bhaiji asked Sri Ma as to why she had made him come to Shahbagh so unexpectedly. Sri Ma smiled and said, 'To test your progress (in obedience versus sense of duty?) during these months. Besides, how else would I have got my name?'

The Bengali population of Dhaka were interested in the worship of the Goddess Kālī, the presiding deity of Bengal. Bholanath had a family-tradition of Kāli-pūjā as had many other people of Dhaka. The annual Kālī-pūjā of 1926 (October) was performed in Shahbagh with considerable enthusiasm by the local people. Many miraculous incidents took place to fill the hearts of the devout. There was more than one interesting sequel to this particular *pūjā*. Firstly the image of Kālī was not immersed in a river as is usual after such annual functions. The clay images are not meant for lasting installations but for quick disintegration in river or lake waters. Niranjan Rai's wife however wished this particular Image of Kālī to be preserved, because it was so beautiful and life-like. Sri Ma said, 'Since it makes you sad at this parting, let Her remain, as long as She wills.'

Secondly the sacrificial fire lighted on the occasion of the *pūjā* was also preserved instead of completing the ceremonial rite of extinguishing it after the last oblation. Nobody saw any future for these happenings, but they were accepted and were made part of their daily routine at Shahbagh.

Among other novel occurrences accruing from this *pūjā* was the discontinuity of the practice of animal sacrifice. Bholanath had understood it to be Sri Ma's *kheyāla* that such sacrifices should not be made - so an alternate form of the ritual was performed. Only those who are familiar with the tradition of Kālīpūjā in Bengal can appreciate the radical nature of this reform.

The most remarkable outcome of this event occurred almost as a misunderstanding. In the early hours of the morning, a few close companions sat with Sri Ma and Bholanath discussing the Kāli-pūjā just completed. Someone remarked that the Image was so life-like that he would be quite afraid to sit alone in the *pūjā* room. The others concurred that the Image was extra-ordinary. Suddenly Sri Ma asked Didi to fetch a little of the fire from the bronze receptacle (*yajña-kuṇḍa*) in the *pūjā* room. Didi put a few pieces of live coal in a suitable vessel and brought it to Sri Ma. Sri Ma took it in her hand and shaking it playfully, remarked, 'The fire of a great *mahayajna* will be lighted from this fire!'[4] After a pause she asked, 'Who can undertake to maintain this fire in Kālī's room?' Nobody said anything immediately because the question was fraught with difficulties. The daily worship of Kali is undertaken by ascetics only as She destroys all bondages. Some householders are even afraid to keep a picture of Kālī in their homes. Maintaining the fire would entail constant vigilance. In short, no person leading a normal family life was suited for this purpose. So expressing the general opinion about it, Didi's eldest brother Birendra Chandra, answered, 'No, Ma, I cannot. I have my wife and children to consider.' The others merely kept quiet. But Sri Ma asked again quite forcefully, 'Who amongst you can do it?' Shashanka Mohan had been dozing a little. He heard the question now and believed it to be in connection with the previous topic of conversation, namely, about being afraid, to sit alone with the lifelike Image of Kālī. He said, emphatically, 'I can. What is there to be afraid of?'

Sri Ma promptly replied, 'Very well. Ask your sons.' Birendra the eldest and Nandu the youngest, were present. Birendra said, 'If father can do it, it will be highly meritorious (*puṇya*).' Nandu had grave misgivings, but he did not speak. Sri Ma then entrusted Shashanka Mohan with the maintenance of the fire which was destined to have a momentous future. Without another word he went away to begin a vigil which was later taken up by others. Sri Ma asked Didi and her brothers to go home.

The First Ascetics

Sri Ma herself went with a blanket to the *pūjā* room, so that Shashanka Mohan could rest for a while. In this almost playful way, Sri Ma guided him on to the path of asceticism. He proved himself worthy of her choice in every way. At this time another transformation was taking place unknown to others. Sri Jogesh Rai was one of the quiet and least known of the visitors to Shahbagh. He was a bachelor living with his mother. He used to visit Shahbagh attracted by the music of *kirtans* rather than the religious activities. One day, during a *kirtan*, Sri Ma happened to touch him while she was in an exalted state of *bhāva*. This was a radicalising experience for him. He thenceforth came to see Sri Ma, although he would stand unobtrusively at the fringe of the crowd. He had, however been chosen by Sri Ma as it were, as one of the select few of her ascetic followers. Sri Ma asked Bholanath to tell Jogesh Rai to take one year's leave from his service. Then he was to leave Dhaka and go on a pilgrimage to distant places where nobody would know him. For one year he was not to make himself known to anybody. He was to inform his mother only before leaving. The friends and relations of Jogesh Rai were astonished to hear of his sudden departure from Dhaka. Jogesh Rai had been told not to take any money, so he was obliged to adopt a mendicant's life. He later said that till he grew a beard and matted locks of hair and his clothes became shabby, he mostly had to starve because nobody would give him alms. Moreover, he did not know how to ask for them. He fetched up at Haradwar where it is easy for the ascetics because it is a town devoted to the other worldly way of life. One day he was surprised to see Sri Ma and many others walking along the road. Nobody recognised him because he looked quite different. Since he was not supposed to make himself known he did not approach them. He stood and watched the whole party walk past and go on ahead. After a short distance the road took a sharp turn. When Sri Ma passed this turning, she looked back at him standing by the wayside, and he knew from her expression that she had recognised him.

After completing one year Jogesh Rai returned to Dhaka. Sri Ma told him to rejoin his service, saying, 'This is enough for the time being.' Subsequently he came to Siddheswari and became an inmate of the newly formed Ashram. After Shashanka Mohan, he was the first man to leave the world to follow Sri Ma. Sri Ma and Bholanath sometimes visited the neighbouring villages and townships at the invitation of their friends and devotees and so the devotees in Dhaka were becoming used to their frequent absences from Shahbagh. In the first week of April 1927 Sri Ma, Bholanath and a big party left Dhaka to attend the *purna-kumbha* at Haradwar. Sri Ma's party included Shashanka Mohan and Didi, Sri Rajendra Kushari and his wife, Matari Pishima, Didima, Dadamashai and Bholanath's youngest brother Jamini Kumar. This was the first long journey undertaken by them.

Passing through Calcutta and Varanasi[5] they came to Haradwar. After taking the ritualistic bath in the holy river they proceeded to other places of pilgrimage in the neighbourhood: Lacchmanjhoola, Hrishikesh and Bhimgoda. They also visited Mathura, Vrindaban and Agra on their return journey.

On the eve of her departure from Haradwar Sri Ma asked Shashanka Mohan and Didi to remain behind for three months and practice *sadhana*. She said, 'It is necessary for everybody to do his own work (*sadhana*) in solitude.' This golden opportunity was not appreciated by Didi, because she wanted to be near Sri Ma and be of service to her. Didi was not interested in *sadhana*. Shashanka Mohan was an old man, the head of almost a clan; he was more used to taking command of a situation and issuing orders rather than to playing a subordinate role. He however, made no demur and agreed to abide by her *kheyāla*. Shashanka Mohan, since he had taken charge of the sacrificial fire, right after the Kālī-pūjā, had been living at Shahbagh. Once a day, he would go in his own carriage to the Medical School. On the return journey he would stop for a while at his home. He had given up home comforts and social relationships. In retrospect it can be seen very clearly that he was the pioneer amongst the early devotees who blazed the trail to the ascetic way of life. He was the first to give heed to what she was saying rather than just be content to follow her around and find fulfilment thereby. Incidentally Didi and her father were recalled to Dhaka after only 6 weeks. Sri Ma was very kind to all those who gave her implicit obedience, as has been the experience of the not very large number of this elite company.

Crowds were still on the increase at Shahbagh. Sri Ma and Bholanath did not make social visits, so a pattern for seeking their company developed which continued throughout her life. People arranged for religious ceremonies, a *kirtan* or a *pūjā* to which they could invite Sri Ma and Bholanath. Wherever Sri Ma went a crowd would follow, invited or not. Different people had different reactions to this phenomenon. Some would consider it a privilege and an honour that 'the dust from the feet of devotees' (*bhaktapadareṇu*) was purifying their homes. Others would be annoyed at the presumption of an uninvited crowd trampling down gardens and making themselves at home wherever Sri Ma might be. Even ladies from conservative homes followed her about without any restraint. Men who could not have imagined themselves running after a 'woman saint' were now jealous of their women-folk when the latter surrounded Sri Ma and they themselves were obliged to catch glimpses of her from a distance. The devotees of Dhaka could not imagine a future without Sri Ma residing at Shahbagh like the presiding deity of the town. They had yet to learn that although Sri Ma would not settle down anywhere she would still be completely at home wherever she might be.

One evening in July 1927, Sri Ma of her own accord visited a number of houses in town. From her manner Didi, her father, Bhaiji and others apprehended that these were farewell visits and that she would be leaving Dhaka again. This premonition turned out to be true. Next day Sri Ma and Bholanath had left before any one of the devotees had come to Shahbagh. Sri Ma visited Narayanaganj, Rajshahi, Calcutta, Deoghar and Vindhyachala. This was her first visit to the hill top resort which subsequently became one of her major halting stations. She returned to Dhaka but very soon was on the move again, this time to her village homes Vidyakut and Kheora. She came to Kheora on August 3, 1927, accompanied by a big crowd of devotees who wished to see her place of birth. The cottage where Sri Ma was born was now in the possession of a Muslim family. The devotees asked Didima to point out the exact spot where Sri Ma had been born, but the surroundings were so changed that Didima felt rather bewildered. Sri Ma was strolling around talking to people. She went round the cottage and stood still near a place where a heap of cowdung had been stored. She picked up a little of the earth from this place and unexpectedly started to weep loudly like a child. Didima now recognised many of the land marks and stated definitely that it was the site of the shed where Sri Ma had been born almost 31 years ago. Bholanath was upset to see Sri Ma cry and wanted to leave immediately. Sri Ma then wiped her tears and called the owner of the house. She said to him: 'It will be beneficial for all of you if you use this place for prayers and meditations only'. They readily agreed to do so. Shashanka Mohan wanted to offer some money so that the place could be maintained in a suitable manner, maybe a platform constructed on the site. The Muslim householder would not accept it saying that he himself would do whatever was necessary. This was a short visit; not many people could come to meet her but Sri Ma came again for longer visits in later years.

The party then left for Vidyakut, where they stayed for a few days enjoying the hospitality of Sri Ma's relatives. On the day of departure Sri Ma caught hold of the arm of one of her old cousins and wept loudly in the time-honoured manner of a young woman going away from the village of her parents to her husband's home. The cousin placed his hand on her head and spoke words of cheer. Didi and the other devotees from Dhaka were amused and charmed to see Sri Ma in the role of a married village maiden bidding farewell to her people.

Sri Ma did not stay in Dhaka for any length of time. She would pay short visits to Calcutta or other nearby towns and villages. She quite often, took many of her relations with her such as, aunts, in-laws, cousins, nephews and elderly persons who wished to travel in her company. In this way the most unlikely of people got the opportunity of travelling to interesting places and many pilgrimages.

Meanwhile the mud hut built at Siddheswari was falling into disrepair. Shashanka Mohan came forward with the suggestion that a more permanent building should be put up. Sri Ma said, 'I realize that you will not be able to preserve the sanctity of 'the hollow' in future. Well, things must take their own course. If you wish to build a concrete building, then brick-up the hollow and make a raised platform over it, so that no one can step on it inadvertently.' All the devotees wished to participate in the cost of the construction so this one-room building may be called the first Ashram which came up in Siddheswari in the beginning of the year 1928.

Farewell to Shahbagh

The devotees of Dhaka came to know that Sri Ma was again preparing to travel forth. Her friend Hiranbala Ghosh said, 'You must come back soon, otherwise we shall close the gates of Shahbagh and not let you in!' Sri Ma smiled and said merely 'Is that so?' On the day of her departure from Shahbagh, Didi saw her walk round the extensive gardens in a particular mood of her own. Here and there she would touch the walls caressingly, but her expression was remote and inscrutable. Didi dared not ask her the reason for this strange behaviour.

While Sri Ma and Bholanath were touring Rajasthan[6] the Estates of the Nawabzadi were handed over to the Court of Wards. As a result Jogesh Chandra Ghosh, Bhudeb Basu, and Bholanath lost their jobs. Shahbagh had to be vacated. The devotees gathered together and rented a house, in the city. Sri Ma's parents, Amulya, his mother and a young boy Kamalakanta came to the new house. The clay image of Kālī was also brought over and installed in a room. Hiranbala Ghosh's words spoken in jest had proved prophetic. When Sri Ma returned to Dhaka, she told the dejected family of Jogesh Ghosh not to worry about the lost job; what had happened was for their future good. Much later, they realized the truth of this statement.

Bhaiji had been ailing for quite some time. He had been away from Dhaka for a change of climate and for rest. Sri Ma had met him in Vindhyachala. He also now returned to Dhaka and rejoined his service. His doctors had advised him to give up his work and lead a retired life of complete rest, as he had not many more months to live. Sri Ma had said, 'Nothing will happen to you for the next few years. Come back to Dhaka and rejoin your service. Then we shall see.'

He, as well as everybody else was convinced that he had received a new lease of life due to Sri Ma's grace. Mr. Finlow, the Director of Agriculture, Government of Bengal, had great regard and affection for his Assistant. He asked Bhaiji one day, 'How did you cure yourself of this fatal disease?' Bhaiji answered, unhesitatingly, 'I have been cured by the grace of Sri Ma. She did not give me any amulets or charms, I have been under medical treatment; the doctors said that the disease (tuberculosis) was incurable, and I too know that without Sri Ma's grace it was so.' Mr. Finlow answered quietly, 'I do not disbelieve you. We have heard of similar cases of divine grace in our country also.'

Sri Ma's Birthday was celebrated with elaborate arrangements at Siddheswari, by the devotees. Bholanath performed the *tithi-pūjā*. This was the second *pūjā*; the first had been celebrated in Shahbagh in 1927.

The rented house was given up as it was not too conveniently placed; another house Uttama-kutir was rented for Sri Ma and Bholanath. All devotees were trying hard to acquire a piece of land on which they could build an Ashram so that Sri Ma and Bholanath would be ensured of a suitable place of residence.

Sri Ma, in the meantime had been travelling almost ceaselessly. She would come to Dhaka for a few days and then leave for distant towns. In late 1928 she came to Varanasi. During this visit she met Mahamahopadhyaya Sri Gopinath Kaviraj, who was at the time the Principal of Queen's College which is now the Sampurnananda University of Sanskrit. From morning till night there would be a constant stream of men and women passing in and out of the house where Sri Ma and Bholanath were staying. Nobody cared to find out if the owner of the house was pleased at this onrush. The people came singly, in family groups, or in crowds bringing offerings of flowers, garlands, sweets, fruits, clothes and incense. They would besiege Sri Ma so uninterruptedly that she did not have time to wash, eat or change or rest. Days and nights flowed into each other, still the people came drawn by the magnetic personality which at last seemed to have emerged out of the restrictive atmosphere of a conservative household. Bholanath tried in vain to persuade Sri Ma not to go on giving unstintingly of her time, leisure and energy. But it was too late. Sri Ma had once said to him in Shahbagh, that he should think twice before he opened his doors to the world. She now reminded him of her warning to him in Shahbagh, saying 'You did not heed me then, how can you now gather the water back which has spilled over!' Bholanath realized that now the tide could not be turned back. Bholanath himself did not dislike the general air of festive rejoicing, so his misgivings were short lived. Perhaps his articulation of his misgivings was necessary because we know now that he at no time sought any publicity for Sri Ma.

Pandit Gopinath Kaviraj was much impressed by her handling of difficult questions, her in-depth answers to all queries and her wit and humour. The *satsang* sessions were not only enlightening but also delightfully entertaining. This was the beginning of Sri Ma's 'talks'. The pattern of questions from the audience and Sri Ma's answers to them became a regular feature of her sojourn in any town. She never spoke at length (like an oration) nor did she volunteer to speak unasked. Her utter stillness in the midst of a crowd was no less remarkable than the hours of untiring replies to unending questions. She would field all types of questions and with unerring judgement as to the understanding of the interlocutor answer. Although she looked like a housewife, dressed in wide-bordered saris, she was not withdrawn and retiring any more. She had come out to the world to which she belonged.

Sri Ma and Bholanath returned to 'Uttama Kutir' in Dhaka but for a few weeks only. 'Uttama Kutir' soon became a miniature form of Shahbagh, but not for long. One day Sri Ma, accompanied by Bholanath walked out of the house and went to Siddheswari. She occupied the small single room of the little Ashram. Bholanath took up his residence in the temple and evidently under Sri Ma's guidance settled down to his *sadhana*. His latent pro-attitude toward the other-worldly way of life found full expression in Siddheswari. Due to Sri Ma's *līlā* at Siddheswari it had become a special site, already recognised as mystically related to Bholanath.

Sri Ma expressed her *kheyāla* not to return to 'Uttama Kutir'. The devotees were taken aback to learn of this sudden decision. This was a more radical change than the removal from Shahbagh. The experience of quick decisions, total changes, the abandonment of pleasant homes and friendly associates was in store for most of the people gathered around Sri Ma and Bholanath. Sri Ma in her own way lived through it all perhaps to prepare them for future instability in their lives.

The arrangements at 'Uttama Kutir' were dismantled. Sri Ma's parents who were visiting them, went back to their village home. Ashu and Amulya were now in services and in other towns. A young boy, a newcomer, Kamalakanta came on to Siddheswari to help out Sri Ma and Bholanath with the simple daily chores of housekeeping. As the people of Dhaka were asked not to stay for more than 10 minutes on their visits, Siddheswari remained lonely and quiet.

Bholanath's Sādhanā

One evening Sri Ma told the visitors that Bholanath was going away the following day. She did not disclose his destination.

Bholanath was observing silence for the last few days, so he also did not say anything. The next day Sri Ma, Bhaiji, Didi and a few others went to the station to see him off by the Calcutta Mail. Jogesh Rai went with him. Sri Ma returned to Siddheswari. So far Sri Ma had never been on her own without Bholanath. One or two of the devotees stayed back at Siddheswari so that she would not be quite alone. In her own natural inimitable way Sri Ma was introducing all of them to the way of *sādhanā*. Siddheswari had an atmosphere conducive to the inwardisation of thought. In this way not only Bholanath but many of the stalwarts of the early days were eased on to the path of yogic practices and renunciation of worldly life.

After some time, a letter was received from Bholanath asking Sri Ma to join him at Tarapeeth a township in Birbhum district. Sri Ma took one or two blankets, a few articles of clothing and made a bundle. For a long time she had not used a bed and had no bedding. Her mode of resting was to wrap herself in a sheet and lie down on the bare floor or sometimes on a blanket. A large crowd gathered on the platform to see her off. Although Sri Ma had left Dhaka many times but never in this strange manner for a destination which awoke strange fears in the hearts of the people. Tarapeeth was a remote place known only for its great Cremation Grounds made famous by the renowned Tantrika saint of Bengal, Sri Bāmākṣepā.

When Sri Ma was seated in her compartment, she took off two of her gold bangles and gave them to Bhaiji, saying, 'Get five rings made out of them and give them to Jotu, Amulya, Sitanath, Makhan and Subodh.' These boys had almost constantly been with Sri Ma and had great enthusiasm for singing *kirtan*.

Sri Ma and her escort Surendra Mohan Mukherji of Calcutta were received at Tarapeeth by Bholanath and Jogesh Rai. Within this short time a change had come over Bholanath. While he was practising his sadhana at Siddheswari he had had a vision of an image of Kālī without a head. When he spoke to Sri Ma about it, she asked him to go to Tarapeeth, although he knew she had no special knowledge about this place. Bholanath, on his arrival found an ancient Temple of the Goddess Tara (an aspect of Kālī) in lonely surroundings. Bholanath did not understand why Sri

Ma had sent him to Tarapeeth; there was no similarity between the Deity in the Temple and the Image of his vision. However, he took up his position on the Temple veranda and settled down to the austere practice of sustained *japa*. In a few days, the priests came to know him well. They were impressed by his absorption and concentration and began to treat him with respect as an ascetic.

One night, while he was sitting in meditation, the priests came to make preparations for the ritual of the evening prayers to mark the end of the day. The priests were now used to Bholanath and did not ask him to leave. He saw them remove the ornaments and outer garments and then he was amazed to see them remove the head itself, leaving just a featureless base. Before opening the Temple doors in the morning they would replace the head, put on elaborate costumes and ornaments and a crown. Only the priests and their families knew that the Image of Tārā was a headless figure.[7]

Bholanath attained a high spiritual state at Tarapeeth. Jogesh Rai was an eyewitness to a major transformation in him. There was a broken down hut near the Temple. Sri Ma took up her residence in this rough shelter. One night strange *kriyās* happened to Bholanath. His body seemed to be wrung out from within. Sri Ma was within reach; when Jogesh Rai felt apprehensive about the strange phenomenon he would look at Sri Ma's calm and benign face and take heart. She seemed to be guiding Bholanath through whatever metamorphosis he was undergoing. Bhonalanath looked a true renunciate now.

After a few days contact was made with the devotees of Calcutta and Dhaka; they arrived in groups, and the lonely surroundings at once assumed a fair-ground like character. Bholanath looked distinguished with his lengthening hair and beard and quite like a *sādhu*. He had been a heavy smoker but now did not smoke at all. He ate very little and rested also for very short periods of time. All his time was spent on the Temple veranda.

Sri Ma in the meantime had so endeared herself to the families of the priests that these simple village women were always with her even as her devotees of other big towns and cities. When Didi arrived in Tarapeeth, she realized how foolish had been her apprehensions regarding Sri Ma's sojourn in this place of desolation. Sri Ma had been cherished with as much love and devotion as anywhere else. The time of parting drew near. The day Sri Ma left Tarapeeth, one of the women said, 'Don't forget us! We are poor people, we can give you a poor man's fare only.' Another said, 'As soon as I heard the horn of a car, I felt depressed thinking that the car has come to fetch you, even as Akrura had come to fetch Sri Krishna away from Vrindaban.'

Sri Ma laughed and said, 'Why do you say such things? I am just like one of you. It is because of the goodness of your hearts that you have been so kind and loving to me.' The woman answered, 'We are the people of Tarapeeth which is a *siddhasthāna*. We can recognize people for what they are. We see many *sādhus* and ascetics. Some are genuine, some are not. You are the Goddess incarnate. Why do you try to hide yourself from us?'

Sri Ma had occasion to return to Tarapeeth many times. Her visits brought about many changes; Tarapeeth gradually acquired a look of prosperity. It became well-inhabited; new buildings and shops came up removing for ever the stark character of the Temple precincts. Sri Ma and Bholanath took to travelling again. After visiting various places they went to Vidyakut for a visit with Sri Ma's parents. Bhaiji, Niranjan Rai, Shashanka Mohan and others had been working hard at setting up an Ashram for Sri Ma and Bholanath. At last they were happy in the possession of such a 'building' in the midst of the green expanse of Ramna. This 'building' so far was a hut only but still a place to call their own and dedicate to the service of Sri Ma. They were now struck by the uncomfortable thought that Sri Ma and Bholanath might not return to Dhaka at all since Bholanath was not in service any more. The elders of the group then went to Vidyakut and persuaded Bholanath to come to Siddheswari for Sri Ma's Birthday Pūjā and the opening ceremony of the Ashram at Ramna.

This was the third time (May 1929) that Sri Ma's Birthday was observed by a special *pūjā* performed by Bholanath and arranged for by the devotees of Dhaka. The next morning Sri Ma and Bholanath came to Ramna from Siddheshwari amidst a lot of jubilant fanfare. Didi noticed that after the crowds had left Sri Ma went round touching the walls of the Ashram. She was sharply reminded of Sri Ma's gesture before she had left Shahbagh for the last time.

Although Didi was apprehensive, she could not get up courage to question Sri Ma, At dawn, the happy throng of people began to disperse after a night of *kirtan* and rejoicings; soon the Ashram was emptied of people. Sri Ma was still up and about. Now she said to one or two of the people who came to take leave of her, 'Why are you going away? Why don't you stay awhile and sing a little more *kirtan*. I see all of you are tired. Where is my father? Ask him to sing some more *kirtan*.' The old man had just retired to his rest, but on receiving this message he came back to the deserted pandal and raised his inimitable voice in *kirtan*. The sound of this music recalled all those who were within earshot and soon a respectable group formed around Dadamashai. To this group Sri Ma announced her *kheyāla* of leaving Dhaka the same day.

She spoke almost in tones of anguish, 'Do not put obstacles in my way, please tell Bholanath not to say 'no' to me. I have to go. Please let me move around according to my *kheyāla* - if you cannot do it then I shall leave my body here with you and go away.'

All protests died before they could be articulated. Someone asked, 'Where will you go? Who will go with you?' Sri Ma answered, 'By the first train available. For myself I do not need anybody, but if it makes you feel better then I may ask my father to go with me!' Dadamashai went inside to collect a few things for the journey. Sri Ma took nothing for herself. Bholanath was visiting Bhaiji, Niranjan Rai and one or two others in the city. He came back to find the Ashram in a state of crisis. He recognised that Sri Ma's *kheyāla* would not brook denials. She had never expressed her *kheyāla* so forcefully before. He was the last man to call into question, the truth of her statement. In great dejection he said 'Very well - but people may speak ill of you if I am not with you when you travel around.'

'I shall not do anything', said Sri Ma, 'which will invite criticism. My father will be with me. Will people speak ill of me?' She looked enquiringly at her companions. Many hastened to re-assure her: 'No, Ma, nobody will say or think anything of it.'

It is true that Sri Ma left Dhaka (May 1929), but in retrospect it seems that she had great difficulty in shaking off relays of people who only obeyed the letter of her *kheyāla*. One or two would join her as soon as they knew her destination. She would send them back, or leave herself. After a while she travelled to distant Haradwar but here also Kunja Mohan from Varanasi joined them. She had Ashu with her now. Leaving behind her father and Kunja Mohan[8] she quietly slipped away to Ayodhya where the ticket collector made them welcome. She eventually fetched up at Varanasi. Her *kheyāla* for a place where nobody would know her was at last achieved when she came to Dr. Girin Mitra's place at Akna, Bihar. Dr. Mitra had met her previously in Calcutta and now saw to it that her retreat was not disturbed by anyone.

Bholanath, in the meantime had visited many *pīthasthānas* of Bengal. He had then fallen ill. He came to the house of his nephew Dr. Girija Shankar Kushari at Chandpur for a rest. His sisters and nephews were always glad to see him.

Sri Ma's *kheyāla* to cut herself adrift from her family and devotees for a short while seemed to have achieved a few purposes. Firstly, she undermined the family-like group of Dhaka who were beginning to think that they were rather exclusive. Secondly, her words regarding the building of an Ashram in Dhaka were found to be true. She had said: 'The whole world is an ashram. Why do you wish to have one of your own?' Later, however, in response to their repeated entreaties, she had pointed out the area which could be suitable for an Āshram. When the building site was being dug up, they had discovered a number of ancient graves of ascetics and their bones. These had not been disturbed; Sri Ma's room had been built over them. The devotees now could hardly take in the fact that Sri Ma had stayed a mere twenty-four hours in this precious little Ashram dedicated to her. The future of the Ashram looked bleak indeed.

References

1. AV, Vol. 1, No. 2, p. 54.
2. Girija Shankar Bhattacharya, 'Mother as I have known Her', *Mother as seen by her Devotees*, pp. 114-115.
3. D.D. Vol. I, p. 103.
4. This prophecy was fulfilled in Varanasi in 1947.
5. At Varanasi the big party was accommodated in the house of Nirmal Chandra Chatterjee, the eldest son-in-law of Shashanka Mohan. This house had the honour of providing lodgings to Sri Ma and her party many times in later years.
6. To relate one of many interesting incidents happening near Sri Ma: In Jaipur Sri Ma's *ṭongāwallāh* (horse-carriage) outdistanced Bholanath. The driver stopped in a lonely spot and getting off his perch came around and advanced in a menacing way toward Sri Ma. When his eyes met those of Sri Ma, he was seen to falter and back away. The fire in the blazing eyes was withdrawn. The man waited quietly by the wayside till Bholanath caught up with them.
7. Worship of Deities is *atmavat*, that is, as you would do for yourself, taking for granted that nothing is necessary for God. The Images are offered meals, beds for rest, refreshments etc.; they are roused in the morning with appropriate mantras. The Image naturally is not moved; generally there is a symbolic representation (*yantra*) in front of the priest. In any case the *puja* with external accessories is secondary. The priest worships in his heart with meditations (*manas pūjā*). The Image is the Form which the pilgrims see from outside. This is the general practice. Every temple has its own tradition known to its priests handed down from one generation to the next.
8. Shashanka Mohan's younger brother - later Swami Turiyananda Giri.

CHAPTER SIX

The Last Years in Dhaka: 1929-1932

Sri Ma was born in Bengal but can any sense of location be ascribed to her? We are told that she had a vision of a Temple of Śivá in the lap of the Himalayas... She arrived at the place of her vision in 1932 and resided in this part of the country for many years... the people of these regions also became enamoured of her magnetic presence and more loving bonds were forged...

- Dr. Pannalal[1]

Apply your reasoning power, your intellect, to the quest for Immortality - all else will follow as a matter of course. It is just like watering the roots of a tree. The tree grows by its own power, throws out branches and leaves, gives forth blossoms and fruits at proper season.

The supreme duty of man is, therefore, to undertake the quest for his true Being - whether one takes the path of devotion, where the 'I' is lost in the 'Thou' or the path of self-inquiry, in search of the true 'I' - it is He alone who is found in the 'Thou' as well as in the 'I'.

- Sri Ma Anandamayi

The Last Years in Dhaka

Sri Ma's random travel in the company of chance-met companions seems especially significant when we consider the effect it had on Bholanath. He was forced to face the fact that he did not understand Sri Ma after all. He did not doubt that she would return to him in due course but he could not but have felt the sudden slackening of the hold that he seemed to have had on her. This loss of confidence coincided with an exposure to the worldly opinions of friends and family. His sisters were fond of him and had his interest at heart. They probably urged him to take a strong line with his wife and not allow her to lead a mendicant's life. So far it had never occured to Bholanath to put the slightest obstacle in the way of Sri Ma. Whatever she had said or done had been completely acceptable to him. Bholanath and his family knew her to be possessed of great yogic powers. They had witnessed many miraculous incidents; they did not doubt that she could make anything happen if so was her *kheyāla*. There was even some talk of acquiring wealth and position in the world. In India many *mahātmās* and *sādhus* are seen to live in luxury. Even in ancient ages, the *ṛṣis* had lived with their wives and disciples in hermitages which were not devoid of home comforts. Further, the *ṛṣis* were certainly the exemplars of the other-worldly way of life. So there was precedence.

That Bholanath had listened to all such talk transpired much later. For the time being, Bholanath came to Calcutta to meet Sri Ma at the same time that she also arrived in the city in response to the message that he was very ill. It was seen that Bholanath was very angry and seemed to be scolding Sri Ma for her irresponsible behaviour. Sri Ma made no answer; she gave no explanations, neither did she try to appease his anger. She looked quite calm and indifferent but rather listless. Her natural radiance was in complete abeyance. Bholanath with Sri Ma returned to Chandpur to the residence of his nephew Dr Girija Shankar Kushari. Bhaiji, Shashanka Mohan, Nishikanta Mitra came to Chandpur to plead with Bholanath to come to Dhaka.

Bholanath agreed to return but not to the Ashram in Dhaka. He and Sri Ma went to Siddheshwari. The devotees were told to keep to the rule of ten minutes only for visiting time. It was at this time that Bholanath repeated to Sri Ma all that was seething in his mind. Sri Ma had occasion to talk at length about Bholanath after his death in 1938. Explaining many things to Didi she said, 'After all these years Bholanath wanted me to cook for him and do the housekeeping at Siddheshwari. It was all the same to me - I tried to do his bidding but as all of you saw for yourselves it was not to be. First Bholanath was taken ill so severely and then I was myself so ill. Bholanath was then only too glad to allow everyone to visit as usual. All of you have seen that his nature was *sātvic*. This clouding of his mind was very short lived and a passing phase only. When I went away he became a prey to random thoughts which were suggested by his family. One cannot blame them either, such is the way of the world. Perhaps it was necessary for Bholanath to pass through the furnace of worldly influence before he could dedicate himself fully to his *tapasyā*.

'Once or twice you had been puzzled by the death-like symptoms of this body at Shahbagh. Whenever he happened to approach me with a worldly type of thought like money matters, or some such thing, this body would respond by as if going away completely. The body would become inert. He would at once be frightened and do whatever, lay within his power to restore me to normalcy. He would do *nāma-japa*, pray or sit in meditation; once, you remember, he called all of you in to do *nāma-japa* near me! These inclinations did not even surface to his conscious mind, he himself was puzzled by such events. Because he was such a pure-hearted and upright person he could treat Maroni[3] and myself in the same way as we lay near him. You have seen how scrupulous his deportment was. I never heard him make an untoward remark in joke or utter any unkind jest about things or people. The few days in Siddheshwari in effect cleansed him of any dross that may have lingered; he made steady progress after this interval.'

As written above, Bholanath did not encourage the devotees of Dhaka to visit or linger at Siddheshwari. Sri Ma did not look well. This was a novel feature because so far, even if physicaly ill, she had never seemed to be so. Didi and the others were very much concerned about her wan looks, but were not permitted to do anything or even stay with them as in Shahbagh.

The conflict in Bholanath's mind, fortunately, was short-lived. While it lasted, Sri Ma looked very ill. Her normal glow and radiance vanished. She, moreover, observed silence although she would say one or two words to Bholanath and sometimes to the others in an indistinct voice. Nobody, however, knew the reason for this change in her demeanour.

After a few days, Bholanath was taken violentiy ill. Sri Ma kept a lonely vigil by his bed-side till people came to know about it. The devotees arranged for medical aid and took turns in nursing him. Sri Ma herself was in constant attendance. Bholanath was removed to Aswini Kumar's house for facility of treatment. Sri Ma, with Bholanath's permission, sometimes went to the Ashram and stayed in the room alone.

In the month of August, Sri Ma started running a temperature which developed into high fever within a few days. But a chart could not be maintained; the temperature would suddenly shoot up to 106 degree and after a few moments come down to 100 degree. A little later, again the thermometer would record 104 or 105 degree, although there was no change in Sri Ma's outward appearance. With her illness Sri Ma appeared to have regained her cheerfulness. She would smile, talk and behave like a healthy person, even when she had very high fever. So, Didi and others stopped using the thermometer as serving no purpose. After a few days of the fever, Sri Ma's body became absolutely limp. She could not use any of her limbs and had to be picked up and carried. Even so, the smallest part of her body that was left unsupported would hang limp in a disjointed fashion. Bholanath now permitted Didi to stay at Siddheshwari to look after her. Aswinini Babu's daughter Chana and other local people came to help Didi. It seemed like a stroke of paralysis, except that Sri Ma spoke and laughted in a normal manner. Sri Ma herself would say, 'Why do you lift the body so carefully? It has become like a bag of flour. You can shove it around.' Didi in sheer desparation appealed to Sri Ma, 'We are unable to look after your body in this condition. Please get well now.'

After this plea, Sri Ma one night lifted her hand without any aid. This was the first voluntary movement of her body after four or five days. The next day, she walked a little by herself and then slowly regained the use of her limbs. But the fever persisted and symptoms of dropsy began to appear besides blood dysentery. Her cheerfulness, however, remained unmarred. Bholanath thought that if she continued to enjoy her illness like this, she would never have the *kheyāla* to get well. So, he said with a show of impatience, 'Illness is nothing to be so cheerful about. Get well now.'

After Bholanath's scolding, Sri Ma's expression became that of a seriously ill patient. She would keep quiet and not talk to anyone. Many devotees from Dhaka were now staying at night at Siddheshwari and the local people also were in constant attendance. Siddheshwari was quite populated now. Housewives would leave their homes and gather round Sri Ma for long hours. If the devotees asked her to get well, she would say, 'I don't ask you all to go away when you come. Why should I send away illness? They will leave in their own time.'

Indeed, the diseases took their own reluctant time to go away from her. The fever continued for many days after the other symptoms had vanished.

A young boy named Atul had come in search of Jogesh Rai from his village. After passing his Matriculation examination he had felt like following in Jogeshdada's footsteps. He now came to Siddheshwari and became one of Sri Ma's ever-increasing family. He was given the task of cooking *bhoga* and looking after the image of Kālī.

It may be recalled that the image of Kālī and the sacrificial fire had been moved from time to time with every change of place of installation. Sometime after the Kālīpūjā in 1926, a hollow was made under Sri Ma's instructions, near the pond in Shahbagh. After consecration of the ground, the sacrificial fire was established in this *kuṇḍa*. Kulada Banerji, a new-comer at that time, was put in charge of this *yajña-kuṇḍa*. He was temperamentally suited for these forms of *pūjā*. For many years he remained in charge of Kālī and the *yajña-agnī* in Dhaka.

At Siddheshwari, the fire had been placed under the *pipal* tree. Sri Ma did not permit it to be taken to any home. Whenever necessary, she gave suitable instructions for its preservation and maintenance.

The devotees were now desirous of establishing the image of Kālī and the *agni* permanently at the Ramna Ashram.

Sri Ma suggested that the Goddess Kālī may be installed where a broken Śiva-linga had been found. A pit for the sacrificial fire was also constructed according to Sri Ma's instruction.

Meanwhile, the devotees wanted to enlarge the Ashram at Ramna. Nagen Babu took charge of the building programme. Several graves were uncovered when the earth was dug up for laying the foundation. Some were in a good condition of preservation. Skeletons, ashes from sacrificial fires and earthen lamps were disinterred. People now recalled what Sri Ma had said about this site, namely, that many ascetics had lived there and practised *sādhanā* in the past.

At Sri Ma's *kheyāla*, the graves were left undisturbed. Three of the main *samādhis* came below the big room of the Ashram. Another became the foundation of the Śiva temple, yet others were under Sri Ma's room.

On Mahālayā, 1331 B.S.[2], that is sometime in October, 1929, Sri Ma and Bholanath came to Ramna. Both were ailing and confined to bed for several days. It took a long time for Sri Ma to get back to her normal behaviour. Once for 15 days she hardly left her bed. She would get up for a few minutes only, otherwise she would lie or sit in her bed all the time. One day, Bhaiji came early in the morning and persuaded her to take a walk in the Ramna Polo grounds. This started off another reaction. She began walking for three or four hours every day.

One morning she did not get up at all. Two days passed, Sri Ma remained lying inert on her bed. Bholanath assembled the devotees for a *kirtan* which was kept up throughout the night. The next afternoon, Sri Ma sat up and slowly resumed her activities of daily life. She would say in answer to inquiries, 'This inert condition is the same to me as an active condition. I feel no difference whatever, so what is there to explain?'

During this time Sri Ma in her own unobtrusive way brought about a major change in Bholanath's life. Bholanath was not indifferent to creature comforts. He had a soft and comfortable bed, whereas Sri Ma had a blanket only. One night Sri Ma roused Bholanath from his fine bed and expressed a *kheyāla* to recline on it. Bholanath being deprived of his bed had to roll up some clothes to serve as a pillow and use Sri Ma's blanket for the night's rest. After a few days Sri Ma rolled up Bholanath's elaborate bedding and had it put away. She took another blanket for herself.

This was a time of sadness for all. Niranjan Rai who had taken the initiative in building the new Ashram at Ramna, had passed away on June 15, 1929 about a month after Sri Ma had left Dhaka. Everyone was keenly aware of the tragedy of his death and his absence from their midst.

Gradually the rhythm of life picked up its usual tempo of happy gatherings. The annual session of the Indian Philosophical Congress was held in Dhaka in December, 1929. The well-known Vedantist Dr. Mahendranath Sirkar already knew about Sri Ma. Many of his colleagues wished to be presented to her. One evening several delegates assembled at Ramna Ashram. Dr Mahendranath Sirkar translated for them. A Professor of the Wilson College led the discussion that lasted for three hours. Dr Mahendranath Sirkar writes, 'All sorts of questions were put, mostly philosophical and Mataji (Sri Ma) was ready with answers spontaneously and immediately. There was no hesitation, not the least conscious thinking, nor the least sign of nervousness in her. Her answers hit directly the point - free from metaphysical technique.' He added that all who were present were impressed by 'the profundity of her wisdom, the fluency of her expression and the luminosity of the smile on her face.'

One of the delegates asked her, 'If the human character changes and everybody becomes unselfish, will the world then become perfect?' Sri Ma at once answered, 'But, such it is, already!' It was evident to the audience that she spoke from her own experience where everything is the perfect expression of the perfect Being.[3]

In the beginning of 1930, Sri Ma asked Bholanath to resume his *sādhanā* at Siddheshwari. One or two *brahmacāris* like Atul or Kamalakanta would stay with him to look after his needs, if any. Otherwise he was practically alone. As in Tarapeeth, here also, he could be seen, sitting in a yogic posture for long hours, in deep meditation. Some of the people of Dhaka were moved to take spiritual initiation from him. His one-time superior officer Bhudeb Basu became his disciple as well as Didi's brother Birendra Chandra. There were many more.

Sri Ma's Birthday celebration of the year 1930 was held at Ramna Ashram. Bholanath came over from Siddheshwari to perform the *pūjā*. Shortly after the Birthday celebration, Sri Ma remarked one day, 'I hear the sound of weeping from every house.' This prophecy became an actuality within a few days. The communal riots in June 1930 brought about a reign of terror. Curfew was clamped on the city. For sometime nobody dared to stir out of their homes. Only Bhaiji came daily to the Ashram as usual. His neighbour told him one day, 'I watch you passing by every day and I cannot rest until I see you return. This has become almost a vigil with me now.'

In August of the same year (1930) Sri Ma and Bholanath accompanied by Shashanka Mohan, Didi, Jogesh, Ashu and a few others started on a tour of South India. This was Sri Ma's first visit to the South. She had occasion to revisit South India in 1952. Sri Ma was seen to be at home wherever she went. The barrier of language did not prevent the local people from crowding round her near Temple precincts.

The party returned to Vindhyachala in October. A small building on top of the Ashtabhuja Hills had been purchased by Shashanka Mohan. This may be called the third Ashram dedicated to Sri Ma's service. With her presence, the lonely surroundings came to life Devotees arrived from nearby Varanasi. For a few days all was joy and festivity. Sri Ma continued to travel. She went to Jamshedpur and then to Calcutta.

In Calcutta, the family of Jyotish Guha including his brother Kṣitish Guha, his daughter Buni, his father-in-law Pran Kumar, headed the concourse of devotees of the town. Their residence became as if, the headquarters for getting news of Sri Ma; they were all gifted singers, so *kirtan* parties formed easily and people tended to gather at this house as at an Ashram. Sri Ma returned to Dhaka after about six months.

In the beginning of 1931 Bholanath heard from his brother who had converted to Christianity. He now was a priest and known as the Reverend K.K. Chakravarty. Bholanath met him and his wife and they were drawn into his ever-expanding family of devotees. Bholanath was very pleased to find his long lost brother again.

In the evening, Sri Ma would stroll in the extensive green fields of the pologrounds surrounding the Ashram. There was always a crowd round her. One day one gentleman asked, 'You were lying in a state of *samādhi*. You were evidently in communion with God. Now you have to descend to our level to talk to us for our benefit.' Sri Ma smiled and said, 'Are you apart from God? I do not feel any ascending or descending. To me it is all the same. Only the bodily reactions are different.'

The devotees of Dhaka were desirous of expanding the newly built Ashram. Knowing that Sri Ma could be consulted about religious ceremonies, it was proposed to install the images of Śiva, Annapurṇā and Viṣṇu in a temple constructed for the purpose. The clay image of Kali} had already been housed in a small room at the Ashram. The image so far had been shifted a number of times with great care; from Shahbagh to the rented house, then to 'Uttama Kutir' then to Siddheshwari and now finally to Ramna. The Devi was an integral part of the lives of the devotees of Dhaka.

On the occasion of the Birthday celebration of 1931 Sri Ma inaugurated a new style in *kirtan*. She remarked 'Why should the men alone perform *kīrtan*? We, women, shall keep awake one night and sing *kirtan*!' Her suggestion was carried out with so much enthusiasm and success that when other women heard about it next day, they asked to be allowed to arrange for another night-long *kirtan*. In the evening nearly 150 women and young girls collected at the Ashram. Sri Ma asked all the menfolk to go home. She nominated a few of the elders to keep watch against intruders or mischief makers as the function would be in the open. Sri Ma always took great care to see to the safety and protection of all young women who crowded round her.

The women decorated themselves with garlands and sandal paste. The fragrance of incense was wafted on the breaze. Quite a few amongst them were good musicians. Bhramara, the eldest granddaughter of Jogesh Ghosh, contributed the leading voice. All of them made the night melodious by their inspired singing. This is how the first all-women *kīrtan*-party was formed in Dhaka. They acted as pioneers for such groups in other towns as well.

After the birthday festivities, Sri Ma left Dhaka for Darjeeling. On her way she visited Bajitpur. Many of the women who had come to see her off, at the last moment climbed into cars and joined Sri Ma's party, amidst much laughter and teasing that they would be considered quite mad by their families and severely taken to task for such impulsive behaviour when they returned home. But nobody was willing to think so far ahead, and adventurously went along with Sri Ma's party to Bajitpur.

A tide of festivity passed over Bajitpur for a couple of days. Sri Ma pointed out old landmarks. Her cottage was there but the roof had fallen in and the walls were crumbling down. From the local inhabitants who collected round them, Didi and others heard accounts of Sri Ma's life during her *līlā* of *sādhanā*. The girl who used to work for Sri Ma came and stood near them shyly. She was so happy to see her mistress again. Didi collected a little of the earth from the corner of the room where Sri Ma used to sit in meditation. She brought it away with her; this was subsequently placed under a platform where Sri Ma used to sit in the Ramna Ashram.

The party returned to Dhaka. Sri Ma with a more conventional group of people left for Darjeeling. From Darjeeling, Sri Ma came to Calcutta and then to Puri. *Ratha-yātrā* or pulling of the chariot of Jagannath is an annual festival held at Puri. Many friends and devotees had come with Sri Ma to join in the festival. A few days before the auspicious day Sri Ma said, 'I see an impending calamity. Do what you can (to prevent it).'

Bholanath conjectured that some sort of accident would occur during the great rush hour of the pulling of the chariot and wanted to leave Puri at once, but his companions prevailed upon him to stay back. Nirmal Chandra Chatterjee and his family had come from Varanasi to be with Sri Ma. On the day of their departure the eldest son Santosh and his sister Tarubala insisted on staying back with Sri Ma's party. Their mother (Didi's sister) said to Sri Ma, 'I am leaving them in your care.' There was reason for some concern about Santosh. He was subject to epileptic fits and had to be watched constantly. He himself knew about his malady and in general, could be trusted to stay in safe surroundings. A week passed. Then one day Santosh was found to be missing. After a frantic search, his dead body was discovered in the well behind the house. The shock of this discovery nearly paralysed everyone. Only Sri Ma remained sitting quietly in her room. Bholanath, Shashanka Mohan (Santosh's grandfather) with help from others, brought the body to the house. Sri Ma's calm demeanour had a salutory effect on them. Many persons who had come to visit Sri Ma were on the point of turning back at the gate, thinking it would be improper to intrude on her grief. When they were told that Sri Ma was her normal self, they took heart and went in to see her.

Death by accident, in some cases, is considered to be inauspicious. Cremation ceremonies are sometimes forbidden, and the body has to be interred in earth. Apart from the tragedy of death, this was an additional crisis which had to be faced. The local people of some authority, rallied to their help and with the permission of the Pandits, the body was cremated. They decreed that in the holy precincts of the Jagannath Temple, no death need be considered accidental with its attending untoward consequences.

After everyone had gone Sri Ma talked about Santosh to Didi and his sister, almost the whole night. At dawn she went to the well to reconstruct the actions of Santosh. Why he had gone there at all remained a mystery. Sri Ma, on leaving Puri came to Vindhyachala. All of them were taken aback to hear that the Pandits of Varanasi had called into question the mandate of those in Puri. The last rites of death which are performed on the 13th day for the spiritual welfare of the soul were not to be performed by them.

Sri Ma now took the matter in her own hands. She sent telegrams to Puri and Varanasi, repeatedly till at last, the misunderstandings were cleared up. She herself arrived in Varanasi to Nirmal Chandra's house on the day of the funeral rites (*śrāddha*). Santosh's father greeted her with composure saying, 'Ma, I gave you two of my children. I see, you have given sanctuary to one of them.' Sri Ma in one of her rare displays of grief, started to weep in a heartrending manner. Nirmal Chandra's wife, who was crying silently all this while now took Sri Ma in her arms and proceeded to quieten her as if Sri Ma were a little grief-stricken girl.

Sri Ma stayed with them for 15 days. It did not appear that this was a house of mourning. The parents were busy looking after Sri Ma and the happy throng which surrounded her. One day the bereaved father asked her, 'Ma, why did you cry, on the first day?' Sri Ma answered, 'Because you did not. I wept to lighten the burden weighing on your heart!'

From Varanasi Sri Ma again returned to Vindhyachala. One day, from the balcony outside her room Sri Ma saw some men climbing the hill. They were carrying refreshments with them and were evidently on an all-day expedition to various places of interest on Ashtabhuja Hills. On arriving at the hill top, they hid their basket under a bush and went away. Sri Ma asked Didi to fetch away the basket. On their return, the gentlemen were non-plussed to find their cache missing. After a few minutes Sri Ma sent some one to invite them to the Ashram. They were highly pleased that Sri Ma had taken away their food (only to be given back with added *prasad*) and congratulated themselves on getting *darśana* in this unexpected manner. One of them Dr. Upendranath Banerjee of Mirzapur became a life-long devotee.

Sri Ma was constantly on the move. She travelled to Cox's Bazar after the annual Kālī pūjā of 1931 in November. She stayed at the sea-side bungalow of Dinabandhu and his wife, an old couple who had been devoted to Sri Ma for a long time. At the request of the old lady Sri Ma undertook another trip to places of pilgrimage. The old lady, who had not travelled at all, was very happy to see the holy places in Sri Ma's company.

In the month of April 1932 Sri Ma came to Calcutta and put up with Bholanath's Christian brother who was now known as Kakababu (uncle). Once more days and nights merged into one another. The unending stream of people eager to see and be with Sri Ma, did not allow her a moment's rest. Kakababu as the host decided to introduce some order by setting fixed times of *darśana*. At noon everybody was requested to leave so that Sri Ma could relax for a little while. After people had gone away rather reluctantly Sri Ma was asked to rest in one of the inner rooms which was cool. April is a hot month. The sun blazed down on the city. The men folk were resting in another room of the house. After a short while Sri Ma got up with a mischievous look on her face. She, followed by Didi and Kakima (aunt) came to the room where Bholanath and Kakababu were enjoying a siesta and asked her brother-in-law to come out for a stroll with her. Kakababu protested against setting out in the scorching heat. He said, 'I told everyone you needed rest, and now you are going out! What will people think of me?' Sri Ma over rode his protests saying, 'Don't you know, there is something wrong with my brain! Alas that I am disturbing your siesta as well.' Sri Ma roamed around, sometimes stopping at little shops to buy some little thing or other. In this manner she arrived at the house of Pashupati Babu. His wife was ill and had not been able to come to see Sri Ma. Now she was overwhelmed with joy as she had been praying deeply that Sri Ma should not leave the town before she could have her *darśana*.

In the evening Sri Ma returned to Kakababu's house. At 9 p.m. Kakababu again requested the visitors to leave. He was determined to ensure a night's rest for Sri Ma. But Sri Ma was still in one of her impish moods. She kept the few people remaining in the house laughing by her entertaining talks. The hilarious laughter made sleep out of the question for anyone. When Kakababu protested, she started to tease him in the manner of a privileged elder sister-in-law. The whole night was spent in a delightful but wakeful manner. The next morning the devotees heard how Sri Ma had 'rested' during the day and night. Kakababu gave up his idea of organizing Sri Ma's way of being with her people.

Didi recalls an interesting incident which occured at his place. Kakima was a Punjabi lady very proud of her athletic figure and physical strength. She would say that she was more than a match for any Bengali girl. In friendly trials of strength she would defeat Didi and others. Sri Ma, one day playfully caught hold of her arm with three fingers only. Much to the amusement of all, Kakima was unable to loosen this slender hold on her arm.

From Calcutta Sri Ma went to Atal Bihari's house at Rajshahi. At night, Sri Ma and her party were invited to a *kirtana* at a neighbour's house. Atal Bihari stayed at home. On her return Sri Ma found that Atal Bihari had retired for the night. He got up when his guests returned. Sri Ma said, 'You are a fine person. Your guests have not dined as yet and you have had your food and are sleeping comfortably.' Atal Bihari said, 'A mother is satisfied if her son is well fed and rested. My dinner should suffice for you.' Sri Ma said. 'Indeed! All right, don't forget what you have said now.' When some light refreshments were brought for Sri Ma, she pushed the dish in front of Atal saying, 'Let Atal eat this on my behalf.' Atal unhesitatingly polished off this plate. Then Sri Ma said, 'I do not need to lie down because Atal's rest will be my rest.' Atal answered, 'All right, you can sit up. I am going to sleep', and with that he marched away to his bed.

The next morning Sri Ma said, 'Atal's stay in the house will be my stay. Let us now go somewhere else.' Sri Ma, accompanied by Didi, Atal's wife and others walked to a riverside temple nearby. Sri Ma said, 'Cook the mid-day meal over here.' Bholanath and Shashanka Mohan fetched the necessary commodities from the market. Didi and Atal's wife cooked a simple meal in the open, consisting of rice and dahl cooked together with vegetables, and a sweet dish of milk with rice (*kheer*). When the meal was ready, Didi poured a little of the *kheer* into a glass and offered it to Sri Ma. After swallowing the first mouthful, Sri Ma asked Didi to taste a little of the *kheer*. Didi obeyed, but had to spit it out immediately because it was still scalding hot. Sri Ma's smile somewhat lessened her discomfiture and remorse. Atal Bihari's wife said, 'I have also learnt my lesson. Very often I offer hot things for *bhoga*, not bothering to ascertain whether they are fit to be eaten or not.'[4]

Sri Ma then returned to the house of her host. It was not in her nature to walk away with a victory over Atal Bihari. So she went back to relieve him of his anxiety and remorse at carrying his playfulness too far.

After travelling around for a few more weeks Sri Ma and Bholanath returned to Dhaka in May 1932. Ramna Ashram was getting ready to celebrate the anniversary of Sri Ma's Birthday. Bhaiji had undertaken the remodelling of the Deities in the Temple. Sri Ma had donated a major portion of her gold ornaments for this purpose. Sri Ma used to be given a lot of jewellery from devotees and relatives but she never kept anything for herself for long. For many years she had worn only a thin gold chain given her by Bholanath. In deference to convention she kept one pair of conch-shell bangles on her forearms and a gold plated iron bangle worn by all married women.

As in previous years, devotees flocked to Dhaka. All day and nearly all night the small red building amidst the green expanse of the polo grounds swarmed with men, women and children. On this occasion yet another facet of Sri Ma's personality was revealed. It was she who with unerring judgement advised how to accomodate the visitors and also how to keep them usefully occupied. She made suggestions about various religious festivals. Everyone had something to do. She herself was everywhere at once, advising, helping, solving problems as they arose. The highlight of the occasion was the installation of the Deities in the Temple. Under Sri Ma's instructions Bholanath performed all the necessary rituals. At Siddheshwari a Śivaliṅga was installed on the platform over the hollow so that it was made safe from desecration for all time.

Sri Ma's advice regarding the Temple had far-reaching consequences as we realize now. The small shrine housing the clay-image of Kālī was left undisturbed. The walls of the new temple came up all around it. The floor of the new room came up to more than half of the shrine which now resembled an inner cell of the new room. A flight of steps led down to the door of the inner sanctum. The roof of the shrine was like a platform in the room on which the Deities were installed.

Sri Ma directed that the door to the shrine would remain locked. Once a year it would be opened so that everyone irrespective of caste or religion[5] would have *darśana*. In the evening after *pūjā* and *abhiṣeka*, the door would be locked again for one year. This arrangement lasted for many years. In 1938, the caretakers were saddened to see that the clay image had started to disintegrate. 1938 also saw the passing away of Bholanath. He was the high priest for ritualistic worship of Deities. Was it a coincidence that the image remained intact while he was alive? Anyway, Sri Ma who was not in Dhaka at the time directed that the shrine should be bricked up for good. Later, when East Pakistan was created, all Temples at Ramna were razed to the ground including the ancient Kālī

Temple where Sri Ma used to sit with her companions. The shrine of Kālī however remained undisturbed and unharmed because it was already buried underground. Sri Ma had had the Deities of the upper temple removed to Varanasi much earlier. Devotees came to understand later that Sri Ma had prepared for future contingencies right from the day when they had been happily engaged in installing Deities in Ramna Ashram.

Towards the close of the prolonged festivities Sri Ma was one day invited to the house of a devotee whose daughter was getting married. This could have evoked the *kheyāla* for little Maroni's future. She pursuaded Bholanath to agree to an engagement for marriage between Maroni and Kulada Charan's elder son Chinu. Bholanath was very fond of Maroni and was somewhat overcome at the thought of this early betrothal. Sri Ma said, 'Do not be sad. It is all for the good of everybody concerned. At the proper time, God willing, Maroni will be married to Chinu.' The ladies of Dhaka enthusiastically assisted at the ceremony and made it as colourful and joyous as it could be.

In retrospect it becomes clear that Sri Ma was making final arrangements whereby Bholanath would be released from his ties with Dhaka and also his one responsibility, Maroni. She visited Siddheshwari one day and touched the buildings as well as the fallen tree in a caressing manner. The same evening, she sat for a while on the verandah of the temple at Ramna Ashram. A small group of people were sitting around her. At about 11.30 p.m. she got up remarking in an undertone, 'I shall go now.' Birendra Chandra was unpleasantly struck by these words. Perhaps with some idea of deflecting her *kheyāla* he said, 'Yes Ma, go and lie down. It is late.' Sri Ma did not say anything. The group of people made their obeissance and left for their homes.

When everybody had left Sri Ma asked Didi to fetch Bholanath. Tired out, he had fallen asleep. Didi roused him and gave him Sri Ma's message. Sri Ma and Bholanath talked together for some time. Didi then saw him putting on his travelling clothes and shoes. Sri Ma sat on the little platform within the grove of the five trees known as the *Pancavati*. She talked to Kulada Charan, Atul, Kamalakanta, Jogeshadada one by one evidently giving them detailed instructions regarding their *sādhanā* and their various duties in the Ashram. She then called Didi to her and said, 'Look, fortitude is the prime requisite of a *sādhaka.* Fortitude is required (of you).' Seeing Didi's distress, she continued, 'Do not be agitated. I have left Dhaka so many times; but because all of you become so upset at my departure I have to come back again and again. Let me move about according to my *kheyāla.* I cannot do so if you put obstacles in my path.' Sri Ma spoke at length in this strain asking Didi to set an example for others. It was a severe blow to Didi to know that she evidently was not to accompany Sri Ma. Sri Ma then spoke to one or two visitors who were staying at the Ashram.

Bhaiji had been sent for. When he came Sri Ma said to him 'You are to come away with us tonight.' There was a pause. When Bhaiji did not answer, she said, 'What is it? Won't you be able to do it?'

It was obvious to everyone that Bhaiji was required to take the most crucial decision of his life. He answered with composure, 'I shall go home first and get some money for the journey.' He must have thought that he would make his explanations to his wife and children, but Sri Ma said, 'No, you are not to go home. Collect whatever amount some of these men over here may have with them.' Bhaiji made no answer to this and quietly walked away by himself toward the Temple.

Sri Ma then sent word to her parents. Bipin Bihari, displeased at this sudden decision did not come but her mother came. Sri Ma, as was her custom when bidding farewell to her, prostrated herself at her mother's feet. She then quietly walked out of the Ashram. She had not allowed anybody to send for a car or a carriage. She went on foot to the station, accompanied by a sad little group of people. Somehow, the few people who were with her got the impression that there was an air of finality about this leave-taking. To such questions as, 'Where are you going?', or 'When will you return?', Sri Ma made no answer.

Thus, on Thursday June 2, 1932 Sri Ma, with Bholanath and Bhaiji left Dhaka for an unknown destination.

References

1. Dr. Panalal, Preface in *Ma Anandamayi* (Hindi), p. 5. (Tr. by author).
2. According to the Bengali Calendar.
3. Maroni was the grand-daughter of Seetanath Kushari. Her parents had given her into Sri Ma's care to safeguard her against all harm. Her parents had lost two children earlier and they were afraid that Maroni too would be taken from them. Bholanath became very fond of the little girl and had adopted her as his daughter.
4. This question and answer was related to the author in 1959 by Prof. J.N. Chubb of the Elphinstone College in Bombay. He had been the the youngest member of the group of professors who had gone to call on Sri Ma. He recalled the same meeting with profound feelings of awe and reverence.
5. Sri Ma frequently suffered from this sort of service from companions. It must be said on behalf of the people who served her that it was difficult for them to judge whether Sri Ma was comfortable or not because her equanimity remained undisturbed even under the gravest provocation. Sri Ma suffered from the scar in her throat for many days.
6. Sri Ma had united all castes and religions as early as 1931-32, much before such movements started in other parts of India.

CHAPTER SEVEN

The Bird on the Wing

The first birthday celebration of Mother that I attended took place in 1951 in Ambala, only a few months after I first met Mother. During the *Tithi-pūjā* I sat not very far from Her. She was lying down straight, as usual on these occasions, apparently far removed from this world. I thought She was in *Nirvikalpa Samādhi* and looked sadly at Her thinking: 'Mother has gone away from us!' While this thought was revolving in my mind, Mother awoke, sat up and opened Her eyes. Her first glance fell straight on me. It was a long and deep gaze full of significance, which I clearly understood to mean: 'No! I have not gone far away from you; I am ever, ever present with you, very, very near you!'

Atmananda ji[1]

This body is like a bird on the wing (*uḍa pākhī*). It sits on random branches for a while, according to its *kheyāla* and then flies off again....

Or if you say '*āshram*' (that I should stay in the *āshram*), then the whole world is an *āshram* for this body, what else!

- Sri Ma Anandamayi

* Raipur, Dehra Dun
* Ananda Chowk
* Kālī Temple at Uttarkashi
* Dhaka Revisited
* The Pioneer on the Path of Renunciation
* The Widening Circle
* *Nāmayajña* at Simla

The Bird on the Wing

Raipur, Dehra Dun

At the Railway Station, the travellers found a train on the point of departure. On being asked where she would like to go, Sri Ma suggested the terminus of the train. Thus, the next day Sri Ma, Bholanath and Bhaiji arrived at Jagannathgunje. Following the same mode of choosing their destination, they arrived in Katihar in Bihar, then Lucknow and finally at Dehra Dun, which is the terminal point for this particular Railway Line. Dehra Dun is situated at the foot hills of the Shivalik mountain ranges just below the hill city of Mussoorie, (7,000 ft.). The mode of travel beyond Dehra Dun was mostly by trekking. There was a motorable road to Mussorie and not much else in those days. The climate was mild compared to that of the plains in hot June. The view of the surrounding mountains was unusual and fascinating; the people and the language they spoke stirred the interest of Bhaiji. They seemed to have come to a foreign land. To his remark that everything about the place was strange, Sri Ma remarked that to her everything was familiar.

From the station they came to a *dharmaśālā*. Bholanath and Bhaiji went out looking for a suitable place. On being told about a small Śiva temple in a remote village called Raipur, they went to see it the next day. Bholanath was immediately enamoured with it. On their return they consulted Sri Ma. She said 'Both of you decide. Just anywhere is good enough for me.'

Thus, on Wednesday morning, June 8th, 1932 Sri Ma, Bholanath and Bhaiji took up residence at Raipur. Raipur in those days was a remote little village. Some distance from the village the ground rose sharply; on top of this hillock was situated a small Śiva temple. The temple was surrounded by an open and big paved courtyard. There was a mango tree in one corner with a raised platform around it. Everything was almost in ruins. From the courtyard or terrace on top of the hill one could command a view of high mountains across valleys glistening with wide and shallow streams flowing over their rocky beds.

While Bholanath and Bhaiji were settling down to a routine of daily life in the manner of ascetics, the devotees left behind in Dhaka were suffering from the painful loss of Sri Ma's presence.

They sometimes foregathered to exchange memories and experiences connected with Sri Ma. They were amazed that everyone had been fully instructed by her about his or her way of life. Nobody had been forgotten or overlooked. Without appearing to make an issue of it, she had taken pains to speak to everyone who depended on her for guidance. This was ever her way then and thereafter. If people did not benefit from her teachings it was not because she was not forthcoming but because of the weaknesses inherent in human nature. She expected everyone to devote themselves to the maximum point of their ability toward the quest for Truth; but alas, people were more keen to spend as much time as possible in her radiant presence, rather than sit in solitude to practice *sādhanā*. Only a few pioneers blazed the trail. Prominent among these apart from Bholanath and Bhaiji was Shashanka Mohan.

Shashanka Mohan and Didi were living in Siddheshwari like ascetics, in solitude. He would sit in meditation for long hours. During evenings and nights his body would be covered by mosquitoes, but evidently this did not disturb him. He had given up wearing tailored clothes and shoes. He was now able to practice breath-control and live the life of intense *sādhanā*. In his old age he had learnt to exercise such extremities of rigour that could be the envy of many a younger man. The *brahmacharis* at Ramna also were fully occupied with the rituals of *pūjā* and *yajña* and had embarked on an other-worldly way of life.

In Raipur, life was simple. There was no electricity or running water. The surrounding jungles abounded in snakes, scorpions lurked in crevices of the walls. Bhaiji went to the village once a day to procure some vegetables and wheat flour. He was able to boil the vegetables; he painstakingly learnt how to make a few *chapatis*. Bhaiji's inexpert efforts were sometimes guided by Sri Ma, more often he was left to his own devices. So late in life, he was required to re-orient himself toward personal habits. He had been served by servants all his life. He knew nothing about the logistics of fetching food-stuffs, cooking and serving. Sri Ma could evidently bring about marvellous metamorphoses in many of her followers!

In time the people of Dehra Dun heard from chance visitors to Raipur, that a Bengali Mataji of great spiritual eminence was living in the *dharmasala* of the Śiva temple. A few venturesome spirits made the journey of four and a half miles through dense jungle and over shallow streams or dry river-beds to Raipur to have *darśana* of Sri Ma. They saw a young woman of striking appearance, not so much in her physical aspect as in her expression of radiant and serene joy. Bholanath received the visitors and made them welcome; he introduced Bhaiji as his 'spiritual son' (*dharma-putra*). Very soon Bhaiji won a place in the hearts of the new comers, because it was he who communicated with them in English. It was always his endeavour to bring people to a greater understanding of Sri Ma. He would encourage the visitors to ask her questions and helped them to articulate the yearning for spiritual solace which was experienced by so many. He would interpret for them Sri Ma's words. To a great extent he was able to bridge the gap between what Sri Ma was and what people could make of her. The devotees of Dehra Dun conferred on him the sobriquet of Bhaiji (respected brother). Bholanath became known as Pitaji (father). Bholanath and Sri Ma picked up Hindi very quickly and very soon the visitors could talk to them directly.

Bhaiji was recalled to Dhaka by his office in August for some urgent work. He had applied for four months' leave some time before he had come away from Dhaka so abruptly; but now that he was asked to return, he wrote to Dhaka directing Kamalakanta to join them at Dehra Dun. He did not like to leave Sri Ma and Bholanath quite unattended. On Kamalakanta's arrival Bhaiji returned to Dhaka. He immediately called on all the devotees eagerly awaiting news of Sri Ma and for long hours described to them her way of life at Raipur.

In late November or early December 1932 Sri Ma, Bholanath, and Kamalakanta travelled to Tarapeeth in accordance with Bholanath's resolve to visit this holy site for three consecutive years at least once a year. From here they came to Nalhati. Didi's youngest brother Nandu came to meet them and with Bholanath's support obtained Sri Ma's permission to inform everyone of her presence in their part of the country. Within a couple of days Nalhati became crowded with devotees from Dhaka and Calcutta. Bholanath looked like a *sannyāsi* now. He was very pleased to see all the well-known faces once more. After this brief interlude of about a fortnight, the visitors, saddened at the inevitable parting, left for their various homes. Shashanka Mohan and Didi returned to their life of solitude at Siddheshwari.

Sri Ma, Bholanath and Kamalakanta returned to Dehra Dun in the beginning of January 1933. Bhaiji remained in Dhaka. Unobtrusively he was engaged in winding up his affairs. From something Sri Ma had said to him at the time of his rejoining his service, he had drawn the conclusion that he had not many more years to live. He was quietly making arrangements for the future financial security of his family. His daughter was married at this time, with all due ceremonies. His son was old enough to know what his father was doing; his wife was not pleased but she made no protest.

In March 1933, Bhaiji again took leave and left for Dehra Dun. His friends in Dhaka surmised that this leave was preparatory to retirement and that he might not return home again. It came to light later that Sri Ma had asked his wife to come away with him so that both of them could live like *vānaprasthis* (that is, couples who retire from the world to live in forest hermitages). Bhaiji's wife Manikuntala Devi had declined to do so, thereby missing the opportunity of being with her husband for the last four years of his life which he devoted to the service of Sri Ma.

Looking back on those times, the role of mediator that Bhaiji played for the people of a different culture seems very significant. The new comers were attracted by Sri Ma's personality but were too much in awe of her to speak to her or behave easily with her. Bhaiji made this possible for them. Since the majority of the new crowd was from Kashmiri or other non-Bengali speaking groups, Bhaiji's interpretative role was of great importance. In this context Bhaiji is reported to have said, 'In my eagerness to make people realize their good fortune, I interpret Sri Ma's personality to them and seek to place her on the highest pedestal. But no matter how high I look up, she remains yet higher and beyond my comprehension!'

In the meantime Sri Ma became conversant with Hindi and talked to the men, women and children who flocked to crowd round her. Sri Ma continued to move around. She, Bholanath and Kamalakanta walked up to Mussorie and then on to Uttarakashi.

In the meantime they had met Hari Ram Joshi, an influential man of these regions. His devotion to Sri Ma was life-long. He was a man of strong conviction and was fired with the zeal of converting all his friends and family to the service of Sri Ma. He knew he had found a treasure beyond the imagination of man. He wished to see the whole world transformed by Sri Ma's divine presence. It was he who brought many notable figures to see Sri Ma. If he felt the slightest reluctance on the part of the visitor, he would scold him mercilessly for not realizing his good fortune! Such instances were, however, rare. The region of Almora, Nainital, Mussoorie, Solon, Simla, became full of devotees within a very short time.

Sri Ma's second trek to Uttarkashi with Bhaiji was arranged for by Jamna Datt Sanwal. Hari Ram made urgent requests to Bhaiji to inform him of their return to Dehra Dun. The fortuitous nature of Sri Ma's presence in different places becomes clear if we follow closely the incidents shaping her travels. If Hari Ram had not insisted on being informed, may be Sri Ma would have passed through Dehra Dun as through many other places; but this one thing led to others, and Sri Ma came to stay in Dehra Dun for a long time.

Bholanath was so fascinated by the scenic beauty of the mountain ranges of the Himalayas that he undertook to walk to different places of pilgrimages. Kamalakanta remained with him. Bholanath was more and more occupied with his *sādhanā*. His food habits had changed. He had given up smoking and was living a life of exemplary discipline. Leaving Sri Ma under Bhaiji's escort, he spent a few months in and around Uttarkashi, like an ascetic. At this time he received many communications from home, remonstrating his and Sri Ma's way of life; but he was not the same man any more. He wrote back in clear and unmistakeable terms that Sri Ma had his full approval in whatever she did and that nobody need concern himself regarding her deportment which was exemplary at all times. Further, that he was fully confident that Bhaiji would look after her to the best of his ability.

We may see from all this that a new image of the little family from Dhaka was emerging steadily; Bholanath now was a renunciate practicing his *sādhanā* under Sri Ma's guidance. Bhaiji also was living like an ascetic and was totally committed to the service of Sri Ma.

A few devotees from Dhaka and Calcutta found their way to Dehra Dun and stayed with Sri Ma for a few days. One such person was Vijay Ratanji Vyas a young medical student from Calcutta. During the summer vacation he came to Mussoorie and went around looking for a 'Bengali Mataji'. He walked from inn to inn on being told that Sri Ma and her companion (Bhaiji) were walking down from Uttarkashi. He came across them at one of the way-side inns. Bhaiji was not too well at the time. Seeing that Sri Ma was cooking and cleaning all by herself, he thought it his duty to offer help. Sri Ma smiled and said that it would be useful if he could fetch milk in the morning. Vyas was willing and he said to her in all innocence, 'I am a late-riser. Please wake me up in the morning when it is time to go.' Vyas recalls with wonder now, how Sri Ma came and woke him up for this little task, and the graciousness with which she served the simple meals she contrived for them.

They walked the mountain paths with great enjoyment, stopping wherever they felt inclined. Sri Ma was never at a loss or put out by any lack of facilities. The shelters for pilgrims were crude in the extreme, but in Sri Ma's company, Vyas never felt the oddness of their haphazard mode of life. It was a delightful interlude during which he came to know and entertain the highest respect for Bhaiji. Incidentally, it may be recorded that he is one of the privileged six, who were initiated by Bhaiji.[2]

Sri Ma had the *kheyāla* that Bhaiji should live like a mendicant whose sole support is God. He was sent out to ask for *bhikṣā* (alms) once or twice. Bhaiji did not succeed too well. Firstly, he looked like the gentleman he was; secondly he did not know how to raise his voice in supplication. If people found him standing at their door, they greeted him and talked to him but did not give him alms! Although he tried to carry out Sri Ma's *kheyāla* his begging expeditions were mostly abortive. If he did not get anything he fasted, as well as Sri Ma. In this manner they walked down to Dehra Dun and took shelter near the Temple of Tapkeshwar Mahadeva. Bhaiji kept his promise to Hari Ram and sent him a note saying Sri Ma had come to his town. Hari Ram and Hansa Datta Tiwari immediately arrived at the Temple and requested Sri Ma to stay in Dehra Dun for some time at a better and more central location.

Ananda Chowk

Hari Ram took Bhaiji and Sri Ma to one or two places seeking their approval. Bhaiji did not like the locations. Sri Ma said, 'Look, do not think about preferences. We shall stay at the next place we come to.' Thus when they arrived at the Manohar Temple at Ananda Chowk, Sri Ma and Bhaiji agreed to take up their residence at this place. Sri Ma settled down on the open verandah of the Temple. Hari Ram obtained permission from the Manager for Sri Ma to stay in the small room attached to the Temple. Next morning when the wives of Kashi Narain Tankha and Dwarka Nath Raina came to the Temple for their daily *pūjā*, they found Sri Ma sitting by herself on the verandah.

This was the unremarkable beginning of the most dramatic era in the lives of these women, their families, friends and acquaintances. This locality of the town was mostly peopled by Kashmiris. Within a very short time almost all these families began to foregather at Sri Ma's feet. Ananda Chowk became another Shahbagh Sometimes there would be *kīrtans* or *yajñas* at the Temple, but most often the visitors would sit quietly, spellbound by Sri Ma's magnetic presence. Household routines went haywire. Wives were not at home to carry out household work. Husbands and children in their turn hurried to the Temple as soon as they returned from their offices and schools. Many Bengali families from the area of Karanpur also found their way to Sri Ma and became life-long devotees.

The women brought food for Sri Ma and Bhaiji, but they were amazed to discover that Sri Ma ate only on alternate days and that too a few mouthfuls only. The fact of her frugality and immense attraction for the people lead to an amusing incident which was related by Sri Ma herself to other congregations. In some parts of the town a rumour gained ground that the Bengali Mataji exercised a hypnotic spell on visitors and that many miraculous events took place in her vicinity at night. In the western regions of India many people believe that Bengal is a land of black magic, most probably due to the prevalence of *tantra* as a mode of worship. Among the group of people who used to come to Ananda Chowk, was a lady known amongst her friends as Barik Mai (the thin one). She was given this nick name because she was rather corpulent. Barik Mai was a public spirited woman. She was a member of the Indian National Congress and a freedom fighter. It was said that once she had been jailed by the Government (British, in pre-Independence days) but the Magistrate hastily withdrew his order when she made life unbearable for all her cell-mates by her raucous voice raised in loud and unending songs. This lady now assured her friends that she would penetrate the secret of Sri Ma's attraction.

She came to stay at the Manohar Temple. There was no formality in the way of life followed by Sri Ma. People came and went as they liked. There were no doors to be closed because Sri Ma was staying on the open verandah. Sometimes one or other of the devotees would sit in meditation near her during the night. Barik Mai became a regular inmate keeping wakeful vigilance when Sri Ma lay down on her blanket on the floor. Barik Mai said she would also eat on alternate days like Sri Ma in spite of all persuasions to the contrary. A few nights were spent in this way. Barik Mai discovered nothing more unusual than the fact that Sri Ma did not sleep like others. She was always found to be fully alert if spoken to any time during the night; sometimes she herself would say something to her companions if they happened to wake up. The next part may be related in Sri Ma's words:

'This vigilance and lack of food naturally put a great strain on Barik Mai's health. One night she collapsed in a fainting fit. I could see that Jyotish (Bhaiji) was petrified with fear. He felt that if the lady were to be really ill her family and friends would think we had done something to her. He sprinkled some water on her face and fanned her till she revived a little. She soon recovered fully and sat up. Jyotish then asked her to take a couple of ayurvedic pills for strength which had been given to him by Dwarka Nath Raina for his own use. In the morning I explained to her that lack of proper nourishment and sleep had brought about a fainting spell and if she wished to stay with us she would have to sleep and eat normally. After a few days, however, to everyone's surprise she stopped visiting me. I knew what had happened. Her friends had convinced her that she had after all been given 'two magic pills' and that was it! I did not say anything to anybody about her suspicions.

'After a long time she came to see me at a *dharmasālā*. I said to her, 'Mother, how about the magic pills?' She was utterly taken aback and then came out with the entire tale of her secret search for miracles. She was very penitent and had to be coaxed back to good humour.'

While Sri Ma was wandering around the foothills of the Himalayas, the Ashram at Ramna wore a deserted look. Sometimes a letter would be received from a visitor to Dehra Dun or Mussoorie which would be read by all the devotees with eager interest. One such letter was from Nirmal Chandra Chatterjee of Varanasi.

'Sri Ma is wearing *dhotis* (the male version of the saree). Her head is uncovered. Her hair reaches to the shoulders. The local devotees have prevailed upon her to use sandals because it is impossible to walk barefoot on these hilly tracks. With her shawl thrown across her shoulders she looks like a young *brahmachari*. Many people are very devoted to her and ready to do her slightest bidding.'

He wrote further that Sri Ma had made enquires about everyone. She had said, how is it that Baba (Shashanka Mohan) has never asked to come to Dehra Dun to see how she did in her new surroundings? Shashanka Mohan had been patiently waiting for instructions from her never deeming that he was at liberty to express a desire of his own. Guessing that it was now time for them to travel, he obtained his permission from Sri Ma. He and Didi came to Dehra Dun in December 1933 and stayed with her for a month.

Didi saw for herself the changes in dress and appearance. She met the new devotees and realised how close they were to Sri Ma. Didi also started to pick up Hindi in order to converse with the bigger family of Sri Ma's devotees. She met Mahalakshmiji[3], Sevaji[4], Maharatanji[5] and also Hari Ram Joshi. Hari Ram in his turn made the visitors from Dhaka welcome. His enthusiasm was boundless. It was his conviction that if the national leaders could see their way to being guided by Sri Ma, the future of the country would be assured. To this effect he asked Kamala Nehru to come to Sri Ma thinking that this would lead to a meeting with Mahatma Gandhi. Jawaharlal Nehru was in jail in Dehra Dun at this time. His mother Swarup Rani, and his wife Kamala were in town also, probably in order to be close to his place of incarceration. His daughter Indira was at school in Mussorie.

Kamala Nehru in spite of Hari Ram's persuasive words, at first did not wish to come to Sri Ma as she knew her husband did not approve of so called religious personalities. Thus it so happened that although she and Indira went in the family car to drop off Swarup Rani at the Temple, she did not get down. Hari Ram visited her and took her to task for, (according to him), this little bit of discourtesy toward Sri Ma. However important the visitor, Hari Ram never compromised on the question of Sri Ma's status of commanding the greatest respect; no one was left in doubt regarding his or her duty towards Sri Ma by this stern stickler for correct observances.

Kamala Nehru acknowledged her mistake and came again especially to see Sri Ma. She came and was bewitched. The very first meeting proved to be of great moment in her life. Mindful of her position, she used to come to the temple late at night, sometimes staying the whole night, going away only at break of dawn. Sri Ma, unlike Hari Ram, quite understood her predicament and used to discourage her saying she should not come if it was thought improper for her to do so. Kamalaji at one time wanted to write to Gandhiji to seek his permission to withdraw from public life in order to stay with Sri Ma. Sri Ma dissuaded her saying the time was not right. The fact that Kamalaji was thinking of Sri Ma constantly and that she attained a high degree of meditative one-pointedness of the mind could be seen by all who were around at this time. She corresponded regularly with Bhaiji when Sri Ma moved out of Ananda Chowk. Once she wrote; 'Bhaiji, you never write enough letters to give me news of Ma. But I 'see' her sometimes. Last night I 'saw' her wearing a sari with a wide red border...'

Bhaiji wrote back from Kankhal to say that indeed on the day mentioned by Kamalaji, some Bengali devotees from Calcutta had pursuaded Sri Ma to put on a red bordered sari as she was in the habit of wearing in Dhaka and Calcutta. The people of Dehra Dun had not seen her dressed like that. Kamala Nehru passed away in Switzerland after about three years. Sri Ma took pains to visit her in Bhowali Sanatorium more than once while she was ill. Till the very end Kamalaji kept in close touch with Sri

Ma through correspondence. It is true that Hari Ram's dream of great events of political moment were not realized from this meeting but who can say if what actually took place was not of greater importance in the lives of the people concerned and the country as a whole.

Kālī Temple at Uttarkashi

Sometime in the summer of 1935 Bholanath wrote to Sri Ma that he was undertaking the construction of a small Kālī-Temple in Uttarkashi. Bholanath had acquired considerable prestige as a dedicated ascetic in these regions. The inhabitants were keen that he himself should perform the installation ceremonies. Hari Ram interested himself in the project. Within a short while forces were mobilised toward a festival of gigantic proportions in the age-old retreat for renunciates.

The installation ceremony was scheduled for August 1935. This occasion may be called a landmark in the lives of Sri Ma's devotees. The new congregation comprising of people from Nainital, Almora, Dehra Dun, Mussoorie etc. organised themselves as hosts for the invited devotees from Dhaka, Calcutta, Jamshedpur and other towns in Bengal and Bihar. The guests were received at the Railway Station and directed to places where arrangements had been made for their stay. Didi writes in her Diary that 'It is a strange zoo that Ma has collected round her - we do not understand each other's languages; no one is quite sure who the other people are, but everyone is happy and ready for the adventure.'

Thus, in the month of August a big crowd of men, women and a number of children as well, started on the trek to Uttarkashi, a distance of about 60-65 miles from Mussoorie. Sri Ma was at the head of this miscellaneous group of Bengalis, Kashmiris, Punjabis, Paharees as well as people from Uttar Pradesh. Many of the Easterners had never before seen mountains, and were quite unused to climbing. The winding uphill road resounded with many exclamations of wonder and awe in various languages as well as with gasps and groans. *Dandees*, mules and rikshaws had been hired for those who would not be able to walk. Many became footsore; some found it difficult to breathe and a few were overcome by nausea. But nothing mattered very much because Sri Ma was constantly moving amongst them. Sometimes she would walk with the stragglers. At every camp she made detailed enquiries regarding arrangements and visited the campers; everyone lay down to rest in the happy knowledge that Sri Ma was with them and that they had nothing at all to worry about! By slow marches the tired but happy throng arrived in Uttarkashi after five or six days.

Bholanath received his old friends with great pleasure. He had sent word to his family priest whose son had come in response to his invitation. The local crowd who saw Bholanath for the first time, paid their respects to him. He was always ready to welcome new-comers. At this time he was pre-occupied with the work of the Temple. With great care and circumspection, he installed the Deities in the Temple amidst great rejoicings. The lonely hillside echoed to the sound of music, conch-shells and *jayadhvanis.*

After this ceremony Bholanath accompanied by his priest and Atuldada went away on a pilgrimage to Gangotri, the visible source of the Ganges. Sri Ma, led her large family down toward Dehra Dun. By now the motley crowd had become a homogeneous group. Some of them became life-long friends. One day they were required to cross a mountain stream. The dry river-beds on the mountains suddenly become swift streams after a rainfall or two. They can be treacherous because they flow over slippery rocks. Sri Ma, seeing the predicament of the women, stood in the middle of the stream and held hands with the nervous, till they were safely across. She went back and forth till all had arrived on the other shore. One of them was so struck by this phenomenon that he wrote a description of it to a friend saying, 'May Ma take us across the *bhavanadī* (river of life) in a similar manner.[6]

Mahalakshmiji, accompanied by a few friends and relations went ahead to Dehra Dun to make arrangements for receiving the tired people. The travellers were charmed by the hospitality of the people of Dehra Dun. Barriers of languages and cultures were breaking down. The impromptu gatherings assumed the orderly look of an organised congregation. This pattern occured wherever Sri Ma happened to be. The harmonious blending of disparate cultures happened as a matter of course. Sri Ma's teachings about the One who appears as many were demonstrated in a practical manner again and again in her vicinity.

Bholanath came to Dehra Dun on his return from Gangotri. Bhaiji took him and Sri Ma to the houses of many devotees and introduced them to Bholanath. They were very happy to have him at last in their midst. In these northern regions he became known as Pitaji (father).

Dhaka Revisited

Sri Ma was being constantly invited to visit Dhaka. In the winter of 1935 Sri Ma, Bholanath, Bhaiji and a few others went to Tarapeeth for some days. From Tarapeeth they came to Dhaka in December 1935. She had been away for nearly three and a half years. The devotees were besides themselves with joy and gave her a tumultous welcome. After a long time Sri Ma again sat out in the green fields of Ramna talking to visitors. The transition from a housewife to a spiritual guide and teacher was complete and yet she remained the same Ma of Dhaka.

While Sri Ma was talking to the people around her, the Registrar of Dhaka University, Khan Bahadur Nasiruddin Ahmed was seen to be out on his usual constitutional. Nagendranath Dutta, the Editor of the East Bengal Times went over to invite him to come and be introduced to Sri Ma. As he approached the group Bhupati Babu said to her, 'Ma, he is a Mussalman.' Sri Ma smiled and said, 'So am I a Mussalman.'

After greetings, the Khan Bahadur asked one of the devotees, 'If Sri Ma has attained Peace why does she keep wandering around?' Probably he did not think it polite to accost her directly but Sri Ma answered the question herself. 'If I stayed in one place, the same question could arise, could it not?' Then she smiled her smile of inimitable grace and charm and said gently, 'Baba, don't you know, I am a very restless little girl! I cannot stay in one place. This is one answer. From another point of view, I may say, it is you who see me travelling from place to place. In reality I do not move at all. When you are at home you do not sit in one corner of it do you? No, you freely walk about in the whole of it and yet remain at home. Similarly I also wander around in my own house - I am ever at home!'

'You have found Peace. We are at the mercy of innumerable distractions. Why don't you be generous and distribute some of your Peace to us?'

'The moment you exclaim in desperation, 'O Lord, how to find Peace!' you are already on the path to attain it.'

Sri Ma said this so spontaneously and humourously, and with such an eloquent gesture of her hands that everyone burst out laughing. Sri Ma, then said seriously, 'If you live with things unpeaceful, how can you hope for Peace? People are affected by things in their vicinity. If you sit near a fire, you feel the heat, if you choose to live amidst distractions, how should Peace descend on you? This does not mean that everyone should retire from the world and stay in forest retreats to find Peace. But what you can do is to live with something which is of the nature of Peace. Wherever you are you should live in the company of that which gives Peace. I say to you, keep God always in mind; God alone is Peace. Whether you call Him Khuda or Kālī is immaterial, because there is One only. The really important thing is to persevere. Relentless perseverence brings about the change in perspective which will establish you in Peace.

'Peace can be attained either in the world or away from it. You say that I have found Peace and should distribute it to others. I say unto you that I am a little child and you are my parents. Accept me as such and give me a place in your hearts. By saying 'mother' you keep me at a distance. Mothers have to be revered and respected. But a little girl needs to be loved and looked after and is dear to the heart of everyone. So this is my only request to you, to make a place for me in your hearts.'

Sri Ma's words spoken lightly and smilingly touched everyone. A solemn atmosphere prevailed. There were no more questions but peace and quiet. After a short while Sri Ma got up and the session came to an end.

Sri Ma again returned to the northern regions of India.

The Pioneer on the Path of Renunciation

Sri Ma's 'choice' for holding aloft the ideal of renunciation as the most meaningful way of life fell upon the oldest amongst her followers. While wandering around in the hills, she had a *kheyāla* that Shashanka Mohan should formally be initiated into one of the monastic orders. Sri Ma's wanderings had taken her to a wayside temple in Salogra near Solon in late March 1934. There is a cave near the temple. It is so small that no one can lie straight or stand upright in it. Sri Ma stayed in this cave for some time. Her attendants were Bhaiji and Hansa Datta Tiwari. Hari Rām's brother Madan L. Joshi was a doctor in Solon. He came to pay his respects to Sri Ma. He found Sri Ma sitting in this cave, looking completely at ease and her usual radiant self. It was bitterly cold after a snowfall in the hills but Sri Ma appeared to suffer no discomfort. Solon is capital of Baghat State. H.H. Raja Durga Singh of Baghat was known to be a Prince of many stirling qualities and also of a religious nature. He was devoted to a sage called Shogi Baba who was residing at Solon at the time. Although the Raja Sahab had heard about Sri Ma, he, in the beginning was not keen to have *darśana* of a 'woman saint'.

Sri Ma was invited by Dr. Joshi to come to Solan but the sudden *kheyāla* for Shashanka Mohan, made her travel to Haradwar instead. She sent word to Dhaka for Shashanka Mohan and also to Varanasi for Swami Sankarananda, a new devotee. Sri Ma was full of enthusiasm and seemed very pleased when Didi accompanied by her father arrived in Haradwar in response to Sri Ma's letter. She said to Shashanka Mohan, 'Some arrangements had been made for us at Solon, but I had this sudden *kheyāla* that you should take *sannyāsa*. These holy places are conducive to *sādhanā* and attract devout and holy men. I have already suggested to Swami Sankarananda that he should look for a suitable Guru for you. Chaitra Saṁkrānti (13th/ 14th April) is an auspicious day. Time is short so all arrangements must be expedited.'

Shashanka Mohan was taken aback at these words. He was not prepared for this radical transformation; moreover it was unthinkable for him to bow his head to some, to him nameless, Guru at this stage in his life. Rather unhappily, he answered, 'I cannot think of any other Guru. I do not think I can commit myself to anyone else. I have always believed and hoped that you will guide me. Why do you ask me to go to another Guru?' Sri Ma answered gently, 'But I cannot confer *sannyāsa* on you,' to which he replied, 'I have no need of anything that you may not do for me.'

Sri Ma then said quietly, 'Well, in that case, there is no need for any further arrangements.' She became grave and said no more. The cheerful look with which she had opened the conversation vanished completely.

It was evening. Shashanka Mohan withdrew from Sri Ma's presence and was seen to go out and sit on the bank of the swiftly flowing Ganga for many hours. On the other side of the river, wooded hills rose to great heights. What thoughts did he grapple with? He was a proud man, more accustomed to command than to obey. The prospect of giving up every prop and support of a long and familiar way of life and to have to embark on a voyage into the unknown must have shaken him to the core of his being. He was the head of a large family, almost a clan. Perhaps he debated whether it would be right to put himself out of their reach forever. He would have no duties towards anyone anymore. He must have considered his daughter and her future also. He could not be a guardian to her and thus she would be alone to fend for herself as best as she could. These however are conjectures. He did not share his thoughts with anybody. All the early devotees were highly cultured and dignified persons. What actually happened was that he came to Sri Ma late at night and said mildly, 'I think I blurted out the thoughts that came unbidden to my mind. I am now ready to carry out your *kheyāla* and do as you say.'

Sri Ma's countenance shone brightly. She was immediately full of plans for the important event. She told him, 'You have no reason to think that you are going to another Guru. There is but One Reality.'

Sri Ma was well known in the Ashram of Bholagiri Maharaj. His successor Sri Mangal Giri Maharaj agreed to initiate Shashanka Mohan into the Order of the Giris. This is one of the most prestigious Orders of *sannyāsis* in India. The disciple is required to perform a *yajña* renouncing connections with the world. In the sacrificial fire are consigned all modes of understanding of oneself as an individual, as a member of his family, society, nation, even his own caste and creed. The 'I', is sought to be set free from all limitations so that it may seek to identify itself with the One and thus with the whole world. A *sannyāsi* belongs to no one and to no place and therefore to everyone and everywhere.

Sri Ma and a handful of her companions watched this solemn ceremony, the highest pinnacle of achievement for a brahmin born and bred in the Hindu tradition. Shashanka Mohan after leading a full and useful life in the world, was eminently fitted now to renounce it for its greater benefit. His name was changed to Swami Akhandananda Giri. Dressed in ochre robes he came to make his obeisance to Sri Ma, She said, 'You have so far rendered constant and unremitting (*akhaṇḍa*) service to your family and to your profession (medicine). From now on devote yourself with the same constancy toward Self-Realization.'

Sri Ma always gave the highest respect to *sādhus* and *mahātmās*, that is, the various orders of ascetics. However, she did not encourage people to give up their duties in the name of religion. An incident may be recorded here which brings out her teachings in this respect. This incident took place some years later in Dehra Dun. While, Sri Ma was strolling near the gates of the newly built Ashram at Kishanpur she saw a *sādhu* standing near them. She spoke to him in Bengali. He answered in Bengali although he did not look like one. She invited him in and asked him to have his evening meal at the Ashram. After the meal he came and sat near Ma, she asked him:

'Are you a *sannyāsi*?'

'No'

'Then why are you dressed like one?'

'For all practical purposes I am. I have renounced the world.'

'In order to carry on your *tapasyā* for Self-Realization?'

'I have not thought of it. For the present I wish to have nothing to do with the world.'

'Does it mean that you have left home for personal reasons and do not wish to go back?'

'Yes'

'In that case you are practicing a grave deception on the public and doing no good to yourself either.'

'I have nothing to do with anybody; it is nobody's business what I do with my life.'

'That is not correct. Your appearance as an ascetic means something to the people. It is our tradition to support a man engaged in intensive *sādhanā* because he has no other means of support. He has given up his own will toward self-support, depending solely on the Divine Will. The people choose to support him as they would any other who is selflessly engaged in some activity for the benefit of the entire society. This garb is not to be adopted to solve personal problems or to escape from difficult situations. If you are not engaged in *sādhanā* to the exclusion of all other concerns, you have no right to accept food and shelter from the lay public who seeing your robes will give automatically without judging your bonafides.'

The young man who looked to be cultured and educated, kept quiet. Sri Ma said to him that he could stay in the Ashram as long as he liked, but it would be better for him to go home and face whatever situation he had run away from. The next morning the young man was not to be seen, so probably he had chosen to follow Sri Ma's advice.

Another incident: A young man belonging to one of the most affluent industrial families of the country, came to ask Sri Ma about his future way of life. At that time he was dressed like a *brahmachari* and had been living in his Guru's Ashram for many years. His problem was this: He wanted to be a *sādhu*, but his Guru after 12 years had asked him to go home and take up the duties of a householder. What should he do? Sri Ma said to him, 'But, I see no problem. At all times you are required to obey your Guru, if you know him as such. If he has asked you to get married and work in the world that is what you should do. Why do you hesitate?'

After some time the young man went away obviously not quite satisfied by Sri Ma's words. Sri Ma in a tone of reflection said to the small group who had witnessed this scene, 'You see, the path of spiritual endeavour is difficult and full of subtle pitfalls. This is the reason why a guide is required at all times. Sometimes a *sādhaka* begins to enjoy the many benefits which may accrue -especially if he has acquired some little yogic powers. The incipient hankerings for name and fame as a *sādhu* may also cloud the judgement of a disciple and prevent him from seeing his duty clearly.'

Sri Ma has said that fortitude and obedience are indispensable to a life of *sādhanā*. When the call came for Shashanka Mohan, he did not fail his Guru. From East Bengal to Haradwar the journey was fraught with changes in more ways than one. How *prasanna* (benign) Sri Ma must have looked when he stood in front of her dressed in the fire-coloured bright ochre robes of the renunciate - the highest stage to be achieved by man in this life according to the spirit of our country.

The Widening Circle

Sri Ma continued to travel. She met hosts of new people. She visited Baijnath near Jogendranagar, Almora, Etawah, Ayodhya, Fyzabad and other places too. In October 1935, on her way to and from Almora, she went to see Kamala Nehru at Bhowali where she was staying for treatment. In Etawah Sri Ma met Dr. Pitambar Panth, a friend of Hari Ram. There is an estate called Doonga near Dehra Dun. The zamindar of Doonga, Chaudhuri Sher Singh and his family became close to Sri Ma during this time. Doonga was like a forest retreat where many people had the opportunity of staying with Sri Ma quietly and listen to her talks. Sri Ma visited Solon also. Raja Durga Singh had overcome his disinclination to visit a woman saint. After his first *darśana,* he had become totally devoted to her. Sri Ma used to say that he was not only a prince in the world but also a prince of yogis. He came to be known as Yogibhai in the circle of devotees.

The names of the above mentioned people became wellknown during these years. The men differed very much in their styles of living, status in the world, temperaments and cultural backgrounds. Such thoughts arise in retrospect. In Sri Ma's vicinity all differences were subsumed under an overall feeling of belonging to the same family.

Sri Ma and Bholanath with their companions came to Tarapeeth in January 1936. For some time past Sri Ma had the *kheyāla* that Didi and Maroni should be given the sacred thread of the brahmins. Girls are not initiated like boys in brahmin families. There was no precedent in this matter. Enquiries about scriptural injunctions had been made in Varanasi; the pandits had said that although no such tradition prevailed there was no injunction to the contrary either. Pandit Sri Gopinath Kaviraj, when appealed to, declared that Sri Ma's *kheyāla* itself was *śāstra* (scripture); no further corroboration about its legitimacy was required. So another pioneering ritual was performed in Tarapeeth. On January 14, Didi and Maroni were initiated into the Gayatri Mantra which is given to brahmin boys born to Hindu parents. They were given the sacred thread which is worn across the body over the left shoulder. Maroni's initiation was given by Bholanath, because traditionally the father is the *dikṣā-guru* for the sacred mantra. Since Didi's father now was a *sannyāsi* his privilege was given to Sri Dinesh Chandra Bhattacharya a revered old man devoted to Sri Ma.

Sri Ma also suggested at that time that Maroni's long standing engagement to Chinu should be solemnised by the marriage ceremony. Bholanath was saddened by this prospect. He was very fond of Maroni; she was like a daughter to him. Although in Hindu marriages, daughters do not go away immediately, it still means a severance of relationships. Judging from later events, it seems now that Sri Ma was winding up his responsibilities and setting him free. Bholanath was a trifle disturbed, not knowing how all the requirements of a traditional marriage ceremony could be contrived in such a remote and desolate place. He should have had faith in Sri Ma. She seemed always to take immense delight in making possible what would appear to be improbable. By the merest chance there came to Tarapeeth just the right ladies from Calcutta, who enthusiastically undertook to make all arrangements; so the marriage actually came to be performed with every kind of elaborate ceremonial extravagance dear to the heart of the women folk of Bengal. Bholanath gave his blessings to the young couple. Now Maroni would be under the care of her father and mother-in-law till she was old enough to join her husband in his place of work.

In February, 1936 Sri Ma left Tarapeeth to its silent contemplation of death and departed with her devotees in a convoy of fifteen to twenty bullock carts to the nearest Railway station at Rampurhat. The slow journey through the moonlit night was made memorable by the melodious singing of Bhramara. The devotees of Dehra Dun had invited all people concerned to come to their town so that Sri Ma's 40th birthday could be celebrated in the new Ashram at Kishenpur. As a result of this invitation, Kishenpur for a while became the venue for joyful festivities. It resembled Ramna in more ways than one because right after the *tithipūjā* (birthday) which was performed by Manmotho Nath Chaterjee a local elderly man of some prestige, Sri Ma left for Solon.

Yogibhai made suitable arrangements for her. Baghat State was small but beautifully situated. The princely treatment accorded to all who had come with Sri Ma was impressive. The lavish arrangements were perhaps routine in such households but the genuine spirit of service in servants, the decorum of behaviour of all attendants, testified to the loyalty and respect they felt for their own prince. In fact, the whole of Yogibhai's entourage became very close to Sri Ma, over the years. The Rani Sahiba, as was the custom then, observed *purda*. She came everyday. She was the sister of the Maharaja of Tehri-Garhwal, a hill-state of considerable importance. In time the family of her brother also became devoted to Sri Ma. Our hillside people are devoted to the many Images of the Goddess Durgā. In later years Sri Ma had occasion to visit the independent states of Suket and Mandi also. Everywhere she was received as the Goddess Incarnate. When Sri Ma had occasion to travel through Madhya Pradesh and to the South many more princes and their families became attached to her. She was as at home in their palaces as on open temple verandahs. Yogibhai, however, had always a special place in the Ashram. He, like Hari Ram, became very close to Bhaiji and assumed many of his responsibilities when the time came.

After a fortnight at Solon Sri Ma had the *kheyāla* to visit Simla.

Nāmayajña at Simla

There was a very spacious *Kalibari* (Temple of Kālī) at Simla (6000-7000 ft. above sea level) It had a number of rooms where visitors could stay for a few days. Simla used to be the summer Head Quarters of the Central Secretariat of the Government of India. The town at this time was at the peak of its summer season. The Bengali population consisted mostly of the officers of the Secretariat who every year spent six months in Simla along with their offices.

The day that Sri Ma arrived at the *Kalibari*, an old *sādhu* named Dayal Baba who was greatly beloved of the people of Simla, passed away. As a matter of fact, Dayal Baba had enquired a short while before his death if Sri Ma Anandamayi who was expected, had arrived or not. Sri Ma on arrival, went to his room and stood near his body for some time. He appeared to be sleeping peacefully. She then came away to her own room.

Groups of people came to pay their respects to Dayal Baba who was held in great esteem in Simla; they heard about Sri Ma and came to have her *darśana* also. Sri Ma's response to these new-comers was as if she were amidst people well-known to her. Within a few days Sri Ma's small room began to overflow with visitors. Many came to the Kalibari straight from their offices. Much fun and good-natured teasing was occasioned by this because some of them found their wives already with Sri Ma instead of awaiting them at home. One lady expressing the views of her friends said, 'Ma, every day we impatiently wait for the office and school hour. No sooner are our husbands and children out of the house than we simply rush here!'

The Bengali officers at Simla were mostly members of the Hari Sabha or attached to it. This society owes allegiance to the Vaiṣṇava Sampradāya of Sri Gaurāṅga Mahaprabhu of Bengal. Sri Gauranga was the propagator of the mode of *kirtan* performed by a congregation which has assembled for that very purpose. In one of the books which is held sacred, the festival of *nāma-saṃkīrtana* is described in great detail; a square and tall altar (*manch*) is erected in an open space (or a big hall); it is decorated with flowers, leaves and pictures of Lord Viṣṇu, Kṛṣṇa, and others of the Vaiṣṇava pantheon. All those who are good singers and drum (*khola*) players are specially invited. In this assembly of devout men the Names of the Lord are invoked on the eve before the day of dawn-to-dusk *kirtan* (*adhivāsa*). This is known as *nāma-yajña*, a *yajña* in the form of singing the Name. In the evening the *kiran*-party goes out on the streets (*nagar-bhramaṇa*); after a short walk-around they return to the alter and amidst songs and hymns of farewell, the sound of the Name comes to an end. The Name is a *mantra* representing God and is so treated the whole time.

In Sri Ma's circle, *kirtan* had been sung in an informal manner. Nobody had so far witnessed a *nāma-yajña*. The officers of Simla had built up a tradition of an yearly festival during summer, at the *Kalibari* which had a big hall. This year they invited Sri Ma and Bholanath to stay for this function to be held on Tuesday June, 23.

A big concourse of people gathered in the *Kalibari* on the eve of the *nāma-yajña*. The hall, the enclosed veranda around it, were decorated with festoons of garlands. The central altar was built up and tastefully adorned with pictures, flowers, leaves and lights. The fragrance of sandal wood permeated the air. The participants assembled: Haran C. Banerjee, Durgadas Banerjee, Charu Banerjee, Manojlal Chatterjee, Deben Chatterjee, Sudhir Sarkar and many others, all stalwarts in this mode of *sādhanā*. Sri Ma, surrounded by their womenfolk sat on the verandah. Bholanath was happily participating in the function.

First of all the altar was sanctified; the musical instruments were acknowledged with gratitude, as it were, for contributing to the invocation of the Names of the Lord; garlands were put on them. The participants were also garlanded and a mark of sandalwood paste put on their foreheads to welcome them. The evening began with the sounding of the musical instruments in unison in rhythmic beats. This music creates the proper atmosphere; at its conclusion a single solemn voice followed by a chorus invokes the presence of Lord Gauranga and Nityananda Mahaprabhu and humbly prays for their participation in the *kirtan* on the morrow. Thereafter the men stand up with their instruments (which are supported by crossbands across the shoulder and back) and slowly walk all around the altar. The main tune for the next day is sung for a while. With this the *adhivāsa* or invocatory session is concluded.

Early next morning everyone gathered again for the start of dawn-to-dusk *kirtan*. This time because of Sri Ma's presence, even those who never turned up till noon, were present. From sunrise to sunset the same mantra would be sung by relays of singers and accompanied by the players of the percussion instruments. Each leading voice is free to change tunes (specially marking the changes of times) but the continuity remains unbroken. The art of changing tunes is also very refined, only to be attempted by experts. Sri Ma sat on the verandah, as before.

The *kirtan* right from the beginning created an atmosphere of sublimity. Didi, and Swami Akhandananda were with Sri Ma this time. They and Bholanath realized that after almost five years or so, Sri Ma seemed to be responding to the rhythm of the music. They had not seen her in a *mahabhava* since she had left Dhaka. Her face was now flushed and there was a look of withdrawal from the world of everyday affairs and a complete submergence into a mood of inner radiant joy. Didi became aware that Sri Ma was trying to check the tides of *mahabhava*; she would talk desultorily to her companions. Once she got up hurriedly and went for a walk. Then again she would go to her room and lie down for some time. Bholanath realizing Sri Ma's condition, came to her room and asked her to check the *mahabhava* if possible. The function was a public one. Bholanath was not happy at the thought that Sri Ma should be seen in a state of exaltation by a lot of strangers who may not understand the phenomenon. Moreover Sri Ma's *bhāva-samādhi* could last for any number of hours, even days. A nameless dread of losing her altogether, during one of these *samadhis* had always made him anxious. He also knew that his words would be obeyed by Sri Ma if they were not swept aside by the force of her *kheyāla* to the contrary. In this case Sri Ma's *kheyāla* was also towards checking the manifestation of *mahabhava,* may be because she had anticipated his reaction to it. The whole day was spent like this. Didi has said that at this time her ordinary comments were shot through as if by streaks of lightning, a look of intense divine effulgence would come and go in a flash on her face. Her eyes would assume a fixed withdrawn look and just as suddenly the expression would be replaced by her glance of recognition.

Evening drew near. The *kīrtan* was reaching its climax before its conclusion at the time of sunset. Sri Ma was in her room from where the strains of the music could be heard faintly. Here her body was seen to roll swiftly and sway up to a standing posture in one fluid movement. Didi took up a position behind her although she knew from previous experience, that no support or help was needed at this stage. Sri Ma's body became buoyant; if she happend to lean against anyone, the feel of impact was as light as the touch of a feather. Sri Ma moving in this style entered the *kirtan*-hall. The men of Simla were well-versed in Vaiṣṇava literature. Although nobody had seen the manifestation of a *mahābhāva* before they immediately recognised it for what it was. They believed that such a display was possible only in the divine form of Sri Gauranga. No human body was capable of sustaining it.

It is difficult to give a description of the *mahabhava.* If Sri Ma fell to the ground and rolled along the floor, nothing actually was seen but a blur of white; she was upright in less than a second. She moved like a 'dry leaf in a wind', or 'a wind-blown cloth'. Her passage through the crowd was so swift that hardly anybody got a full view of her. Some saw a radiant countenance, some a hand raised in a graceful gesture, others a beautiful posture of the body for a split second. Bholanath need not have feared that the people of Simla would not understand. They were enthralled and overwhelmed.

As before in Dhaka, after the few moments of ecstatic movements, Sri Ma sat in utter stillness on the floor of the hall. The *kirtan* in the meantime had been concluded. The silence was broken by Sri Ma's voice pronouncing mantras in an enchanting voice. As before the language sounded similar to Sanskrit. After a while she sat motionless with her eyes closed. It was a divine image; the congregation with one accord bowed profoundly and with full hearts. Some of them hurried home to fetch such members of the family who were absent.

Bholanath himself had stayed with the *kirtan* the whole day without resting or breaking his fast. All the participants had greatly enjoyed his encouraging and supportive presence. Altogether this *nāma-yajña* marked a turning point in the lives of the people of Simla. One of them summed up the general feeling by saying, 'We have been performing this function for many years. Today our prayers for Divine Presence has been answered, blessed are we indeed!'

Next morning, it rained heavily. Some women came to the *Kalibari* notwithstanding the rains. They wished to sing *kirtan* near Sri Ma. At first the novelty of the experiment, prevented them from becoming a group to be led by a single voice. Then Sri Ma herself came to the hall and started to walk round the altar which was still in position. Within a few minutes the singing was unified into a *kirtan*. There were many gifted singers among the women; the percussion instrument (*khola*) was no problem because many young boys could play it well. Young boys like Tulu and Khokon got no chance to play them when their elders did so and were happy to be able to accompany their mothers and sisters.

Thus a *kirtan*-party of women was inaugurated by Sri Ma in Simla, as she had done in Dhaka. This was a more organised group. When the men came to the temple in the evening they were informed of this proud achievement, by their women-folk. A few men were sceptical about the future of this programme because they did not think that women would have the physical strength to carry the instruments and stand singing for many hours. In this they were totally wrong. The *nāma-yajña* became a regular item of celebration on all festive occasions. Sri Ma introduced a new feature; the women took up the refrain from the men after the invocatory prayers (*adhivāsa*). They kept up the singing the whole night till the men came at dawn to receive the Name from them. At this time Sri Ma said to the men, 'Do not keep the women away from this aspect of your life. Let them join their efforts with yours otherwise you may face unnecessary obstacles.'

Sri Ma returned to Solon. The officers also came down to be with Sri Ma for another day. Yogibhai's great courtesy and generous hospitality captivated the hearts of the visitors. They promised to hold a *nāma-yajña* at Solon in the near future.

Sri Ma took to travelling again. Bhaiji had been at Dehra Dun all this while. She went to Dehra Dun and returned back to Simla, this time to attend a *nāma-yajña* which was being performed just in her honour. Her photographs now adorned the altar along with those of the Deities.

Sri Ma had the *kheyāla* to keep on moving. In Solon she asked Bholanath, 'Where shall we go now?' He had no suggestion to make. Then she asked Bhaiji, 'Where would you like to stay in the meantime?'. The question made it clear that he was not to accompany her. Since he also had nothing to say to the question, Sri Ma asked him to reside in Solon for the time being. Yogibhai was delighted that Bhaiji would remain with him.

Sri Ma asked Swami Akhandananda to stay in the new Ashram at Kishenpur. She then came on to Vindhyachala. She said to Didi, 'Stay here and take charge of this Ashram. You have chosen this way of life, so you should get used to being on your own; moreover you must learn to be independent and also to travel alone and without escorts.' Didi since leaving home had never stayed alone or been without the support of her father. This was a new experience for her. Sri Ma, however, somewhat softened the impact of the drastic changes by arranging that a reliable family servant would come from Dhaka to stay at Vindhyachala Ashram.

In the last week of July 1936 Sri Ma and Bholanath left for Calcutta. Bholanath had been suffering from a pain in the stomach for sometime. Sri Ma asked him to stay at his sister's house and get himself examined and treated properly by the doctors in Calcutta. She took his permission to set out on her travels accompanied only by Virajmohini Devi. Virajmohini was a widow and had been travelling with Sri Ma for sometime. Since the marriage of her two daughters she had considered herself free to lead a life of renunciation. She had come to Sri Ma in order to take guidance for her life of *sādhanā*. She was a woman of good sense and dignity of manner. Her ready appreciation of the unusual must have stood her in good stead because Sri Ma now started on a course of travels strictly *incognita*. Bholanath wrote to all concerned that it was Sri Ma's *kheyāla* to move about by herself and that nobody should seek to discover her whereabouts. She would return to them in her own time.

For about four months Sri Ma moved around at her *kheyāla*. She visited Puri, Bhuvaneswar, Gomoh, Adra and many nearby places. She then travelled to distant Agra, Mathurạ, Vrindavan, Sultanpur, Ayodhya, Barabanki and to Bareilly. She went up to Nainital also. Sri Ma's travels took her to Lahore, Amritsar and Garhmukteshwar. She returned to Bengal at the end of the year. From Tarapeeth she sent word to those anxiously awaiting her return that they could come and join her.

References

1. AV. Vol. VII, no. 3, pp. 113-114.
2. The other five are Sadhan Brahmachari, Maharatanji, Sevaji and her sister and Ranadeva Ghosh of Delhi.
3. The wife of Kashi Narain Tankha.
4. Dr. Sarada Sharma who had a well-established practice in Dehra Dun.
5. The wife of Sardar Balwant Singh Jaspal. She and her eldest daughter Billoji (Swarna Kumari Jaspal) lived in the Ashram for many years.
6. This friend Swami Asitananda came to see Sri Ma later saying he wished to see the *bhavanadikarṇadhāra* (the pilot of the ship of the river of life).

CHAPTER EIGHT

The Pilgrimage to Kailasha

For Sri Ma the question of pilgrimage does not arise. She has come here to bless everyone and to enhance the sanctity of the holy places. She comes to the Temples to visit Herself.

(Address bv Mrs. Talyarkhan at a reception in the Temple precincts of Minakshi Devi, 15th Nov., 1952)[1]

The Himalayas - indescribable beauty!
The visible concretization of Eternity - Infinity!

(D.D. Vol. V. p. 28)

* From Didi's Diary
* Garbyang: Base Camp
* The Last Days of Bhaiji

The Pilgrimage of Kailasha

In the beginning of June 1937 Sri Ma and her party arrived in Almora to begin on the trek to the sacred Mountain Kailasha. The journey, ordinarily, would not have entered the consideration of Sri Ma's companions, but for the coincidence of her visit to Almora and Nainital earlier in the year. Many young people from the villages and townships in the Himalayas came to Almora for their studies. Some of these students had become very attached to Sri Ma and Bholanath. One such student, a married young woman, Parvati, was specially devoted and had broached the idea of a jouney to Kailasha, promising to guide them on the way since her own home was not distant from the Holy Mountain. Other students from Garbyang, a halt of some importance on the way, leant their support to the scheme. Bholanath had for long entertained a wish to undertake this most hazardous of pilgrimages. He was so fired by enthusiasm at the prospect that he was ready to leave as soon as he heard about the plans. It was decided, however, to wait till proper preparations could be made and the roads became more negotiable in June.

At that time Kailasha (22,000 ft. above sea level) was still accessible from India. No passports or visas were required from independent Tibet under the rule of the Dalai Lama. It is approximately 240 miles from Almora. The journey was considered arduous because for people of the plains to walk on such unfamiliar terrain and at such great heights without training was difficult in the extreme. Kailasha, for all Hindus is the visible abode of Śiva. The pilgrimage consists in going round the Mountain, (a *parikarmā* of 60 miles or so) and then bathing in the waters of the lake Gaurikunda (18,400ft). Kailasha itself towers over the famous lake Manas Sarovar (apprx. 15,000ft). This beauteous site has inspired the imagination of poets and the admiration of travellers since the ancient times of the Epics. This location is sacred to the Buddhists also; as such it has been the habitation of ascetics of both faiths for centuries.

The details of this remarkable journey, made especially memorable for the devotees by the event of Bhaiji's death at the end of it, have been preserved in Didi's diary, which she contrived to write under trying conditions. Didi's accounts, as always, are prosaic and down to earth. Reading her fast moving travelogue one cannot but get the impression that Sri Ma was looked upon as the central figure of a close-knit family. It is apparent that Didi views with interest and understanding the attraction, others feel for Sri Ma, but there is here, no attempt at guiding them to a better understanding or a seeking toward an enlargement of the family. Didi was content to be at hand to serve Sri Ma and be an onlooker of her *līlā* as it were.

At this point of the narrative we make a change in the format. Didi's diary is translated here, for a more realistic approach to the journey and its aftermath. We have heard these accounts many times from Didi, as well as Sri Ma. The translation is close, but not verbatim.[2]

From Didi's Diary

Thursday, June 10, (1937) we have arrived in Almora.

Arrangements are being finalized for our journey to Kailasha. The Bengali people who have come to see us off are not at all happy with this scheme and are expressing doubts about its feasibility: whereas the people of this region are very enthusiastic and encouraging. Parvati and the other girls were eagerly awaiting our arrival. They will accompany us.

Friday, Saturday June 11th, 12th.

I feel dizzy to look at the pile of necessities which are accumulating as our baggage. Water proofs, rubber sheets, snow glasses, warm clothes, torches, lanterns, all kinds of antidotes for breathlessness and dizziness; dry fruits and other kinds of food stuff for days when cooking will not be possible - and a hundred other things - the list seems unending. For many years now I have been used to carrying the minimum of personal belongings. I just could not see how I could deal with this pile of luggage. Moreover all these things have to be organised into portable weights. Each coolie (porter) will carry not more than 25 seers (about 50 lbs), so the boxes and knapsacks have to be weighed very carefully. At my wits' end with this problem I requested Ma to come and sit near me in the room where we were doing the packing. She made a few suggestions about a redistribution of the items; we accomplished the task in no time at all, or so it seemed to me. None of the pieces had to be repacked when we weighed them. The job I had been dreading was not so difficult after all.

Sunday, June 13th

To-day we started on our pilgrimage to Kailasha. The devotees who had come to see Ma off bade us a sad farewell. Apart from Ma and Bholanath, and the highland girls, we were a party of six: Swamiji (Didi's father) Bhaiji, Dasubabu from Varanasi, Tunu (Prankumar Babu's son from Calcutta) myself and Keshava Singh, Swamiji's attendant. There are about a dozen porters to carry the baggage. It was considered advisable for us to engage a few *dandees*[3] as well.

Since none of us is used to mountain climbing, it was felt that *dandees* should be at hand to carry those who could not walk. There are 25 coolies for the five *dandees,* as each crew of four is accompanied by a fifth man as relief. The porters are to be paid Re 1/- per day.

Starting at 8 a.m. we arrived by 11 o'clock at Barchhina, a distance of about 8 miles only. The natural scenery is very beautiful. After resting for a while we proceeded further for our overnight's stay at Dhawalchina which is about 5 1/2 miles from Barchhina. I cooked a meal in the open and we spent the night on the open verandah of the Dak Bungalow.[4]

Monday, June 14th

We made an early start at 5 in the morning. We had found the sun too hot and wished to avoid the afternoon heat. Midday camp was at Sheraghat, a distance of about 11 miles from Dhawalchina. The river Sarayu flows alongside the road. The surrounding scenery is picturesque. Tall trees provide plenty of shade. So we cooked and ate under the trees and rested during the afternoon. The coolies also cooked and ate their meal and rested for a while.

We had occasionally come across small shops where we could buy pulses, rice, ghee and salt. We are told that none of these things will be available as we climb higher. We have brought with us dry fruits, black-pepper powder, tamarind, pickles and other items that various knowledgeable people advised us to carry along.

Bholanath seems full of energy and has walked ahead of the party most of the time. Ma and Swamiji also have walked some miles. Only Bhaiji and I have used our *dandees.* Our concern for Swamiji, because of his age, seems unfounded. We started again at 3 p.m. and at sunset camped at a place called Gonoi, about 7 miles from Sheraghat. We have been provided with permits for staying at Dak Bungalows along this route, so we spent a comfortable night at the local one.

Tuesday, June 15th

We started at 6 a.m. for a place called Berinag, a distance of 13 miles. We found the heat and the climb too strenuous and decided to camp at Rani for a rest and our midday meal. Berinag was another 3 miles or so. The road was so steep that though starting in good time, we managed to arrive at Berinag only at sundown. This seems a big place with many shops, a school and a dispensary. The Dak Bungalow is situated above the village, so we decided it was not worthwhile to climb up to it, instead we took shelter on the open verandah of the school building.

Wednesday, June 16th

Camping tonight at Thala about 11 miles from Berinag. After every couple of miles or so the men carrying the *dandees* need to rest for a while. At one of these rest-camps Bhaiji declared in great good humour that Swamiji was the Raja (king) of the expedition and he himself the Yuvraj (prince). After a few miles, Swamiji's *dandee* broke down and Bhaiji also met with a slight accident and was hurt. I laughed and said, 'You've been rightly served for thinking yourselves the leaders of this party.' I had of course spoken in jest but Bhaiji in half-serious tones replied, 'You are right! Make a note of this incident in your diary.'

At one such way-side camp Ma called out in greeting to an old woman who, accompanied by a few children was going in the opposite direction. The old woman, not slackening her pace, answered over her shoulder. She then stared at Ma for sometime and slowly retraced her steps back to where Ma was sitting. She squatted near Ma and there was a longish conversation. Then it was time for us to resume our journey. When we had come quite a distance, I looked back and saw the woman standing still on the road and gazing back at Ma.

We arrived in Thala around 10 o'clock. The road was comparatively easier. We had seen the river Sarayu at Sheraghat; at Thala we found the Ramganga flowing noisily over its rockstrewn bed. We had never before seen such a vista of mountain ranges. I have no language to describe the feeling of exaltation which is induced so naturally by these majestic surroundings.

Thursday, June 17th

We have travelled a distance of 10 miles today to a place called Didihat. It is still quite hot in the sun but the water for the last two days has been rather cold.

We met the Raja of Askote on our way up to Didihat. He had been on the look out for our party he said, having heard that Ma was travelling on this road. He was going to Almora, but gave us some letters for officials at Askote and requested us to contact them on arrival.

At sundown, we reached Askote (7 miles) and put up at the *dharmaśālā*. We have found it more convenient to stay as near the road as possible instead of making the extra effort to go up to the Dak Bungalows. We were drenched in a sudden shower this morning. We are now happy to be able to spread out our clothes for drying. All of us are feeling quite well. The air is invigorating.

The officials at Askote made kind enquiries regarding our requirements. The ladies of the palace came to visit Ma and invited us to the midday meal next day. I have noticed that the princely families of these Himalayan States are very pious and observe all the rules of orthodoxy. I have seen this at Tehri-Garhwal and at Solon and now at Askote also we noticed the same distinguished manners of a devout princely family. The Rani of Askote expressed the wish to have Ma visit her home and bless it by her presence.

It transpired that the Rani's brother and another official's son were studying at Almora. They had written to their families to look after Ma and her party. This explained the concourse of people awaiting our arrival at Askote. It occured to me that Ma indeed belonged to all and it was very short sighted of us to think that she should stay in Dhaka or in Calcutta and not travel to far-off places. I now see that all places are the same to her. Even total strangers are able to communicate with her easily. Dasudada told me that once when Ma was walking, a small boy had gathered a few wild flowers from the mountainside and had placed them at her feet. As Ma stood and smiled at him, he folded his hands and recited a prayer. In general we all get off our *dandees* whenever Ma does so, but this time a bend in the road had hidden them from my sight, so I had missed this interlude. It is amazing indeed to see the hill people accepting her so naturally as the Devi incarnate and paying her the reverence they would to the Deity in a Temple. Who can say who is closer to Ma, we who are with her most of the time, or these wayside strangers who become friends so quickly!

Friday, June 18th

After our midday meal at the Palace, we started around 1 p.m. We arrived at Baluakate (10 miles) a little after sundown. Five miles from Askote we saw the Kaliganga. After the Ramganga we had been accompanied by the swiftly flowing Gouriganga. The confluence of the Gouri and Kaliganga is known locally as the 'Gateway to Kailasha'.

Today's trek was uncomfortable because we had to walk in the heat of the day. There was intermittent rain also. The sun beating down on the bare road is unbearable. Approaching Baluakote we realized that we had missed the road to the village in the dusk. We decided to stay where we were for the night and camp in the open. Parvati had very thoughtfully brought a tent for just such a contingency, so that Ma could be made comfortable. Ma, however, elected to stay in the open with us. All our baggage, at her suggestion was stacked in the tent, instead, in case of more rain. We now realize that it is the greatest discomfort to get the luggage wet.

The headman of the village was on the lookout for us. He now came down with a little fresh milk, which was most welcome, but we declined his offer of the rooms prepared for us near the road. It would not be worthwhile to strike camp again and climb up to the village.

Saturday, June 19th

We spent a most uncomfortable night. It rained most of the time and the wind became blustering and cold. Some of us sat huddled in our dandees but it was not really any better than being under the trees. At the first sign of day-break, we came away, leaving the porters to follow with the baggage later. We came to the little Dak Bungalow of Dharchula around noon. We had stopped for a drink of fresh milk at one of the wayside villages. We were obliged to cross two mountain rivers. It was out of the question for us to negotiate the cold waters flowing swiftly over a bed of slippery rocks; so we (excepting Bholanath) were unceremoniously slung over the backs of coolies in a kind of basket-chair and carried across the rivers. It seems this is how the local people take the pilgrims across streams. They are wonderfully surefooted, not even staggering under such unwieldly loads. Only Ma's *dandee* was very carefully brought across by seven or eight men. There are rope pulleys over some narrow streams. The way the locals fling themselves across, hanging on to the rope which is manipulated by a pulley from the other side is also quite fearful to watch.

At Dharchula the bright sun was very welcome. Our clotnes could be dried, the baggage unpacked and aired. This seems quite a big village. The Kaliganga can be heard from afar. The music of its rushing waters has kept company with us for many miles. Still mountain peaks surround the little rest house. The unseen river sounds like the continuous roar of breakers of the ocean. I do not know what (if any) benefit may accrue from a pilgrimage, but this journey is more than worth its while for the experience of the sheer beauty of nature. It comes to my mind that these still and vast spaces are a fit background for Ma's divinely mysterious personality.

After our midday-meal I got some time to write in my journal. We are all feeling somewhat relaxed today because we do not need to start again immediately. Our coolies are tired. A local man of some standing called Rai Sahab came to call on us. He has received letters from the Raja of Askote and also Sri Krishna Panth of Nainital regarding our party; he wished to be of service to Ma. He advised us to dismiss our porters from Almora (considered almost plainsmen by the locals). He said that the terrain to be negotiated now is so difficult that only local coolies could do it. Porters are to be engaged in relays as we climb higher. The coolies could be paid waiting wages which is a little more than half their carrying wages; but the hill people are so poor that it seems unfair to keep them sitting idle here until our return whereas they could earn their full wages if set free. So we shall pay off our porters tonight. They are so tired that they are happy at the prospect of relief. Tomorrow a new set of coolies will take charge of the baggage.

Sunday, June 20th

Everybody rose rather late today. Bhaiji while spreading out his bedding last night had remarked, 'What I say is that to keep a balance between enjoyment (*bhoga*) and abstention (*tyāga*) is the best thing to do!' Ma at once said, 'I do not agree. Unless you try to give up looking for pleasures they will haunt you to the end of your days. Renunciation alone helps to conquer desires.'

Ma and the others went for a walk, while I with the help of Parvati and the girls prepared the midday meal. Swamiji sat in meditation for a long while. The noon-time meal was enjoyed by everyone as there is no anxiety that we might be obliged to start again on our journey. The coolies of Dharchula look robust; they will even carry a slightly heavier load, that is, about 70 lbs or so. We have engaged six dandees; the crew is of 6 men each and not 5 as earlier. We are taking two tents also. Nine porters will carry our baggage. The entire group of porters elected a headman from among themselves, who was addressed as 'Mate'. All these preparation went on till midnight. The local people said that not since the Raja of Mysore had gone on this pilgrimage five years ago, had such a big party as ours negotiated the journey.

Monday, June 21st

The road was so steep that we preferred to walk rather than sit in dandees which are tilted at uncomfortable angles. Although the carriers are very very sure footed, I could not rid myself of the nervousness that they would slip with such a cumbrous, swinging burden on their shoulders. Once Ma and I outdistanced the others a little. While we waited for them to catch up with us, Ma sat on a rock and sang a few lines of an old Bengali song which begins: 'Let us go back let us go back to our home!'[5] Was she saying that Mount Kailasha was home to her!

These words in Ma's voice evoked in one an indescribable joy. Even without Ma's presence to increase the effect a thousand times, the majestic grandeur of these mountains is overwhelming. This panorama of high mountain ranges exercises such a strange attraction that I am sure every pilgrim is gripped by a feeling of homecoming. The world left behind seems shadowy and unreal. Here one knows the meaning of peace and tranquility.

We met on the road here a very devout lady called Ruma Devi. She is held in great respect by the natives of the place. She is a disciple of Sri Sarada Devi. She is a *sannyasin*, dressed in saffron-coloured robes. Ruma Devi has an Ashram at Khela our destination of today's journey which is 10 miles from Dharchula. Narayana Swami from Mysore also stays in this Ashram sometimes. Many of the girls who study in Almora travel under the escort of Ruma Devi or Narayana Swami while going to and from their homes from the surrounding area. Two of these students from Khela who were at home now came running to Ma as soon as we reached the small *dharmaśālā* for our night's camp. Ruma Devi postponed her journey for a while; she walked back with us and sat talking to Ma for a long time.[6]

Tuesday, June 22nd

It rained a little in the morning. Ruma Devi and a few students bade Ma a lingering farewell and resumed their interrupted journey to Almora. Before leaving, she advised us against starting in the rain because there might be danger from falling rocks and landslides.

We started a little later than usual, at 7 a.m. The road was not too bad but steep, or maybe we were getting used to it. The Kaliganga after staying with us all these days, receded to a distance. The change to sudden stillness from the ever-present music of its rushing waters was felt by everyone. Ma frequently left her dandee to give rest to the coolies. We also walked with her along the steadily climbing mountain path.

At Pangu, Parvati's husband's village, we stopped for a while. Parvati was very keen for her husband and his family to meet Sri Ma and Bholanath and had prepared them for this visit. We were invited to their home for the midday meal. Ma has shown us a way how to observe the rules of orthodoxy with regard to meals without giving offence. On such occasions (which arise frequently) we accept the grains, vegetables and other items of a meal and cook it ourselves and then all of us eat with the hosts who are served by us along with everybody else. In this way not only the togetherness of a meal eaten in a group is maintained but adds to its enjoyment as the presence of Ma inevitably knits everyone together into a big family.[7] Thus it was that at Pangu a big meal was cooked by me with the help of Parvati, and everyone partook of the repast with great pleasure. Parvati was happy. She now took leave of her family in order to complete the pilgrimage to Kailasha with us.

We left Pangu at 3 p.m. and came to Sirkha about 11 miles from Khela. We have taken up quarters on the open verandah of a school house.

Wednesday, June 23rd

It poured almost the whole night. The narrow verandah was iashed by the slanting rain. We were drenched inspite of our umbrellas, waterproofs, rubbersheets and what not, but the strain of walking this road is such that I think we all slept through the rain, curled up in our protective clothes. Today's camp is at a place called Deepti (11 miles). For the last two days we have been rewarded by glimpses of snow-capped mountains. It looks beautiful when the sun makes the snow shine like silver.

We found the road slippery after the rains. We have taken shelter in a small room near the village shop. The floor of the room is anything but clean but we have no mind to be fastidious. We merely spread oilcloths over the floor and made ourselves as comfortable as possible.

Thursday, June 24th

Camp at Malpa after only seven miles. This short journey will live long in my memory. The road was so steep and precarious that no one could use the dandees. In fact it was difficult to climb even on foot without support from the coolies. It was either almost a perpendicular ascent over slippery rocks or a descent down an equally precipitous incline. To add to our discomfort, we had to share this path with herds of sheep either going up or down. The sheep negotiate this treacherous path in a nimble-footed way which could have evoked admiration had we been in any condition to appreciate their skill. Neither did we, (or at least I did not) admire the beauty of the shining waters cascading down the mountain sides.

We generally choose the site for the night's camp before sunset. By the time we have finished with the business of unpacking, cooking, eating, cleaning etc., it becomes dark. If we make a midday camp then this later meal is cooked only for Dasudada, Tunu and Keshava Singh. We are all feeling the effects of the strain of climbing, excepting Bholanath. He alone says, 'It was not that difficult after all!' Bhaiji looks strained and tired. I have not been able to look after Swamiji or Ma at all, but she looks the same as usual. The serenity of her face and Bholanath's enthusiasm sustain us and perhaps save us from thoughts of abandoning the trek.

Friday, June 25th

A place called Bodhi, about 8 miles from the last camp. Path a little better, since we could use our dandees for short stretches. Sometimes the chairs swing out and strike against the mountainside; although some of the dandees broke down, none was hurt. We reached Garbyang at sundown.

Garbyang: Base Camp

As soon as we arrived in Garbyang, the local people came and surrounded us. This is quite a regular feature of our trek; I suppose they are naturally curious about travellers from other lands but there is one peculiar feature about these village encounters. Wherever we stop, if there are people around, they invariably find their way to Ma and surround her even as the crowds in Calcutta, Delhi or Dehradun. It is possible that they make out that Ma is the most important person in our group from our attitudes towards her; but this does not explain why they eagerly stay with her the whole time she is available. Ma, on her part, appears completely relaxed and happy amid these strange groups. We have now come so far into the interior of the Himalayas that there is no common language between us. We have learnt to distinguish people of different regions, such as Bhutias, Nepalis, Garhwalis etc. The coolies at times act as interpreters since they know a smattering of Hindi. Ma sometimes playfully holds the hands of the women and children and her smile of course, wins all hearts. I am sure she communicates with them in some fashion because they are always reluctant to see her go. A few walk along with her *dandee* at times. Who can tell if they do not get more from Ma than any of us who are more constantly with her!

On our way to Garbyang a mishap occured; one of the coolies was bitten by a black snake. Bholanath and some of his own companions tried a few remedies. Ma pointed out some herbs growing on the hillside and made him chew the leaves; this seemed to ease his suffering considerably. He was carried in a *dandee* by his friends and it seems he will survive the ordeal.

Garbyang is a township. It has a post office. Bhaiji fetched a bundle of letters from it. All friends and devotees had made enquiries regarding our safe journey. One Sri Nandaram came to see us. He is the father of Randra Devi of Almora. Parvati's parental home is nearby. She will go to visit her parents and then return to join us for the rest of the trek. We are to stay here for a couple of days, which is welcome news.

Saturday, June 26th

We are enjoying the respite from walking today. Bholanath alone seems not to be tired at all. In fact his enthusiasm and energy is a matter of wonder for all of us. We had been warned that this journey is so exacting that not even a father can stop to look after his son, but Bholanath is indefatigably concerned about the entire party. He walks down again and again to see to the stragglers and encourage those who are losing heart. The porters are moved to admiration saying that they have never seen a plainsman walk so comfortably and skilfully as Bholanath.

We have come 135 miles from Almora in 12 days. The height of Garbyang is 10,000ft.

Sunday, June 27th

We are at the Schoolhouse. The Dak Bungalow is already occupied by more than one party of pilgrims. Some of them came to visit Ma. Amongst them were Swami Jnanananda, a veteran on this trek, accompanied by the Kumar (Prince) of Dinajpur. We are given to understand that it is usual for two or three parties to combine for this last stretch of the *yatra* (pilgrimage), because of the dangers not the least of which is an attack by robbers.

The Kumar and his party are starting today and came to Ma to seek her blessings before proceeding on their way. Ma smiled and said, 'He alone directs everything. Whatever happens, know it to be His will. Keep your own *mantra* in constant remembrance so that you may take things as they come.' The Kumar bowed in *praṇāma* and said, he would do as she had said.

The reverberating sound of the river is again with us. This sound matches the beauty of the vastness around us. Now that we have time to admire nature we see how beautiful the surroundings are. The mountains are not at all drab or grey. They are full of colours. Flowers of infinite variety and many hues seem to have been cultivated to decorate the mountainsides. It does not seem a haphazard wilderness but truly a beautiful and fragrant garden.

Preparations are being made as if for a battle. Our second set of porters will be paid off and a new set engaged here with a guide. Ponies will be required, rather than *dandees.* The baggage will be carried by mules. The next big camping station will be Taklakote in Tibet. We shall cross over to Tibet over the Lipu Lekh Pass which is 17,000ft but we descend to Taklakote on the other side. The round trip from here to Kailasha and back is estimated to take 20 to 22 days. The charges are as follows: For each pony Rs. 20/-; another 12 annas daily for his groom. A guide will now take charge of every thing. He will be paid Rs. 25/-. We will pay for his horse as well. We are to carry sufficient food stuff for the round trip, as nothing is available beyond Taklakote. The men will do the same. We are to take tents for us and also the men because there are no resting places beyond Garbyang. We have decided to take a *dandee* for Ma. We are to take a tent for the crew and also pay for the mules carrying their baggage and rations.

Monday, June 28th

We were happy to be greeted by a strong sun today. It has been foggy the last few days. The sun disappeared soon and it rained the whole day. Anyhow we are at last rid of the flies which had made life miserable for quite some days.

Many of the inhabitants of Garbyang are coming with various kinds of offerings for Ma. Conversation is difficult although Bhaiji does his best. I daresay they communicate with Ma entirely to their satisfaction, because that is how they look.

Tuesday, June 29th

We left Garbyang early and walked to Parvati's village. Her mother had come to invite us. We spent some time at their village. Parvati is happy that Ma and Bholanath could come to the home of her parents.

Wednesday, June 30th

It rained last night. We are getting used to the discomfort of damp clothes and beddings. It was afternoon before we could resume our journey. Our guide Sendel Singh organised the train of 21 ponies and mules. We noted that he was fully armed and so were many of the porters. We were now obliged to dress for riding the ponies, that is, in warm trousers, coats, caps, gloves etc. The novelty of the dress, the strange experience of sitting on horseback, brought home to us with great vividness the actuality of this pilgrimage.

The guide called a halt after 8 miles at a place which he said was Kalapani. This was the strangest journey. We saw no road. The ponies stumbled over a bed of stones and pebbles in single file following the guide. The mountains have receded leaving vast empty tracts of land. Sendel Singh says tomorrow's trek will be difficult, so we are to make an early start.

Thursday, July 1st

We could not start before 11 o'clock. It had rained incessantly during the night.

A lonely trek. There is practically no road to be made out now. We are given to understand that sometimes even the shepherds lose their sense of direction. At such times they allow their herds to lead. The sheep unerringly find their way back to their villages. It rained. We were drenched and numb with cold.

At about 1.30 p.m. Sendel Singh announced camp. We saw some stone huts. These are shelters for sheep. I was glad to get inside one. Parvati has thoughtfully brought firewood. She now managed to get fires lighted in one or two of the huts. I saw Bhaiji, Bholanath and Father trying to dry out their clothes over one of these. I sat crouched over another. After a while I realized that I was sitting on a floor practically made of packed and dried dung of animals. It did not weigh with me, I was so glad of the roof overhead. This place is called Dobra.

Friday, July 2nd

It is still raining heavily. The porters brought the ponies down from their grazing grounds but the guide decided not to venture on today; the road would be too slippery and dangerous, he said.

Father and Bhaiji are not too well. The air is so thin that all of us are suffering from varying degrees of breathlessness. Tomorrow we are to cross Lipu, a climb up to 17,000ft and a descent to 16, 000ft to Taklakote. We have heard fearful stories of this part of the journey. It is too late to think of the hazards now; besides Ma is with us, nothing can go wrong. In spite of many drawbacks, all of us are under the magic spell of the Himalayas. We feel an uplifting of the spirit and an inner joy quite unrelated to our physical condition.

Under Ma's direction, I made separate packets of antidotes for dizziness and breathlessness for each one of us. Everyone from now on, is to carry his own share. Ma, like the others, had no previous experience of climbing to this height but with amazing forethought she had made me bring the exact items which we find so useful now, like camphor, lemonpickles etc. It is a constant source of surprise to me as to how she can anticipate our needs and provide for them. She herself seems her usual self, very much at home in these, to us, novel surroundings. She always speaks words of cheer which make all the difference between hopelessness and a renewal of courage. It is too cold to write legibly.

Saturday, July 3rd - Crossing the Border

We started in a drizzle and climbed steadily. The path we traversed is too fearful to contemplate. The guide decided to risk the journey; probably because it is not profitable for him to lose days of travel as his contract is for the round trip. Or perhaps this weather may hold for days. We somehow traversed the slippery precipitous path, most of the time with the help of the grooms. We gradually came onto snow-covered ground. I have no words to describe the magnificence of the sight of fields upon fields of dazzling white snow broken only by many hued rocky projections. The mountains are really very colourful.

The vista of Lipu Lekh Pass was truly breathtaking. It seemed to me that we were traversing a narrow bridge through an ocean of snow. The ponies picked their way stumblingly and precariously over this narrow path. We were glad of the packet of antidotes provided beforehand by Ma, which enabled us to ride in some comfort. For the descent we got off our ponies because the incline was too steep. There was many a stumble in the snow but no one was hurt. Bholanath with undiminished enthusiasm kept track of the entire train, moving up and down the line to see if everyone was allright. When we arrived on level ground again he clapped us on the shoulders and congratulated us on our achievement.

We arrived in Taklakote at sundown. The guide had gone ahead and our tents were pitched and ready by the time we staggered along. Some people came and stood around silently watching our preparations for the camp. They did not seem to welcome us as at other places. Later we were informed by our men that they are robbers and dacoits, a constant source of threat and danger to pilgrims. The Government does nothing to suppress them and they are a very powerful community. This is why the guide and some of our men are carrying fire arms, because they like to be prepared for emergencies.

On our way to Taklakote we saw many caves. Nearer to the town we saw temples and stone terraces, decorated with coloured strips of cloth, gaily fluttering in the wind. We could see some cultivated land as well. In this remote region Ma had visitors. Two women disciples of the lamas came and stayed with her for sometime. I cannot imagine what they knew of Ma and what was the result of this encounter but it is apparent that with Ma everything is possible everywhere. She was as kind to these women ascetics as to any of the people well-known to her.

The road that we traversed today seems like a dream now. The beauty of the changing colours of the bare mountainside amidst an expanse of snowy fields is truly sublime. It is no wonder to me now that pilgrims attempt this journey year after year. By Ma's and Bholanath's blessings we have arrived safely.

Sunday, July 4th

We started around 11 a.m. and arrived at a place called Ringung at Sundown (10 miles). This is a village of ordinary friendly people. They came as usual to stand around Ma's *dandee* and gaze at her with reverence. A few bent down to touch her feet. Ma smiled at them and for sometime held their fingers lightly in her hand. We could not talk to them at all.

We saw many temples. Some letters and words were carved on stone walls. One particular letter seemed to be repeated all along. One of the grooms said, it was the letter OM. All housetops are decorated with strips of coloured cloths. Today's trek was not bad. We were made to keep close together by the guide as precaution against attack by robbers.

There were no trees or shrubs. I cannot imagine how Sendel Singh plans the trek. It seems unchartered land. A small group of pilgrims wending their way slowly through a vast silent valley of snow with towering mountains on all sides. There are no special landmarks that we can see; the journey takes on a quality of endlessness. Then all of a sudden, the guide calls a halt and camp is pitched. For one night this is home. Again it is time to move on through the same silent scene of magnificent vastness. The overwhelming impression of this scenery is that of stillness, it is no wonder that ascetics down the ages have come to the Himalayas to concentrate on their *sādhanā* for self-realization.

Monday, July 5th

Father is suffering a little from breathlessness. Ma pursuaded him to sit in her *dandee*, while she rode his pony. After a very short trek we pitched camp at 2 p.m. Sendel Singh chose to halt at this place because there was food and water for the ponies and mules. We also were glad of the extra time.

Tuesday, July 6th

We started comparatively earlier to-day and carried hot tea

in flasks as no fresh milk is available now. Ma was on horseback again so that father could use the *dandee*.

We had been meeting odd-looking riders as we traversed this lonely 'road'. These, we were told, were the robbers who are a menace to the pilgrims. This morning two riders came alongside and rode with us for a while. They were armed. I was surprised to see that their right hands were uncovered even in this icy cold. Sendel Singh told us later, that they take off their gloves at the approach of strangers so that they can use their firearms quickly if necessary. After some time we saw two more men on top of a hill watching our approach. The first two raised their hands and moved their fingers in a peculiar manner, evidently some kind of signal between them. The other two, then came down and joined their friends. They collected at a spot which we would pass following in the wake of our porters. Sendel Singh must have been watching them for some time; now he broke out of the train of ponies and cantered ahead and joined this group. He stood talking to them while we slowly rode by, one by one. After we had gone a little distance, he again cantered on and caught up with us.

Probably all guides are known to the dacoits. A little further on we saw a few men sitting at a small camp of two tents. Sendel Singh again went ahead, dismounted and sat talking to them while we passed by. Then grinning broadly, he rejoined us on the road once more. The sudden appearance of these unfriendly looking armed men had been disconcerting. Sendel Singh evidently saved us from some unpleasantness at the hands of these men.

All such things were forgotten when we quite suddenly got a glimpse of the Manas Sarovar. The immense sheet of water was the colour of the blue sky overhead; the two blues merging together at the horizon made us feel as if we had stepped into a world where sky and earth were one. An unforgettable experience!

Ma, Bholanath, Bhaiji and myself were a little in advance of the rest of the party. Sendel Singh and the coolies had gone ahead to pitch camp at a suitable site. On our way to this camp at the lake-side, Ma suddenly dismounted from her pony, saying she would wait for Father's *dandee.* She asked the three of us to ride on to the camp. We were very reluctant to leave Ma unattended at such a lonely place but we had no choice. Her *kheyāla* was not opposed even by Bholanath. Tunu and Dasudada also had not arrived. So our party was split into different groups.

For some time I was alone at the camp as Bhaiji and Bholanath strolled off in the direction of the lake. I decided to utilize the time by writing in my journal. Our destination is still a matter of three days but we already feel rewarded by the *darśana* of the snow-covered top of the holy mountain which is visible from here. As I sit and write I can see swans of many colours gracefully riding the rippling waves of the lake. The encircling august mountains are crested by the silver dome of the sacred mountain, truly the presiding deity of this beautiful scene. It was no wonder that, when the rest of the party came up, they spontaneously burst out in great shouts of joy, '*Jai Kailashpati, jai Kailashpati*!'

I think I have so far not written about a strange phenomenon. From Taklakote a black dog has joined our party so to say. The odd thing is that he invariably trots behind Ma's pony or *dandee.* He takes no notice of anybody else. When we pitch camp the dog stays close to Ma. When we are ready to resume our journey, he continues to sit near Ma while others are riding off. He only moves when she is ready to proceed. One day I saw Ma put out her hand and stroke his head. The dog does not look like one of the shaggy mountain dogs. He has a more sleek coat, yet he seems to be managing well in this cold climate.

With the help of others, I started the business of preparing a meal. Ma, Bholanath and Bhaiji were still at the lake-shore. There has been no firewood for the last two days. The grooms procure for me a kind of thorny little bushes and dried dung. The wind is so strong that it is not possible to use oil stoves, although the guide says the wind is mild in comparison to the usual gale which blows here. We somehow managed the task.

Ma has spent most of the day near the shore of the lake. Bholanath took her aside and spoke to her for sometime. Bhaiji also spent sometime with her. Parvati wanted to be initiated. In Ma's presence, she was given the much coveted *mantra* by

Bholanath. She was radiant. This young girl has impressed us all by her piety and her devotion to Ma and Bholanath. We all bathed (except Ma) in the lake.

Wednesday, July 7th

We started around 11 o'clock. On the way we visited a cave dedicated to the worship of Lord Buddha. These caves are in very good condition. Our camp was at Ju-gumpha where we could not light a fire at all. So all of us took a little *sattu* (flour of roasted gram) for our one meal. Much later I discovered that I had given Ma raw wheat flour instead of *sattu*. My hands were so cold that I could not distinguish between the two. Ma, realizing this, did not say a word but suffered the infliction with her usual calm and serene look. Had she protested I would have known immediately but that is not her way. She just accepts what is given her. When I was remorseful, she made a joke of it.

The cold is overpowering. Even the coolies are feeling it. They are in the habit of drinking alcohol to keep warm, but even this is now ineffective it seems. With all these discomforts we could not but admire the brilliant effect of the flowers and the heart-warming glimpse of the sacred mountain from time to time. We camped at a place called Boond.

Friday, July 9th

Today we start on the *parikramā*. It is now snowing quite often, a novel experience for us. We are now meeting herdsmen and also other people sometimes. There are beggars also. They raise their thumbs at pilgrims which is supposed to be a gesture of supplication. It is customary to give them food-stuff which we did at Sershung camp.

Saturday, July 10th

Today's camp is like a base camp for the last lap of the journey which is the trek to Gaurikunda. The holy mountain would have been gone round on its three sides, with Gaurikunda at the end of it; this completes the pilgrimage. We have to climb another 2500ft to reach Gaurikunda which is 18,000ft. The road by all accounts is hard. A dandee is out of the question. There was some talk of leaving father behind at this camp but Bholanath would not hear of it. We made preparations as if for a battle.

Sunday, July 11th

We could start early as everyone wanted to keep a fast, so there was no delay with cooking etc. We went up in a steady incline for about 3 miles and were, at last, rewarded with the glimpse of our goal. Gaurikunda is simply a lake of ice. There are no temples or shrines. The pilgrims bathe in the lake and this concludes the ritual *parikramā* of the Holy Mountain.

We dismounted near the lake. A little water is visible near the shore. The pilgrims have to break the ice to make a space to bathe in. Bholanath and Dasudada bathed in the lake. We contented ourselves by sprinkling the water over us. Ma had asked me to bring bundles of joss sticks. These came in very useful now. We did *ārati*, with them; those who had bathed were glad of the little heat from these flames for a while.

It is a tradition, we are told that all companions should be treated to a meal on completion of the main objective. This was not possible, for us here. At Ma's suggestion we distributed from our stock of dry fruits and *halwa* to the porters, which pleased them very much.

By Ma's grace and Bholanath's unfailing encouragement we have indeed accomplished a most difficult pilgrimage. I cannot describe the magnitude of the Himalayan scene. I can only say that it is not all surprising that people from all over our country come to this site, for it is truly a most fulfilling experience.

(End of Didi's Diary)

The Last Days of Bhaiji

The return journey in a way was more difficult than the ascent. All the travellers were tired and looking forward to walking again on flat ground. Bhaiji especially was very quiet and seemed not to be too well. After a couple of days of the steep descent they came to more negotiable terrain; the dandee was again available. Clothes could be dried out in the hot sun.

At Taklakote they were met by a devotee who was awaiting their arrival and gave them a bundle of letters. The camp was as usual surrounded by the local residents. Sri Ma took out a pair of cymbals which somebody had given her sometime back and gestured to the women and children to sing to the beat of its melodious sound. The grooms obligingly translated for her. The women delightedly joined hands and formed a ring. So there were dances and songs in these unusual surroundings, but Didi had already realized that for Sri Ma no place was strange and no one an alien. At Sri Ma's suggestion, Didi distributed amongst the people the remaining stock of dry fruits - almonds, raisins, cashewnuts etc.

At Parvati's suggestion they climbed up a mountain side to visit the caves of Buddhist lamas. They were admitted to the presence of the chief lama. Bhaiji spoke on their behalf saying, 'Give us strength (to remain on the path to God)', Parvati translated Bhaiji's words. The Lama seemed pleased with them and there was an exchange of gifts. Bhaiji took interest in the scrolls which were stacked on shelves. He pursuaded an old lama to sell him one of these parchments.

From Taklakote the path ascended to the Pass and was negotiated with some difficulty. After crossing Lipu, they were on easier ground. Garbyang was reached on Tuesday, July 20th. The grooms were happy because they had completed their contract and now were free to go home. Many people came to pay their respects to Sri Ma. Another bundle of letters was received from the Post office. Parvati and the other students now bade farewell and departed to their various destinations. Sendel Singh and the grooms also took their payments and said good-bye to them. After the togetherness of a most difficult journey - the separation now caused its inevitable wrenching of hearts.

The pilgrims, with a new set of grooms started on the trek to Khela the last major camp before the final trekdown to Almora. In between they met Ruma Devi who was waiting for their return very anxiously. Now she told Sri Ma 'Ma, I had decided to spend my life in the service of others - but there is no end to it. Now that I am old, it does not appeal to me any more. I wish to carry on with my personal *sādhanā* in solitude now. I would like to stay near Ma for the remaining years of my life.'

This wish was granted by Ma because Ruma Devi did accompany them to the plains and lived in Dehra Dun in Sri Ma's Ashram for many years. She was delicately built and had a charming smile and very pleasing manners. Everyone became very fond of her and she acquired a position for herself amongst the devotees.

The descending trek was accomplished in very slow marches because Bhaiji became ill with fever which persisted even with medication and medical advice at wayside dispensaries. Sri Ma was constantly at his side, advising Didi and others how to make him more comfortable. She was quiet and it was noticed very soon that she had become *maunam* (silent). With a great sense of relief they arrived in Almora on Tuesday August 10th. Devotees were awaiting their arrival with great eagerness. Manik and Juthika were already there; Maharatanji arrived very soon. All responsibilities for Bhaiji's treatment and care were assumed by Hari Ram and his friends and relatives. The joy of a difficult journey accomplished and the pleasure of meeting friends was tempered by the shadow of Bhaiji's illness. Those who would have been overjoyed to find Sri Ma again in their midst were saddened to see her observing silence and Bholanath and the others so worried about Bhaiji's health.

The best doctors of the town were fetched to Bhaiji's bedside. Didi now had dozens of people she could call upon for help. Bhaiji's wife was communicated with but she neither responded nor did she come to Almora. The person who came by the first train available was Bhaiji's personal servant Khagen. Bhaiji was very pleased to see him. Bhaiji's condition fluctuated. The doctors embarked on a struggle with imminent death, trying their best to stem the ebb of waning energies. One day, while the attendants and visitors were sitting in a dejected group round Bhaiji's bed they were startled by the most unexpected sound of Sri Ma's ringing joyous laughter. It is impossible to describe Sri Ma's *aṭṭahāsa*; a reverberating peal of sound which sets at naught all expressions of human predicaments. Divine laughter in the face of human tragedy?

Bholanath, Swamiji and Didi knew that Sri Ma's compassionate understanding, care and concern for her people knew no horizons; they now suddenly awakened as it were, to the almost forgotten fact that life and death, health and sickness were accepted by her with complete equanimity. Their prayers for Bhaiji's recovery, perhaps, were not going to be answered. The new members of the crowd of devotees were awed by this phenomenon; they did not doubt her concern for Bhaiji but caught a sudden glimpse of a dimension of total freedom from the emotional overtones of the situation. They seemed to understand a little of the way of her being with them as one of them and yet remaining quite untouched by all problems endemic to the human condition.

Bhaiji knew he was dying. He tried to dissuade the doctors from trying out last minute measures of saline and glucose injections. The doctors, however, could not and would not accede to his request. On the eve of the day of his death, Bhaiji looked at Didi and perhaps in a gesture of farewell and also perhaps in acknowledgement of her devoted nursing said clearly to her, 'Khukuni (Didi's nickname).. finish! (in English).'

The next day Hari Ram, Didi and many others repeatedly prayed to Sri Ma to bring her *kheyāla* toward Bhaiji's recovery; but she made a gesture indicating that no such *kheyāla* was occuring to her. After her negative response, everyone abandoned hope. Sri Ma sat quietly by the bedside of the patient occasionally wiping his forehead with a cool cloth. This day Bhaiji seemed to have brightened and was in full possession of his faculties. He spoke aloud a few Names of God and then just went on repeating 'Ma, Ma, Ma ...' After a short period of silence he suddenly remarked, 'How beautiful!' (*ki sundara!*) Then again in a tone of great conviction he said, 'There is One only. There is naught except the One.'

Hari Ram perhaps thinking that Bhaiji had already gone to a region beyond their grasp, called out in a tear-choked voice, 'Bhaiji?' Bhaiji responded to him immediately saying, 'Remember friend, always, that all is One, there is the One only. Ma and I are one, Baba (Bholanath) and I are One, all of us are One: there is naught else but the One.'

A few minutes before his death he was alone with Sri Ma for a minute or so. When Didi and the others came into his room he said in a clear voice and in a very calm and composed manner, 'Ma has asked me to sleep now. I shall go to sleep.'

These were his last words to his devoted attendants. He breathed his last soon after, at 3.30 p.m. on August 17, 1937. The serenity of the manner of his death, held them in thrall for some minutes. Into this stunned silence and before anybody could react in any way, fell the soft voice of Sri Ma speaking in low tones. She broke her silence of many days to say to them these words:

'I will now tell you about some incidents which took place in the Himalayas near the Holy Mountain Kailasha. When I arrived at the shore of the Lake, I was met by Bholanath who took me aside and spoke in agitated tones regarding Jyotish. He told me that Jyotish after bathing in the Lake had discarded his clothes and had come up to Bholanath and placed at his feet all his belongings which he was carrying on his person at the moment. Kneeling at his feet he had expressed his wish to take leave of all of us and walk off towards the mountains in the manner of an *avadhuta* (an ascetic who belongs to none of the established orders). His manner manifested an urgency as if he could hardly brook any delay. He only had enough thought regarding his position to seek Bholanath's permission before trekking off alone into the unknown regions of the Himalayas.

'Bholanath, not unnaturally, was frightened by this phenomenon and did not know how to deal with it. He resorted to admonition, exclaiming, 'What is all this that you are saying? Get up and put on your clothes immediately. Your Ma is not here. How can you talk like this? What would everybody say to us if we returned without you?'

'Thereupon Bholanath was relieved to see that Jyotish obeyed him without further protest. He put on his warm clothes and waited quietly near the tent for the rest of the party to come up. When I arrived, Bholanath told me about this incident at the first opportunity. Everyone went about doing his own thing. I walked by myself for a while near the Lake. Jyotish finding me alone repeated to me in a very determined voice all that he had already said to Bholanath, and then added, 'Ma, I know I have not many more days to live in this world. I have a great yearning to spend the few days remaining to me in one of these caves in the heart of the Himalayas. I wish to walk off just in any direction from here and be by myself till it is time for me to leave the world. May I take my leave of you, now? Allow me to bid farewell for ever. Please pursuade Baba (Bholanath) to give me his permission.'

It was obvious that he did not expect me to deny him this choice of action on his part. At that moment I saw in him the manifestation of that pure spirit of renunciation which is the coveted goal of all pilgrims on the path of spiritual life. I saw all this, but what I said was, 'Nevertheless, you must stay with us for the time being.' Jyotish did not speak anymore but followed me in grave silence. After a while he said with an effort, 'I have one small request. Please permit that I take a vow of silence from now on.' To this I answered, 'No, that will not be convenient while we are on this journey.' He said, no more.'

The listeners to this account of Bhaiji's attempt at disassociating himself from the world, felt that they had caught a glimpse of the magnitude of his self-surrender at the feet of Sri Ma. In the most crucial moment of his life he had not failed to subsume his will to her *kheyāla*, and that without demur. He had experienced *vairāgya* (dispassion); it was inevitable that he should receive that for which he yearned so fiercely. Sri Ma resumed, 'After a little while, I heard what you call *mantras* issuing from my lips. Jyotish who was walking behind came forward and flung himself at my feet exclaiming in an exultant voice, 'Ma I have got the sanyāsa mantra that I wanted, my yearning is fulfilled!' He thereupon had performed certain *kriyās* in the waters of the Lake (*tarpan* etc.) and was seen to live, as it were, with his *mantra* from then on.'

Sri Ma resumed her narration after a while, 'Since Jyotish wanted to be *maunam* and since he had received the *sannyāsa mantra* in the high mountains, I gave him his ascetic name 'Maunananda Parvat.' His body is to be treated as that of a *sanyāsi* (renunciate) and interred with due ceremonies. Jyotish had asked me not to disclose to anyone all that I have narrated to you just now, but I had told him that I could not promise, and if necessary I would tell the people concerned about these matters. I think the time has come for this disclosure so that you may act rightly as far as the remains are concerned.'

The listeners were deeply moved. They were proud of their ideal; the examplar of all devotees had to the last breath of his life demonstrated how man may sustain the knowledge of God in this very life.

Hari Ram went away to look for a proper place for a *samādhi*. A place called Patal Devi was chosen. It transpired that on a previous visit Bhaiji had expressed a wish to stay there. Now his body would be interred in his chosen place. To the inconsolably grieved Hari Ram, Sri Ma said, 'All of you loved him so well. The concurrence of events has been such that his body now remains in your part of the world.' Sri Ma directed Swami Akhandanandaji as a renunciate to perform the last simple rites of the burial of an ascetic.

To grief-stricken Khagen, Sri Ma spoke again and again and at length about the last days of Bhaiji. The simple ceremonies over, the small group of people with saddened hearts left for various destinations. Sri Ma, Bholanath, Didi, Swamiji and Hari Ram came to the Ashram at Dehra Dun. From all the towns where Sri Ma was known came letters expressing the sense of a poignant loss. A bulwark had fallen. It was felt that now there was nobody to take his place and mediate Sri Ma's *kheyāla*. An exemplary identification with Sri Ma's *kheyāla* was unique with him. Sri Ma herself had said that many times Jyotish would do things and deal with people according to her *kheyāla* without the necessity for her to speak to that effect. Many had found his guidance invaluable and now felt deprived of this sustaining source of encouragement.

Bhaiji was typical of the well-educated man occupying a responsible position in the world, well aware of the demands of modern times and yet firmly established in the traditional heritage of his own culture and background. He had not found easy solutions to his questions. He had had to do the work of a pioneer breaking new ground all along the line. In his day Sri Ma was an unknown quantity - the followers were not at all admired for their devotion to her. The faithful followers themselves needed to be guided toward understanding the extraordinary personality who had captured their hearts.[8] Bhaiji had played a considerable role in explaining this extra-ordinariness for the people who were flocking to visit Sri Ma. The exemplary self-surrender seen in Bhaiji is not something which happens of itself but is also a matter of constantly lived effort. His life will always remain a source of inspiration for those who feel the yearning for a life of renunciation.

It may not be out of place here to refer to Bhaiji's own words regarding his wife and his attitude toward his family obligations. Directly after leaving home, Bhaiji had occasion to live alone for a month or so at Solan. He was in the habit of recording his thoughts in his diary. The following words are taken from this account written in Solan:

'When I met *Mataji in 1924-25*, my wife and I were both equally drawn in devotion to her. However, as I surrendered more and more at the feet of Ma, my wife withdrew herself from these contacts. She was unable to sympathize with my state of yearning for, even I did not know clearly, what! She would remonstrate with me saying, 'Surely, it is not necessary to go about like this in order to lead a life of devotion. You do not take care of your health, you have no time to pay sufficient attention to your son and daughter. Is this a way of life for a householder?'

'My wife comes from a well-established, highly cultured family and has always had a great sense of self-respect and dignity of deportment. Throughout the years, to this day, the memory of her upright behaviour and straightforwardness remains undimmed in my mind. I did not wish to hurt her in any way. I tried to explain to her that any disruption in the ordered rhythm of life would necessarily appear to be irresponsible behaviour; yet how else was one to strive for something which would take him beyond settled values? My friend Niranjana tried many times to plead with her and to explain to her my point of view, but she was not receptive in this matter.

'One day she said with some impatience, 'You are so indifferent that as far as we are concerned, it is all the same whether you stay at home or leave us and go away altogether.' I made light of the remark, saying with a smile, 'Then you won't mind, if I leave home as a *sanyāsi*?' In a hurt tone she answered, 'Of course not!' My son and daughter were also present. Although neither of us had spoken seriously, for me this conversation was significant and I made a note of it in my diary.

'When I fell ill, my wife nursed me with a care and concern which is beyond human conception. Her nursing and untiring service were no doubt large factors in my recovery from that terrible disease. At about this time she lost her younger brother to whom she had been deeply attached. Her grief further alienated her from Ma. She became a prey to dejection and in this mood grew increasingly antagonistic to my attitude of devotion to Ma. She found an ally in my elder brother who also did not sympathise with my way of life.

'I was helpless in the face of so much misapprehension and opposition. I myself did not know what was happening to me, how could I explain it to others? I had discovered a new world and I recognised the people of this world as fellow-travellers, but I could not inspire my own family with any enthusiasm for this venture into the unknown. My wife, at this time was wrongly advised into making many unworthy statements regarding me. I however, was not displeased at this turn of events. It was a blessing in disguise. In this way she helped me greatly on my chosen path of *sādhanā*. It gave me the opportunity to isolate myself more and more from social obligations and meaningless occupations of the world.

'It was never my aim to renounce the world as something unreal. Neither was I educated to take my responsibilities lightly. It was obvious to me, that while I was real to myself, everything else was equally authentic. However, to establish oneself in the pursuit of that Reality which is the Ground of all and through and by which everything else assumes reality, requires a turning around to a certain degree. For bringing about the desired 'recovery', the medicine of meditation must be supplemented by the invalid diet of solitude.

'My family charge me, saying, 'you have left us!' How have I left? I have removed only my body to a remote region. In every other way I remain where I was or so it seems to me.

'When I think of my wife, I realize that although she has outwardly severed all connections with Ma, in her inner life, because of her antagonistic thoughts, she is engaged in a formidable *sādhanā* of deep concentration. She is a person of strong will-power, deep religiosity and purity of heart. It is quite possible that with her greater powers of single-minded concentration, she will reach the feet of Ma much sooner than I can with my desultory efforts. So be it, let Ma's *kheyāla* be fulfilled in every way in our lives.'

Those who came after the era of Bhaiji were always eager to hear Sri Ma talk about him. Amongst these, Anil Chandra Ganguly, could specially invoke Sri Ma's *kheyāla* regarding Bhaiji. He writes:

'This time in Vindhyachala, Sri Ma talked very often of Bhaiji. All topics seemed to converge upon some aspect of Bhaiji's life. His life of dispassion was extra-ordinary. Sri Ma sometimes says, '(To suffer the) annihilation of hope is to be truly bereft.'

'Bhaiji had wished to be bereft. The last years of his life found him in ruined health, disturbed family atmosphere, suffering the disapproval of his kith and kin. He never prayed for redress, he never sought to use Sri Ma for his own wellbeing; his surrender at Sri Ma's feet was for knowing Sri Ma for herself alone. So, what an ordinary person would feel as despair, he welcomed as a boon from Her who for him was the plenum of Blessedness' (AV. Vol. VIII., No. 3, pp. 151-152. Tr. by author from Bengali)

References

1. D.D. Vol. XI, p. 50.
2. I have read Didi's diary and have transcribed some of the pages. Didi's diary was written in school exercise books; this particular one had become sodden and then dried out. I could imagine her crouched over a smoking lantern, wearily fighting sleep to pen a few lines. At times the lines sloped away to an illegible scrawl, but the meagre accounts have a vividness and credibility not to be found in more formal writings, so I decided to keep to this form for this chapter. (Author)
3. A sort of chair of canvas and wood, swinging between two shafts carried by four coolies on their shoulders.
4. Government quarters along public roads. These are used by officials touring on duty. Sometimes other travellers are permitted to stay in them as well.
5. '*phire cholo phire cholo apano ghare!*'
6. Ruma Devi joined them on their return journey and stayed at Kishenpur Ashram for many years.

7. Didi does not say, but her cooking is so superb that that also is an attraction at such feasts.
8. As for example, Bhaiji was close to my parents. We had seen them talking together for long periods. As children we were under the impression that he had given Initiation to my parents. This was not so. My mother explained later that he had guided them to a clearer understanding of Sri Ma, answering many of their questions about Her. (Author)

CHAPTER NINE

Ramani Mohan Chakravarty: Bholanath

Dhaka, January, 1938: Bholanath seemed inspired. His tall figure dressed in silken ochre robes easily commanded admiration. He moved along with the *kirtan*-party adding to their enthusiasm; they derived fresh impetus from his whole-hearted participation. His retinue of small boys and girls was constantly around him singing and dancing along with him.

Truly this time he gave great pleasure to the devotees of Dhaka. Although Sri Ma was not with him, they were happy to have Bholanath with them for a while. He was the greatly revered Baba Bholanath, beloved of them all, an unfailing friend and guide. It was good to remember this last visit when news of his passing away was received in April 1938.

'All the years I was with Bholanath I did not hear about the many worldly desires which beset mankind. I was effectively shielded from the knowledge of weaknesses of character which create so much unhappiness in the world. It is now that I hear so much about this side of human nature. All of you know that he was prone to fits of great anger. It is said that even *ṛsis* were subject to the emotion of anger. Not that I am saying Bholanath was a *ṛṣi*. If I did, people would think I was praising my husband!'

- Sri Ma Anandamayi

* Sri Ma's first visit to Gujrat
* Sri Ma's illness
* The passing away of Bholanath
* Sri Bholanathji

Ramani Mohan Chakravarty: Bholanath

Sri Ma's first visit to Gujrat

From Dehra Dun Sri Ma sent Didi and Swami Akhandananda to Vindhyachala and then on to Calcutta and Dhaka. There was a great feeling of disorientation amongst the devotees after Bhaiji's death. Sri Ma asked Didi to go and talk to all of them, describing to them the last days of Bhaiji. With a heavy heart Didi parted from Sri Ma. When asked if she could convey any message from Sri Ma to the devotees she said, 'Tell everyone that they should live constantly and uniformly in God-remembrance with their attention firmly fixed on the One Goal.'

After coming from Almora Sri Ma had subsisted for almost a month on water only. Her body had been very still as if in *śamādhi.* The new devotees from Dehra Dun quickly learnt not to identify her bodily condition with illness because they saw that Sri Ma was otherwise quite her normal self. She conversed with visitors showing no fatigue or other ill-effects from a complete abstinence from food. Ruma Devi looked after her simple needs with the help of local visitors. Sri Ma, at the invitation of Manmotho Nath Chatterjee and others attended the annual Durgā Pūjā festival of the Bengali community in the city on October 13, 1937. After the *pūjā* she said to her companions, 'Now that we have come away from Kishenpur (the Ashram) let us not return but go on to Haradwar.'

As usual in Mataji's presence improbable things were made possible with comparative ease. Sri Ma's retinue, quite considerable at all times, enthusiastically accepted the plan and travelled down to Haradwar with her immediately. Changes of clothes were improvised, money collected from voluntary contributors. All such impromptu arrangements created an atmosphere of holiday and festivity quite peculiar to Sri Ma's presence because there was always the over-all atmosphere of a *satsang*. Perhaps by calling into question the staid conventionality of accepted norms, she opened up a dimension of freedom for many people. On such occasions things so arranged themselves that Sri Ma's *kheyāla* could be carried out smoothly and everyone would be happy. As for example, there would be a sufficient number of conveyances, sufficient money, clothes and food for a sudden exodus in such big numbers. At first Didi and others used to think it a coincidence, then the regularity with which they encountered such phenomena led them to the conviction that it was best to comply with Sri Ma's *kheyāla* no matter how improbable or impractical it sounded. If a more reasonable mode of engaging on a course of action were pointed out to Sri Ma, she would acquiesce immediately but nothing would go right thereafter, and the counsellors themselves would veer round to the original suggestion. Over the years this fact had emerged so clearly that no one who knew Sri Ma well, consciously tried to modify or deflect her *kheyāla*.

In Haradwar she visited the Ashram of Mangala Giri Maharaj and also called on Swami Ashimananda. She reminded Swami Ashimananda that he had once offered to escort her to the holy sites on the banks of the river Narmada in Gujrat. He expressed his readiness to do so at any time convenient to her. He had reckoned without his guest, because Sri Ma said immediately, 'Let us then start today, by the first available train!'

Initially thrown into considerable disorder by her suggestion, everyone rallied round and when they finally steamed out of Haradwar they realized it was not such an impossible scheme after all. The party which arrived at Chandod on the shore of the Narmada on October 18, 1937 was small enough. Most of the people who had been with Sri Ma had gone home when she left Haradwar. Didi and Swami Akhandananda had returned to be with her for this trip.

Swami Ashimananda was quite well known in this part of the country. He took Sri Ma and her party to many places of interest. This visit was in the nature of a very quick flight from place to place. In later years Gujrat became one of the major provinces where Sri Ma acquired a great following. She passed through Ahmedabad, Baroda and came back to Vyas and Karnali. Crowds assembled wherever she stayed for a few days. Gujrat has a distinct culture of its own. People spoke a different language and had a more practical approach to life; but Sri Ma evoked the same response of a friendly familiarity as if she were a person well-known to them and a devotion which was not less than that of the people of Dhaka, Dehra Dun or Almora. Men and women thronged round her singing kirtan, asking her questions or just sitting in silence around her.

This period of a quiet life on the banks of the holy Narmada was made specially memorable by the devotional music sung by Bipin Bihari (Sri Ma's father). Both her parents were with Sri Ma on this trip. On many evenings he filled the hearts of the congregation by his rendering of devotional songs. Sometimes Sri Ma would join in as she had done in her childhood. The moonlit sandy shores of the beautiful Narmada very often echoed to the sounds of what the people felt was divine music.

This quiet period on the banks of the holy Narmada were also especially remembered because these were Bipin Bihari's last days with his daughter. Sri Ma and Bholanath travelled to Tarapeeth right across North India while the rest of the party left foı Calcutta and other destinations. Bipin Bihari was taken ill. Bholanath and Sri Ma came to visit him. While Sri Ma stood near him, he went on saying, 'Ma, Ma, Ma...' In Bengal, little girls are addressed as 'Ma' by their fathers, but this time it seemed to the onlookers that he was addressing the Deity of his heart. Perhaps he was experiencing the reality of the songs he had sung for her many times. After a while Sri Ma sought his permission to leave which he gave with a tranquil gesture of farewell. He died on December 16th, 1937 at the age of 71. Thus ended a life of great dedication towards the One only, so constantly on the lips of Sri Ma.

Sri Ma's illness

As written earlier Sri Ma had travelled *incognita* for a few months attended only by Virajmohini (August to December 1936). Passing through Etawah, she had developed a few symptoms of stomach troubles. Dr. Peetambar Panth, the Civil Surgeon and Chief Medical Officer of the town had brought some medicines to her when Virajmohini got in touch with him. Sri Ma received him kindly but said it was not her *kheyāla* to take any medicines. She added with a smile that if ever there was a question of medical treatment she would put herself under his care.

The beginning of the year 1938 found her in Dehra Dun. She went on travelling continuously to different places in these hilly regions, although suffering from a fever which had persisted for over two months. Many devotees requested her to bring her *kheyāla* toward recovery. She smiled and said, 'Why do you have an anti-attitude toward illness? It is not causing me any trouble.

Everything is joy.' The fever however caused great anxiety amongst the devotees. The new crowd at Dehra Dun, not knowing Sri Ma so well, began to demur at Bholanath's reluctance to put her under medical treatment. At length, he gave way in the face of general opinion and agreed that Sri Ma should be treated by the much respected Dr. Shome. When this topic was raised, Sri Ma recalled her words spoken to Dr. Panth in Etawah. Somebody came up with the information that Dr. Panth had retired from service and was living in nearby Haradwar. Sri Ma then had the *kheyāla* to go to Haradwar and contact Dr. Panth. He was happy to see her again but very troubled to find her ailing. He agreed to prescribe medicine for her but he did this with great hesitation. He said, 'I can prescribe only for ordinary people. My medicine is not going to be effective unless you have the *kheyāla* to terminate this illness.'

Sri Ma became bed-ridden from the first day of her taking the medicines. To her alarmed companions, she said smilingly, 'The illness wants to be with me for some time. I don't ask any of you to go away, do I? I am not ill; but if I take medicines then naturally I have to be 'ill', isn't it?'

According to Dr. Panth's request Sri Ma came to his house Peetkuthi situated on the banks of the Ganges, in the last week of February. It was very spacious and slowly began to fill up with visiting devotees. Sri Ma gradually began to walk about a little. Her illness and recovery, as always, followed a pattern of their own, not correlating with the intake of medicines. Sometimes she would look normal, receive people, talk to them as usual. At other times she would look as if tired and ill. The doctor was puzzled and mystified. One day Sri Ma asked Didi to bring her the midday meal from whatever had been prepared for everyone. The chief dish that day happened to be *taker dahl* that is, *dahl* cooked with unripe mangoes and thus very tart in taste. It was nowhere near an invalid diet. Sri Ma asked Bholanath if she should eat this heavy combination of *dahl* and rice. He realized it was her *kheyāla* so he gave his permission. She then asked him to feed her. After she had taken one or two mouthfuls, she said, 'I shall tell Pitaji (the Doctor) that Bholanath has asked me to eat this *dahl* and has fed me himself!'

Bholanath joined in the laughter and said, 'What else! The blame should always be mine!' But Sri Ma seemed to recover a little after this unsuitable meal. Dr Panth realizing that medicines were ineffective prayed that she should cure herself. Sri Ma was seen to go through certain *kriyās* one day. Her companions deemed that perhaps she had the *kheyāla* at last to bid farewell to the illnesses. She seemed to improve slightly.

This was the year of Pūrṇa Kumbha Melā at Hardwar. The town was teeming with *sādhus* and *mahātmas.* There were daily processions toward the Ganges. Bholanath very often led *kirtan* parties through the streets of Haradwar. His figure was imposing and easily attracted attention. Many strangers came to swell the crowd round him. He often hoisted Bindu, a small boy on his shoulders so that the boy could lead the kirtan. Bholanath was especially fond of Bindu because of his melodious voice. The kirtan party from Delhi arrived to sing their special *nāmayajña* at Dr. Panth's residence. This was their mode of praying for Sri Ma's recovery.

On the day of Holi (mid-March 1938) the strains of *nāmasaṃkirtan* permeated the precincts of Peetkuthi (the house of Dr. Panth). Even the passers by on the streets felt drawn to it. An eyewitness[2] writes, 'The *kirtan* brought together a grand concourse of people. The sadhu abandoned his *daṇḍā* and *kamaṇḍaḷu,* the officer forgot his assignment, the beggar his begging bowl and the common man his errand; all were drawn to it as if pulled by a magnet. Sri Ma came to the Hall and by her graceful presence added to the waves of ecstasy rising and falling in a glorious rhythm. Bholanath was always at the centre of the *kirtan* party adding to their zest and at times raising flagging spirits.'

The elements are seen to love *kirtan.* There is always a down pour when *kirtanas* are being sung by crowds. This occasion was no exception. The main gates were closed because of the storm. After some time Sri Ma was seen to hurry to the doors, through the rains and open them again, saying, 'Pitaji you are wet through, come in, come in.' The person for whom Sri Ma had hurried across was seen to be Maulana Talatuff Husain, a Muslim devotee from Dehra Dun who had come to see her hearing of her illness.

The kirtan ended on a triumphant note because Sri Ma was seen visibly to regain her normal radiance. She had said once to this group, 'It is all of you who by your devout thoughts maintain the health of this body. The *nama-japa* that you do is medicine for it and a *kirtan* is like an injection for a quick recovery!'

The Passing away of Bholanath

On April 13, the final day of the Kumbha, Bholanath accompanied by a great crowd of devotees went to Brahma-Kuṇḍa for the ceremony of the bath. He was spontaneously acclaimed by the other ascetics gathered there for the same purpose. They did not know who he was but must have perceived in him an exalted personality commanding respect. When he related the incident to Sri Ma on his return from the river, she said, 'You live in self-forgetfulness, but others recognize you for what you are!' Unknown to others Bholanath, while bathing in the river, had performed certain rituals for formally adopting a life of renunciation. He had already accepted his *sanyāsa mantra* from Sri Ma in the Himalayas on the shore of the Lake Manas Sarovar. He had expressed his wish to enter the state of *sanyāsa* formally to Sri Ma. Sri Ma had endorsed his wish. He had thereupon got in touch with a prestigious Ashram where he could be given the Initiation. It was however the wrong time of the year and he was required to postpone all arrangements for a few months or so.

On the occasion of Holi in Haradwar the crowd of devotees was in a festive mood. They wanted to take photographs of Sri Ma and also of Bholanath. In great good humour they asked Sri Ma to bless her principal devotee Bholanath and asked him to sit at Sri Ma's feet. Bholanath and Sri Ma entered into the spirit of the joyous crowd. Bholanath smiled and sat at the feet of Sri Ma who was sitting on a higher level. Sri Ma placed her hand on his head in the manner of patting the head of a child. She said, 'May your renunciation be auspicious!'

Nobody really marked her actual words which were spoken softly to Bholanath. It does seem that she indicated in her own inconspicuous way the future events which were soon to overwhelm the entire family of devotees.

At the conclusion of the Kumbha the pilgrims are always in a great hurry to leave the town, creating difficulties with travelling arrangements. The devotees thought it better that Sri Ma should leave immediately by car for Dehra Dun. At the conclusion of a function Sri Ma in general moves out first because so long as she is in residence, people also linger, at times causing inconvenience to those who are in charge of the board and lodging sections. In Sri Ma's vicinity all arrangements were temporary; managers always hoped for the best and it may be said that they were never short of money although it was strictly forbidden to ask for it from anyone coming to visit Sri Ma. It would be more correct to say that the people near Sri Ma never knew from day to day where the money was going to come from, how much would be required to meet the expenses and if anything would be left over for the next stage of Sri Ma's journey! To this day nobody actually can say how the huge expenses were met and how Sri Ma's *kheyāla* was always borne out satisfactorily.

Bholanath stayed back to escort all those who had come to be near Sri Ma and travelled with them to Dehra Dun by bus. He returned again to Haradwar on April 24th to attend the *sanyāsa* ceremony of Didi's uncle Kunja Mohan. Bholanath was feeling indisposed but did not regard it seriously. Sri Ma said to Didi, 'Bholanath is going to be very seriously ill.' Didi, alarmed at these words, wished to persuade Bholanath not to undertake the trip, but Sri Ma said again, 'You may try, but he will insist on going and the illness is also inevitable.'

Bholanath returned from Haradwar with a high fever and complaining of pain in the stomach. The fever persisted. Doctors diagnosed chicken-pox. Sri Ma said quietly to Didi, 'It does not appear to me to be chicken-pox. You see, diseases also reveal themselves to me just like persons. The personification seen by me I have heard described by all of you as being much more fearful than chicken-pox.'

Within a short time nobody was left in doubt about Bholanath's illness which turned out to be the dreaded small-pox. Bholanath was given the best medical treatment available in the town and the very loving care of the devotees but the terrible nature of the disease made him suffer excruciatingly. Sri Ma visited his room at frequent intervals and made such suggestions for his care and comfort as she alone knew how to do.

Bholanath's condition deteriorated rapidly. Everyone was in despair at this sudden calamity. At this crucial time Sri Ma unexpectedly asked Didi and her father to leave Dehra Dun immediately and to take Didima (Sri Ma's mother) with them. She had already sent away Abhaya[3] and one or two others to Raipur Ashram. Sri Ma had spoken quietly; in order to forestall any attempts at deflecting her *kheyāla*, she said 'It must be either all of you or myself. If you do not leave I shall.' Didi knew that they could do nothing without Sri Ma's guidance in the matter of Bholanath's illness so with a heavy heart she started to pack her things. Swami Akhandananda expressed his bewilderment by saying, 'Ma, why are you sending us away when we require as many as we can have here to look after Bholanath?'

Sri Ma said gently, 'You are a *sanyāsi*. You are not required to render Bholanath any physical service. The only way you can be of help to him is to engage steadfastly in your own undertaking of the contemplative life.' To Didima, she said, 'Is it not agonizing for you to watch Bholanath's suffering? At this time he does not require your physical presence. You can help him by your prayers and healing thoughts. Do that for him now.' On Didi, to whom nothing at all made any sense apart from Sri Ma, she could only enjoin patience and fortitude. Didi writes in her Diary that Sri Ma seemed to be shrugging off all encumbrances, as it were, to make herself free to be wholly with the patient who was now, like a child in distress, constantly calling out to her, 'Ma', 'Ma'.'

Bholanath, missing Didi and the others, enquired about them. Sri Ma said, 'I have sent them away to Varanasi. Was I not right to do so?' To which he immediately answered, 'Yes, that was the right thing to do.'

Sri Ma was almost constantly in his room the last few days of his life, fulfilling all his expressed wishes. Once he wanted to have her *prasāda*. When the thin gruel was brought for him, she took one spoonful of it and fed him the rest slowly. Once he wanted to hold her hands for a while. Bholanath now seemed not to be self-conscious in showing his total surrender at her feet.

Sitting by his bedside, on the last day of his life, Sri Ma asked him, 'Are you in great pain?' Bholanath answered that he was but that he could not quite locate where the pain was. His entire body was under the influence of the dreadful disease and his suffering was great. He was lying on his side, facing Sri Ma. She got up and was seen to pass her hands over his entire body from head to toe, thrice; she was also seen to perform some *kriyas* with her hands. She sat in her seat once more. Bholanath seemed to relax. In answer to a question, he said, he did not feel any pain anymore and that he was quite at ease. Since the beginning of the illness this was the first time, he was at peace. Everyone heard him murmur quite clearly, '*ānanda, ānanda*.' (Bliss, Bliss!)

Some time later, he said, 'I am going.' Sri Ma responded by saying, 'Why do you think so? There are no comings and goings but just the one totality of being in which there is no scope for any separation.' Bholanath seemed to agree and said quietly, 'Yes, so you have always said.'

Sri Ma's hand was on Bholanath's head when he breathed his last on the night of May 7, 1938. His death was so calm and peaceful that the *brahmacaris* who were attending on him, and a *kavirāj* (doctor of Indian medicine) who had come from Varanasi and was in the room, were not aware of the passing away of a great soul. They were sitting in meditation as if experiencing a great upliftment of the spirit. The quiet atmosphere prevailed till Sri Ma herself spoke softly to the *kavirāj*, 'See Pitaji, if all is not over as far as your science goes?' Everyone as if awoke to the realization of the ultimate mystery of life. The man who had so joyfully and so completely given of himself to the entire community of devotees, was no more.

The bewildered group of attendants looked to Sri Ma now for her guidance. She said that Bholanath was a *sanyāsī* and endorsed his chosen name of Tibbatananda Tirtha. The people of Dehra Dun took their beloved Pitaji to Haradwar to conduct the time-honoured rituals for the burial of a *sanyāsī*.

Bholanath's passing away brought about many changes in the lives of the devotees; firstly, because it was an irreparable personal loss to every one of them, and secondly all of them had in some measure or other to reorient themselves in their understanding of Sri Ma.

In the beginning, as in other cases of bereavement, the local people hesitated to intrude upon Sri Ma, but they soon realized how ludicrous it was for them to think that she would be found grieving over the death of her husband. She had once said in another context, 'What is the occasion for grief? Nobody is lost to me. Do you feel sad when you go from one room to another?' The ladies of Dehra Dun felt a little ashamed of themselves for attributing their own emotional reactions to Sri Ma. The general opinion was voiced by one of them who said, 'It is due to our limitations that we see you go through changes in time, like growing up, or changes in status, like being married and widowed. You are always the same and just what you are in yourself. Please continue to do according to your *kheyāla* now as always.'

Thus no drastic changes were brought about in the mode of Sri Ma's life. Didi anxiously waiting in Varanasi for news of Sri Ma, got reassuring tidings that all was well. Sri Ma remained quietly in Dehra Dun for some time. Ruma Devi looked after her simple needs. Abhaya, a young newcomer remained the most constant companion of these days. Didi went on to Calcutta and Dhaka. At the time of the Birthday Celebration, the devotees of Dhaka were glad to have Didi with them. The shocking effect of the news of Bholanath's passing away was mitigated considerably by Didi's presence in their midst.

Sri Bholanathji 1881-1938

One of the many mysteries which was integral to Sri Ma's way of being in the world was the role of Bholanath in her life. He was her first disciple and he was her husband. He combined both positions with ease and without any tension.

It has already been written that it was Bholanath who made it possible for visitors to approach Sri Ma. He, however, was not looking for publicity. On the contrary; he was careful to satisfy himself that only those with genuine questions regarding their spiritual quest should find their way to Sri Ma. It is true that very soon the little groups began to swell to crowds but still they were all of a kind, friends of relatives, or friends of friends and so on. All those who felt devotion toward Sri Ma began to gather round them and became a family of the faithful.

How did they orient themselves toward Bholanath? It is difficult to focus on him because he was rather taken for granted, even as the priests are when we visit a temple. We forget entirely that the availability of the Deity is made possible only by virtue of their painstaking care and devotion at all times. Further, if some of us wish to know how to conduct ourselves in front of the Deity we look to the priests to guide us with regard to our offerings of flowers and sweets etc. It may be conjectured that

that something akin to this happened in Dhaka way back in the early twenties. Sri Ma's enigmatic and ethereal personality was attractive but it also had an aura of unapproachability. Everyone looked to him when in doubt regarding their own proper method of approach. When Sri Ma lay in deep *samadhi* for many hours, Bholanath would decide whether to try and recall her to the everyday world, or just sit in silent vigil around her inert body. Sometimes he would ask the women to rub Sri Ma's hands and feet, or just sit closeby doing their own *nāma-japa*. If it were too late in the night they would quietly lay Sri Ma down on her bed and leave her to his protective care, and go home. Sometimes Didi and others would stay overnight to be at hand if necessary; in this way the number of residents at Shahbagh also were augmented day by day.

The few years in Shahbagh (1924-1928) were good and rewarding for Bholanath. He had a satisfying job; his employers were respectful towards them and ready to make many concessions for their comfort. He could afford the schooling of his two nephews Ashu and Amulya. He could and did invite many of his relations and Sri Ma's parents to visit them and stay with them for as long as they liked. He was a family-oriented man. He was immensely pleased when Sri Ma got in touch with all his brothers and sisters. They were reunited again in Shahbagh after many years. This gathering of the clan reached its climax when he performed the Vāsanti Pūjā (April 1926) in Siddheswari with considerable pomp and ceremony. His family-priest from Vikrampur came for this purpose. His sisters undertook to cook the large meals for three days. All the devotees of Dhaka gathered in Siddheshwari. It was a memorable occasion for many of them for more reasons than the magnificence of the celebrations.

Bholanath had once expressed his wish to Sri Ma that he would have liked to own a house, where he would perform the Vāsanti Pūjā. This dream was at least partially fulfilled at Siddheshwari. Bholanath had a natural openness toward the rituals and ceremonial *pūjās* offered to Deities especially to the various Images of the Devi. He himself was well-versed in these *pūjā*-forms; his invocatory prayers could create an atmosphere for the devout to feel the presence of the Deity. His robust and outgoing personality delighted everyone during big functions, feasts and the joint singing of *kirtans.* He did not have too melodious a voice but he made up for it by his sense of rhythm and enthusiasm. He never seemed to tire of dancing along with the participants filling them with his own high spirits.

Kirtan and *pūjā* were easily seen to be his *métièrs.* They could always inspire him. He had another major interest and that was to visit places of pilgrimages. In his time he probably had visited all the major *pīṭhasthānas* dedicated to the worship of the Devi. He was fond of people. His genial personality welded the enlarged family of devotees together. He made them feel welcome not differentiating between the elite of the town, or the humble folk from villages. In time he became especially attached to Bhaiji. As written earlier when they were in new surroundings he introduced Jyotish Rai to new comers as his son-in-spirit (*dharma-putra*).

The days of festive gatherings at Shahbagh had come to an end rather abruptly. Luckily, for everyone the small room at Siddheshwari could become a focal point for the gathering of devotees, especially as the venue for the celebrations of Sri Ma's Birthday in 1928. Bholanath was requested to perform *pūjā* on their behalf as in the previous year. The people were gathered round Sri Ma who was lying in a deep *samadhi.* The people of Dhaka believed that Bholanath's dedicated worship could invoke the presence of God in a clay image. How much more uplifting and inspiring was the worship of the person who was the living image of God in all their hearts.

Perhaps, nothing need further be said regarding Bholanath's position in the eyes of the devotees of Dhaka. He was the screen through which Sri Ma allowed the splendour of her effulgent presence to be felt by all visitors. He bore the first impact of her supra-natural aura like his namesake the Divine Bholanath who had positioned himself on the Himalayas to sustain the first impact of the descent of the Heavenly River to earth.

Immediately after the Birthday Celebrations of 1928 Sri Ma and Bholanath had taken to travelling once more. When his job was terminated he was not in Dhaka. Bholanath rode the waves of these radical changes without any visible adverse effects. The Nawabzadi had requested him to continue at Shahbagh but he it was not Sri Ma's *kheyāla* and so nothing had come of it. During this time Sri Ma travelled so widely and rapidly from place to place that Bholanath did not get time to sit back and take stock of his situation. Many years later Sri Ma told Didi that this was one of the reasons for these journeys to distant and interesting places when life at Shahbagh came to an end.

Bholanath was now without means of support, and without a place to call his own. Due to Sri Ma's presence, however, and over-all *kheyāla* for the guidance of his affairs, he did not seem to have felt any kind of wrench during this period of transition. There was a change in the lives of the devotees as well. They had been visitors at Shahbagh. Now they found themselves in the privileged position of making decisions for Sri Ma and Bholanath. This group of people became firmly united, inspired by the one goal of being desirous of rendering service to Sri Ma and Bholanath.

As written earlier, in response to the request of the delegation from Dhaka Bholanath returned to the town with Sri Ma but stayed aloof from everyone for sometime at Siddheshwari. This was the most difficult time of his life. Sri Ma was with him exclusively, nursing him when he was physically ill, guiding him in his *sādhanā* and sustaining him through his mental turmoil. She suffered his disquiet in silence, till he could shake it all off and emerge in possession of himself once more. She also sat with him while he underwent the crucial period of his *sādhanā*, when a wrong move can have disastrous results. It may be said that he never looked back. Everybody saw for himself that Bholanath led an extra-ordinary life of self-denial and rigorous asceticism. Only Sri Ma knew about his problems when they happened; he himself took nobody else into his confidence. Sri Ma kept his confidence secure all his life only saying a few words to Didi after his death in order to explain away a few puzzling incidents as has been written above.

Mahamahopadhyaya Pandit Gopinath Kaviraj wrote his views regarding Bholanath in a letter to Didi, which he wished her to read out to Sri Ma. The letter is translated here. The translation is not verbatim but close:

'It is indubitable that Sri Ma's mortal frame is unlike any other human body. Ordinary people, even gods are subject to the influence of personality traits or qualities (*guṇa*). All bodies are *karma*-

oriented. Ordinarily all human beings are born to expend themselves in living out their *prārabdha karma.* After being born they work out the consequences of their previous actions. Since they are possessed of the I-sense and they are identified with their will power they go on performing new actions and so accumulate further *karma*-sequences.

'The gods or perfected human beings (*mahāpuruṣa*) who are born out of compassion for suffering humanity are Blissful Persons. They remain on earth to guide human beings on to the path of *ānanda* or joy. Compassion is felt as a reality by people on this path. It goes without saying that the great souls are pure and shining in their own light. They are *sātvic* in nature. Ordinarily men are constituted of all three *guṇas* (qualities) *satva* (light, purity), *rājas* (action, energy etc.), *tāmas* (heaviness, darkness) - the Great Persons are *sātvic*, effulgent, of the nature which is full of all goodness.

'I understand Sri Ma's body to be beyond all qualities, that is why she is completely aloof and beyond understanding - yet from another point of view all humans are understood by her. She responds to each according to his own propensity. What is the meaning of this? Just as a crystal reflects any colour brought close to it, maintaining its own pristine purity without any loss, so Ma is not limited by any predilections. All those who draw near see their own feelings and thoughts understood fully and responded to. People see her in different ways - as daughter, friend, *Iṣṭadevatā* or God. Since she is not bound by any particular attitude all is possible with her. I think the difference between one who is pure, good, and he who is beyond every quality (beyond good and evil) may be stated in the above terms.

'Now the question is, Bholanathji who lived with Ma at such close quarters, why was he not purified of his worldly inclinations at one stroke? It may be said that because Sri Ma was totally beyond the realm of mortal qualities, she neither indulged these inclinations nor did she repudiate them. Whatever Bholanathji felt at times was the manifestations of his own previous *karma-saṃskāras* (predilections).

'To say this, is not enough because it is indubitable that Bholanathji attained to a height of perfection in his life which is exemplary.

'I think the resolution of this question is possible. The difference between the 'state' of pure-goodness and the 'state' of being beyond all qualities is just this that under the influence of the former all dross is overcome and a life of goodness is achieved. The dross is not totally eradicated. Whenever the powerful influence of the *mahāpuruṣa* (Great Soul) is withdrawn then again that which was in abeyance may become visible again. The Good gains a temporary victory over evil and that is all. But, under the influence of Quality-less-ness, all propensities get impetus to express themselves to the full. Such exposure is conducive to their total annihilation. Therefore, this purity is permanent and not temporary. As a last step, when the quality of *satva* (good) also becomes inactive then the creature attains liberation. Under the influence of Great Souls man may attain to a life of pure goodness but liberation remains within the sphere of influence of one who is beyond all qualities. I think the mystery of Bholanathji's ultimate state of *ānanda* could be explained in this way. He began as a *yogi* of remarkable ability and attained to a state which is the gateway to liberation. In Sri Ma's vicinity alone is this metamorphosis possible.

'This is my understanding of Bholanathji's position. If Sri Ma makes any comments, please let me know.'[4]

Sri Ma made no comment, but Didi got the impression that she agreed with his interpretation.

References

1. D.D., Vol. V, p. 248.
2. Dhirendra N. Datta of New Delhi, the moving spirit behind the festival of *nāma-yajña*.
3. A young boy who had recently joined Sri Ma's entourage.
4. D.D., Vol. XII, pp. 17-18.

CHAPTER TEN
The Changing Order

I have yet to mention how very thoughtful it made me that although millions of men and women of all strata of society fell at Her feet, I could never detect even the faintest trace of pride, neither also of humility in Mataji. Probably there is a connection betweem this and what I stated when I first met Her, namely that she seemed beyond good and evil. I must confess that, to this day I am unable to understand this fully. ... According to the Christian doctrine, Christ is the most perfect child of God - the Son - because His Love for God and men was most perfect. The ocean or the mountain cannot testify to Divine Love, but men, if he is what he should be, gives evidence of God's Love. This is so with Mataji. Hence She is one of the important religions figures, as a proclaimer and a witness.

Melita Maschmann[1]

'Why, you haven't changed at all!'

Spoken by Nirmala Devi, Sri Ma Anadamayi's playmate and namesake at Kheora, 1939

* Swami Paramanaṇdaji
* The Vidyapeeth and the Kanyapeeth
* Jamnalal Bajaj
* Sri Ma meets Mahatma Gandhi

The Changing Order

Sri Ma had once described her sojourn on earth as a five faceted event, a *pañcasaṃyoga*. Naming the four, other than herself she had mentioned her grandmother (of Kheora), her parents and Bholanath. Within the short period of a couple of years, both her father and Bholanath passed away. Her grandmother had died sometime before her marriage. The only anchor remaining for devotees to rely upon to rivet Sri Ma's *kheyāla* for her continuance on earth, was her mother or Didima. Didima remained with us for another thirty years. During this time Sri Ma became so widely known as almost to become a tourist attraction for India! She continued to travel widely, attend functions of a varied order and speak continuously, tirelessly and undeviatingly on the subject of the human quest for God.

Didi and Swami Akhandananda would have remained with Sri Ma but as a matter of fact this did not happen for any length of time. Sri Ma entrusted Didi with the carrying out of her *kheyāla,* so that Didi was continuously travelling away from her. She had said once, 'I know that you are always thinking of my convenience and comfort; but I am sending you to do more important work. Remember that a sincere effort toward *sādhanā* is more pleasing to me than any personal service.'

Sri Ma accompanied by Ruma Devi and Abhaya went up to Simla in July 1939 to attend the annual event of the *nāma-yajña*. Since none of her usual attendants was with her, she seemed more approachable. The people mixed more freely with her. This happened in all the places she visited, such as Moradabad, Bareilly, Lucknow, Faizabad and Burdwan. In the beginning of August 1939 Sri Ma came to Calcutta. She went to the house of Jyotish Guha. Instead of allowing Abhaya to inform the devotees of her arrival, she stood at the door and sang a few lines of *kirtan* in the manner of street singers. The inmates tumbled out of the house in great joy and excitement. Accompanied by this group, Sri Ma went to other houses to announce her coming to the city in the same way.

News of her arrival spread to all concerned like wild-fire. Within a short time, Birla Mandir, where Sri Ma had put up, was teeming with a crowd of happy men, women and children.

Many people appealed to her to give them spiritual guidance. Sri Ma said, 'I am your child. You have not even educated your child properly. What guidance can she give you now? However, you can always hear the tones that you yourself play on this 'bell'. You can listen to the words that you so much desire to hear from me. I shall speak to you about the *saṃyamavrata* which I have already repeated at many places. Once a week one should make a strong resolve to live in the sphere of Truth only. On that day, one should eat sparingly, watch one's speech and action carefully to avoid the least incorrect utterance or unworthy behaviour; emotions should be controlled. One should look upon the children as child-manifestations (*bāla-gopāla*) of the Divine; one's wife or husband as not only an object of love but reverence as well. One should render services to all the members of the family (including servants) in a spirit of humility. Even if there should be occasions for anger or other provocations one should respond with calmness and not be jolted out of a tranquil frame of mind. In spite of a few or many failures in the beginning one should persevere till the goal of perfect *saṃyama* in thought, speech and action is attained. If one member of a family practices this *vrata* then the entire family will feel the calming effects of that one day.' Sri Ma paused for a few moments and then added amidst laughter, 'May be, some naughty children will take advantage of you, but it will pass. When you feel confident, you may increase the number of days. The aim would be for it to become a way of life rather than for it to remain a special occasion. During the chosen day, some time should be given to the reading of scriptures, meditation or *nāma-japa*. In short this will enable you to turn inward, to be in tune with the rhythm of your own life-breath which links you to the cosmic *prāṇa*. In this way, you may hope to realize your own Self, because who knows at what auspicious moment you may not be caught up in that universal rhythm of Perfect Harmony.'

Sri Ma stayed for only a few days. On August 19th, she came to Dhaka, also for a very short visit. From Dhaka she travelled to Kheora, the village where she was born almost 43 years ago. Outwardly many things had changed; Sri Ma, now, definitely was on her own. There were no other people who would naturally know how best to arrange her affairs. In one way; in another she was as free as she ever was and in no way any different in her behaviour. All this was expressed by her childhood friend and namesake, Nirmala Devi, who said in astonished tones, 'Why! You haven't changed at all!'

From far and wide the villagers arrived at the small village to welcome the now famous 'Ma of Dhaka.' Sri Ma visited the cottages of those who had known her in her childhood; Mukunda Chowdhury, Vaikuntha Das, Mohin Das. Introducing Mohin Das's wife to her companions, she said, 'This lady used to teach me embroidery ...' A big contingent of devotees had accompanied her from Dhaka. They travelled in boats threading their way through rice fields; sometimes they sought shelter from the afternoon sun under large overhanging trees. Proceeding in this leisurely fashion they came to Vidyakut on September 10th. Sri Ma had spent most of her childhood in Vidyakut before and especially after her marriage. Sri Ma greeted all the villagers in suitable terms, speaking in the dialect of the place. The elders addressed her in the familiar form of the second person (*tui*) and then became self conscious, not knowing if the throng of devotees would take offence!

In a couple of days a change came over the people of Vidyakut. They were in a quandary. They could not quite keep up the tone of familiarity although Sri Ma did nothing to dissuade them. The people, gradually began to ask her for her guidance in spiritual matters. Even the elders requested her to say something to them. Sri Ma was quick to respond to the changed mood. She spoke to them about the *saṃyamavrata* and spent hours listening to their problems and guiding them into new patterns of daily behaviour.

Sri Ma returned to Calcutta from Dhaka by the middle of September. Leaving this part of the country altogether, she went up to Solon. From there she went up to the state of Suket via Baijnath. The Raja of Suket had been very pressing in his requests for Sri Ma to visit his state. He was one of those rulers who had the welfare of his people closest to his heart. It was his conviction that Sri Ma's presence in his state would sanctify it and be of immense benefit for its people.

Sri Ma's companions had never before experienced such lavish arrangements and ceremonial receptions as they met with as soon as they crossed the border into the state of Suket, about hundred and fifty miles from Pathankot. The Raja and his family could not do enough for Sri Ma and her retinue as well. Sri Ma's room had been decorated with as much care, concern and splendour as if it were the Temple of the presiding Deity of the Palace. After a few days of the usual joyous activities which characterised the presence of Sri Ma, anywhere, it was time to go. From the metropolitan city of Calcutta, to Vidyakut the village in East Bengal, to Suket an independent state near the Western borders of India, the perches for the 'bird on the wing' were varied indeed.

On the day of departure the Raja placed before Sri Ma costly ornaments, silk clothes and many other offerings suited to his princely state. Sri Ma said to him gently, 'These things that you have presented to me are now mine. So I should be free to bestow them on anybody I choose? I shall entrust them to deserving people who will take good care of them on my behalf...' In this way having forestalled any objections, she started distributing the gifts among the assembly comprising mostly of the Raja's family and important members of the court. She did not discriminate between the distinguished company and the retinue of servants standing to one side. The heap of costly ornaments, gold and silver coins, brocades and silks etc. vanished in moments. The Raja of Suket, extraordinary devotee that he was, remained totally obedient to Sri Ma's expressed *kheyāla* about his princely gifts, as about everything else.[2]

Sri Ma left for Baijnath where she attended the installation ceremony in a new Temple which had been constructed by Swami Tarananda. Sri Ma had stayed in Baijnath before while travelling with Bhaiji. Many of the village women who had known her, now met her other companions. Sri Ma spent a day in Amritsar and visited the Golden Temple. She also stayed in Bareilly for a while on her way to Almora. In Bareilly Sri Ma was known to a cross-section of society where women took the leading role. Maharatanji at that time resided in Bareilly. Her friends, Mrs. Dikshit, Mrs. Amba Prasad, Mrs. Beharilal, Mrs. Dwarka Prasad etc. were all educated women, involved in community projects of various kinds. They had their own special way of celebrating the presence of Sri Ma in their midst. The untutored village women of Almora on the other hand, also had formed a group. They used to call themselves the *sahelis* (friends) of Sri Ma. Their special song of *ārati* (*Ambe Gauri Maiya*), in time became known to all devotees, all over India. They became known as the *aṣṭa-śakhis* (the Eight Friends). Sri Ma's way of communicting with every cadre of Indian society was easy because she was accepted everywhere as one's very own.

Sri Ma came down to Vindhyachala on 4th November 1939. The war had been declared. Although India was not directly involved it felt the impact in many ways. Food and clothing were rationed. Big cities were put under the 'black-out' regimentation. The fight for Independence gathered strength. The Indian leaders said, in effect, that a free India would join the Allies; that the British Government had no moral right to deploy Indian troops to different theatres of war, without the consent of an Indian Government. All this was, of course brushed aside by the War Cabinet. Winston Churchill was reported to have said that he would not 'preside over the liquidation of the Empire'.

Sri Ma remained in Vindhyachala for almost a month. It was most probably at this time that Swami Paramananda came to the Ashram.

Swami Paramananda

Sri Ma had said that while Bhaiji lay ill in Almora, she had seen' (a vision) the face of a young *sādhu*. She knew she would meet him in the near future. Some time later Sri Ma was in Dehra Dun. One day Bholanath met the young *sādhu* he had already met in Uttarkashi, coming out of the Sri Ramakrishna Ashram. They got into conversation and walked over to Sri Anandamayi Ashram next door. Sri Ma recognised him as the person of her vision. This was Paramananda. Sri Ma said to him, 'Whenever you feel like it you may come to me.' She remarked to her companions later, 'One has gone (Bhaiji) another has come!'

Paramananda was not ready to settle down anywhere as yet. He went away to Uttarkashi where Sri Ma met him again. At the end of the year 1939 he came to Vindhyachala in search of Sri Ma and stayed on. He gradually became an integral part of the Ashram. His phenomenal organisational powers are remembered to this day in wonderment. Many surprising stories could be related of his achievements under the most trying conditions. Sri Ma came to rely on his judgement and people got used to her off repeated utterance, 'Ask Paramananda.'

Paramananda had left home as a boy of twelve. He had wandered all over the Himalayan ranges. Once he had lost his way completely and then luckily he met up with a herd of sheep and so arrived at a village. He had stayed for many years at Uttarkashi, studying the scriptures with the learned ascetics, notably Sri Debigiriji Maharaj. At this point in time all devotees will remember his gentle ways, one-pointed devotion to Sri Ma, his readiness to help those in need of it, his generosity and his undoubted ability to make something out of nothing!

Sri Ma started out again on her travels in December. This time she stayed in Calcutta over the Christmas Holidays. Physically she was showing symptoms of ill health causing concern to her devotees. They appealed to her that she should put herself under the treatment of well known doctors. Sri Ma acquiesed, remarking with a smile, 'I shall have the *darśana* of many doctor *pitājis* and *kavirāj pitajis*!'

The medical practitioners, Eastern as well as Western, however, did not prove to be of great help in the matter of Sri Ma's treatment. The Kaviraj who tried to study her pulse rate, desisted after a while, saying that he had never felt a pulse which would be racing for one minute and slow down to a dead stop the next. Adding to his bewilderment Sri Ma extended her wrist again, saying, 'Now you will find it quite normal.' Dr. Devendra Mukherjee was equally puzzled by the erratic appearance and disappearance of a few clinical symptoms. After a few days of this anxious activity Sri Ma, herself spoke to the medical practitioners, 'The fact of the matter is that this body does not follow the usual rules of good or bad health. Sometimes it so happens that its normal activity due to a lack of *kheyāla* slows down. At such times the intake of food acts as an impediment; this is why you find symptoms of 'liver' or 'stomach disorder'. The reason why these 'symptoms' disappear suddenly is that the body, in its own time, returns to its normal rhythm. This body does not suffer from diseases which can be 'diagnosed' or 'cured' by the usual methods.'

The doctors had realized as much already and now with humility acknowledged the correctness of Sri Ma's explanation. In a lighter vein, she added, 'You may have given rise to another problem! People have seen so many doctors being consulted; they will think Ma is suffering from some terrible disease and her attendants are trying to keep it secret from the public!'

After her longish sojourn in Calcutta Sri Ma, accompanied by Paramananda, Ruma Devi, Jogesh Rai, Keshavbhai (a Parsee young man from Tatanagar) and Abhaya left for Puri and Bhubaneswar. The middle of March 1940 found her travelling to Delhi via Vindhyachal. For the next few months she moved around in this part of the country: Dehra Dun, Haradwar, Vrindaban, Mathura, Solon etc. She stayed frequently at Doonga, the country seat of Chowdhry Sher Singh. She also went to Jullundhar at the pressing invitation of Sardar Sadhu Singh, a Punjabi devotee. She spent some time in Dehra Dun also, attending the festivals of Durgā Pūjā and Kālī Pūjā. Although these festivals are mostly observed by Bengalis, due to Sri Ma's presence non-Bengalis also became involved.

At the end of the year (1940) Sri Ma travelled down to Gujrat. Here also she kept on the move: Chandod, Rajpipla, Omkareshwar and also Ujjain, Baroda and Ahmedabad. Sri Ma was quite well known now in these places. She was made welcome everywhere by the local people. She returned to Dehra Dun sometime in March 1941. During the summer, she stayed in one or the other of the three Ashrams - Kishenpur, Raipur and Doonga. Generally many visitors could avail themselves of the summer vacation for staying with Sri Ma. To accomodate this influx, she did not travel too widely during this time.

During these years, many college girls and boys came to stay with Sri Ma along with their parents. This was now possible, because of the greater availability of accomodation. A new way of life was beginning for many. Sri Ma herself now gave many directions for the greater comfort of visitors. From the very beginning strict rules of segregation of the young boys and girls were inculcated. She personally made sure that no adverse comments regarding free mixing in the Ashrams could arise. Once she said to the youngsters, 'It is all the same to me if people criticise me, but will you like it if you hear on all sides that Sri Ma's Ashrams are places where young people mix freely with each other and obey no rules of correct deportment as are current in conservative households?' So all new comers learnt to be circumspect and aware of the possibility of public censor. Sri Ma, at times, was obliged to assume the role of the chatelaine of a large family, who had to keep an eye on every member of the household. Even if she were busy with crowds or special dignitaries, the young girls under the care of the Ashram would always feel her attention drawn to them if they were being neglected by others. As for example: Once Sri Ma went to Bahrampur at the invitation of the devotees who had arranged for the festival of Durgā Pūjā in their town. Sri Ma and her companions, including two young girls Buni and Renu travelled to Bahrampur by steamer. When they neared the pier, thousands of people, singing *kirtan* waded into the river to welcome Sri Ma on to the platform erected for the purpose. A sea of men surrounded them. Renu and Buni were left behind. They lost sight of Sri Ma and did not know where to go. Suddenly they found themselves with Sri Ma, who had made her way back to the girls through the pressing throng and took them by hand in each of hers. She held on to them till they arrived at a clearing, where they could get into cars for going into the city.

Sri Ma explained her strictness at times by saying that since parents entrusted their daughters to her, her *kheyāla* was always with them. It is entirely due to Sri Ma's uncompromising insistence on purity in behaviour that the young people surrounding her remained rooted in their own tradition of good department. Modern times are permissive and living in ashrams also is in vogue. Modern ashrams do not go against the times. Sri Ma on the other hand adhered to the rules of conservative behaviour and easily inspired the young people on to the path of chastity and dispassion. Her uniqueness lay in creating an atmosphere of togetherness; young men and women, worked as teams for all functions without overstepping any of the barriers of a strictly orthodox society.

During the decade of the Forties the Great War came close to India as well. One day a visitor asked Sri Ma, 'Who will win this war? Is it going to have an adverse effect on India?' Sri Ma burst out in one of her ringing laughters (*aṭṭahāsa*). With an expression on her countenance not entirely of this world she said, 'Is there a war? How can there be a war without an 'enemy'? Is there more than One, that there should be two contestants? The war you talk of is like the clapping of one's two hands, so where is the question of defeat or victory? There is naught else, except He. It is His Will that you see displayed in this form. Pitaji, why do you worry? Try to accept whatever happens as a manifestation of the Divine!'

Sri Ma's words were spoken to a person who was capable of understanding the profound ideas thus expressed. She was not trivializing the enormity of the war-situation. According to an eminent devotee Birendra Chandra many of Sri Ma's inexplicable sufferings were reflections of the agonies being experienced in other parts of the world.

The annual Birthday celebrations of 1941 were held in Raipur. As before, the *tithi-pūjā* was performed by Manmotho Nath Chatterjee. He had been given this position by Bholanath himself in the last year of his life.

A few days before the *tithi-pūja* Sri Ma was in Kishenpur. Late at night her body underwent a change. Abhaya alone was near her at this time. Seeing Sri Ma assume yogic postures, he ran to fetch Prajñananda Brahmachari who was staying in the Ashram at the time. Didi also came over - Sri Ma's entire body seemed activated by a spontaneous rhythm in obedience to which her limbs were assuming beautiful postures. Her hands expressed many *mudrās* all marvellous to behold. She uttered various mantras in a clear, soft tone, to the accompaniment of these yogic *āsanas.* There was a bright look on her face. An exalted atmosphere prevailed. The three people watched in reverent silence.

After a while Sri Ma became still and spoke in a low voice, 'I asked Abhaya to go to bed. Not only did he not heed me but he woke up Pitaji too.' Prajñananda denied any sense of inconvenience. On the contrary; he considered himself fortunate to be vouchsafed this rare opportunity. He said, 'I had the good luck to witness a similar phenomenon once before at the residence of Kunja Mohan Babu at Varanasi. At that time Sri Ma's body had lain in a samadhi. Today's *kriyās* are specially remarkable to me because Sri Ma somehow appeared to be quite her normal self. It is indispensable for faith to be given the opportunity to actually witness what is written in the scriptures!'

Sri Ma said, 'These *kriyās* are also normal. Just as I talk and laugh and walk around, so these postures which seem so extraordinary to you, are equally natural... These *kriyās* take place of their own accord. I remain as I am.'

The decade of the Forties, saw the coming of nearly all the *sanyāsis* and *brahmachāris* who occupy important positions in the Ashram today: Swami Swaroopananda, Prakashananda, Bhaskarananda, Nirvanananda, Sivananda; Nirmalananda was a student in the Vidyapeeth. Panu Brahmachari, Chinmayananda and Swaroop Bhai came as tutors for the boys in the Vidyapeeth. The seniors among the young women who joined Sri Ma's entourage also came around this time. Savitri Mitra in 1942, Buni (Juthika Guha) was already travelling with Sri Ma; Udasji, Renu Mukerji and Billoji (Swarnalata Jaspal) came a little later. After them came many others. Didi's dream of founding a place where young women from even highly-placed families could come and stay with confidence and comfort was nearing fulfilment, not only near Sri Ma but also in an Institution. During the year 1941, both the Vidyapeeth and Kanyapeeth were formally established, the former in Kishenpur and the latter in Haradwar.

The Vidyapeeth and the Kanyapeeth

After the death of Bhaiji in Almora in 1937 his admirers were wishful of concretising the high ideals he had upheld for them to follow. In the last few days he had talked at length with Hari Ram regarding a special school for boys on the lines of the ancient *gurukul* system but where modern subjects would be taught as well. When Hari Ram had broached this subject in Sri Ma's presence, she had said:

'If you wish to undertake a work of this order, you are certainly free to go ahead with it. I have nothing to say in this matter. As you know I have no *kheyāla* for undertakings of this kind. Jyotish, as you know, had some thoughts regarding the establishement of an exemplary school where the teaching of the fundamentals of the tradition would be combined with instruction in all modern subjects. What I say is that any good work which is undertaken with a sense of commitment and service is worth while. I am pointing this out because all of you now have a great desire to do this work of benevolence and merit. All good and selfless enterprises everywhere in the world are services to the One. All of you are as a rule engaged in work for your own selves, so it is desirable that you should become involved in altruistic work also to take you out of the narrow limits of self-centredness. However, one must constantly remember that unflagging endeavour is to be directed towards the realization of Truth alone. Man cannot stay inactive and it is not practically possible for him to spend all the 24 hours in meditation and *japa*, therefore all such works are to be undertaken which are conducive and helpful towards this end. Service to humanity, studies, engaging in good actions are necessary for purifying the mind which is to be engaged in *sādhanā*. Enterprises which help one toward God-realization are alone worthwhile. Similarly anything which proves to be a distraction is to be rejected. Discrimination is required. All action must be undertaken with a view to increasing and expanding the sphere of God-rememberance.'

Taking these words to signify Sri Ma's approval of the scheme, Hari Ram with the help of a few devoted friends of Bhaiji, subsequently laid the foundation of an Institution for eligible boys which came to be known as the Vidyapeeth. Yogibhai (Raja Sahab of Solon) was its main supporter for many years. Another founder member was Shachikanta Ghosh of Calcutta. The Kanyapeeth remained a Charitable Institute. It was organised on the same lines as the Vidyapeeth.

Jamna Lal Bajaj

Seth Jamnalal Bajaj, the right-hand man of Mahatma Gandhi came to Dehra Dun in August, 1941 to visit Jawaharlal Nehru who was in jail and also Indira Nehru who was in Mussoorie. After discharging his obligations, he came to meet Sri Ma. At the very first encounter Bajaj seemed to have arrived at some sort of journey's end. For the last few years he had been restless under the yoke of political activities. Mahatma Gandhi seeing his disquiet, had asked him to go and meet Kamla Nehru's 'guru', Sri Ma Anandamayi. Bajaj could not tear himself away from Sri Ma's presence. He wired to Wardha for Gandhiji's permission to stay on in Dehra Dun. His total dedication to Sri Ma and his appropriation of her companions as his family, touched the hearts of the inmates of the Ashram. They came to know him well and responding to his desire that he should be accepted as one of them, gave him the title 'Bhaiyaji' (respected brother).

One day while conversing with Sri Ma, he began a sentence, 'When I was in jail...' Sri Ma interrupted: 'You are still in jail! Are you under the impression that you have gained freedom?' She continued in a more serious vein, 'One must strive for real freedom. A little time, just a little time, has to be set apart every day for God-rememberance . If one looks upon one's activities as His work which he is getting done in His own way, then one avoids the coils of bondage. Otherwise action can not lead to freedom.'

Jamna Lal Bajaj, in many ways, reminded people of Bhaiji. His total self-surrender to the *kheyāla* of Sri Ma was exemplary. He was ready to give up his life of dedication to the service of his country and his people; he wanted to send a wire to Gandhiji, to this effect, but Sri Ma dissuaded him. She said to him, 'You must return to Wardha and take up your responsibilities. Nobody knows how long one is permitted to live in this world. It may be six months, or it may be six years. The future is ever uncertain and it is best not to plan too far ahead.'[3]

Bajaj had evidently understood Sri Ma to mean that he had not many more years to live. On his return to Wardha, he shifted to Gopuri, where he lived by himself in a small mudhut, practicising his *sādhanā* in his spare time. It was his dearest wish that Sri Ma should come to Wardha and meet Mahatma Gandhi. He had repeatedly invited her and had his invitation endorsed by Gandhiji as well, but Sri Ma had no *kheyāla* toward it. She continued to travel far and wide.

In the beginning of the year 1942, Sri Ma agreed to visit Pundri, a village near the town of Mainpuri. Chowdhury Sher Singh's daughter Darshi and son-in-law Nauratan Singh had made elaborate arrangements for Sri Ma's reception. The occasion was the consecration of a newly built Temple in the village. Sri Ma and her party were received at the nearest Railway station, Etawah. They set off in two cars to cover a distance of about 36 miles. After an hour or so, Sri Ma's car came to a stop. The driver on investigation was staggered to find that the petrol tank was empty. The other car with Paramananda had gone ahead and was nowhere to be seen.

The village road was quite unfrequented and so there was no hope of immediate help. Sri Ma descended from the car and remarked cheerfully to Didi and Abhaya her two companions, 'Never mind, what has happened is all to the good. Let us walk. We are sure to come to a village where we can ask for food and shelter if necessary.'

The driver abandoned the car and came along with Sri Ma, hoping to be able to borrow a bicycle from someone and thus go ahead to Pundri to inform them of this mishap. After a mile or so they came to the village of Kimini, where a kind brahmin villager provided them with refreshments, but there was no bicycle! So they rested under a tree by the roadside. Soon, Nauratam Singh came looking for them in another car, much mortified that Sri Ma had been put to such inconvenience, however little she made of it. Sri Ma arrived at the village, and all was again happiness and rejoicings.

In the evening, Sri Ma sat surrounded by a group of people. One of them asked, 'Mataji are you an orthodox Hindu or an Aryasamaji?'

'What do you think I am?'

'If you countenance the installation of deities in a Temple then you must be called an orthodox Hindu?'

'Whatever you say, Pitaji, and also anyone else, that is what I am.'

'Mataji, there are so many creeds; it is bewildering when everyone starts preaching his own faith and decrying those of others.'

'To denounce another man's way of worship is quite uncalled for and profitless. Imagine a man on a pilgrimage. If he repeatedly interrupts his journey to enter into disputes regarding the value of it, the inevitable result will be great delay in achieving his own goal. It is best to advance with steadfastness in one direction.'

After a fortnight at Pundri, Sri Ma took her leave. The villagers who had come to regard her with great love and reverence within this short period of time, stood with folded hands and tearful eyes around her car. Sri Ma bade them farewell and came to Lucknow in the beginning of February 1942. Dr. Pannalal was in Lucknow at the time. He, Seetal Prasad, Hari

Ram Joshi, Ashu Babu etc. hoped that she would stay for a long while. On february, 10, Sri Ma expressed her *kheyāla* for leaving town the same day. On enquiry it was ascertained that the last train to leave Lucknow would be the Express for Jhansi. At the station, since Sri Ma did not say anything about her destination, Hari Ram bought tickets for Kanpur. While they were waiting for the train to start they were surprised to see Kamalanayana, Jamnalal Bajaj's son. They were shocked to learn of Bajaj's death the same afternoon at Wardha. Kamalanayana thought it providential that Sri Ma was travelling by the same train to Jhansi (as he thought) and asked her to come to Wardha with him so that his father's last wish could be fulfilled. But Sri Ma, gently dissuaded him from insisting on her visit at the time. Didi, Abhaya and others had become very close to Bajaj. Hari Ram was a friend. They were grieved at the news of his death and not a little hurt at Sri Ma's aloofness. Sri Ma said later, 'Why are you so sad at this event? To me he is not lost at all, so I see no occasion for sorrow.' Hari Ram and Didi could not share in Sri Ma's equanimity and continued to regret the fact that she had not gone to Wardha while he was alive. It was exactly six months since his meeting with Sri Ma in Dehra Dun.

Sri Ma went on to Jhansi. After one week she gave her consent for proceeding to Wardha. Sri Ma, on arrival, was met by Kamalanayana, who took her to Gopuri as desired by her. Here she was met by the widow Janaki Ben, who with tears in her eyes, inconsolably went on recalling her husband's repeated requests for Sri Ma's visit. She said, 'Had you come even a week earlier, he would have been here to welcome you.' Sri Ma in her own inimitable fashion assuaged the pangs of bereavement of the sorrowing family. She said, 'Even now, I have come to visit him. Now is the right moment for my visit. Whatever comes to pass is the best thing to happen. If you can live with this thought then there will be no occasion for grief.'

Sri Ma spent many hours talking to Janaki Ben, Kamalanayana and their friends about Bajaj. Sri Ma said, 'Death is just another state of existence. Do not be anguished at the thought that he is parted from you forever. If you do not stop grieving, he cannot proceed up on to a higher stage. It behoves all his people to render assistance to his journey by doing as he would have you do, had he been alive.' Janaki Ben said, 'Ma, I do understand what you are saying but it is difficult to overcome this dreadful wrenching of the heart.' Sri Ma spoke again, 'It is but natural to be grief-stricken. Do not think I do not understand how difficult it is to contain one's sorrows.'

Death is inevitable, but Sri Ma's presence in Gopuri took away a large measure of the trauma of the sudden loss. Since Bajaj had surrendered so completely to Sri Ma, she took upon herself the responsibility of guiding his dear ones out of their paralysing grief. From this point of view, even he might perhaps have preferred Sri Ma to come to Wardha at this time rather than when he was alive. Janki Ben related to Sri Ma that her husband's last days were happy ones. After coming back from his meeting with her, he had changed considerably. Much of his time he spent in solitude; he had carried out his tasks in a detached spirit. Altogether he seemed to have been at peace with himself.

Sri Ma's Meeting with Mahatma Gandhi

Mahatma Gandhi, at this time was away in Calcutta, where he had gone to meet Chiang-Kai-Shek. He returned to Wardha on the 18th. On February 19th, 1942, a meeting had been arranged at Sevagram in order to delegate the considerable responsibilities which Bajaj had been shouldering alone so far. Gandhiji sent a messenger, specially inviting Sri Ma to attend this meeting. Since Sri Ma had no *kheyāla* to go to Sevagram, Janaki Ben and others went without her. In the meantime Sri Ma asked Didi and Hari Ram to make arrangements for going away from Wardha if it could be contrived without causing too much commotion.

On their return from Sevagram, Janaki Ben and Kamalanayana were taken aback to hear that Sri Ma wanted to leave so soon. They said they had assured Gandhiji that Sri Ma would be staying for a few days, otherwise, he would have come back with them inspite of being very tired after his long journey. Sri Ma smiled and said, she was ever with Pitaji (Gandhiji) and one specific meeting did not matter. Luckily for Kamalanayana, who was preparing to go to fetch Gandhiji, knowing this was what he would wish to do, it was announced that all train services for civilians for that evening were being cancelled due to troop movements. Sri Ma could leave next morning at the earliest.

In the evening Acharya Vinoba Bhave, Dr. Rajendra Prasad and a few others came to meet Sri Ma. From them she gathered that Mahatma Gandhi would be coming to meet her after that day's prayer meeting.

After a little while Sri Ma walked out of her cottage to go to Sevagram. Kamalanayana was only too delighted at this change of her *kheyāla*. When they arrived at Sevagram, Gandhiji was sitting in his room, surrounded by many people. As Sri Ma mounted the steps of the hut, he extended both arms in welcome, as if to a small girl. Sri Ma responded suitably, going up to him and sitting down close to him. He spoke first, 'Do you know who sent Jamnalal to you? It was I. He told me frankly that the inner peace I had not been able to give him during our long association of thirty years, he had obtained from you.' Gandhiji continued, 'It was Kamala Nehru who told me about you.' Looking around at the other people he said, 'Kamala used to regard Mataji as her Guru.'

Sri Ma said, then, 'Pitaji, I am no one's guru. How can I be? I am a little girl!' Gandhiji accepted this statement with great enjoyment, saying, 'Yes, yes, you are my little girl; I made a mistake in calling you 'Mataji',' Gandhiji seemed very pleased with Sri Ma. He said to her, 'I am told that you want to leave tomorrow morning. This cannot be. You must stay for a few more days.' It was obvious from his confident tone that Gandhiji had no fear of being disobeyed by his 'little daughter.' Sri Ma, however, rejoined, 'Pitaji you must know that this small child is a little crazy. She cannot always mind the words of elders. And after all, why not? This child has acquired the nature of her father in this respect!'

Everybody in the room burst out laughing but Gandhiji made another attempt, saying, 'If you disregard my wish, everyone will make fun of me. They will say, 'He could not pursuade a crazy child, how will he influence Chiang-Kai-Shek? I shall be made to look utterly ridiculous!' Sri Ma laughed and said, 'As if Pitaji cares about what people might say; besides what is the harm if people enjoy themselves a little at Pitaji's cost?'

It became clear to everyone, including Mahatmaji that Sri Ma did not have the *kheyāla* to change her programme. He then asked if adequate arrangements had been made for the travellers to go to the station, the next morning. Sri Ma and Janaki Ben spent the night in Gandhiji's cottage. Once during the night, Sri Ma suddenly addressed the five or six persons who were attending on Gandhiji, in some capacity or other, saying, 'What will you do if I take Mahatmaji away from all of you?' All declared without hesitation, 'We shall all go with him!' Sri Ma smiled but did not seem to pay attention to the answer. She spoke softly to Gandhiji, addressing him directly, 'I shall fetch you at the right moment. What do you say Pitaji?' Gandhiji, evidently understood Sri Ma's intended meaning because he replied in the affirmative in the same tone of voice, quietly and gravely. Didi and Hari Ram, who were present, exchanged a quick glance of apprehension; was it possible that Gandhiji would not be with them for long?

Next morning, Sri Ma left Wardha. At the time of parting she said, 'I know Pitaji will not be displeased with this little girl for disobeying him?'

'As if you care about my displeasure!'

'Pitaji, if I have the *kheyāla*, you will find me entering your hut without any previous notice and without waiting for an invitation.'

'Yes, thieves and dacoits enter silently by stealth, without the knowledge of the householders.'

'Fine! Pitaji has called me a thief! I shall steal everything belonging to you. Shall I?'

Gandhiji smilingly nodded assent murmuring softly, 'Such theft is a rare fortune.'

At Wardha station, Sri Ma again reverted to the topic of the previous night. She said to Janaki Ben, 'Tell Mahatmaji to be prepared. After all the time for going home is drawing near.'

Hari Ram recalled that it had been Bajaj's ardent desire that Gandhiji should come in close contact with Sri Ma. The entire nation's hopes of achieving freedom lay with Gandhiji; it was only right that he should have Sri Ma's blessings for this momentous task. Hari Ram knew that Bhaiji also had hoped for a meeting between the two. But the best of devotees had not been able to penetrate the inscrutibility of Sri Ma's *kheyāla.* Just as, way back in Bajitpur, Janaki Sen and Nishikanta Bhattacharya had failed to see the significance of Sri Ma's miraculous powers, so now Hari Ram and others could not quite gauge Sri Ma's tremendous impact on all the builders of the Indian Nation who came in close contact with her before, during and after the year of Independence.

Sri Ma met Gandhiji again in New Delhi in 1946, about a year and two months before his death. At that time also he, with all the emphasis at his command, asked her to stay with him and not wander around. Sri Ma, with matching emphasis answered smilingly, 'Pitaji, believe me, I am ever with you.'

References

1. 'Mataji Gives Darshan' AV. Vol. XI, No. 2, p. 61.
2. Only one of a pair of silver anklets was left because Didi felt that at least one little memento should remain with Sri Ma.
3. Was it a coincidence that Bajaj died after 6 months of meeting Sri Ma and Mahatma Gandhi after about 6 years?

CHAPTER ELEVEN

Sri Ma and the Sādhu-Samāja

One who has seen Mother even once, cannot doubt that there is such a thing as Perfect Bliss or Ananda. One really feels in Her presence something like an unmixed joy which is pure and unique, a higher and nobler happiness than the transitory pleasures of the sensory plane. Her illuminating discourses show unmistakeably the presence of a *jñāna*, a realization or an *anubhava* that is not due to the training of the intellect and which is above the piecemeal working of the faculties...

Dr. Nalini Kanta Brahma[1]

Question by Swami Dayananda of the Bharat Dharma Mahāmaṇḍala:

'Mother, what are you in fact? People hold different views regarding you and no agreement seems to exist.....?

Sri Ma: You want to know what I am? Well, I am what you consider me to be - not more not less.

Question: What is the nature of your *samādhi* then? Is it *samādhi* then? Is it *savikalpa* or *nirvikalpa*? Does mind, then, persist?

Sri Ma: Well it is for you to decide this question. All that I can say is that in the midst of all apparent changes of states in body and mind. I feel I am aware that I am always the same. I feel that in me there is no change of states. Call it by any name you like. Is it *samādhi*?[2]

* *Sādhu-sammelan* at Jhunsi

* Haribabaji Maharaj

Sri Ma and the Sādhu-Samāja[3]

After leaving Wardha, Sri Ma, Didi, Abhaya, Hari Ram Joshi and Paramananda came to Saugor. Some senior members of the royal family of Nepal, were living in retirement in the town. Hari Ram was known to them, He contacted the elder Rani, who was only too happy to be of service to Sri Ma. She wanted Sri Ma to come to her palace but deferred to Sri Ma's *kheyala* of retreating to a more remote location. The Rani, took them to a small *dharmaśālā* on the river Vyas. A huge banyan tree dwarfed the small cottage. After Sri Ma, Didi and Abhaya had settled in Hari Ram and Paramananda left for Raipur. The Rani also departed renewing her offers of any kind of help that might be needed.

Sri Ma spent a quiet fortnight in this retreat. This sojourn was made memorable by the repeated recurrence of the phenomenon of spontaneous outpourings of mantras from Sri Ma's lips. Almost every day she would pronounce these syllables of a divine language (*deva-bhāṣā*) indescribably beautiful in their rhythmic sequence and exquisite melody. Abhaya tried to write down some of the verses but his version of the sound-forms remained inadequate.

Didi, ever practical, tried to engage Sri Ma's attention toward her correspondence. Ordinarily letters addressed to Sri Ma are read out to her, the same day if possible and her answers to them are taken down verbatim. Whoever reads the letters is responsible for posting the answers. At times Sri Ma is too busy to listen to any but a few urgent ones; the letters keep on accumulating in a bag. It is not unknown for it to take six months or more for a letter to be responded to. The bag of letters remained one of the indispensable items of Sri Ma's baggage on her travels. In later years the letter sessions became quite well-organised. Sri Ma would ask five or six people to sit around her and start reading the letters in turn. They were sometimes divided according to the languages they were written in. Everybody was required to be ready with the salient points of the letter (if it were very long) and present them to Sri Ma as soon as it was his/her turn to read out. Sri Ma would dictate her answer. She always gave her full attention to each and every letter. Sometimes the same correspondent, impatiently would have written half a dozen letters in the meantime. All of them were read out scrupulously. The letters which found their way to the bag were mainly not such as needed to be answered immediately - Didi, now with Abhaya's help tried to dispose of as many letters as she could.

Sri Ma travelled around for a while, and then returned to the little *dharmaśālā*. Here they were joined by Kantibhai Vyas (Swami Bhagavatanandaji). The tale of his quest for Sri Ma and the miraculous manner in which he had found his way to their forest dwelling, was interesting in the extreme.

Sri Ma left Gujrat toward the end of March and came back to the United Provinces. She was in Lucknow, Varanasi, Vindhyachala, Delhi and then Dehra Dun. She remained in Dehra Dun for the entire summer. In August the country experienced an upheaval when the leaders of the nation were arrested following the Civil Disobedience Movement announced by Gandhiji. The Eastern Front of the War was close enough to India. In answer to a letter from a devotee in Calcutta Sri Ma said, 'There is no occasion for faintness of heart. Nothing is achieved by being nervous of what might happen or being afraid of events which come to pass. Whatever is happening is what has to happen. One must bear the present with fortitude and face the future bravely.'

At the end of October, 1942, Sri Ma left the district of Dehra Dun and set out on her usual unplanned travels. Conditions were unsettled. The British Government in India was ruthlessly stamping out the 'Civil Disobedient Movement'. Troop movements were given priority. Travelling for civilians, was fraught with uncertainties. Pursuasively, allaying misgivings, Sri Ma accompanied by Paramananda, set forth, first for Solon, via Ambala, and then on to other places. After a couple of months of this aimless (or seemingly so) wandering she came to Vindhyachala at the beginning of the year 1943. The small ashram on top of the Astabhuja Hills immediately filled up with guests from nearby places and daily visitors from Mirzapur.

At this time Sri Ma came in close touch with Sri Prabhudatta Brahmachariji of Jhunsi near Allahabad. He was a Mahatma of considerable reputation in this part of the country, mostly known for his work of spiritual upliftment among villagers and also for his promulgation of a greater awareness of Hindu thoughts and ideals. He came to Vindhyachala to Sri Ma's Ashram for a couple of days in March in the company of Protima Devi of Allahabad. His liveliness and childlike delight in everything amused everybody. He became very devoted to Sri Ma but would hide his allegiance by an off-hand manner which was quite his own peculiar style.

After this visit, Sri Ma set out again on her travels. This time she went to Calcutta and also to Dhaka and Deoghar. These were all flying visits but still Sri Ma delighted the hearts of all her devotees in this part of the country which was under some stress from a fear of the uncertainty of Japanese intentions regarding the Indian border. In Sri Ma's company all such concerns receded to the background. For the duration of her visits in all towns, the devotees were able to concentrate on the timeless, forgetting the immediate demands of the moment.

Leaving Bengal, Sri Ma came to Lucknow and proceeded to the ancient, holy site of *Naimiśāraṇya* near Sitapur. On arival at *Naimiśaraṇya*, Sri Ma took up her seat near the sacred tank and expected her companions to take this opportunity of visiting all the temples in the vicinity; but alas! the lure of her magnetic personality was more powerful than the silent appeal of her precepts. After a while Sri Ma got up and walked to the nearby ancient temple of Śiva. She took a garland from the basket of a flower-vendor and put it with great care on the *liṅgam*. Now, of course, everybody wanted to do the same!

The devotees of Delhi were desirous of performing a *nāma-yajña* in honour of Sri Ma. At their invitation Sri Ma came to New Delhi. Arrangements were made for her to stay at Dr. J.K. Sen's house. Dr. Sen was an elderly person, very much dedicated to the service of Sri Ma. His house in subsequent years became a focal point for the gathering of devotees as Jyotish Guha's house in Calcutta.

In the last week of April, 1943 travelling through Bareilly and Haldwani, Sri Ma came to Almora. Yogibhai (Raja Durga Singh of Solon) had financed the construction of a beautiful *samadhi-mandira* over Bhaiji's grave at Pātāl Devi and also a small cottage nearby. It was a secluded place, nestling at the foot of high mountain ranges. Another house was taken on rent in case Sri Ma remained for some time and there was an overflow of visitors.

Almora, at that time, had the distinction of housing the famous dance-school, the Culture Centre of Uday Shankar which happened to be quite close to Patal Devi. A great bond of friendship was forged between the inmates of the Ashram and the School. Uday Shankar, his wife Amala Devi, his brothers Rajendra Shankar and Ravi Shankar, the French dancer Simkie, Prabhat Babu, Sati Devi and many others became frequent visitors.

On May 3, Sri Ma's Birthday, Uday Shankar arranged for a performance of his famous shadow-play of the Ramayana at his Culture Centre. They professed themselves honoured that they could have Sri Ma as audience. The precincts of the centre were very beautiful. Sri Ma visited it sometimes, holding conversations with Uday Shankar and the various members of his troupe on the subject of the dance-form as a mode of *sādhanā*. One day she said, 'This body is, of course, quite ignorant of what you call dance. But would you believe it, Pitaji, when this body was engaged in the play of *sādhanā* it went through so many of the postures and motions I have seen here, and many more. Once in Bajitpur, I said to Bholanath, 'Sit here in front of me. I shall perform *ārati* to you.' I did not have any physical accessories for the *ārati*. It was all bodily movement and gestures with the arms and hands. It was quite like what you call a dance performance. Bholanath was amazed, because he knew very well that I had never been taught anything like it. There is of course, a difference between learning and spontaneous expression. After all, the origin of all that exists, is the One alone. There is only the one rhythm pervading everything. If one knows the One, all is known. The One that is Bliss, expresses itself in this exuberant form of the Dance.'

Abhaya promptly asked, 'How about the forms which depict sorrow?' Sri Ma answered, 'They also grip the attention. If executed perfectly, such dances give rise to a kind of sympathetic understanding which is a quality of happiness.'

From Almora, Sri Ma accompanied by Hari Ram, Sher Singh, Hansa Datt, Govinda Pandey and many others went to attend a *Bhāgavat Saptāh* at Sahasradhara, at the insistent invitation of Prabhudatta Brahmachariji. Here she met other well-known *sādhus* like Haribabaji Maharaj, Udiya Baba, Chakrapaniji and Sharananandaji.

Sri Ma returned to Almora. On June 25th, she went to see Jashoda Ma at Mir Tola. Arun Babu from Lucknow escorted her to his Guru's Ashram. Jashoda Ma was not at all surprised to see Sri Ma. She said, 'I have just finished reading Didi Gurupriya's books on Ma. Since yesterday I had an overwhelming desire to see Sri Ma. I knew that since I could not go to her, she will come to give me *darśana*' The Ashram was delightful. The inmates, Sri Krishna Prem, Sri Hari Das and others became well-known friends at Sri Ma's Ashrams over the years.

Sri Ma travelled away from Almora for a while in the month of July but she returned back after a fortnight or so. This was definitely, the year of Almora. She stayed here for the Annual Durgā Pūjā in October as well which every year used to be celebrated at the Culture Centre. This year due to the sudden passing away of his Guru Udaya Shankar could not engage in this festive programme. At his request the *pūjā* was celebrated in Sri Ma's āshram on his behalf. The worship of the Daughter of the Himalayas among the Himalayan ranges, touched the imagination and moved the hearts of all devotees.

Sri Ma's prolonged sojourn in one place produced its inevitable consequences. Buildings were constructed to provide greater accomodation for visitors. Parashuramji undertook to expand the little ashram. A big terrace came into being. Sri Ma would walk on it; sometime she sat surrounded by visitors answering their questions:

'How is it that no sooner one attempts to sit in meditation than sundry thoughts begin to impinge themselves on the mind?'

'Don't you know why one cannot concentrate? Desires act as repellents. Just as when you enter the sea, the waves keep on throwing you back to the beach; if you persevere and attain a deeper level then the waves cease to hinder.' Sri Ma paused for a while and then added:

'It is necessary to realize that there is nothing but One alone. Desires are the return-tickets, that ensure one's comings and goings in the world of duality. If you perceive Śiva, you do not see a stone. And if you see a stone, you do not perceive Śiva. Further, just as He is known by the name 'Śiva', He and no other is indicated by the word 'stone'. Neither can be extraneous since all expressions and manifestations are His only.'

Sādhu-sammelana at Jhunsi

In the beginning of 1944, Sri Ma at the invitation of Prabhudattaji, came to his Ashram at Jhunsi on the other side of the Ganges at Allahabad. He was organising a big meeting of all the *sādhus* of reputations in Northern India. He received Sri Ma at the Railway Station with a *kirtan*-party and escorted her to her room with a lot of ceremonious fanfare. Brahmachariji told her that he could accomodate a thousand of her devotees! In fact preparations on a very grand scale were under way. There were provisions for the housing of hundreds of visitors. Brahmachariji himself looked to the comforts of everyone and supervised all arrangements.

There was a big Satsang-Hall in the middle of the courtyard which was a formally laid out garden as well. Every morning the visiting dignitaries would assemble in the Satsang-Hall. Some of them gave discourses on religious subjects to the big gathering which assembled to listen to them. The *sādhus* in their resplendent ochre-robes sat facing the audience; women on one side of the hall and men on the other. Since Sri Ma was not one of the speakers she sat at the head of the group of women, dressed in her spotless white garments.

Sri Ma had met many of the *sādhus* in Sahasradhara in the previous year. She also knew about them from her many visits to Vrindaban and other holy places. So far, the *sādhu samāja* had not given her formal recognition; not only was she a woman, but also she did not belong to any of the ascetic orders. She was not learned; she did not have a Guru, so she did not belong to any known *sampradāya*. It lies to the credit of Brahmachariji that he recognised Sri Ma's aura of divine presence; he made it possible for the *sādhu-samāja* to come to her and pay her homage as the spirit of the Upaniṣads, the very fountain-head of all *sampradāyas* (brotherhoods).

The Satsang-Hall at Jhunsi in the evenings, wore a more informal look. Sri Ma would converse with the visitors in her own style of a dialogue. Sometimes, some of the *mahātmās* would come and join in. The main concern of Brahmachariji was to plan for a jointly sponsored festival of *nāma-samkirtana* later in the year. These were difficult times. The Government was highly suspicious of any concerted activity and discouraged assemblies of any kind. The *sādhus* felt it to be their duty to participate in the life of the people and this could be done by them through the medium of religious festivals alone. So the festival of *nāma-samkirtana* was decided upon as a function which would touch the largest number of people at the simplest level of religious activity.

There was much discussion regarding the details of this event. During one of the evening sessions, after an agreement had been reached regarding the manner and extent of the festival, Sri Ma was requested to choose the site for it, Sri Ma, who had been liṣtening to the deliberations silently so far, broke out into a spontaneous peal of ringing laughter.

We have tried to describe this *aṭṭahāsa* once or twice before. Sri Ma's whole body seemed to radiate the joyous sound, which was totally arresting as a supra-natural phenomenon. The poet Ravindranath has used this word *aṭṭahāsa* to describe the awe-some clap of thunder emanating from the swiftly spreading and lowering dark clouds of the monsoons of Bengal (*kāḷa-vaiśākhī*).

In the *maṇḍapa* (Hall) there was total silence till the echoes of this sound ebbed away. For Sri Ma to laugh, when a lot of eminent men were seriously engaged in organisational work of some moment under trying conditions? The much revered *sādhu* Swami Sharananandaji, who was blind, had not 'seen' Sri Ma. He now said in very grave tones, 'I have studied a lot about *ullāsa* (joyous ebullience) in the scriptures, the manifest form of the unmanifest Divine Bliss. We are fortunate and honoured that today we've heard the utterly thrilling notes of this divine sound.'

Haribabaji said, 'It is right that Mataji should laugh at our question. She who belongs everywhere and therefore 'nowhere', how should she choose a particular site for a particular event since she accepts all that happens as the only way of its occurence.'

Sri Ma herself was now serious and silent. She, as usual volunteered no explanations for her laughter. When the *mahātmās* looked to her for her final response, she said gently, 'He, who has manifested Himself in your hearts in the form of a wish for this joint celebration will further reveal Himself in the choosing of a place acceptable to all of you. A good resolve is actualized by the Good Itself. As far as I am concerned, I, as your little child belong to all of you; whatever decision is taken by all of you, know that to be my suggestion.' The assembly seemed pleased with this pronouncement. Jhunsi, itself was quickly chosen as the venue for the proposed function.

The *sādhu-sammelana* or the concourse of ascetics at Jhunsi marks a water-shed event in the life of Sri Ma and her way of being in the world. Every country has a tradition which is sustained by those who are considered its exemplars. The ochre-robed ascetic is for an Indian community an ideal, a person who shows them that their tradition is a living force which is able to sustain them forever.

The ideal of renunciation as a form of knowledge has been thematised in the Advaita Philosophy of the Ādi Śaṁkarācārya. All other schools of thought in India subscribe to it as a high ideal but it is not integral to their philosophy. Śri Śaṁkarācārya on the other hand has placed it in the very heart of his writings on the identity of Ātman (Self) and Brahman (Supreme Being). The sphere of the world together with its knowing subject, the I-consciousness is, as if, superimposed on this unity and needs to be cancelled so that Brahman may shine forth as Bliss Supreme. Sri Ma's call to dispassion seemed to be a continuation of this classical exegesis of Upanishadic thought. The difference lay in her own personality, her own way of living in the world which was a compassionate involvement and not a withdrawal which somehow, leant greater credibility to the *mantra* of *sanyāsa* running like a thread through the garland of many flowers which is Hindu tradition.

The *sādhu-samāj* were quick to recognise her as the personification of *brahmavidya* the quintessence of the Upanishadic wisdom. They were not deceived by her humility in their presence. Moreover, they reoriented themselves toward her affirmation of the entire gamut of devotional attitudes toward God. Sri Ma on her part was always ready to respond to their invitations and paid them the highest respect when they came to visit her.

In the meantime Didi had been trying hard to acquire a piece of land in Varanasi near the river bank, so that a small Ashram could be built for Sri Ma's convenience. Sri Ma used to visit Varanasi very often during those years. She would stay in *dharmaśālās*, or houseboats, or temple verandahs, or in the small mud hut in Nirmal Chandra Chatterji's garden in Ramapura.

Didi succeeded in her efforts and a piece of land in Bhadaini was bought for this purpose. In the month of April 1944 the first Vāsantī Pūjā was celebrated on this site. Subsequently Varanasi Ashram grew to be the Head Quarters of the Sri Sri Ma Anandamayi Sangha which was formed in 1950. Although the Head office is now in Kankhal, it remains one of the major Ashrams.

Sri Ma returned to Almora during the month of May. All the *mahātmās* who had come in contact with her had assembled in this Ashram for Sri Ma's Birthday celebrations. Haribabaji Maharaj from the very beginning saw in her the fulfilment of all his yearning for spiritual bliss. He was a man who truly did not waste a second in futile conversation or activity. His one-pointed concentration seemed a carrying out of Sri Ma's *vāṇī*,

'To talk of God alone is worthwhile; all else is in vain and pain.'

Swami Akhandanandaji passed away in Varanasi in the month of August. For many months he was living in a rented house which had been hired to house the girls of the Kanyapeeth. Savitri Mitra and others were looking after Swamiji who was there as a guardian for them. He did not require much tending or nursing. On learning about his indisposition Sri Ma sent Didi to Varanasi. Didi asked her father, more than once, 'Shall I send a telegram to Ma?'. He invariably answered, 'It is not necessary.' It was clear to his attendants that he felt himself to be living constantly in the presence of Sri Ma and felt secure in the refuge he had sought and found. His last moments were calm and peaceful. A great loss for the family of devotees.

In her many visits to Allahabad, Sri Ma had met Kanhaiyalal, a devout Vaiṣṇava and a man of some position in the city. He was the owner of a big Hall which was hung on all sides with the portrait of Krishna. All the portraits were copies of the same huge canvas hung in the middle of the end wall facing an audience. The portrait depicted a young Krishna leaning against a tree, with the flute in his hand, a beautiful white cow standing near him. It was related that Kanhaiyalal had had a vision of such a scene. He had commissioned an artist to paint it and make copies of it also. The Hall was known, therefore as Krishna-Kunja (the bower of Krishna).

The annual Durgā Pūjā in the month of October 1944 was celebrated in the bower of Krishna, at the invitation of Kanhaiyalal. Such commingling of opposites was ever possible near Sri Ma. Another special feature of this year's Durgā Pūjā was that Sri Ma came to Satya Gopal Ashram in Allengunj for the first time. Sri Gopal Thakur Mahashaya was a disciple of Sri Satya Deva Thakur of the renowned Sadhana Samar Ashram. This *sampradāya* has a distinctive way of performing this *pūjā*. Sri Ma had been invited to this *maṇḍapa* (place of *pūjā*) also. When Sri Ma arrived, Sri Gopal Thakur in an exalted state, made her welcome with flowers and songs and *mantras*, as the living Devi, he had invoked in the clay image.

This first meeting was the beginning of a long association between Sri Ma and Sri Gopal Thakur and his family. In commemoration of her visit Sri Ma was asked to visit Allahabad for three days every year around *pūjā* time. Sri Ma kept Sri Gopal Thakur's request for many years. After his death, the tradition was kept alive by his daughter Kalyanididi. His entire family and his devotees were very close to Sri Ma.

Haribabaji Maharaj

Sri Ma had been receiving many messages from Haribabaji Maharaj, the much respected *sanyāsi* of Vrindaban. He and Udiyababaji were well-known *sādhus* in this part of India. Their prestigious Ashram in Vrindaban was the meeting place for many heads of ascetic orders.

At this time Haribabaji was in Bhirauti near Aligarh. He had sent a personal messenger to escort her to this rather remote village. The messenger, Sri Premraj, told her that the whole countryside had heard about her and was eagerly awaiting her visit. Haribabaji had put enthusiasm in the hearts of the people saying if they prayed sincerely Sri Ma would give them *darśana*! The people had started a programme of continuous *kirtan* till such time as Sri Ma would visit their village.

In response to this appeal Sri Ma with a large contingent of devotees left for Bareilly enroute to Bhirauti after the Durgā Pūjā at Allahabad. At Bareilly they changed to a local train and came to a small station called Dhanari. Bhirauti is 7 miles from Dhanari. This distance was usually covered by bullock-carts or simply on foot.

The atmosphere of the miraculous had always surrounded Sri Ma. One rather nice incident took place at this time. A gentleman, Kamal Malaviya of the house of Madan Mohan Malaviya at Allahabad, wished to accompany Sri Ma on her journey to Bareilly. At one of the many stoppages, he along with others gathered as usual in front of Sri Ma's compartment for her *darśana*, returning to his own at the very last moment when the train was in motion. His compartment in the meantime had become full of more travellers many of them standing at the entrance itself. He stood on the footsteps trying to work his way in. The train had picked up speed. After a while there was an extra rough scuffle amongst the set of ruffians who were making trouble; Malaviyaji lost his precarious hold and fell on the stony embankment from the speeding train. As he lay stunned and bruised, he saw dimly the figure of a lady dressed in white, who seemed to be urging him to get up and walk! He somehow managed to do this and followed her shadowy figure along the train track till the twinkling lights of a station became visible. He saw the lady no more. At the station the officials were frankly incredulous of his statement that he had fallen off the running Punjab Mail and had not only survived to tell the tale but had walked some distance also. On examining his ticket, however, they flagged down the next train (the Doon Express) to an unscheduled stop and found a seat for him. On arrival at Bareilly, he was taken to the Railway Hospital on a stretcher because he was, by then, suffering from delayed shock. Some of Sri Ma's people, recognised him as one of their own party and went along to the Hospital to do what they could for him. On his rejoining the party, he was accommodated in Sri Ma's compartment in the local train. Apart from a slight bruise, he had sustained no damaging injury. Later, he related his tale to Didi and others.

At Dhanari, all was ecstatic jubilation. The whole countryside seemed to have assembled to give a fitting welcome to Sri Ma. There were decorated bullock-carts surrounded by *kirtan*-parties. The men-folk in Sri Ma's entourage elected to walk. The women got on to the carts. Sri Ma herself was pursuaded to climb up on to an elephant; she was told that otherwise the people awaiting her arrival so eagerly, would not be able to see her. This regal procession complete with other insignia of a very important personality, advanced toward Bhirauti. It was met half-way by Haribabaji himself with his own *kirtan*-party. Keeping his face toward Sri Ma he walked backward the whole way!

In this style they arrived at Bhirauti and were taken to their resting places. Baandh, the final destination, was another ten miles from Bhirauti. Sri Ma and her companions were taken to see this place also. They went in a procession of bullock carts. The villagers in their enthusiasm unyoked the bullocks and pulled along the carts themselves.

At the first opportunity when Sri Ma could sit with her companions in her room, she started to tease Didi for riding in a cart which was being pulled by men instead of bullocks. She went on laughing at Didi's embarrassment, saying 'Didi, how could you! Sitting there like a *mahārāṇī* while the village people were pulling the cart along!' In vain Didi protested that she never knew that in their enthusiasm the villagers themselves were pulling the carts. She said, 'All I could see was a sea of heads. How was I to know that they had unyoked the animals!'

This entire tract of land comprising of nearly 800 villages at one time used to be inundated by the yearly flooding of the Ganges causing untold misery in terms of loss of life and property. Seeing that the Government was not ready to render help, the two saintly men, who were very close friends, set about the task of erecting an adequate embankment of earth to hold the waters at bay. The entire countryside was mobilised. The *sādhus* themselves carried baskets of earth on their heads to build up the barrier, along with the villagers. All able-bodied men and women and even children took part. In time the 10 mile long *baāndh* (barrier) came up to a height which prevented the flood-waters from ruining the villages. As a consequence the two saints were looked upon as saviours of their land. The life of the villagers was planned around the central event of an ongoing *satsang,* as it were. There was a big hall for daily assemblies, where *kirtan* took place. There was a simple village troupe of artists under the tutelage of Premraj. Each evening short dramas were enacted in the hall based on the lives of Sri Krishna or Gauranga Mahaprabhu, the *Iṣṭa-devatā* of Haribabaji Maharaj. It was discovered that Premraj was very well-read and had done considerable research into relevant Vaiṣṇava literature. Moreover he had a captivating melodious voice. He himself sang the preludes and what may be called 'fillers'.

Sri Haribaba had so set the routines of the *satsaṅga* that villagers had barely time to work in their fields or attend to other household affairs. He kept a strict tally of regular absentees! Sri Ma was told all this by the prominent men of the village knowing that she would appreciate the situation. It was apparent to everyone that they loved Haribaba and would do anything to please him so that he would continue to stay with them. He was in every way the life and soul of Bhirauti and Baandh. Haribabaji played a very crucial role in the development of the way the Ashrams in Sri Ma's name came to organise functions in subsequent years. He became a frequent visitor. Everything was geared up to the standard he himself had set at Bhirauti, in the matter of receptions, arrangement in *satsang* halls, scriptural discourses and so on. He had seemed to be pleased with paper decorations. So whenever he came, Sri Ma would expect the young people of the Ashram to put up banners, festoons of paper-chains, colourful flags and what not. It was very festive. *Sādhus* were received at the station with *kirtan* parties. The daily routine, if Haribabaji was in residence, followed his timings.

On return from Baandh and Bhirauti Sri Ma came to Vindhyachala. Many festivities took place on top of this lonely hill. It was always a matter of astonishment how a large contingent of people were accomodated and provided for in this remote place, but with Sri Ma all things were possible.

The young girls of the Kanyapeeth[4] were now in Vindhyachala for a change of air. Sri Ma would go for walks with them and join in many a game of relay races. Once she visited Varanasi for a short while and attended the *yajña* being performed by Karpatriji Maharaj, Vindhyachala, however remained the venue for a lot of activities over the Christmas holidays.

At the beginning of the year 1945, Sri Ma became *maunam*. Didi understood her *kheyāla* of going to Vrindaban, so the camp at Vindhyachala was abandoned for the time being. At Vrindaban, she met Haribabaji Maharaj again and also Udia Baba. Sri Ma's *maunam* was not quite like other times. Once or twice she would speak for a few minutes.

Sri Ma left Vrindavan soon to travel to Gujrat. She stayed in Ahmedabad for a while. She spoke a few words in Gujrati which delighted the local people. Somebody asked her, 'Ma, why did you become *maunam*?' Sri Ma answered, 'Was I *maunam*? *Maunam* means, to give the mind totally to God. Here, there is no question of a mind - so when I am talking, it is also a case of *maunam*!'

After a couple of weeks it was noticed that there was a pattern to this *maunam* as Sri Ma was observing it; she would speak on Thursdays and next day also but only till the evening. This routine was observed for many months.

From Ahmedabad, Sri Ma travelled to many other places escorted by Kantibhai Munsha and his brother. Sri Ma's *maunam* raised no problems. People would gather to sit in silence for long hours just looking at Sri Ma. Since Sri Ma sat in her usual serene beauty, the people displayed no restlessness. Sometimes the devotees marvelled at Didi's capacity to understand Sri Ma's *kheyāla* under these unusual circumstances, because while Sri Ma was *maunam*, she did not make gestures to make herself understood. Didi would say that it was no credit to her. Sri Ma as if by a mere glance could convey her meaning to the persons concerned. Didi, however, could, and did carry out many complicated programmes, which were an expression of Sri Ma's *kheyāla*. They travelled to Bombay; stayed there for a few hours only. From

Bombay they came to Delhi. Next day Sri Ma travelled to Agra for a few hours. Returning to Delhi they again started for Allahabad the very next day. Here also Sri Ma stayed for just one day. She came to Varanasi and from Varanasi to Vindhyachala. It was just more than one month since she had left it on January 12, 1945. Some of the newcomers in Gujrat had asked Didi as to why Sri Ma kept moving around in this bewildering fashion. Didi replied that many times she had discovered very good reasons for Sri Ma's lightning visits to random places but naturally she could not explain fully Sri Ma's *kheyāla* for the ceaseless wanderings which seemed to be a way of life for her.

Since the *sādhu-sammelana* in Jhunsi, Sri Ma had been almost constantly in the company of the *mahātmās*. Either they visited with her or she was invited to grace many of the functions organised by them. It seemed that they had penetrated the rather off-putting disguise of her female-form; just as way back in Dhaka, the gentlemen had, after a while ceased to be deterred from coming to Shahbagh because Sri Ma was, at that time, a beautiful young woman. Bhaiji had called it 'an effective disguise.'

Haribabaji Maharaj with his formidable entourage of villagers, accompanied Sri Ma on a tour of Bengal in the beginning of 1946. He wished to visit all the sites sacred to the memory of Gauranga Mahaprabhu. This tour was astonishing in its scope, because it tapped the ingenuity and resources of the managers to the utmost. Firstly, the Hindi speaking villagers were truly terrified at the idea of going to Bengal, in their imagination the dark abode of the black magic of Kālī-worshippers! Secondly, the language barrier was impenetrable for many. Thirdly, food habits were wildly dissimilar.

Sri Ma arrived in Bahrampur with this motley crowd and at once an atmosphere of merriment swept over the town; somehow the Bengali populace rose to the challenge of entertaining these devotees of Haribabaji competently and satisfactorily. The mingling of cultures was harmonious. The visitors saw the highly evolved *yātrās* of the Life of Gaurānga Mahāprabhu. Sri Premraj was delighted and learnt the richly stylised tunes of the many *kīrtan*-forms of Bengal. He added to his repertoire, the scenes from the *yātrās*. The Bengalis, on their part watched the *rāslīlā* of Vrindaban; they heard the robust and resounding recitations of the *Hanumāna-chālisā*.

Haribabaji went on to Calcutta and also to Dhaka to visit the Ramna Ashram. This was, incidentally, Sri Ma's last visit to the city where her devotees were living in a state of utter uncertainty. While she was with them they forgot their troubles and crowded round her as usual. Days and nights became one. Sri Ma sat up, talking to them tirelessly. No doubt all of them received advice and instructions regarding their future because right after her visit most of them started to move out of Dhaka.

Haribabaji came to join Sri Ma again in Solon, in the Summer of 1946. Here again occured that commingling of cultures which was so common in Sri Ma's vicinity. Raja Durga Singh was the ruler of his independent Baghat State. His devotion to Sri Ma affected his princely household and all his people. The devotees coming to Solon from all over, for the summer vacation of 1946 will remember the dedicated spirit of service displayed by Deviramji (Raja Sahab's Secretary) Ruparama, (personal servant) and a host of others.

The coming of the *mahātmās* played a significant role in the lives of the devotees. The impromptu nature of Sri Ma's travel itineraries became rare, rather than the norm. Greater stability was given to her programmes. At Solon Haribabaji stayed for more than a couple of months. *Satsangs* became a regular part of the daily routine. It was his practice to start a *satsang* by reading from the Scriptures. At this time Haribaba began to read from the Diaries of Didi Gurupriya regarding Sri Ma's early days in Dhaka. Sri Chakrapaniji and Swami Sharananandaji were also in Solon. Sri Ma spoke at length about her *sādhanā* at Bajitpur and also other matters in answer to their penetrating questions regarding herself. Such *satsangs* came to prevail whenever *mahātmās* came to visit Sri Ma. The management got into the habit of preparing for these visits on a mammoth scale.

References

1. 'Mother Anandamayi - A Great Mystic', *Ma Anandamayi*, Varanasi, 1956. p. 37.
2. Pandit Gopinath Kavirajji 'Mother Anandamayi' *Mother as seen by Her Devotees*, Varanasi, 1946. p. 16.
3. The ochre-robed ascetics form a 'society of sādhus' or a *sādhu-samāj*. All ascetics belong to different brotherhoods originating from the Upaniṣadic tradition. The founders of different brotherhoods or *sampradāyas* are recognised as the great '*Acāryas* or Teachers such as Saṁkarācārya, Rāmānujācārya, Mādhvācārya, Nimbārkacārya and Bhallabhācārya. The *sampradāya* of Gauraṅga Mahāprabhu is not always recognised by the Orthodox systems. Some ascetics wear white clothes.
4. The Kanyapeeth is now permanently housed in the Ashram at Varanasi.

CHAPTER TWELVE
A Harmonious Presence

(Mātṛ - Satsaṅga)

Sri Ma arrives and sits down in her usual place winning everybody's heart by her sweet and gentle smile. For a while there is pin-drop silence. We are spell-bound. No questions occur to us. We feel as if all our problems have already been solved, as if, we had gone beyond the level of questions and answers.

Swami Bhagavatananda Giri
(Kanti Bhai)
June 20, 1955

Sri Ma with Sri Padmanabhan

Sri Ma with Swami Akhandanandaji of Vrindaban.

Sri Ma and Pandit Gopinath Kaviraj

Sri Ma and Swami Muktananda Girī.

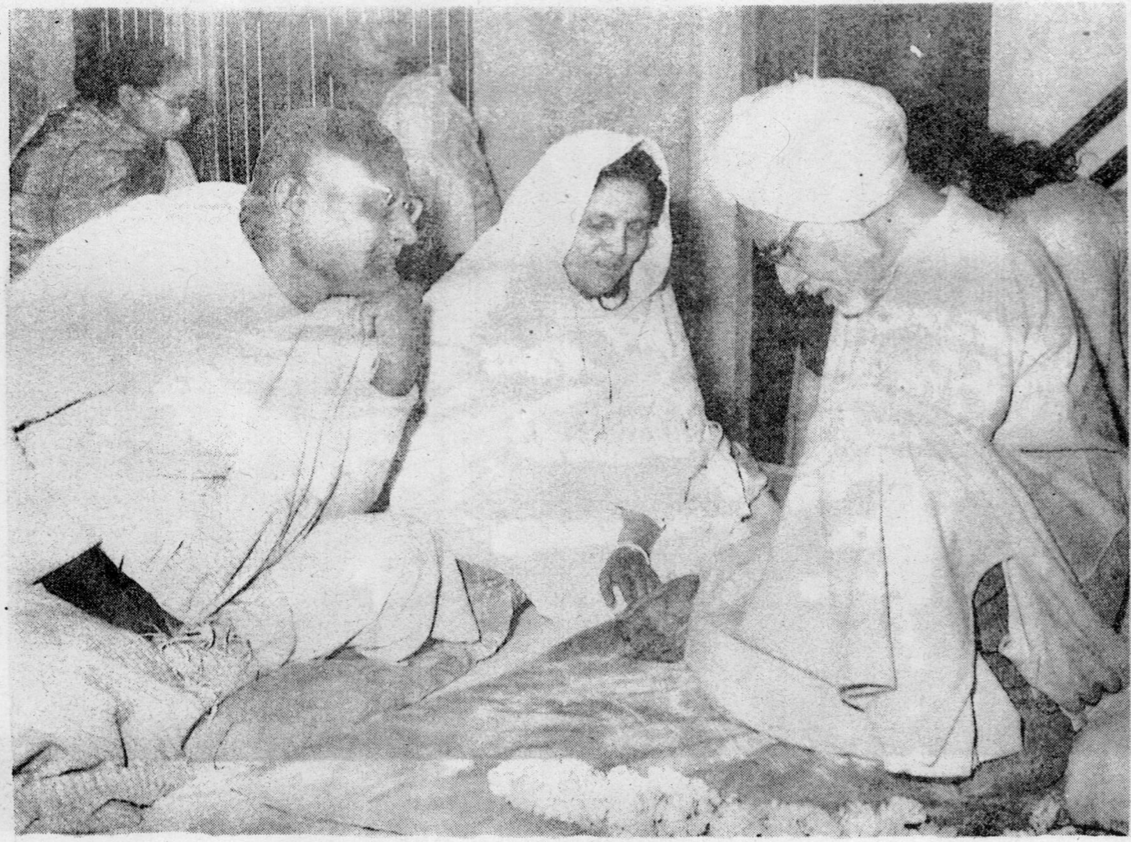

Sri Ma and Haribabaji Maharaj.

A Glimpse of the Sudden Attahasa.

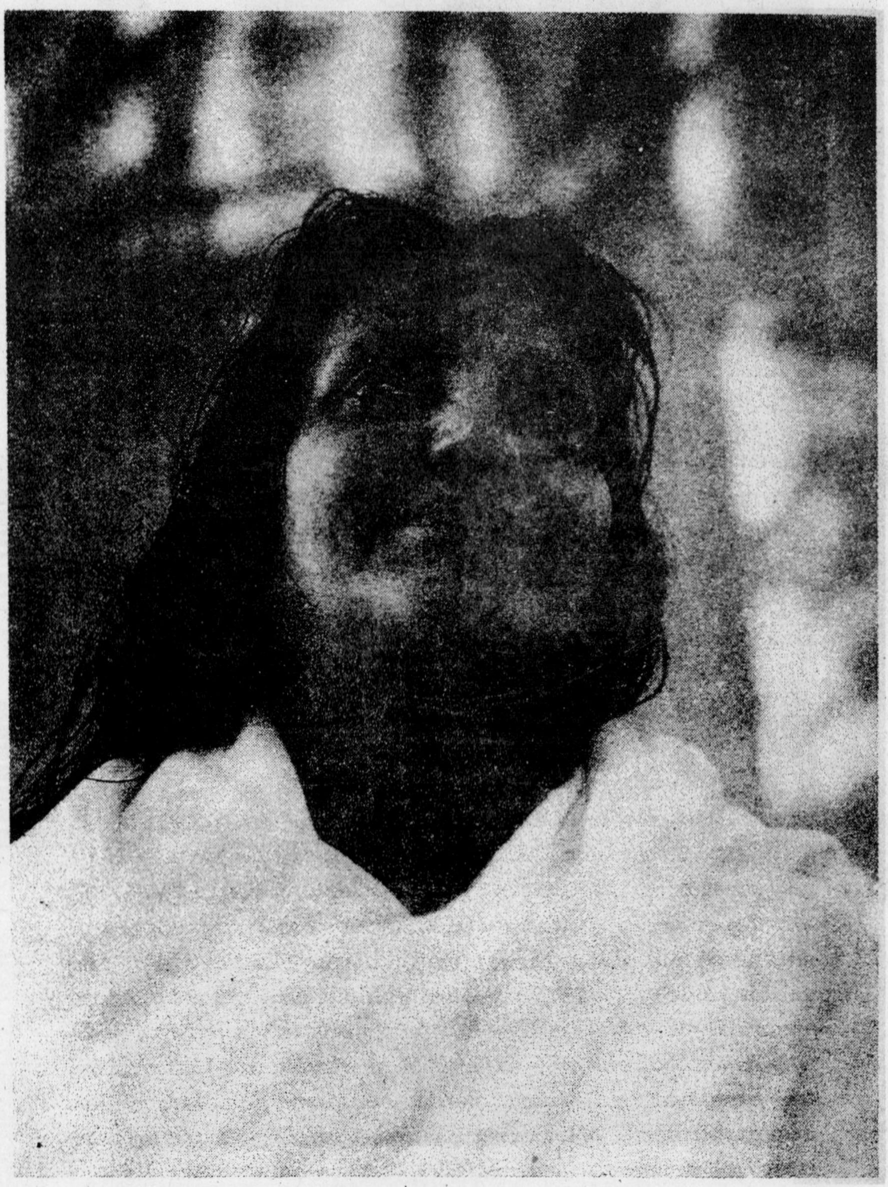

Alone.

See, abstention and indulgence, both are necessary. For example, when a child starts to learn there is only encouragement for him. When he has learnt a little then mistakes are pointed out. Then again when a child is well on his way toward reading correctly, he is given a new lesson to read even if he has committed one or two mistakes in the old one.

So don't sit back thinking I am not ready yet - the errors will fall by themselves. Abstention drives away the springs of desires. Do not waste time!

- Sri Ma Anandamayi[1]

- The Sāvitrī Mahāyajña
- The Conclusion of the Mahāyajña
- Saṃyam Saptāh

A Harmonious Presence

The decade of the Forties was crucial. The war had ravaged Europe. In India the 'Quit India' movement of 1942 had failed with its terrifying consequences of ruthless suppression. Next, India was galvanized when news started filtering in about Subhas Chandra Bose's Indian National Army operating almost on the borders of the country. Japan was crushed by the atom bombs. The Indian National Army or the I.N.A. were not successful in marching on to India to set her free from the British yoke, but they contributed to her freedom in an oblique fashion. The officers of the I.N.A. were brought to India under arrest in 1946 to undergo trial as rebels. They were to be made examples of for the rest of the Army by being court-martialled as deserters. This turned out to be a costly error of judgement on the part of the British. The nation rose as one man to the defence of the Officers. The bulk of the Indian Army had been engaged in various threatres of the war under Allied Command. They were now a force to be reckoned with and did not support the rulers in this matter. Given a chance they would have also become the I.N.A. The trials at the Red Fort in Delhi were hastily brought to an end and the Officers were released to become admired heroes.

History will record whether the deciding factor which made the British quit India in August 1947 was Gandhiji's *satyāgraha*, or the I.N.A. trials or President Roosevelt's pressure or perhaps a combination of the three. Unhappily for India they did not quit gracefully. The conditions of Independence were such that India will be required to pay a price for it for all time to come or so it seemed to those who had the ability to judge such matters. Freedom was not a matter of great jubilation because the country had passed through the heart-breaking carnages in Punjab, Bihar, Bengal especially Noakhali. The massacre of the Hindus prepared the ground for the creation of Pakistan.

Sri Ma was in Varanasi. On August 14, 1947, she sat quietly on the terrace of the Ashram. The inmates decided to sit in meditation all around her at midnight to pray for the new nation which was emerging to face a number of on-going problems.

Varanasi, for many years, before and after Independence remained the venue for various activities. On January 14, 1947 a *yajña* was begun in the newly established Ashram.

The Sāvitrī-Mahāyajña : 1947-1950

A series of fortuitous circumstances so arranged themselves near Sri Ma, that there was serious talk about performing a *yajña* at Varanasi. One devotee promised the supply of fire-wood, another, the *ghee* (rarefied butter) for the purpose. The war had just ended - conditions regarding food and other necessities were far from normal. Didi however, very courageously initiated the undertakaing which at the time seemed to be beyond their meagre resources. Her trust was in Sri Ma's *kheyāla* of a *mahāyajña* which she had spoken about way back in Shahbagh nearly twenty years ago.

A temporary building came up in the middle of the courtyard of the Ashram. Nepal Chandra Chakravarty (later Narayana Swami) was chosen as the main priest for the *yajña*. He was helped by Kamalakanta Brahmachari and Sadananda Brahmachari, one of the students of the Vidyapeeth. From these simple beginnings it grew to be one of the most spectacular events to be organised by the Ashrama because the scope of the *yajña* was vast. The *saṃkalpa*, that is the aim of the *yajña* was 'for the well-being of mankind' (*viśva-kalyāṇa*). For three hours every morning, the inmates of the Ashram got used to the beautiful rhythmic sound of the Gāyatrī Mantra being pronounced in unison by several voices. All details of a Vedic *yajña* were adhered to scrupulously. The *yajña* continued for three years, finishing on January 14, 1950.

During these years Sri Ma visited Varaṇasi very often. The *yajña* was one reason; the other was without doubt the rehabilitation of the many families who had been uprooted from East Pakistan and came as refugees to India. Notwithstanding the difficult conditions sometimes bordering on the dangerous, Sri Ma had not desisted from her programme of ceasless travels. She had repeatedly visited Bengal; Calcutta, Bahrampur, Dhaka and other nearby towns saw her quite often. While she was in residence, the townspeople forgot all their worries and lived in peace and happiness. Where ever she happened to be, her gracious and compassionate presence exercised a beneficial effect. She met all the Indian politicians who rose to power after Independence. Her understanding of all kinds of problems, facing the nation, no doubt gave relief to those who brought them to her.

Amulya Kumar Datta Gupta, used to maintain a diary in which he noted the conversations that took place near Sri Ma. His words written during this time in his journal echo the cries of distress ringing everywhere.

'Drastic changes were taking place in India. The policy of the British was to divide and rule. The implanted seed of hatred for the Hindus in the Muslims was so nurtured under the leadership of Jinnah that it had grown into a gigantic tree which threatened to darken the horizons for ever. Man had descended to a level many degrees lower than animals. The terrifying carnage of Calcutta, Bihar, Noakhali made us come to the unhappy conclusion that in this divisive holocaust, whatever is distinctive would perish in the tradition of Bharatvarṣa (India). Mahatma Gandhi and the other leaders agreed to the partition to save the country from a further blood-bath. ... this did not happen ... instead of the cruel killings coming to an end they increased in intensity. Realizing that Punjab had become nothing but a theatre for the barbaric atrocities indulged in by Pakistan, thousands began to flee across the border .. In East Pakistan those who were clinging to their own ways of life, felt compelled to uproot themselves...'

Prabhudatta Brahmachariji was almost beside himself with grief. He said to Sri Ma, 'I wish I could help my people, but what can I do ... I am an ascetic and a mendicant... But at least I can go and mingle my tears with theirs....'

From the vantage point of the ninetees it becomes clear that Sri Ma's emergence into the limelight of general recognition all over the country was of considerable moment at this time. Like a sure-footed gazelle She travelled lightly from one corner of the country to the other. She did not assume the role of a Guru or even a Teacher of spiritual knowledge. She was more like the mirror-image of one's innermost being (*antaryamin*) glimpsed imperfectly but recognized immediately as such. For thousands she was the one source of courage and hope when the future seemed lost in uncertainties.

Many more of the devotees of Dhaka came away leaving their homeland under the direst conditions. Amulya Kumar's friend Manmohan Ghosh, the Steward of Dhaka University also came to Varanasi. The two friends decided to settle down in Varanasi in the hope that they would be able to see Sri Ma quite often. The Images in the Temple at Ramna Ashram had been brought over to Varanasi; the statue of Baba Bholanath was taken to Calcutta.

A new era in *satsangs* began with the coming of Amulya Kumar. It so happened that a congenial group of men began to gather in the Hall at the Ashram. Sri Ma would sit there for many hours, holding discussions or answering questions. Sri Ma knew that this was a rewarding way of life for many, especially Amulya Kumar. After the satsang he would go home and write out in longhand the entire discussion complete in its question/answer form.[2] This became the mainspring of his life till his death in 1972. If not in actual fact then in spirit both he and Manmohan Ghosh became renunciates, more dedicated than many in formal ochre-robes.

The nucleus of the *satsang* remained rather constant: Amulya Kumar, Deva Shankar, Vaidyanath Shastri, Swami Shankarananda and Sanyal Mahashaya. Sometimes Dr. Pannalal, Gopal Thakur from Allahabad and others would augment the group of interlocuters. The audience which generally participated by listeing only was always such as to overflow the Hall. We quote from some of Amulya Kumar's books:

'Deva Shankar Babu has been worrying this theme for the last few days. He again asked, '*japa* and meditation depend upon an object. So if one continues with a duality how can one be established in the One?'

Sri Ma: Your question is: 'The mantra is after all a sound, and meditation is merely an imagination of a form. Man being thus bound by the name/form syndrome how does he overcome it?'

Deva Shankar Babu: 'Yes!'

Sri Ma: 'Don't you apply soap to cleanse yourself? First the soap, then the water. If there is no water available nobody would use soap!

'How wonderful is God's creation. If one proceeds on a spiritual path aiming at God-realization, devoting onself to *nāma-japa* and meditation, the Ganga of knowledge wells forth; it washes away nescience and reveals The Truth of the Self. If one is devoted to the aim of God-realization then he can rid himself of duality. This is one way; there is the other way of discrimination, 'not this,' 'not this', but discrimination is at the level of the mind; the mind is synonymous with duality. Therefore, while one is a pilgrim engaged in *sādhanā* no matter which path one follows, one perforce must work with the mind - at the proper time - the pilgrim attains the state of no-mind and that is, when Self is realized.'

'What about the pilgrims who walk on the path of enjoying a duality - the *līlā* of creator and creation?'

'The duality inherent in *līlā* is not a hindrance to the realization of the One. Where it is found to be a hindrance, know that to be the stage of seeking for fulfilment. It is *bādhaka* (hindrance) for the *sādhaka* only; not for he who has arrived at the goal!'

On another day, a young man from the audience asked a question.

'In order to find God, is it necessary to inflict suffering on the body?'

Sri Ma said, 'Under no circumstances is it necessary to inflict suffering on the body.'

'Can God be found without suffering?'

Sri Ma: 'God-realization is a different matter. One has no right to make the body suffer under any condition. Why not? There is a reason for this. To whom does the body belong? He, who has created this body, He has given this form, so that you may render service. The body is God's dwelling place, keep it clean, keep it pure, keep it undefiled. God resides in this body, it is His abode. Try to live in His presence, yearn for His presence. You have no right to inflict suffering on the body.'

Question: 'If the body has been defiled, one may feel like finishing with it altogether?'

Sri Ma: 'No. Even to think of such a thing is a grievous sin. True repentence is a cleansing agent of infinite power. Do not the saints say that man cannot possibly commit so much sin that it may not be washed away by God's Grace?'

'Do not be thinking of sins; nobody should think of themselves as sinners. You are in reality the 'sons of Immortality 'but you don't know this at present. God's mercy is all-encompassing. If one concentrates on living steadfastly in the light of God's presence, fills his heart with thoughts of Him, then there will be no danger of erring. He Himself will see to the cleansing of His devotee. Faith is all that is required of you.'

Another extract from the same writings:

Gopal Thakur had come from Allahabad on the occasion of the *Gītā-jayanti.* He performs this function with great devotion and dedication. His conversations with Sri Ma are always enjoyable:

Gopal Thakur: 'We all have been talking away for so long... not it's your turn.'

Sri Ma: 'Baba! this is a clean slate - there is nothing here!'

Gopal Thakur: 'And we are very knowledgeable! Yet everyone flocks to you, why?'

Sri Ma: 'Oh! The people come to listen to the *Gītā-jayanti.*'

Gopal Thakur: 'Indeed! Actually I arrange to hold the *Gītā-jayanti* here, because I know I shall get a large audience!'

Sri Ma: 'You know, there could be a reason for people to come to me. Isn't it true that those who drink like to get together - so those who have nothing, come to me who also is in that group!'

Gopal Thakur: 'A person with such understanding will be rare. Most people come here in the hope of getting something from you but they have to go back empty-handed.'

Sri Ma: 'But this coming also is not entirely unprofitable?'

Gopal Thakur: 'No doubt. But if one comes to an ordinary person and receives a little something, it is a matter of satisfaction. If one goes to a Royal presence and comes away with a penny it seems rather like a joke!' (Everyone laughs)

Sri Ma: Looking round at his disciples- 'Remember these words spoken by Baba. Don't be satisfied by a penny, extract the riches from his store.'

One of them said: 'We are not capable. Why don't you forcibly give us your blessings?'

Sri Ma: 'See Baba, you are required to give of your plenty to your disciples!'

Gopal Thakur: 'This is most interesting! How did the whole thing devolve on me? And is it possible to give forcibly? If one enters the water to bathe, it is one thing, if he is flung in, it is quite a different matter!'

Sri Ma: 'Not really, because he does get wet, doesn't he?' (Everyone laughs)

I saw that to-day we would have no serious conversation.

The uprooted people of East Pakistan gradually came to believe that perhaps 'the distinctive tradition of Bhāratvarṣa' would not disappear without a trace in the seething cauldron of changing times. No doubt a future generation will be able to assess the true value of Sri Ma's steadying influence on our country at this time.

The conclusion of the Sāvitrī Mahāyajña

The best years for the new Ashram at Varanasi began with the concluding function (*pūrṇāhuti*) of the Akhaṇḍa Mahāyajña on January 14, 1950. Around 5000 devotees from all corners of India flocked to Varanasi. The concourse of ordinary people mingled with the princely families from the Independent States of India. Above all, the mammoth gathering came in touch with eminent Sādhus and Mahātmās some of them from their remote retreats in the Himalayas. Sri Ma's invitation to witness the final function of the Vedic Yajña was answered by all who received it. Panu Brahmachari and Mrinmaya Brahmachari (Chinmayananda) made arrangements for the board and lodging of all guests, a marathon task accomplished successfully as they experienced from day to day, due to Sri Ma's *kṛpā* (grace) alone.[4]

This splendid function brought the family of devotees together in an unprecedented manner. The need for a central body or committee was felt keenly which resulted in the creation of the Sri Sri Anandamayi Sangha in 1950. Later, a quarterly magazine called *Ananda Varta* came into being in 1952, in order that news about Sri Ma's travels and other information could reach all concerned.

The decade of the fifties was a time of Sri Ma's response to various invitations for her presence at many functions throughout the country. Whoever invited her knew that at least one hundred or more people, men, women and children would have to be provided for. The extent of the festivals grew in scope day by day. The range of hosts was also varied, from eminent *mahātmās,* to ruling Princes, wealthy business men and also common people who pooled together their resources. Sri Ma was also seen to visit any devotee's house who singly had made arrangements on a small scale. At such times she arrived with just one or two close companions.

A new orientation in festivals was marked by Sri Ma's Birthday Celebration in the Punjab in May 1951. Haribabaji and Sri Krishnananda Avadhootji made all arrangements for her reception on a gigantic scale. The whole countryside was mobilised for the purpose. Sardar Sadhu Sing of Jullundhar and his four sons who had been named Ram, Lakshmana, Bharata and Satrughna by Sri Ma, were already well-known to the family of devotees. They received Sri Ma at Jullundhar Station. Thereafter she was taken in a suitable procession to the Savitri Ashram. In this Ashram, Sri Ma was given the same place of honour as the Holy Granth Sahab.[5]

Sri Haribabaji was waiting for her with a band party as well his own *kirtan*-party. Thus Sri Ma was taken in a procession to his Guruji's Sacchidananda Ashram. After a welcome *ārati* and *pūjā* Sri Ma was escorted to a newly constructed house. Perfect arrangements for board and lodging had been made for Sri Ma's retinue of a heterogeneous crowd. All this was very remarkable because the entire festival was being arranged by *sādhus*! Generally, the lay public caters to the comforts of the *sādhus.* Now matters were reversed. The devotees who had come from other towns were amazed to see the quality of management at every level. Sri Krishnananda Avadhutaji was not only a renunciate of utter dispassion but also a remarkable man of action where a large-scale organization was concerned.

Sri Ma's Birthday Celebrations were observed in Hoshiarpur, Jullundhar, Doraha and finally concluded at Ambala on May 24, 1951. There was a crowd of more than 10,000 people in the Sanatana Dharma Sabha Temple, to hear Sri Ma's voice and have her *darśana*. The flower decorations, the music and the orations of the Mahatmas captivated all hearts. It was a very successful function.

As one of the features of the manifaceted celebration, food and gifts were distributed to many Institutes for the poor including a Leper Colony. When Sri Ma entered the precincts, the inmates gave her a heartfelt welcome. One boy stood forth and recited hymns in Sanskrit with a perfect pronunciation. Sri Ma approached him and embraced him lightly, touching his head with her hand.[6]

After the Birthday celebrations Sri Ma travelled to Amritsar and thereafter to Mandi. The Raja Sahab and his officers were waiting for Sri Ma at Gurdaspur. The party reached Baijnath from Gurdaspur on 29th May. At the earnest request of the Rani of Kashmir, Sri Ma was escorted to her residence by the Raja Sahab of Mandi. Thereafter he himself drove her to his capital city. He stopped the car at many places, where people had gathered to have a *darśana* of Sri Ma. It was 10 p.m. when the palace was reached. Sri Ma stayed here for a fortnight. All arrangements were on a princely scale. At the request of the Rani of Mandi the Delhi Party of *kirtan* singers arrived to perform their special programme of a *nāma-yajña*.

The State of Suket adjoins Mandi. Sri Ma visited the Raja Sahab of Suket also for one day. She returned to Mandi and stopped again at Baijnath to be with the Rani of Kashmir, on her way down from Mandi to Amritsar. Sri Ma and her considerable party arrived at Kishenpur on 22nd June. After only two days Sri ma left for Varanasi. From 30th June Bhagavat Saptah was observed at the Ashram. After this programme Sri Ma accompanied by only a few people went to Chhapra (Bihar) at the pressing invitation of Krishna Sheopuri. This was a simple household where arrangements were just adequate. To Ma it was the same whether she was at Mandi, Ambala or at Chhapra. She returned to Varanasi on 17th July. Guru Pūrṇimā was observed on 18th July at the Ashram.

On August 9, Sri Ma went to Deoghar. Sri Pran Gopal had been ailing for some time. Sri Ma visited him for a short while; she left for Calcutta the same day and returned to Varanasi the very next day. Sri Ma paid her annual visit to Allahabad for three days in the beginning of September. A Bhagavat Jayanti was celebrated in the Varanasi Ashram by Sri Kumar Bhattacharya. After this function Sri Ma went to Vindhyachala for a rest, but after only three days she travelled to New Delhi to see Dr J.K. Sen who was seriously ill. After a day at the capital, Sri Ma went to Etawah for three days. She returned to Varanasi before the Annual Dūrgā Pūjā which was celebrated here by the sons of late Sri Pran Kumar of Calcutta in October 1951.

Saṃyam Saptāh (week of austerities)

In answer to Sri Ma's constant requests for a daily routine which would include a prayer session, many people were heard to say that they found it very difficult to break the habits of a life time. Busy schedules held a rhythm of their own. Even if one tried to snatch a few minutes, the mind was nowhere near a peaceful state.

Sri Ma frequently spoke words of encouragement for such problems: All right, if your time is taken up by your everyday. occupations and thoughts at least you can set apart certain days and dedicate them entirely to the 'supreme quest'. She would elaborate on the *saṃyam-vrata* for one day for everyone. Out of this originated the idea of a *saṃyama-saptāh* to be organised by the newly created central Body of Organizers, named the Shree Shree Anandamayee Sangha. The Raja of Solon, Durga Singh had been unanimously elected to the position of President after it was vacated by the First President Rajmata Ananda Priya of Tehri Garhwal. Yogibhai (as he was known more familiarly) submitted his proposal that a week-long programme of *saṃyam* be chalked out; all devotees would be invited to join in. The first venue and dates were decided upon after due consultation with concerned organisers. The first week of *saṃyam-saptāh* was held at the Varanasi Ashram from August 6, 1952.

This initial experiment proved such a success that even now it is the most well-attended function in the Ashram. All devotees feel the living presence of Sri Ma once more; the Mahatmas, dutifully attend the Saṃyam saptāh, demonstrating that they also believe in Sri Ma's all-permeating grace for this occasion when for a short while, everyone becomes an ideal ascetic

A quote from the diary of a participant:

The '*saṃyam vrata*' started after a night of vigil, entirely spent in *kirtana* and meditation, as it was both Jhulan Purnima and a lunar eclipse; and the week terminated with *pūjā* and *Kirtan*, throughout the night of Janmasthami.

Every morning at 3.30 a.m. the rising bell called us from our short rest. Several times Mother Herself attended the *usha kirtan* at 4 a.m. After the usual morning ablutions we were at our individual *pūja, japam* and meditation and at any other time we could spare throughout the day.

Two and three quarter hours were spent daily in silent meditation in Mother's presence; 8-9 a.m., 3-4 p.m., 8.45-9 p.m. and 11.45-0.15 a.m. After the reading from the Gītā in the morning, Mother usually replied to questions, or related incidents from Her early life (on being asked) or Sri Krishnanandaji Avadhut spoke. In the afternoon the Bhagavata was read and then Sri Krishnanandaji Avadhut gave some inspiring and instructive talks explaining the meaning of *saṃyam-vrata* about *sādhanā*, about the attitude of the *sādhaka* and other similar topics which gave much practical help to the aspirants.

Sri Gopinath Kaviraj had written out a few simple but very useful instructions about *āsana, japa* and meditation which were read out and discussed. He also came in person on two or three occasions. Many residents of Banaras joined the *satsang* enthusiastically and kept up the food restrictions and rules of behaviour in their own homes.

Mother was present regularly at the long hours of Satsang from 7.45 to 11.30 or 11.45 a.m.; from 2.45 to 5.30 p.m. and at the evening kirtan for at least an hour or more. Again at 9.30 p.m people gathered round Mother informally for half an hour or so on the open platform overlooking the Ganges. There the happenings of the day were discussed and suggestions made for the next day.

There were three categories of diet to choose from. Class A kept fasts on Ganges water on the 1st and 7th days, had one meal of rice and fruit boiled in milk, without sugar, on the 2nd and 6th days and rice with vegetables once daily on 3rd, 4th and 5th days. Class B had rice, *roṭi*, vegetable stew and curds at midday and milk at night. Class C the same with *dāh.* added.

There was no time to feel hungry in between, and in general everyone felt fitter and stronger than usual. Mother herself gave minute instruction as to how the food was to be prepared and by whom, and went round daily whilst meals were served. As usual, but more obvious than at other times Mother was everywhere, supervised everything and gave everyone the guidance and assistance needed.

I do not think it an exaggeration to say that in that week we gained something lasting, a new strength in the search after Truth, a greater certainty of purpose. We got a taste of how wonderful life can be, when it is spent in Satsang, every minute dedicated to the search of God.'[7]

Surprisingly, the largest group of the participants opted for class A. One day after the session of meditation in the morning Sri Ma broke the silence humming in a soft voice a bewitching tune. After a few minutes some words could be made out namely:

he hitaḥ, he pitaḥ, he brahmatattvaṃ
he hitaḥ, he pitaḥ he brahmabhutaṃ
he hitaḥ, he pitaḥ he brahmasvarūpaṃ

Sri Ma signalled to Bibhu Brahmachari to pick up the tune and sing the words with her.

Later Sri Ma said that she had 'seen' a young boy sitting near her, dressed in brownish clothes and singing these words in the tune which she had repeated audibly after the hour of meditation was over. The tune somehow was difficult and nobody but Bibhu Brahmachari could repeat it after her. Sri Ma incorporated this item for all such future weeks; Bibhu Brahmachari alone would sing it in his very melodious and deep voice. Later she named other singers who were entitled to sing it but only during the *saṃyam saptāha* and in Bibhu's absence. These were Brahmacharini Pushpa or Kanti or Chhabi Banerjee.

Another 'First' happened during this *saṃyam saptāh*. The well-known ascetic Sri Shankar Bharati of Lalita Ghat, Varanasi came to the Ashram during a *satsang* session. He stood quietly near the staircase for a few minutes and then went away. Only Sri Ma took note of this short visit. The scholars of Varanasi held him in high respect for his vast knowledge of the *śāstras*, his ascetic way of life and his simplicity. He came very close to Sri Ma over the years. Once, his disciples had called in Dr Gopal Dasgupta, an eminent doctor of the town to treat him for some stomach trouble. The doctor was amazed to discover that his meals consisted of a boiled concoction of the leftover vegetables from a daily market near Lalita Ghat. Dr Dasgupta reported this to Sri Ma who arranged for a wholesome simple meal to be taken to him every day and this he accepted till the time of his passing away.

He was not in the habit of minding anyone regarding his own welfare except what he knew to be the 'will' of his *Iṣṭa-devatā*, the Goddess Lalita of the Temple where he lived. He came to identify Lalita Devi with Sri Ma and abided by her instructions during the short period of his remaining days. Because of his erudition he was regarded by the scholars as an incarnation of the Ādi Śaṁkarācārya.

References

1. D.D. Vol. III, p. 651.
2. These invaluable notes have already been published in many volumes as *Sri Ma Anandamayi Prasanga*.
3. These families were known to us because they came to Varanasi. Many more would have similar tales to relate regarding Sri Ma's continuing sustaining grace on families settling elsewhere.
4. Didi Gurupriya wrote a book called *Akhanda Mahayajña* (in Bengali) describing the amazing concurrence of events which brought about the fulfilment of Sri Ma's *kheyāla* of a *mahāyajñā* expressed in Dhaka after the Kālipūjā of 1926.
5. Even now Sri Ma's room and chair is maintained in the same reverential manner, in this Ashram. Many devotees go to Jullundhar on a pilgrimage to this site of Sri Ma's *līlā*.
6. Sri Avadhutaji wrote to say that a miracle had been witnessed by the people of Ambala. The leper boy had been cured completely. This amazing incident had been written up in the daily News Papers. Ananda Varta Vol. I, No. 2, p. 34.
7. Atmanandaji, *Ananda Varta* 1953, pp. 50-52.

CHAPTER THIRTEEN

A Confluence of Many Streams

It happened that I was asked to speak before the gathering one evening. I was told that Mother would give me part of her time in the programme. I was introduced to the assembly as a disciple of Pitaji Yogananda. I told the audience about Master's limitless love for the Divine Mother, about his great task in the West to spread the message of Yoga. Then I dwelt on the duty of disciples - the duty to take up the mission of the Guru with ever-increasing zeal and selflessness. Having seen in India how devoutly saints are worshipped, I reminded the gathering that it is not enough to praise these saints and to seek their *darśana*; that we the devotees and disciples must use our lives rightly by striving to follow in their footsteps... The best way, by which we can truly appreciate what the great ones like my blessed Gurudev and Ananda Mayi Ma and other holy ones have to give us, is to become like them. I finished by saying that the only mission of such holy beings is to rouse in us the desire to find the Beloved in us.

- Daya Mata (Feb., 1959)

President, Yogada Satsang Society of India and Self-RelizationFellowship of America

How much more time will you spend at a wayside inn? Don't you want to go home? How exquisite it all is ... One is in his own self, the wanderer, the exile, the home-coming and the home... oneself is all that exists...

- Sri Ma Anandamayi

* Sri Ma's second visit to South India
* The Pūrṇa Kumbha at Prayāg

A confluence of Many Streams

Sri Ma's second visit to South India

Sri Haribabaji was keen to see the Temples of South India and an elaborate itinerary was drawn up by knowledgeable people. Sri Ma's devotees took it upon themselves to make all suitable arrangements. Sri Ma, when travelling at her own *kheyāla* never depended upon anyone for anything but she was very mindful of the conveniences of the Mahātmās travelling with her. Apart from Sri Haribabaji and many of his disciples, the party also consisted of Sri Avadhutji, Swami Paramananda, Brahmacharis Kusum, Bibhu and Kamalakanta, Didi Gurupriya and Buni.

Sri Thakurbhai and Kantibhai Munshaws of Ahmedabad had organised the first and last parts of the journey. On arrival at Waltair, they found a reception committee waiting for them, who escorted them to a *Dharmaśālā*. While everyone was busy settling down, Sri Ma quietly left the inn with Shashadhar Bhattacharya (a devotee from Calcutta) and after wandering round the city arrived at a place called Shanti Ashram. The inmates were full of joy at Sri Ma's unexpected visit. They said that at first all arrangements had been made for her to stay at Shanti Ashram but much to their disappointment plans were changed at the very last minute!

Sri Ma strolled on to the settlement of the fishermen and started a *kirtan* to attract them out of their huts. Soon a crowd was round Ma singing *kirtan*. Sri Ma invited them all to come to the *Dharmaśālā* in the evening, which they did with their wives and children. A lot of fruits and sweets were distributed to them as *prasāda*. Sri Ma and the fishermen and their families were happy with each other.

Sri Ma and party went on to Bezwada and from there to Guntur. The devotion of the reception committees was heart-warming, although language became a barrier for conversational exchanges.

Sri Ma and Sri Haribabaji arrived in Madras on 27th October 1952. Ms. Talyarkhan had taken it upon herself to look after this phase of Sri Ma's journey. She had given thought to every detail of it. Sri Ma was received at the Railway Station to the sound of a band and the attendance of the elite of the town. The well-known scholar, Professor T.M.P. Mahadevan had written an article about Sri Ma and her visit which had been published in the Sunday Times, so that Madras in a way was ready for her *darśana*.

When Sri Ma had taken her seat in front of the rooms prepared for her, ten brahmins recited hymns from the Vedas and gave her the traditional welcome of the *purṇakumbha*. From the next day visits began to one famous temple after another - the first naturally being the Kapaleshwar Temple in the heart of the city. Thereafter the Temple of Venkateshwara. The northerners were impressed by the magnificence of these Temples, permanent monuments to the devotion of the Kings of the South.

In the evening Sri Ma visited Sir C.P. Ramaswamy Aiyer in response to a pressing invitation from him. He seemed very devoted and his family made her especially welcome and in turn the people in her party were glad to make the acquaintance of this exceptional man.

Sri Ma had a busy schedule. She visited the Sri Ramakrishna Mission where Swami Shuddhasattvanandaji received her with great pleasure. He conversed with her for a while and made her eat a little fruit from his hands. Ms. Talyarkhan took the whole party to Adyar to visit the Theosophical Society. She had not informed anybody about Sri Ma's visit - so here Sri Ma walked around for a while in very peaceful and quiet surroundings.

Next day, that is on 29th October they went to Kanchipuram a distance of about 60 miles. Sri Ma and her attendants had *darśana* of the Śiva and Viṣṇu Temples. Everywhere the priests were ready to receive her and show her the Images with special care. The vast Temple precincts are awe-inspiring. There is no electricity inside the inner sanctums. The Images are made visible by lighting oil lamps or camphor *āratis*.

They were told about an old mango tree in front of the Temple which is considered to be the repository of the four Vedas, because the same tree produces mangoes of four different kinds. One mango is taken from the tree every day for offering to Śiva inside the Temple.

After Śivakāñci and various other smaller shrines they had *darśana* of Kāmākṣi Devī. The beautiful Image captivated the hearts of the onlookers.

The Temple of Viṣṇu was equally gorgeous and overwhelming. Sri Ma was shown the fan which Sri Yamunācārya used to wave for a while near the Image everyday. It is preserved carefully in the Temple. The Image was huge, more than life-size. It was so covered with precious ornaments that it seemed to emanate an aura of light. This is the visible Image for the *darśana* of the pilgrims. There is another Image of Sri Varadarajan above in an inner sanctum. There are 25 steps to this room. It is said that each step symbolizes the sacred syllables of the Gāyatrī Mantra.

Ms. Talyarkhan had enlisted the help of the Minister concerned, Sri Vishwanathan who had himself come to visit Sri Ma and made kind enquiries regarding her requirements. In consequence the management committees of Temples knew beforehand Sri Ma's probable time of visit. Everywhere the priests received her with all due Temple honours. Sri Ma was taken to see the residence and birth place of Sri Ramanujacharya the great Vaiṣṇava Teacher of the South.

Sri S.S. Cohen wrote an article about Sri Ma's visit to Madras and Tiruvannamalai.[1] Some exerpts are taken from this article:

'Ms. F. Taleyarkhan of Ramanashram had met Sri Mataji last year in Delhi, and had taken a promise that if she ever blessed South India by a visit, she (Taleyarkhan) should be given the chance to serve Her by making all the arrangements necessary for Her stay etc... The people of the city (of Madras) poured in their hundreds to have Mataji's *darśana* ... Her appearance, Her magnetic personality and Her sweet conversation charmed everyone and attracted big audiences (p. 55). On the night of October 29, Sri Mataji for the first time answered questions in public. The talk was opened by a young lady who wanted to know the remedy for the fainting spells she had contracted almost from childhood, and which used to seize her whenever she heard *bhajans*, attended *pūjā* or concentrated on the statue of Sri Krishna in her house. Mataji cross-examined her, and for ten minutes gave her full explanation of the import of her complaint and finally extorted her to practice self-control. 'As' she argued, 'you remain unconscious during these spells, and as they have after all this long time caused you no spiritual progress, nor furthered your *sādhanā*, you should consider them unfavourable and you should therefore make an effort to steady yourself whenever the impulse to faint begins to be felt. Take to *japaṃ* and strengthen your mind by repeating God's name', and placing Her hand on the shoulder of the young lady, Mataji smilingly and with extreme tenderness, said, 'You have had the *darśana* of Sri Krishna, now I must have your *darśana*', and folded her hands in salutation. The young lady burst into tears out of excessive joy. At this stage a voice asked:

'What is the easiest way to God?

'Profuse tears!' (Everybody laughed with Sri Ma)

'And if tears do not come?'

'Then you should seek the company of those who shed tears, namely *satsang*. This is the easiest way to God through love and devotion.'

On 30th October Sri Ma and the Mahatmas visited the Gaudiya Math; Haribabaji was specially pleased to see the Temple of his own *Iṣṭa-devatā*.

A disciple of Sri Ramana Maharshi Sri Rama Rao (A judge of Madras High Court) had invited Sri Ma to grace the monthly meeting of Raman-Bhajanas at his house. Sri Ma sat on a sofa in a flower-decked marquee which had been put up in the extensive gardens of the house. Scores of Brahmins recited Vedic verses and Upadesa Sāraṃ, a composition by the saint himself. It was a very beautiful function.

The next day Sri Ma and her companions visited Mahabalipuram and the renowned Pakshitirtham. The legend says that two rishis are continuing with their *tapasyā* (austerities) in the visible form of the two large birds which come daily to partake of the food offered to them flying in from the Himalayas.

Sri Haribabaji and Avadhutaji went on an extensive tour of other famous sites on November 1st; Sri Ma had the *kheyāla* to stay quietly at Abbotsbury, the name of the house where she was putting up. The local people were becoming a little disheartened that they had no opportunities to sit with her or talk with her. May be this brought about her *kheyāla* of staying in. In the evening some questions were asked in the *satsang*:

Q: 'How much striving is necessary in order to reach God? Is it not better to put one's trust in God instead?'

Sri Ma: 'Unless He makes it possible for you to put your trust in Him, you cannot do it. What is striving? (Willed action) Whatever action He makes you perform can be converted into your striving.'

Q: 'Ma, tell us why we are attracted to transient objects? Why don't we feel attracted toward the permanent source of Peace?'

Sri Ma: 'This is His *līlā*. He is having a game with Himself. Even so, does not the *Dūrgā-Saptaśatī* say, 'In the guise of delusion it is You only.' It is He who is manifest in the form of these distractions. It is to be remembered, however, that if one is attached to worldly things, he is going toward losing himself; if one is attracted to God then that leads to liberation! Bliss! If you stay with the world, it means you are purchasing a 'return-ticket!' An endless rhythm of going and coming, coming and going!'

Sri Ma paused for a while and then said,

'You see, it is all infinite. Non-finite, that which has no end (that is in both directions). This is the reason why I say to all of you to persevere with God's name. Do it quietly, hiding it within yourself. Public demonstration (of *sādhanā*) is not desirable. This human body is a precious gift. Do not waste it away recklessly. Just as you breathe normally, so try to practice the *nāma-japa* (a constant rhythm). The body, after all is changing all the time. First it was small, now it is an adult. This development, this growth should be directed toward that which is good, auspicious, beneficial otherwise it will be just suicide - nothing else (the failure to realize the Self in this life).

This small girl does not know how to give lectures or discourses. As your little daughter and friend (to young people) it is my childish demand that you stay with His Name always.

The congregation became silent and contemplative after these words.

The next few days were spent in touring nearby places. Sri Ma and the Mahatmas visited Pondichery and had an audience with the Mother at the Ashram.

The next major place of pilgrimage was the world-renowned Temple of Cidambaram. Cidambaram is 75 miles from Pondichery. Five Śivaliṅgas are extolled in the South as the representatives of the five elements of the cosmic process: In Śivakāñci, Śiva is in the form of Earth (*kṣitimurti*), as Water in Jambukeshwara (*apmurti*) as Energy in Arunachalam (*tejamurti*) as Wind in Kalahasti (*marutmurti*) and Space (Intellect) at Cidambaram (*vyomamurti*). Śiva is here identified with Formless Intellect (enlightenment), therefore, the Temple is called Cidambaram (*cit* Intellect *ambara* sky). The legend says that Śiva disappeared in Formless-Intellect after his Dance of Annihilation or the Dance of Creation of all forms. The Temple contains the Image of Śiva as Naṭarāja.

Next to the Temple of the Nataraja there is the equally massive Image of Govindaraja, a Viṣṇu murti. The northerners were interested to see that Saivaites first visited the Śiva Temple turning aside from the Image of Viṣṇu. On their way out they paid their homage to Govindaraja. The Vaiṣṇavites followed the opposite procedure, but both Images are in the same Temple and worshipped by everyone. The Temple precincts were impressive; all Temples were of exquisite workmanship and built on grand scales. Every pillar, every hall or corridor was replete with legendary history coming down from pre-historic epic times. An overwhelming experience for all pilgrims.

On November 4 Sri Ma and her company came to Tiruvannamalai.

S.S. Cohen writes, 'Mataji was scheduled to arrive at Tiruvannamalai the same day, the 4th, at 12.30 midday. Taleyarkhan in concert with the Trustees of the big Arunachaleshwar temple and the local officials prepared to receive Her with temple honours. But exactly at 11 a.m. i.e 90 minutes before the scheduled time, Her car quietly glided into Ramanashram; thus leaving Trustees, officials, elephants and priests cooling their heels in the shade of trees on the Cidambaram high road, waiting for Her, totally unaware of Her early arrival.

'A few minutes afterwards She went around the Ashram to see the places sanctified by the holy presence of Sri Ramana Bhagavan in His life-time. Before His *samādhi*, She reverently stood with folded hands, and enquired about how the sacred body had been buried, and whether there was a *liṅgaṃ* on the *samādhi.* The *liṅgaṃ* She could not see because it was covered with flower garlands...

'All the Ashram devotees and many members of the Managing Committee who had come from Madras, gathered in the Ashram at 9 a.m. on the next day, the 5th. The ceremony of laying the foundation-stone of the Meditation Hall was performed and at its end Sri Anandamayi Ma approached and strew flowers over the foundation stone to the joy of all present. (ibid p. 61-62)

'On the same night (6th), She delighted the Maharishi's disciples by leading the *bhajan* in calling the name of Bhagavan - 'Oh Bhagavan, he Bhagavan, ha bhagavan' etc. for about 10 minutes amicably changing the modulations of the tune and the words of the appeal at each call.' (p. 62)

At the end of Sri Ma's stay, one of the Managing Committee members approached Sri Ma and with folded hands begged Her to visit Ramanashram again. Sri Ma smiled and said, 'I am not going anywhere. I am always here. There is no going nor coming - all is *ātman.*'

S.S. Cohen refers to a miracle performed by Sri Ma. He writes, 'Although it was very early in the morning, a number of admirers had collected earlier to bid Her farewell. Their hearts were full and heavy at parting from Her. I looked at a particular face usually imperturable, in which I was interested and read in it a solemn, pensive emotion which a month ago. I could not have dreamt it was capable of feeling for any saint or any religious institution and I heartily rejoiced. It was one of the miracles Mataji had performed in the short space of only one week: she had relieved the long pent-up sorrow of my friend.' (p. 61)

Sri Ma's healing touch had wrought a miracle in Ambala in the physical sphere. In Madras, the metamorphosis of a heart is also called a miracle by the onlooker; there were other such cases of a coming together in self-giving devotion all over the countryside. Didi Gurupriya writes with wonder in her diary. 'It is amazing how close we feel to the people in Ramanashrama. One *sādhu* said,

'Bhagavan (Sri Raman Maharshi) is no more but in Mataji we seem to recognize his ways and his way of being with us.' We also feel quite at home, as if we all know this place well and recognize these people as fellow-travellers.'

One of the new devotees was the wife of Sri Padmanavan, Srimati Kalapakkam. She sang to Sri Ma whenever possible. One hymn (*he jagatrāṭa*) was specially liked by everybody. Sri Ma herself sang it with her and added her own modulations. Bibhu picked it up and it became a very familiar and popular song when they returned to the North.

Sri Ma visited the Temple where Sri Ramana Maharshi had practiced *tapasyā* for many years. Ms. Talyarkhan told them that the Temple Committee had given them permission to keep a life-size photograph of the Maharishi in the place of his *sādhanā*. Mrs Talyarkhan, by her one-pointed devotion and magnanimity of attitude had won the right of entry to all Hindu Temples, although she was a Parsi lady. She now accompanied Sri Ma everywhere. Another new addition to the group was Topaswami of Ramanashrama. His identification of Sri Ma with the Maharshi was such that he unreservedly gave her the same allegiance as to his Guru.

On 7th November Sri Ma arrived at Kumbhakonam. From there they came to Sri Rangam, visiting enroute the Samādhi of the famous saint-poet Sri Tyagaraja. The devout believe that he had the *darśana* of Rama, the presence being invoked by his devotional music. They stopped again to visit the Temple at Tanjore. The massive Nandi of nearly 12 feet in height was appreciated by Didi very much. Nowhere else in India such an impressive Image is seen.

The temple of Sri Rangam is the pride of South India. Mahaprabhu Gauranga, on his pilgrimage through the South had stayed near the Temple for four months. The profusion of architectural masterpieces, the vastness of spaces enclosed, the gold encrusted pillars and other beautiful ornamentations held the visitors spell-bound. The priests, with extreme circumspection made it possible for Sri Ma and the Mahatmas to visit the Inner Sanctum.

In the evening the usual *satsang* was held in the wide open courtyard of the Temple. A crowd estimated at much more than 10,000 waited in pin-drop silence for Sri Ma to come and occupy her seat on the rostrum erected for the purpose. There was no unseemly jostling, no mad scramble for getting closer to Sri Ma or no yellings which created more disorder than order. Didi and others, used to Sri Ma's visits in Calcutta, Dhaka and Varanasi etc. wished that the people from those towns could be with them to see and learn how to be disciplined in the presence of Sri Ma. There was no lack of devotion in these crowds. They were anxious to hear Sri Ma's voice. Sri Ma overcame the language barrier by singing *kirtan* for them at Sri Rangam as well as at all such *satsangs* arranged at other Temple precincts.

Sri Ma and the Mahatmas went on to Rameshwaram, Danuṣkoṭi and Kanyākumarikā. On November 13, in accordance with Sri Ma's *kheyāla*, Didi arranged to have one lakh (1,00,000) *bilvapatra-pūjā* at the Śiva Temple of Rameshwaram. All the priests were invited to a meal. Next day, the Manager of the Temple along with other officials came to say farewell to Sri Ma. He remarked that he saw Didi as Sri Ma's Nandi. Sri Ma laughed at this and said, 'What a coincidence! You should know that Didi has always been an admirer of Nandi because he sits for ever in timeless waiting for his *Iṣṭa-devatā*.'

In Madurai Didi was once more awed by the spectacle of a gathering of nearly 10,000 people sitting in a disciplined way, awaiting Sri Ma (D.D. Vol. II, pp. 48-49). Sri Ma again sang for them. In response to many requests she said, 'I have this to say to you, 'To talk of God alone is worthwhile, all else is pain and in vain'.'

A voice from the crowd: There has been no rainfall here for a long time - a draught is imminent. So many prayers are being sent up! What will happen to us?

Sri Ma: He who has created the world, is sustaining it, is to be dependent upon for everything. You yourself are the head of a family. Do you need your children to tell you what is best for them? He who is the Father of the world knows what arrangements to make. Try to leave everything to His care. Let His Will reign supreme.

(The congregation seemed pleased with this answer. Incidentally it may be written that a profuse rainfall was recorded in South India right after Sri Ma's visit. The News Papers reported that the devout were convinced that it was due to Sri Ma's *kheyāla*).

Ms Taleyarkhan spoke a little about Sri Ma in the meeting. She said 'In effect the question of pilgrimage does not arise for Sri Ma. Out of Her infinite mercy She has come to the South to bless the country and its people. Everyone should try and observe the routine of *nāma-japa* or *maunam* for 15 minutes, which Sri Ma requests all to do at least once every day, in memory of Her sojourn amongst us.'[2c]

In this congenial manner Sri Ma and the Mahātmās started on their return journey by way of Suchindram and Trivandrum. Sri Ma was invited to grace the Palace of the Maharaja of Travancore because the Ranis were obliged to observe the orthodox tradition of not appearing in public amidst crowds. The Private Secretary to the Maharaja came to make his obeissance to Sri Ma dressed in unstitched silken clothes, as he would do for a *darśana of* Meenakshi Devi in the Temple. He said to Didi that Sri Ma was being accepted by many in Madurai as the Goddess herself. It was a far cry from the days of Dhaka when Sri Ma was treated as *mānush-Kālī.* The fearsome Image of Kālī and the very beautiful Image of Meenakshi Devi were synthesized in the winsome person of Sri Ma Anandamayi.

They visited the Temple of Sri Padmanabhan next day. The image was most impressive. The splendour of the precincts was truly awe-inspiring.

Sri Ma and the Mahatmas came to Kaladi on 23rd November. They heard the legend about the river which flows near the Math. The place radiated a palpable atmosphere of peace and quietude. Sri Ma stood in front of the statue of Jagadguru Bhagavan Sri Ādi Śaṁkarāchārya for some time. Was it possible that he could have visited distant Siddheswari in his time? (c-7th century A.D) After staying at Kaladi for one day the party came on to Coimbatore, a distance of 150 miles.

All arrangements for their comfort had been overseen by Devaraj Babu, a friend of Kantibhai Munshaw. The elder brother of Subhas Chandra Bose, Sailesh Bose a resident of Coimbatore, spent the whole day in Sri Ma's company. Didi writes that the question 'When will you come again?' rises like a refrain wherever Sri Ma spends a little time. They proceeded on to Mysore visiting the well-known Ashram of Satya Sai Baba at Shirdi on 26th November.

Sri Ma and her entourage came on to Mysore. Ms Talyarkhan had arranged for the personal royal tent of the Maharajah for Sri Ma. He and his family came for *darśana.* The travellers spent some time in Mysore.

Sri Ma spent another two months in a leisurely tour of the Southern places of pilgrimages. They had *darśana of* Viṭhāldeva at Pandarpur. They spent a couple of days in Pune where Sri Somnath Nanda had his first darśana of Sri Ma. Subsequently, due to his interest and efforts, Sri Ma visited Pune many times and thus the foundation for the future Ashram was laid. In Bombay Sri Ma was the guest of Sri Krishnananda Swamiji of the Sanyasa Ashram at Villeparle. Sri 1008 Swami Maheshwaranandaji the Head of the Institute is a renowned saint and scholar of this part of the country. He became a regular visitor to Sri Ma's Ashrams in later years.

Sri Ma and Haribaba stayed for more than a fortnight at Bombay. Another contact which remained not only constant but grew to closeness was established with Swami Svatantranandaji. He remarked one day 'After these 12/13 days of acquaintance with Sri Ma, I have come to the belief that she is a knower of Brahman."

From Bombay the travellers went down to Ahmedabad and from there to Dwarka, breaking their journey at Junagarh at the request of a devotee of long standing, Sri Deogan. After visiting Bhalka, Prabhas Tirtha and Somnath, they came on to Dwarka on the last day of the year. The pilgrimage to Dwarka in a way concluded the tour of South India.

Sri Ma initiated a beautiful confluence of Northern and Southern traditions when she received a small image of Sri Padmanabhan with great ceremony in 1971 presented by the Elia Raja of Travancore. She detailed Bharat Bhai (Bhaskarananda) to learn all the rites of worship from Southern Priests.

It was also Sri Ma's *kheyāla* to instal a statue of Bhagavan Sri Adi Śaṁkarāchārya in the Hall at Kankhal Ashram. It is a unique and very beautiful installation. On a graded platform, the central seat is occupied by the great ascetic in the typical posture in which he is always depicted. Southern brass lamps decorate the four other platforms lower than the central one, two on either side. The four front faces of the lower platforms are four panels depicting the four regions where the Four Maths were established by the Jagadguru. Badrinath (North), Sringeri (South) Puri (East), Dwarka (West). The panels are executed by the well-known sculptors of Bengal, Nitai Pal and his disciples. A merging of traditions, cultures and an upholding of the ideal of renunciation. Sri Ma's words, travels, actions, all go toward this very end or so it seems when we peruse the shining trail of her *kheyāla* throughout her life.

The Pūrṇa Kumbha at Prayāg

1954 was the year of Purṇa Kumbha at Prayag (Allahabad). Sri Ma calls the Kumbha Melā the flag of Hindu Dharma. Just as a flag denotes from afar the presence of the goal to travellers from a distance, so is the Kuṃbha Melā a time of renewal of all ideals held sacred by the devotee. All the ascetic orders of India congregate on the occasion of this festival. The processions of *sādhus* are seen by thousands of people gathered for the same purpose of bathing in the holy waters at an auspicious hour.

The camp-site for Prayag is very extensive because of the two rivers Ganga and Yamuna. For one month, a town comes into existence on their banks, with an independent water and electricity system, a post office, the police control towers and even Banks. Rows upon rows of tents and shops cater to the pilgrims. Decorated fluttering banners proclaim identities of various camps. It is very beautiful and festive. It is the biggest concourse of people, a *melā,* in the entire world.

The Kumbha Melā of 1954 was marred by an accident of tragic proportions. Hundreds of people were trampled to death in a stampede. This was the first Kumbha after Independence. The new Government was not as experienced as it became later in controlling such mammoth crowds. Although the *melā* has grown in size and elaborate arrangements, such a disaster has not occured again.

On the day of the ritual bathing, Sri Ma kept to her small cottage, while relays of campers went in groups to the holy river. Sri Ma watched them set out, gave them practical advice regarding mishaps. She said, everyone should loudly pronounce a few words, such as 'Jai Siva, Jai Ganga' etc., so that if anybody got separated from the group, he may locate it again. The devotees chose to sing aloud the words, 'Jai Ma, Sri Ma, jai jai Ma.

After everybody had left Sri Ma lay quietly in her hut. Suddenly she sat up and exclaimed, in anguished tones, 'There, there, they are being crushed, choked, they are being suffocated!' Didi, who was sitting nearby, felt a terrible sense of calamity overhanging their own parties of pilgrims. She could think of her own people only. She said, 'No, no, nothing will happen to anyone in our party!' Sri Ma said, 'Are you sure?' Didi remembering Sri Ma's mode of repetition of an assurance three times, emphatically repeated her conviction twice more. Sri Ma said no more but lay down again. After a while, she made a few sounds of excruciating pain and said again, 'Didi, I see apparitions - they are horror-stricken.. they are clearly visible.' Didi was very alarmed. She knew from experience that whenever Sri Ma 'saw' apparitions (*murtis*) it presaged death and disaster. Didi, now thoroughly non-plussed tried to divert Sri Ma's *kheyāla* away from the site of the *melā* and give it a wider range.

After a few hours Sri Ma accompanied by Yogibhai, Dr Pannalal, and Didi went to the Sangam by car. She was taken in a boat to the confluence of the rivers, but her mood was aloof. It was apparent she had no *kheyāla* of bathing. She touched the waters and sprinkled a little of it on herself and her companions. When they returned to their camp they met with groups of people returning from the *Sangam*. Sri Ma asked 'Is there any news?' Everyone responded with their own tales of adventure - some had lost their bearings in the crowd, some others had had no difficulty etc. Not till evening the news of the catastrophe spread all over the camp-site. Hundreds of pilgrims had been trampled to death on the slopes of the *bāandh* (levee of the river). A pall of gloom descended on the entire township. Devotees now understood Sri Ma's words which she had uttered right at the time (early morning) when the accident had occured. Someone asked her, 'Did you see only those who were being suffocated?'

Sri Ma answered, 'I saw those who were saved as well. I saw pile upon pile of human beings crushed and choked, and completely suffocated. Many who closed their eyes and opened them again, and others who shut their eyes forever. It was as if this body itself were being crushed and suffocated. I saw those who were being stifled to death and those who were trampling on them - and all the time I was lying on my bed in my hut.'

Dr Pannalal asked, 'Why did you feel all this? Did you take their suffering upon yourself?'

Sri Ma said, 'What I felt was not suffocation in the worldly sense. I seem to laugh as you do, speak your language, yet I remain what I am. Who is it that appears as suffocation? Who is it that appears as distress? To take upon onself the agony of another is a different matter. Every kind of action is possible everywhere. Where in very truth all is THAT, where, in the shape of misfortune and suffering, in the shape of laughter and play, is the ONE who also manifests as suffocation, in that state there is no such thing as taking on the tribulation of others, there is only perfect identity, sameness (*sama*).

'Participation in another's sorrow implies mutual relationship, one talks to another. There is a place for that also. To take suffering upon oneself means to share it; this is possible only when one can still speak of give and take.'[4]

Sri Ma's ceaseless travels continued after her sojourn at Allahabad. The Birthday Celebrations were held in Almora, where Sri Ma remained from April 14 to June 27th, quite a long duration as far as she was concerned. Her movements were now a little restricted because the Mahatmas, especially Haribaba liked to stay in one place during the summer months. Since Sri Ma herself had no preferences, she, in general catered to the convenience of these exalted personages who came to attend functions and celebrations in the Ashram.

Sri Ma, on leaving Almora visited many towns. She came to Ranchi where a new Ashram was established. The house being a gift from Dr P.R. Ghosh (Priyaranjanda of the Ashram). Sri Ma travelled all the way back to Hoshiarpur at the invitation of Haribaba. Mahatma Triveni Puri more popularly known as Khanna Baba was no more, but his disciples and devotees made suitable arrangements for Sri Ma's reception and the Birthday Celebrations of 1954.

The *saṃyam-vrata* of this year in November was observed in Bombay due to the great enthusiasm of S.N. Sopory. On this occasion many new families came to Sri Ma and became integrated in the community of devotees: Sri B.K. Shah and his family, Dr Surabhai Seth, D.K. Kania and Jaya Ben and many others.

Gurupriya Didi had been stricken with arthritis and was in indifferent health for the last couple of years. The end of 1954 found her bed-ridden in Varanasi. Haribaba who had a great regard for Didi came to Varanasi and initiated various ritualistic ceremonies for the express purpose of bringing about her recovery. Didi did make a partial recovery much to everyone's relief.

1955 proved to be the year of Vrindaban. The new Ashram came up gradually. A new temple was built to house the very beautiful Images of Lord Gouranga and Nityananda Mahaprabhu. The eminent sculptor Nitai Pal of Calcutta had quite excelled himself. Sri Ma said, 'Due to Haribaba's great devotion and his *kirtan*, Mahaprabhu has manifested Himself in this Form.'

The summer of 1955 was spent in Solon. Jogibhai had constructed a very spacious Ashram on a flat piece of land just below the Palace. The views over mountains and valleys were marvellous. The *satsangs* were well attended. It was a restful interlude in Sri Ma's busy programme. In Solon, whenever Sri Ma walked out for a stroll, a dog, Moti would come and walk with her in spite of all attempts to chase him away. Sri Ma said, 'Give him some sweets.' Thereafter, he was given his share of the *praśāda* every day. Moti became a regular *satsangi*! So much so that on the day of Sri Ma's departure from Solon, everyone noticed his absence. Word was brought that he had met with a slight accident on the road and was lying quietly in a corner of the long curving verandah. Sri Ma herself approached him with a sweet in her hand. He did not take the sweet but licked her fingers instead. Yogibhai reported later that Moti had died soon after Sri Ma left Solon.

During the month of February 1956, Sri Ma went to Vindhyachala from Varanasi, to give some time to Dr M. Boss, one of the leading psychiatrists of Europe. Other foreigners came to Vindhyachala to be with her away from crowded cities. This became a recurrent pattern; some of the Ashrams proved to be very congenial to people unused to the hectic and haphazard way of life prevailing near Sri Ma. Such Ashrams were Rajgir, Vindhyachala and also Bhimpura in Gujrat, near the holy river Narmada. Thanks to the foreigners, who enjoyed Sri Ma's proximity in condition of 'retreats' she also sometimes got a much needed rest for a few days or even a few weeks.

In 1956 Sri Ma was 60 years old. The Birthday Celebrations were held in Varanasi. In spite of the heat of the plains, the function was fully attended by all devotees. Sri Ma's *aṣṭasakhīs* (eight friends) from the villages of Almora came with offerings of home-made puffed rice and other such humble items of food prepared with loving care. Sri Ma made them open up their bundles and ate a little of the items with every appearance of relish and gratification. The Princes and their families came with valuable gifts. The big business houses of India provided the means for the board and lodging for the large crowd of devotees. Scholars and savants came to give learned discourses during the sessions of *satsangs.* Musicians of great reputation like Ravi Shankar, Ali Akbar, Omkarnath Thakur and Siddheshwari Bai gave recitals in the evenings. Throughout the day many religious rites were performed like, Chaṇḍī Pāṭh, Rudrābhiṣeka, Rāmāyaṇapārāyan, Viṣṇu-yajña etc. The big pandal from morning till night resounded to the sounds of Vedic *mantras,* discourses on Scriptures, *kirtan,* instrumental and vocal music. The last item held in thrall, the entire congregation and for which it waited the whole day; this was *mātṛ-satsang,* a half hour of conversation with Sri Ma.

Professor Tripurari Chakravarty, the outstanding expert on the Mahabharata said, 'I have talked so many times of the Rajsuya yajña performed by Yudhisthira, in the age of Dvāpara. Here now is another Rājsuya yajña in the age of Kali, and Sri Ma is the presiding Deity of this one as Krishna was of the other.' It was indeed a magnificent achievement by the organisers of the Celebrations.

This celebration opened up a new dimension for the future of all activities in the Ashram. The Mahatmas came to hold a position of priority. Gradually Sri Ma's movements came to be guided by their presence at the Ashrams. Haribaba treated her as the visible embodiment of his *Iṣṭa* Mahaprabhu Gauranga Deva. He spent more and more of his time in Sri Ma's Ashrams or he would invite her to his own. His own entourage were also devoted to Sri Ma. They came to her on their own to consult her about Haribaba's welfare. He was an ascetic of uncompromising strict observances. Even in his old age he did not relax any of the dietary rules or accept anything but the minimal amenities of daily life. All his waking hours were devoted to one or the other form of *sādhanā*.

Once he had come away alone from Bāandh to Sri Ma's Ashram in Kishenpur, Dehra Dun. He said to Sri Ma, 'My people are not serious about the devoted way of life. I keep telling them that we shall all, strive together. All of us together shall ford the river of life, but they have no real unity of purpose. They only do something desultorily in order to please me. It is best for a *sanyāsī* to be alone.' According to his request Sri Ma did not send word to his people in Bāandh regarding his whereabouts.

He was given a room in the Ashram. Sri Ma herself would work out a menu for his midday meal. She would sit in the kitchen and arrange the *thāli* (plate) with different dishes served in separate *kaṭoris* (small bowls). After two or three days Swami Paramananda, who used to take in the food for Haribaba happened to come by when Sri Ma was carefully arranging it on the plate. He said, 'Ma it doesn't matter at all. Your Baba is going to mix all the items up before eating!'

Sri Ma said, 'What? Even the chutney and the *payas* (pudding)?' Paramananda confirmed that all the different flavours were jumbled together by the Mahātmā. Sri Ma then said, 'Well, let Baba do what he likes. We have to send food arranged in its proper way.'

Haribaba's devotees guessed his destination; they found out Sri Ma's whereabouts and accompanied by several important people from their villages came to Kishenpur to plead with him to return to Bāandh. The villagers confided in Sri Ma their own problems. They said to her, 'Ma, Baba does not understand our difficulties. He expects us to attend all the *satsangs* and programmes of religious activities. We work in the fields, the whole day, look after the cattle; we also have our families to consider. Sometimes we are too tired or distracted to listen to scriptural readings or sit in meditation without falling asleep. Baba is disappointed in us. Please ask him to forgive us and come back to Bāandh. Only you can prevail upon him to do this.'

Haribaba did return to Vrindaban and Bāandh after a few months at Dehra Dun. There were other Mahatmas, whose devotees confided in Sri Ma about their Gurus. The much revered Khanna Baba (Triveni Puriji Maharaj) in his old age was advised to eat fruits which he did not relish. His devotee said to Didi, 'We only have to tell him that these fruits have been sent by Sri Ma for you, then he like a docile child eats them without any fuss.'

Avadhutaji Maharaj spent the last days of his life in Sri Ma's Ashram in Vrindaban. He chose a room from the windows of which he could see Sri Ma's cottage. He was sitting in a yogic posture, looking at this cottage when he breathed his last.

Udia Baba of Vrindaban, at first had not quite liked the idea of being associated with a woman saint. Later he had remarked, 'Yes I did not recognize her at first. I am impressed by her equanimity under all circumstances. Her behaviour of complete dispassion is very agreeable.'

Once Udia Baba, Haribaba and Sri Ma were expected in Bāandh for a function. On the day of their departure from Vrindaban Udia Baba felt unwell and decided to cancel the trip. Haribaba had already left to see to the arrangements for their reception. Sri Ma sat in her Ashram playing with a pair of cymbals (somebody had brought for her) striking them in rhythmic beats. She said, 'It is not right for *sādhus* to go back on their words. I shall go to Udia Baba and say to him, 'Baba, why do you worry about the body? The body after all, will go sooner or later. The spoken word will remain.' After a while, word came from Udia Baba that he was well enough and would accompany Sri Ma as planned. Some of the devotees standing around felt that as if, the resonance of the cymbals had eddied over to Udia Baba's ears and made him change his mind.

Other Mahatmas made it a point to attend each function at Sri Ma's Ashrams, or wherever she happened to be in response to invitations from people desirous of her *darśana*. In this manner, *satsangs* became a regular feature of Ashram activities. Big congregations assembled to listen to the Mahatmas and to see Sri Ma for many hours at a time. The common people at first rather resentful of the ascetic orders who took away so much of Sri Ma's time, later came to regard their advent as a blessing because Sri Ma was at least visible for long hours, although it was difficult to approach her for leisurely conversations.

Another aspect of the spectacular functions which came to stay was that only the very affluent could afford to host them. The big business houses of India belong to very devout people such as Birla, Singhania, Dalmia, Modi, Jaipuria and others. Again the common people, overcame their prejudices against an order of society beyond their own orbit of competence. They only had to be grateful that Sri Ma was available to them because the rich people alone could afford to entertain hundreds of devotees for a prolonged period of time. When Sri Ma had wandered around the country, not many people could stay with or travel with her. The towns she visited also, had never been called upon to provide for her retinue for a long time. Moreover, the common people could not afford to travel long distances to have *darśana* of Sri Ma. So thanks to the large-hearted generosity of Princes, business magnates, and the Mahatmas Sri Ma became available to hundreds and thousands of ordinary folk all over the country.

References

1. Ananda Varta, Vol. I, No. 2, pp. 59-61.
2. D.D. ibid, p. 50.
3. D.D. Vol. II, p. 79.
4. AV, Vol. II, pp. 182-183.

CHAPTER FOURTEEN

Through a spectrum of Rainbow Colours

There is a movement in the cluster of figures and She is leaving the room now. We watch Her go outside and standing on the step, She pauses for a moment, not looking at anyone, but beyond them, quite still, and we notice with what perfect beauty She stands, and we are close enough now to see Her face clearly. It ripples: there is a kind of fullness, a richness of modelling, it is as if we were looking at a Rembrandt, with every line and slightest variation of modelling containing behind it a tremendous power, so that the volumes, their density, their delicacy, their lightness are the shape of the character itself, a power which is both dark and mysterious and also radiant.

Richard Lannoy[1]

Madras

Question: At what age and by what *sādhana* did you attain Enlightenment?

Sri Ma: laughing, said - Am I enlightened? I know no time when I was not as I am. I have not performed deliberately any *sādhanā*! No sudden spiritual illumination came to me as something which was a new achievement. Whatever I am, so I have been always. This is what I have to say to your question. You may draw your own conclusion.

S.S. Cohen; AV 1953, No. 2., p. 61.

* Sri Ma and visitors from abroad
* Sri Ma in the company of scholars
* Sri Ma travels *incognita*
* Sri Ma with the leaders of the country
* Sri Ma and children
* Sri Ma and *janatā-janārdana*
* The *līlā* of being a woman

Through a Spectrum of Rainbow Colours

Sri Ma continued to be busy and her travel itinerary was as bewildering as ever. Functions and ceremonial rituals multiplied Many scholarly brahmins of the priestly caste, who had begun to look upon their profession as somewhat dispensable in modern times, regained a new confidence and developed new interest in their vocations. Sri Ma showed a great appreciation for the erudition of those who had a profound knowledge of the *śāstras.*

The deserving but very poor brahmins came into some prominences almost in all the towns she visited very often.

The resurgence of Vedic rituals and Paurāṇic festivals were felt everywhere. People came in close touch with the *yajña* in various forms and in many ways it was a time of renewal of faith in the Upaniṣadic tradition. *Pūjās* were performed everywhere in order that Sri Ma could be invited to attend the occasion and enhance its joyousness a thousandfold.

Sri Ma and visitors from abroad

Sri Ma, however, easily made a transition to a quiet contemplative interlude for people who did not quite feel happy with the sound and lights of exuberant pageants. The main groups for these occasional retreats consisted of Europeans who very often spent Christmas with Sri Ma in Vindhyachala, Rajgir or Bhimpura and other such remote places. As early as 1937, Sri Ma had been in contact with the West in the person of Mrs Jennings who had come to attend the Conference on World Religions sponsored by the Ramakrishna Mission. Since that time there had been a regular influx of seekers of spiritual guidance from the West. All foreigners will remember Atmanandaji (Miss Blanca Schlamm) who was so helpful in corresponding with them and in editing the *Ananda Varta* till the time of her passing away. She was an Austrian by birth and had been 'interned' in India during the years of the war, that is, she was obliged to stay in India. This was congenial for her because she had been very fond of India and things Indian since her childhood. She became very close to Sri Ma; she was able to 'communicate' with Sri Ma without outward help of physical means. When Sri Ma sat in meditation at the request of her foreign visitors, she would choose Atmanandaji to sit in the room with her; sometimes also Billoji, knowing these two would not be overcome by sleep as soon as they were required to sit still, as it happened with her other women companions.[2]

Other Europeans who came and became members of the family of devotees were Swami Vijayananda (Dr A. Weintrob from Alsace-Lorraine), Jayananda (Jack Unger from America), Premananda (Colin Turnbull from England), Satyananda (Henri Petit from France) and many more. Arnaud Desjardins and his wife Denise were regular visitors. Their daughter Muriel was a lovely little girl who wished to be dark complexioned like her other friends in India. Sri Ma said to her 'You are beautiful' in English to console her for her lack of the dark skin. Muriel was very fond of Didima. Often she would be seen gathering wild-flowers (in Vindhyachala) and bringing them in a bunch to Didima's feet. Didima always put out her hand and touched the child's head. Muriel also visited India again when she was a grown up young woman and brought her husband with her.

In France, America, Spain, Germany, Italy, and England there are families who are as close to Sri Ma as any of the Indian families who have never travelled abroad. The readers of Ananda Varta, would be familiar with the writings of Melita Maschmann, Richard Lannoy, Jean Herbert and others. Alexander Lipsky's book on Sri Ma (published by Motilal Banarsidass, Varanasi) remains a very readable one. Amongst all these very close companions, Vijayanandaji stands out as the person about whom Sri Ma herself said 'There is the look of a *ṛṣi* (Upaniṣadic sage) on his face.'[3] His *tapasyā* (austerities) in the Himalayas was an example of obeying Sri Ma's spoken words, rather than choosing the more congenial way of travelling around with her for her daily *darśana*. Sri Ma's call toward an one-pointed, undeviating and relentless effort was practised by him for nearly thirteen years in Dhawalchina. He came down when Sri Ma herself recalled him to the plains.

In more recent years there were other visitors too numerous to be recorded in this book. Sri Ma was as spontaneous with her answers to them as she was to anyone who could communicate directly with her. At Ranchi, she was invited to visit a plant of heavy industries being set up in collaboration with a foreign country. An engineer from Czekoslovakia said to her, 'I do not believe in rebirth. Does it really matter?'

Sri Ma: 'You believe in this life don't you? There is only one genuine life namely, the one that is dedicated to the search for God, only one genuine death which is the annihilation of death itself. After that there are no more births and deaths.'[4]

A group of people from the West were talking with Sri Ma. One of them asked 'What is right for me? Should I live an active life in the world or a contemplative life in seclusion?'

Sri Ma: 'To whichever of the two you can give your heart and soul, that is right for you.'

Another question came from a young woman who had come to India to study Buddhism: 'Have you anything to say to me?'

Sri Ma: 'Live the teaching that you profess.'

A third question: 'How can I avoid saying the wrong thing at the wrong time?'

Sri Ma: 'By pausing before you speak. If you wait for a little while, you may think better of it and never say it at all.'

Another young woman who was a well-known actress travelling incognita asked: 'I know that certain people have a bad influence on me. Yet I fall victim to it. Is there a way of saving myself from it?'

Sri Ma: 'Curtail to a minimum the time you spend in their company.'

'How can I? My work is such that I have to be with them for long hours.'

Sri Ma: 'How can you then save yourself from their influence? If you go near fire, won't you feel the heat? If you put ice on your hand won't it freeze?'

When taking leave the spokesman for the group said, 'We feel greatly honoured to have had Mataji's *darśana.*'

Sri Ma: ''Honoured?' When you meet a stranger you may feel honoured, but when you come to your own self there is only joy and happiness!'

Sri Gopinath Kaviraj asked a young American Mr Phillips to visit Sri Ma and put his personal questions to her instead of to him. Sri Ma heard him out and then said 'You wish to know, what really determines your thought-processes and your behaviour. He who has created you is the sole director of your thoughts and actions. This, however, is a matter of inner experience, not something to be stated orally. The realization of Truth is possible only if one can depend fully on one's Guru.'

The young man asked, 'I have no Guru. Who will assume charge of my affairs?'

Sri Ma: 'Are you married?'

Mr Phillips: 'Yes, and I have two children.'

Sri Ma: 'I see. Do this if you can: become a manager. Just as a manager looks after another man's property with great care but without a feeling of ownership. Whenever you have time, occupy yourself with the reading of good books or good thoughts. Behaviour must be good and exemplary. Practice meditation. Thus you can make out a path for yourself...'[5]

Didi Gurupriya writes that once Sri Ma said to an elderly American couple when they were about to leave- 'Your baby!' They came back from the door and embraced her and caressed her again and again. The lady kissed Sri Ma like a child![6]

Sri Ma was equally close to her Western as to Indian disciples. They had no difficulty in communicating their innermost thoughts. The Western perspective on life and times, is sometimes hardly understood by even well-educated Indians; Sri Ma was never nonplussed or astonished by their questions. Once an English follower of Acharya Rajnish asked her, 'The states of *bhava* can be induced by drugs. One may choose in live in such euphoria for as long as one likes.'

Sri Ma, 'Yes but these *artificial* means are not without there repurcussions and also very transient and need to be induced again and again. The real bliss transforms the very being of the *sādhaka*. His goodness and moral equilibrium shows, he is on the path to permanent felicity.'

When talking to a Westerner, Sri Ma was one herself, so that no one complained of a sense of lack of communication. Melita writes:

'At Poona recently when I was talking to a South Indian academician who suffered severely from his mental blockagees, Ma caught my eye with a glance whose loving ironical charm showed me how amusing she found the situation. Unfortunately this made me laugh for no reason that the young man could see. He must have thought that I found his intellectual pains amusing, and indeed I did find them rather funny. Though actually, I was sorry for him. I said, 'You have no idea how much more relaxed I feel since I gave up searching for the secret of holiness with a dissecting knife.'[7]

The Western devotees did not look upon Sri Ma as a Guru full of the wisdom of the East. They also found a Friend who understood their innermost thoughts and responded accordingly so that 'knots of the heart' were dissolved at even the first encounter.

Lynn Dalton (Jyotipriya) writes her first impressions of Sri Ma. She had been in touch with Sri Ma's devotees in her own country and had corresponded with Atmanandaji. At last the day came when she could fly to India to visit Sri Ma. She was prey to disturbing thoughts also, along with feeling an elation at the prospect of the first *darśana*: supposing Sri Ma was not all what she was said to be; supposing she did not at all feel anything at the time of this meeting?

'At last I am to meet Her. We are at the Hardwar railway station at 5.30 a.m. Although exhausted, I feel no tiredness; I am very much on edge... Then the train windows were flashing before me. Shraddha (an American friend) having spotted Mother in one of them, was running alongside the train and we were following her. It was just a moment's wait, and then Mother alighed on the platform.'

'My fears dissolved immediately and forever. In my mind, I said, 'Yes, there's Mother', with a ring of complete familiarity. Never had anything seemed so completely real to me as Her very presence. My recognition was instantaneous.'

After an audience at the Ashram, Lynn writes:

We were wreathed in smiles on our way back to the bungalow. Words cannot convey my sense of relief and satisfaction. As Shraddha was going into her room, I stopped and said to her, 'Now I can...'; and she finished my sentence for me, 'Now you can die!'[8]

Many people wrote to her from different countries. Atmanandaji could read and answer letters written in French, German and English. For other languages, she took help from competent people. One letter she published is given here:

A letter from abroad:

Mother, are we frineds?

Mother, do you love me?
Can you reach me here?
You have said you are here, so would you please appear?
Am I too impure?
Am I not sincere?

Sri Ma's answer to this letter:

God is the Supreme Father, Mother, Beloved, Friend, Companion. Of course He is a friend, He is indeed the friend. Everything that appears is the manifestation of the Supreme Lord, He is the true friend. All pain and sorrow are due to the sense of 'I' and 'mine'. The world is God's creation. In God is everyone and everything. Where is He not? This is how Ma is always near although the body does not go everywhere. In the *paramātmā* (Supreme Being) there is no possibility of impurity or insincerity at all.'[9]

Sri Ma in the company of Scholars

The end of the nineteenth and the beginning of the twentieth centuries are said to have witnessed the renaissance of Indian Classical Philosophy. The Universities brought forth a new generation of scholars who while grounded in their own tradition learnt much from the West and were influenced by it. Pioneers like Dr S. Radhakrishnan gained renown as spokesmen for the Neo-Vedanta of contemporary times.

Sri Ma had come in contact with a group of professors trained in academic philosophy in 1929. These professors, such as Dr Mahendra Nath Sarkar, Dr Nalini Kanta Brahma, Dr Girija Shankar Bhattacharya and others, kept in touch with Sri Ma over the years. Dr Nalini Kanta Brahma wrote to demonstrate that her message was not an universalism but a perfect synthesis of two of the tenets of Advaita philosophy which seem to contradict each other, namely '*sarvam khalvidam brahma*' (All here is Brahman only) and '*neti, neti*' (not this, not this) that is, nothing here is Brahman.

Other well-known scholars who came to know her quite well were Dr T.M.P. Mahadevan. He met her in Madras in 1952 when he was asked to translate for her. Although he did not know

Hindi at all, Sri Ma's language was so philosophic that he made a success of this interpretative task. S.S. Cohen writes, 'On November 1st, Dr T.M.P. Mahadevan, Head of the Department of Philosophy of the University of Madras undertook the difficult task of translating Mataji's answers on the spot and on the next day he gave the following written record of the talk.

'Where questions arise, there is answer too. Who questions whom? There is only one Atman everywhere: you are that. Where there is duality there is misery. You are non-dual, eternal. You seek and desire truth, knowledge, bliss; because you are that. No one wants *mṛtyu, ajñāna, duḥkha.* True, evil has a fascination for man, who, attracted by it, falls. This is due to *vāsanā* which means non-recognition (*na*) of the existence of God (*vasa*). To counteract it, one must be attracted towards God, one's true Self.'

A question: 'How do we know there is rebirth?'

Sri Ma: 'Yes, there is ignorance, why go so far as rebirth? One does not know what will happen the next moment. Yet there is knowledge. Those who have crossed the veil of ignorance tell us that we are the eternal *ātman.*'

In 1955 Dr Mahadevan requested a message from Sri Ma for The All Faith's Conference in Madras. After repeated efforts Didi managed to elicit the following *vāṇi* (utterance) in response to his request:

O Thou, Immortal Self!

Be Thou a pilgrim on the way to Immortality.

O Immortal Self, O Immortal Wayfarer, abide

Thou ever in Thine own Self.

The enumeration of names is incomplete because Sri Ma met many more scholars during her travels all over the country. Dr Rama Chowdhury came close to her. Sri Ma herself went to visit Pandit Vidya Vinod Vidyabhusan a great Vaiṣṇava scholar of our times.

Once she was visiting one of her devotees who was ill in the P.G. Hospital at Calcutta. On her way out she was told that Dr S. Radhakrishnan was in the next room. Sri Ma, at her own *kheyāla* entered the room and touched lightly the sedated person of the scholar and came out quickly, before the nurses realized what had happened.[10] When Dr Radhakrishnan heard about this visit, he was overwhelmed. On his invitation Sri Ma visited him at the Rashtrapati Bhavan (Presidential House at New Delhi) also when he was well and able to receive her with due ceremony.

Among all the scholars of this country, the name of Pandit Gopinath Kaviraj, by the sheer extension and depth of his learning, comes most easily to mind. We need not enumerate his many Eastern and Western titles or his many decorations which an admiring Government and several Universities bestowed on him. We quote here the tribute of another scholar, himself a *yogi* of great ability, the well-known writer Sri Anirvan:

'Gopinath was the personification of the articulate sound-form of the immortal soul of India, the living image of the learning of the ancient land; the light of his genius was not confined to the shores of India but illuminated the universal mind. He knew no difference between his homeland or alien lands. Wherever man's consciousness has attained a high understanding there went his appreciation which was as wide as it was deep.'[11] (Tr by Author)

Kavirajji records his first impression about Sri Ma: 'The recommendation of my colleague: Mahamahopadhyaya Pandit Padmanath Vidya Vinoda, a person who was known to be a fastidious critic of men and things and who spared none from his attacks, seemed to me to carry special weight.'

Kavirajaji met Sri Ma in early September 1928. He writes: 'She used to reply to each question resolving the doubts of the inquirers with a few short sentences in Her sweet and inimitable manner. As enquirers hailed from different cultural levels and represented different intellectual and spiritual points of view, it is only natural that the questions should range over many different topics and be of varying interest and value. It was wonderful how Mother tackled all these questions with the same ease and spontaneity without requiring a moment's reflection to deal with even the most abstruse and knotty problem brought before her. Her replies were, as a rule, very pertinent, going straight to the heart of the questioner, couched in a language remarkable for its terseness and expressiveness. Every word that fell from Her lips carried weight; and humour too was not wanting when occasion demanded it.'[12]

Sri Ma travels *incognita*

Sri Ma sometimes travelled *incognita*. Although this *kheyāla* was incomprehensible to everyone, they in time came to accept it without demur. Sri Ma went into a prolonged *ajñātavāsa* (unknown places of residence) on August 3, 1936. Her companions were Kamal (Atal Bihari Bhattacharya's nephew from Rajshahi) and Virajmohini.[13] After a few days Kamala[14] was sent back home by Sri Ma. Virajmohini alone remained with her. She herself was fond of the unusual and must have appreciated Sri Ma's unstructured travel itinerary without visible means of support or even minimal accessories like a change of clothes or a glass for drinking water.

After about four months Sri Ma and Virajamohini fetched up at Tarapeeth. Virajamohini wrote to the people concerned that all who wished to see Sri Ma could come to Tarapeeth. Within a couple of days a large group of devotees arrived from far and near. With great eagerness they made enquiries from Virajmohini about Sri Ma's travels during the preceding months. How did they manage, who gave them money, where did they stay, were they put to any difficulties; these and many more questions were asked from all sides. Virajmohini tried her best to satisfy everyone. Although she had not much money with her when they started she had never been short of it. At opportune moments exact sums needed had come their way. She had always managed to prepare their simple meals, at times nothing more than boiled vegetables and most often a little milk and fruit. Sri Ma had been recognised in a few of the towns, but as she left the place immediately, crowds could not gather round her. From Virajmohini's accounts the following itinerary was pieced together by Didi and the other listeners:

Sri Ma's first destination had been Puri. Triguna Chakravarty (from whose house Sri Ma had set forth) not being reconciled to Sri Ma's adoption of complete mendicancy, quietly gave Virajmohini a *dhoti* and a blanket for Sri Ma. A devotee at the Railway Station presented a rather beautiful *sāri* which Virajmohini bundled up with her own meagre effects. In Puri they put up at the Goenka *dharmaśālā* (pilgrim's rest house). All the rooms being occupied they stayed on the open verandah. At the time of going out to visit the Temples Virajmohini left her few belongings with a family in a nearby room. When on their return she went to collect her things, the lady asked if she would sell her the *sāri*. Since both Sri Ma and Virajmohini were dressed in dhotis, she thought the *sāri* would be of no use to them. Virajmohini, however, refused saying it was a gift and could not be sold. Thereupon Śri Ma herself entered into the discussion and pursuaded the lady to accept the *sāri* as a gift from her. She became their daughter and said that a daughter had every right to present a *sāri* to her mother. Next day Sri Ma's 'mother' brought her a dhoti as a gift, so now Sri Ma had a change of clothes.

While she was strolling on the beach, a young boy recognised her as 'the Ma of Dhaka' and ran off to inform Makhan Babu of Jatia baba's Ashram. On her return to the *dharmaśalā*, Sri Ma remarked, 'I see Makhan Babu with a lantern in his hand looking for me.' After a while Makhan Babu arrived carrying a lantern; he had gone to the beach to look for Sri Ma and had been wandering around in search of her. He was joyful at having found her at Goenka *Dharmaśālā*.

At Puri, the meeting of Shyamdas Babaji and Sri Ma was of some significance. Shyamdas Babaji was an old man, devoted to his *sādhanā* and had been living in retirement in Puri for a long time. A few months earlier he had suddenly become very keen to have *darśana* of Sri Ma. Although his health was not good, he had made enquiries about Sri Ma's whereabouts with a view to going to Dehra Dun if necessary. One of his friends, seeing this uncharacteristic agitation on his part remonstrated with him saying, 'How is it that you have become so disturbed about this *darśana*, you who are so steadfastly established in your own way of life? If Sri Ma Anandamayi is all that they say, she is, then, I am sure she will come to your hut to give you *darśana*.' Now this is exactly what happened, Sri Ma went to see this old man on the brink of death. His urgent desire for *darśana* was fulfilled through the most unexpected concurrence of events. Didi wondered if Sri Ma had gone to Puri, just for this purpose.

From Puri Sri Ma and her two companions went on to Bhubaneswar. After visiting Gomoh, Ardra, and other nearby places Sri Ma undertook the long journey to Agra in Uttar Pradesh.

At Agra Sri Ma asked Kamal how much money he had. On learning that he had only Rs. 10/-, she told him to purchase a ticket for Calcutta and return home. He tried to plead with her to allow him to stay on but all to no purpose. With Kamal was sent back the surplus (!) baggage which they had acquired *en route*, because Virajmohini had purchased one or two small utensils at Puri. Sri Ma cut a piece of about 5.5" feet in length and 2 feet in width out of the blanket which had been given by Triguna Babu. She kept this piece of blanket one dhoti and a *loṭā*; Virajmohini was similarly equipped. Leaving them in this state of freedom from encumbrances, Kamal departed for Calcutta. He was able to inform everyone in Calcutta about Sri Ma's wellbeing upto the time he had been with her.

Sri Ma and Virajmohini stayed in Mathura for three days in a *dharmaśālā*. After this time (as is the rule for visiting pilgrims) they vacated their room and sat on the bank of the river. Virajmohini purchased some fruits. After washing them in the river, she fed Sri Ma a few pieces of the fruit. The passers by seeing a grown-up person being fed by another, stopped to watch the spectacle and a few were highly amused. Sri Ma laughed aloud to see their amusement and so they went away probably thinking that she was a mentally disturbed person. When it became dark Sri Ma asked Virajmohini if she would be afraid to spend the night in the open under the stars? Before her companion could answer in the negative, a devotee of long standing happened to pass by. He was thunderstruck to see Sri Ma and Virajmohini. He congratulated himself again and again on this chance encounter and escorted them to a more suitable habitation.

Next day Sri Ma set out for Vrindaban and then on to Etawah. At Tundla Junction, a young man said to her, 'Ma I have seen you in Sultanpur. Please come with me to Sultanpur now.' On learning that they had tickets for Etawah, he went to the ticket counter and got them changed for Sultanpur.

At Allahabad Junction they changed trains for Sultanpur and entered a ladies' compartment. A Muslim woman got in at Pratapgarh. In the time-worn fashion of Indian women, she immediately wanted to know all about her fellow travellers. She asked Sri Ma, 'How many children do you have?' Sri Ma answered, 'I am myself your child (*bachā*), how should I have children?' The woman appeared much struck by this answer and within a short while they were deep in conversation about many matters. Virajmohini had purchased a toy for Sri Ma from one of the vendors. Sri Ma had been fiddling with this for some time. Now she gave it to the woman saying, 'Keep this toy safely for me.' The woman was overtaken by tears when time came for her to get off the train. She gave her address to Virajmohini and requested Sri Ma again and again to get in touch with her if she should pass their way in future. May be, this Muslim woman was the reason for Sri Ma's fortuitous change of plans!

From Sultanpur Sri Ma boarded a chance-met bus and came on to Ayodhya. She stayed here for a week. Just as the host of devotees found her out she left for Lucknow. In the train a lawyer from Barabanki, invited her to visit his home town. She said she would keep it in mind. Sri Ma came on to Etawah where she stayed for nearly twenty-five days. Virajmohini got in touch with Dr Pitambar Panth. It was here that Sri Ma told him that if she should ever have the *kheyāla* to take medicines he would be the first doctor to prescribe for her. Every evening he and some of his friends would visit her at the Temple where she was staying and held long conversations with her. She Ma often went out to stroll on the river bank and visit a gypsy family's campsite. They were extremely poor. They would give her a papaya leaf to sit on and talk with her quite freely as with a friend of many years. Who can say if the gypsies were not closer to her than the elite of the town?

As soon as visitors began to multiply, Sri Ma left Etawah for other towns. She came to Barabanki. Virajmohini contacted the lawyer they had met earlier. He was very pleased to make suitable arrangements for her. He and his friends had the opportunity to talk about spiritual *sādhanā* with Sri Ma for four days.

Sri Ma came to Bareilly. What was the joy of Maharatan who so unexpectedly found Sri Ma in town. Maharatan was grieved to see Sri Ma travelling like the poorest of poor pilgrims. She immediately went to the market and brought woollen clothes, blankets and other items as seemed necessary to her. After a few days, Sri Ma said, 'Now that we have so many warm clothes, let us make use of them. Let us go to Nainital.'

At Nainital (5000ft.) they were met by Krishna Panth at the bus-stop. By the merest chance he happened to be there and was amazed to see Sri Ma getting off from the bus. Sri Ma stayed at the Temple of Naina Devi for a few days much to the joy of the people of this region. She moved out of Nainital and passing through Bareilly, Agra, Delhi came to Lahore. After one day at Lahore's Temple of Kālī, she proceeded to Amritsar and Garhmukteshwar via Meerut. From Meerut, a young man Manik had accompanied her to Garhmukteshwar, where she remained for fifteen days.

Travelling in this seemingly haphazard manner Sri Ma came to Deoghar, but did not allow Virajmohini to get in touch with Pran Gopal who would have been transported with joy to have her *darśana*. Sri Ma found a room in a *dharmaśālā* instead.

In the next room of the *dharmaśālā* a woman had a sudden attack of some kind of seizure. The manager, sympathising with the husband in this trouble, advised him to approach 'a Mataji' who was staying in the next room. The man came and knocked at their door. When Virajmohini understood his request she answered with some annoyance that Sri Ma was not a doctor and would say nothing about such illnesses. The man thrust past her and falling at Sri Ma's feet begged her to do something for his wife. Sri Ma said to Virajmohini, 'Let us see what the matter is.' The woman in the next room appeared to be very ill. Her lips were bluish and her hands and feet cold. She was trembling uncontrollably. After watching her for some time Sri Ma asked Virajmohini to prepare a little fruit juice and give it to the woman to drink. Sri Ma had the window opened and after seeing the patient lying comfortably in her bed, she came away to her room. The next morning the woman was quite normal and well, much to the surprise of Virajmohini who had not expected her to recover so soon.

From Deoghar Sri Ma had gone to Tarapeeth. Sri Ma had travelled without a retinue for about four months; now she was surrounded by a huge entourage but it was all the same to her. Like an expert commander, she moved her army of devotees from place to place travelling lightly. The midday meal was cooked in one big pot which contained every kind of vegetable, rice and pulses. This meal was served on banana leaves, so cleaning and washing up was accomplished quickly. Eddies of people surrounded Sri Ma. Some were new comers, greeting her on arrival; those who had stayed for a day or two were going away, bidding her farewell.

On another occasion Sri Ma disappeared for a while, with only Ruma Devi as her companion. She stayed in Navadweep on a boat for about 15 days. The boat was taken to mid-river during the day and brought back near the banks at night. The local police came to make inquiries regarding the 'two strange women.' The boatman Ramraj reported that they were *mahātmās* and their behaviour was exemplary. The policeman thereupon enjoined upon Ramraj the responsibility of looking after the gracious ones to the best of his ability. When the devotees at last found their way to the dilapidated boat in Navadweep, Ramraj was overwhelmed by their gratitude in words and kind. Sri Ma used to slip away quietly like this sometimes but never for very long. It will require intense researching to find out even the apparent purpose of these retreats as well as the reasons for her random choice of places to visit. Sometimes she chose the houses of devotees, such as Aptap Mitra's near Calcutta, 31, George Town in Allahabad, Harish Banerji's in Varanasi or the Jaipuria House in Naini and many more. Her entourage sooner or later discovered her whereabouts. Sri Ma with her usual equanimity accepted the quietude as well as the renewal of activity.

Srī Ma with the Leaders of the Country

All men and women in positions of power came close to Sri Ma at one time or another. Her busy schedule with ordinary people and the Mahatmas did not prevent her from allocating time for them. India's first Prime Minister Pandit Jawaharlal Nehru, his daughter Indira Gandhi and her entire family became very devoted to her. They were initially drawn to her by their memories of Kamala Nehru's association with her.

Vallabha Bhai Patel, came with Pandit Nehru. All of the Governers and Chief Ministers (any exceptions would be more due to Sri Ma's speed of travel through their provinces) came to her when she passed through their provinces or on visits when she was in New Delhi. Sri Ma, herself went to see a few eminent people when and if they were not in a position to come to her. One such person was Sarojini Naidu, the first Indian Governor of Uttar Pradesh, right after Independence in 1947. She was at her summer residence in Nainital when Sri Ma was visiting the hill-town at the invitation of Dr Pannalal. Sri Ma went to the Government House to see the somewhat ailing lady who received her in a specially decorated marquee put up on the lawns for the purpose. Sri Ma approached the Governor as a friend and greeted her warmly. After some introductions, Sri Ma said to Sarojini Naidu, in Bengali, '*Hari kathāi kathā ār sab vṛthā vyathā, ki bolo mā? tomār banglā bhāṣā mone āche*?' (to talk of God alone is worthwhile, all else is in vain and pain, isn't it so, ma? Do you remember Bengali?)

The Governor inclined her head, saying softly that she could understand quite well, although she could not speak fluently. Somebody suggested that perhaps Sri Ma would like to stroll through the extensive gardens. Sri Ma and her considerable entourage left on this expedition. When Sarojini Naidu was sitting alone except for the various officials in attendance on her, her daughter Miss Lila Naidu approached her and asked, 'Who is she?' Lilaji had been astonished to see Dr Pannalal in attendance on Sri Ma. Dr Pannalal had been a figure of considerable authority during the British Regime; he was one of the fine brains of the era and undoubtedly a man of great ability. Mrs Naidu said to her daughter:

'She is the quintessence of the spirit of India. She is the tuning fork, the touch stone, the ultimate criterion for distinguishing between what is our tradition and what is not. She is just perfect as she is. It is only possible in India to experience perfection personified.'[15]

Although this meeting was the first and the last (because Sarojini Naidu passed away very soon after it), it becomes apparent that Sri Ma's powerful impact did not depend upon prolonged companionship. For many, one *darśana* was enough.

Netaji Subhash Chandra Bose came to see Sri Ma while she was visiting the Dakshineswara Temple near Calcutta (1935). Sri Ma was seated under a big tree on a platform. Sri Ma's companions and Subhash Chandra sat in front and around her on the ground. Neither Sri Ma nor Subhash Chandra spoke, so there was complete silence for a while. Somebody introduced Subhash Chandra to Sri Ma. She said, 'I met your brother in Ahmedabad.' He said, 'You have been visiting Ahmedabad?' Sri Ma, 'Yes'. Again, there was silence. Evidently Subhash Chandra had nothing to ask and Sri Ma had nothing to say.

Amulya Kumar, in response to quiet nudgings from others in the audience, broke the atmosphere of quietude and raised a relevant topic: 'Ma, can one find God by serving one's country?' Sri Ma said to Subhash Chandra, 'Pitaji, you answer this question. Can God be attaind?'

Subhash Chandra: 'Do I keep track of God?' (every one laughed)

Sri Ma (also smiling): 'You keep track of, what?'

Subhash Chandra: 'The question was not put to me!'

Sri Ma: 'You are the reason for this question. (looking at Amulya Kumar) Isn't that so?'

Amulya Kumar: 'Yes'

Sri Ma: 'Now, say something! Let me put it this way. Why do you work for your country? If you can tell us the benefits of this service then everyone will become involved. I have heard that you are a marvellous speaker. Say something to us.'

Subhash Chandra: (Smiling) 'I have not come here to give an oration; I find happiness in serving my country and that is why I do it.'

Sri Ma: 'Is this happiness permanent?'

Subhash Chandra: 'The word 'permanent' is a difficult one.'

Sri Ma: 'What lasts forever is permanent. Engagement in the service of one's own self generates permanent happiness. Moreover, if this service is genuine, then everlasting happiness is ensured. Pitaji, are you engaged in a service of this quality?'

Before Subhash Chandra could answer, one lady broke into the conversation and engaged Sri Ma's attention away from the previous topic. After Sri Ma had addressed herself to her problem, she turned to Subhash Chandra again and said, 'Pitaji, won't you say something?'

Subhash Chandra: 'But I have come here to listen, not to talk!'

Sri Ma: 'Only to listen? Will you listen to what I say? Will you do what I tell you to do?'

Subhash Chandra: 'I cannot promise. I can only say that I will try.'

Sri Ma: 'See, Pitaji, whatever action is done by us is done because of a sense of lack; it is true that when that lack is fulfilled, we are happy. All actions in the world, however, generate fresh wants... This is why it is said that action in relation to the world is ever incomplete and gives fragmented joys only. Action relating to the Self gives true happiness... You are a great soul. Try to elevate your capabilities still higher. The service to your country is also because of a sense of want; the happiness it affords will be transitory. Everybody looks for that continuing Bliss which is unending. Only such work as is aimed at finding your true nature will lead to Bliss or Supreme Joy. But you may object, 'What is the use of my attaining the state of Bliss when the whole world is suffering endlessly!' To this it may be said that if one attains that Bliss, one can impart it to others as well.'

Subhash Chandra: 'What is that action which pertains to the search for one's true nature?'

Sri Ma expatiated on true nature and also ways of being, which take one away from one's own nature, not quite answering this question. He again said, 'You are not telling me the way to this attainment.' At this time, the lady who had spoken before interrupted the conversation, giving her own understanding of Sri Ma's words. Amulya Kumar, Bhupati Babu, and Nagen Babu and other serious minded men felt that the session remained unsatisfactory and incomplete because Sri Ma had no opportunity to answer Subhash Chandra's question. After a while Subhash Chandra made his *praṇām* and bidding farewell, left for Calcutta.

Sri Ma and Children

Children always crowded round Sri Ma. In Dhaka, in Bareilly, in Dehra Dun, in Uttarakashi and in Cox's Bazar, Sri Ma and Bholanath were followed everywhere by their retinue of small girls and boys. In later years Sri Ma continued to give her concerned attention to children. To relate just one incident:

In the beginning of December 1936 Sri Ma happened to be travelling toward Assam. While her train was standing at Pandughat, Sri Ma looked out of the window and saw a young boy walking along the railway track with books under his arm. She spoke to him and asked him to come into her compartment. When he climbed up into her compartment she entered into a friendly conversation with him. He was a very well-behaved child and seemed to be intelligent also. His name was Mukul Datta and he was the son of a Railway Officer. He and other boys and girls of the Railway Yard went everyday to their school in Gauhati by this train. Now his friends, seeing him in the compartment, climbed on to it also. Soon all of them were conversing with Sri Ma as with a friend of long standing. After a while, Sri Ma said to them, 'All of you must think of God every day for a while. He has many Forms and many Names. You can choose any one you like. Tell me, which Name do you like best?' Many Names were mentioned: Hari, Rama, Krishna, Lakshmi, Sarasvati, Śiva etc. Two of the boys turned out to be Muslims and said 'Allah'. To all of them Sri Ma said, 'Take a new exercise-book. Write the Name of your choice five times, ten times, or twelve times (in accordance with their ages) every day. This you must do the first thing in the morning after you wash your hands and face etc. When the exercise book is full, consign it to the river in the name of God and start another one. Can you do this? I am now your friend. Will you remember me?' They said they would.

In Dibrugarh, Sri Ma again addressed another group of children in similar words. At her suggestion Didi now purchased a dozen exercise books and distributed them among the children, writing each child's name on the cover. One child asked Didi to write Sri Ma's name on the first page. So all the others also had Sri Ma's name written on the first page. The next day, the children brought their exercise books to show to Sri Ma their written efforts. This *līlā* continued whenever Sri Ma had leisure and time for the children throughout her travels.

On this stretch of the journey to Assam Virajmohini had left Sri Ma's party to visit her daughter and son-in-law at Nougaon for a couple of days. She came to Pandughat to await Sri Ma's arrival by the motor route, so that she would rejoin the party for embarking on the steamer for crossing the river. The Railway Yard children came running up to her thinking they would see Sri Ma also. When they heard that Sri Ma was expected to come by bus, they stood around the bus-stop, eagerly scanning the faces of all who descended from cars and buses. It was rather late when Sri Ma arrived. The disappointed children were not there. On hearing from Virajmohini that they had been looking for Sri Ma the whole evening Akhandanandaji and Bholanath went to the Railway Yard and tried to find them. Didi, unfortunately had lost the list of names, so their vague enquiries were not fruitful. Just as they were obliged to leave for boarding the steamer, Sri Ma herself beckoned a young man standing at a distance. At his approach she asked him if he knew Mukul Datta. He replied that he did. Sri Ma left a message for the children saying that she had come and had looked for them but because time was short she had had to leave without waiting to see them.

Saccidānanda

In Cox's Bazaar, there was a school in the vicinity of the house in which Sri Ma stayed for some time. The children, whenever free before or after school or during recess would come running to Sri Ma while she strolled on the sea-shore. They gathered cowrie shells and brought them to her as offerings. One day she said to them, 'Let us play a game with all these cowrie-shells. The name of the game will be *Saccidānanda*.' The rules of the game were formulated by Sri Ma herself. There would be two teams of equal number of players, sitting alternately in a circle. Each player was entitled to a single throw of seven cowrie-shells. If there were three face-ups then the score would be *sat*; if five then, *cit* and *ānanda* would need a throw of seven face-ups. The team which arrived at *sat, cit* and *ananda* in order would win; if *ananda* cause before *sat* or *cit* before *sat*, then it would stand cancelled. The team to win would sing *kirtan* and the losing one would do *japa* for 108 times before joining in the *kirtan*.[16]

Usually, Sri Ma and Bholanath would be the two team leaders. The children were very fierce in their loyalties to their team leaders; counts would be kept very carefully. Even grown-ups became like children. Sometimes grave controversies arose which needed to be settled by the team leaders. As soon as the neighbours heard the sounds of *kirtan*, they would know that the children were playing *Saccidānan*with Sri Ma and Bholanath on the sea-shore.

Sri Ma easily understood the predicaments of foreign children who accompanied their parents but could not relate to things happening around them. One young German girl writes about her own experience during a session of the *Saṃyam-Saptāh*:

'For me, the whole *saptāh* was a study in boredom. I could not understand why all these people would crowd into a big hall and sit, watching a collection of old bald men sitting on a stage wrapped in old blankets, with their eyes closed for a whole hour. And if that wasn't painful enough they would sit for another couple of hours giving lectures in Hindi and read out of books!'

Gopalpriya Radich later met Sri Ma in private and was given a magic formula for an interest in life; she continues: '... I realized then the lucid accuracy of the statement that after coming in contact with Mataji, I would never be bored again!' (AV (1988), April pp. 147-148).

Sri Ma sometimes spoke to clusters of children. Addressing them as her friends, she would say, 'Now that we are friends, you will mind what I say won't you? I shall tell you five things which you must always remember: The *first* is, 'Always speak the truth, the *second*: Obey your parents, and teachers; *thirdly*: Remember God every day. When you get up in the morning, pray to God to make you a good boy/girl. Before going to bed pray also and beg for His forgiveness if you have been bad; *fourthly*: study hard to the best of your ability and *fifthly* if you have observed the first four items then you can be a little naughty if you feel like it and play as much as you can!'

The children would always agree enthusiastically to the five-point programme. There should be many middle aged or old people now who have grown up with these principles of a happy childhood.

Sri Ma and *janatā-janārdana* (the populace)

Sri Ma seemed to have close affinity with the simple people of our country. It would not be realistic to say that she worked toward a more harmonious state of the social order. As with everything else she never made an issue of such matters. Each human being was important to her; she responded to the total person when answering questions or dealing with social problems. A thief caught red-handed in Vindhyachala Ashram was not denounced publicly because Sri Ma would not so demean the person concerned. The thief was allowed to keep up appearances and depart in peace.

Sri Ma had repeatedly broken across caste rules, in Dhaka to create what is known as *Jagannāthkṣetra*. In Puri, the *prasāda* from the Jagannāth Temple is treated as blessed food which may be shared by Brahmins and non-Brahmins alike. It may be served by anybody and thus orthodoxy is given up when pilgrims go to this holy city. Sri Ma many times went out among a concourse of people sharing their food, serving them and eating from their hands. In Dhaka, Calcutta, Varanasi and Vrindaban, many mammoth gatherings at times enjoyed this festive air of togetherness.

Sri Ma always mingled freely with the people who are known as *dalits* in our country. We have already written about the women in Atpara, who were her friends. At Paruldia and other villages, she moved amongst the cooks and servants to bring them forward and make them join in with the main *kirtan*-party. In a village near Ranchi, she made a special point of including the people of the soil in the festivity of the *saṃyam-saptāh*. She was never oppressed by crowds or impatient with their demands for her *darśana*. At Varanasi Ashram which is surrounded by the habitation of fishermen, she was always mindful of their interests. One great *Jagannāth kṣetra* was created in the lanes around the Ashram when Sri Ma sat on the steps with a pot of *khichiri* (pulses and rice cooked together) distributing it tirelessly to relays of the fishermens' children who clustered round her, hugely enjoying themselves. How the pot of *khichiri* sufficed for the hordes was a miracle in itself!

Sri Ma's *vāni* that she belonged to everyone was demonstrated by her again and again. From the hill tribes of Taklakote to remote villages in Bengal, Bihar, Uttar Pradesh or Gujrat she endeared herself to people of the soil as one of their own.

For many years, crowds were a constant feature of her travels. She had her own unique way distributing *prasād* to each and everyone of the company.

She would throw *batasās* (sugar puffs) or fruits into the crowd. The range of her throws was truly spectacular especially as they seemed so effortless. The fringes of the crowd would begin to press forward to catch a fruit and then scramble back when they found the shower falling behind them. Sometimes she added to the fun by making a feint, her poised hand would suddenly change direction. Every time it so happened that the fruits and sweets would be adequate for the assembled crowd. We do not think there are any records to the contrary.

Once Sri Ma had to stopover at Hardoi Railway Station for a few hours (17th March 1969). She began to sing a *kirtan*. In a few minutes there was a crowd round her, the Railway Staff, sweepers, cleaners, also the travellers to various destinations surrounded Sri Ma and joined in singing the chorus. Just before she was ready to board her train, she acquired the fruits and sweets from all the vendors who were also standing around and threw them into the crowd in the above mentioned manner. Some of the vendors took money for their wares (from devotees), others contributed their shares. For a couple of hours Hardoi Station knew the ecstacy of *nāma-yajña*

The Līlā of Being a Woman

The *līlā* of Sri Ma as a 'woman' was especially enjoyed by the multitude of housewives surrounding her most of the time. Women always felt really understood and appreciated by Sri Ma. Men, on the other hand were always impatient with what they considered were trivialities when they were excluded from all-women sessions, sometimes jealous also!

When Sri Ma had the *kheyāla* for Didi and Maroni to acquire the privilege of the sacred thread, it was an innovation of considerable moment. Subsequently many more young women joined them in acquiring the rights as well as the rather strict regimentation of the twice born, such as Purnananda (Kumari Shanta Pathak); Brahmacharini Chandana Bhattacharya, Kumari Geeta Banerjee and Kumari Jaya Bhattacharya of the Kanyapeeth were also given the sacred thread.

Sri Ma brought about major changes in unobtrusive ways. Once it so happened that a girl from the Kanyapeeth was asked to read a sacred book in Sri Ma's presence. While she was reading this book Sri Ma put a garland round her neck. At a sign from her a small *chowki* (lectern which can be used while sitting on the ground) was placed in front of the reader on which she could place the book. A sandal-paste mark was put on her forehead. She now looked like a *pathak* (reader) who has been chosen for the role. The girl shyly read a page or two of the book. These simple beginnings have lead to amazing results. Many girls of the Kanyapeeth are now scholars, well able to speak in public on religious subjects. In September 1995 Kumari Geeta Banerjee was anointed the speaker on Srimad Bhagavatam for one week at Varanasi. She occupied the *vyāsāsana* with confidence and for seven days gave entrancing discourses on the sacred book. A worthy offering for this year of celebration of Sri Ma's Centenary. (1995-1996)

In June, 1982 the Jagadguru Samkaracārya the Head of the Sringeri Peetham, Sri Abhinava Bharati Tirtha and his chief companion Chhote Maharaj came to Kankhal to visit Sri Ma. The entire Ashram turned out in force to accord him the welcome suited to his exalted position in the hierarchy of our *sādhu-samāj*. Flower decorations and the sound of *kirtan* announced an imminent festivity. All the rituals pertaining to the reception of a great Mahatma were observed.

Jagadguru Sri Samkarācārya seemed very happy. When he sat with Sri Ma in the Hall, she introduced many of the girls standing at her side. First it was the turn of Kumari Jaya Bhattacharya, the Principal of the Kanyapeeth. Listening to her academic qualifications he asked a question in Sanskrit from the abstruse treatise *Khandanakhandakhadya*. Jaya made a very polite rejoinder also in Sanskrit, 'With Sri Ma's and Maharajji's blessings, it is true that I have read this treatise but I have not had time to meditate on its intricacies.' Jaya added, 'We are happy that you have visited us. Please come again.' Maharajji seemed pleased with this answer. Sri Ma then presented other academically qualified girls, dressed in their sober yelloy robes looking like *brahmacārinis* of Upaniṣadic Age. Dr Padma Mishra, the President of the Kanyapeeth came in last. Sri Ma said, 'Pitaji, all credit for this school rests with Padma.'

The Jagadguru was visibly impressed. He turned round to his companion and said in Sanskrit 'All things are possible with Sri Ma!' One of the onlookers seeing Sri Ma's glowing countenance thought, 'Truly Sri Ma's 'girls' are persons to be proud of!' His wonderment was shared by many because for well-educated girls to be following the words Sri Ma's oft repeated *vāni* 'To talk of God alone is worthwhile all else is in vain and pain' is an amazing and uplifting example.[17]

As with all other teachings, it is not quite easy to construe Sri Ma's *kheyāla* regarding the position of women in our society. It was obvious that Sri Ma made no distinction between men and women, as regards rights and obligations, although she was heard to say that to demand an equal share in the sphere of possessions was an unworthy aim of life. She encouraged all women to bring an independent spirit to the business of finding their places in the world; but she advocated a way of life which was guided by a spirit of service as distinguished from subservience. Sri Ma always cited her own mother whenever she wanted to demonstrate an ideal behaviour. She would say, 'My mother used to say', or 'My mother would not allow us to do such and such', or 'My mother did not do this.' The life of Didima however was an orchestration of fortitude, dispassion, spirit of service, self-confidence under difficult conditions and a total identification with God's will in life. Her sense of humour fortified her against any attempts at trivilaizing her position or dignity. She could not be pitied for her poor circumstances or shown sympathy for her hardships. She was taken at her own valuation and that was the dignity of complete self-sufficiency.

Sri Ma appreciated all this and spoke about it to many housewives. She wanted a woman to understand that she was the fulcrum of a well-knit family. The brunt of various outer forces are withstood by a family if the centre is strong and has enough resilience for the give and take of relationships. She, however, did not advice an endurance which went beyond the fitness of things. Once or twice she has endorsed the separation of husbands and wives although in general, she always spoke in favour of a harmonious togetherness between a pair. Conversations regarding human relationships took place very often in her vicinity:

A question: 'Ma, do people, who come to you, find peace in their lives?'

Sri Ma: 'Ask them!'

One lady: 'Yes, we are at peace.'

Sri Ma: 'Is it true? May be for the time being. But as soon as you think, your husband is neglecting you, you will weep; and so also with husbands. If he thinks his wife is uncaring, he is angry. Then? Sulks, breaking off of communications, for ten minutes in some households, for ten days or ten months or even ten years - Isn't that so?'

Everybody laughed at Sri Ma's way of describing family problems. They shamefacedly acknowledged the truth of her statement. Sri Ma continued, 'Some wives look up to their husbands, are mindful of their ways of doing things; some wives are more full of their own importance: why won't he listen to me? If he doesn't do as I say, I shall also not do as he wants, - a typical trader's attitude, a *pukka sethji* (shopkeeper)!'

The audience joined in her laughter. Sri Ma said more seriously, 'A household also is an ashram. Don't you say *gṛhasthāśrama*? Where there is no *śrama* (hardship), no pain. Where a husband will pay heed to his wife, a wife will mind her husband - an agreement, a mutuality, a unity of purpose should be evident. The spirit of service should prevail, otherwise there will be discord. The mother should look to the son, the son be mindful of the mother- if everyone renders service in the belief that He alone is being served, then you have hope for peace. Is it not said, *janatā-janārdana*, - God in the form of people. The aim should be to see your own *Iṣṭa* in everyone; in pleasing all, you please your own Iṣṭa. If your family life is not congenial or peaceful, it is difficult to make progress in your spiritual endeavour- another point - do not consider anyone an adversary or enemy. There is only the One- there are no 'others'. All are friends.'

The question of superiority and inferiority came up sometimes in Sri Ma's presence. At one of the *Samyama-Saptāh* sessions, a provocative statement was made by the controller of the *satsanga*. A participant asked Sri Ma, 'The controller just now stated that morning and evening *kirtans* are not well attended by brothers. The sisters are more regular for all items throughout the day. Does he mean women are more devout and that they will reach God sooner?'

Sri Ma smiled and answered, 'Women are more self-disciplined; they are mothers after all. The mother knows how to serve and how to persevere. One receives according to one's capacity to give. Whether you are here or at home!'

Question: 'Is our capacity to give less than theirs?'

Sri Ma avoided a direct answer. She said, 'I am reminded of a legend. When God created the world and made arrangements for everything Evil asked Him, 'Where is my place?' God answered, 'Make your place in such hearts where there is no room for godliness or devotion.' Whosoever is devoted to God, will gain freedom.'

Question: 'Are women likely to get ahead of men in the quest for God?'

Sri Ma: 'Whosoever is able to concentrate more profoundly will forge ahead.'

The questioner persisted: 'Women are less intelligent; that is why they are devout by nature!'

Sri Ma made none of the obvious rejoinders. She asked, 'Are you saying that those who are intelligent will go ahead sooner? Is it not true that ego and intelligence are to be surrendered to God?'

'Yes'

'So?'

'Now you have confused me!' Everyone laughed.

Another person asked rather bluntly, 'Who is more important, a woman or a man?'

Sri Ma answered, 'Both. Don't you say Hara-Parvati, or Radhey Shyama or Sita-Rama? One is incomplete without the other. Where would you be yourself without your *śakti*?'

Sri Ma was never seen to involve herself in social problems as such. People who sought advice and redress for their predicaments were heard as individuals and Sri Ma always spoke directly to their own particular situation. She dealt with such interviews in hundreds and thousands. There are no set patterns of her responses, because she spoke to the individuals concerned. The only generalization possible is that she seemed to put the onus of holding together the constructive forces of life on women. She seemed to make a distinction between parity of opportunities and an unrealistic demand for equality. She always upheld the quality of friendliness which could bridge all chasms of misunderstandings. She herself, above all, was an unfailing Friend to everyone.

References

1. 'The Golden Orange', AV, Vol. II, No. 3, p. 267.
2. No blame attaches to them because in general they were too busy during the day and also late in the night; truly meditation needs much practice (*abhyāsa*).
3. Ananda Varta (Hindi Ed.) April 1988, p. 106.
4. Ananda Varta Vol. XIII, No. 2, August 1965, p. 56.
5. AV. Vol. 36, No. 3, pp. 193-95.
6. D.D. Vol. 13, p. 135.
7. AV, Vol. XXI, No. 1, p. 94-95.
8. AV. Vol. XXI, No. 7, p. 249-251.
9. From the Collection of Atmananda.
10. A similar incident occured when Sri Ma was visiting the ailing Pandit Gopinath Kaviraj at Jaslok Hospital in Bombay. In the general ward outside his room she stopped near the bed of an Arab invalid. He had been travelling alone in India and had no kith or kin near him. She spoke to him about 'Allah' and touched him lightly on his head. The invalid although surprised seemed pleased with his visitor and promised to remember 'Allah' at all time.
11. AV. Vol 24, No. 1, p. 3.
12. Pt. Gopinath Kaviraj, *ibid*, pp. 5-6; 9-10.
13. Many people will know her better as Brahmacharini Visuddha's grand mother.
14. At present Swami Virajanandaji.
15. This is from personal diary notes. I had not gone with Sri Ma to see the gardens but happened to be sitting behind the dais. I am sorry I cannot quite reproduce the beautiful eloquent language used by Sarojini Naidu. Her utter command of the English language was beyond my powers of retention at the time. (Author)
16. This is from my own recollection of the game as we played it with Ma and Bholanathji in Bareilly 1936-37. It is possible that it had more rules for deciding controversies. (Author)
17. Swami Prakashananda; AV Vol. 29, No. 4, p. 313.

CHAPTER FIFTEEN
Swami Muktananda Giri

Sri Ma is leaving Didima and myself in Vrindaban. She is going to Varanasi. She made her *praṇām* to Didima and said, 'Ma, do keep well.' Didima answered, 'You also. Come back soon.' Sri Ma said, 'Ma, due to your blessings alone this body is here. If you keep fit and continue to bless me, then this body also will keep well!' All of our soliticious enquiries were silenced by this statement. Sri Ma went away saying with folded hands, '*namo nārāyaṇa*'.

Didi's Diary 25th Oct., 1966[1]

14th April 1939. Didima becomes Swami Muktananda Giriji Maharaj at the prestigious Bhola-Giri Ashram in Haradwar.

Sri Ma said, 'You always say that I never give you any advice as I do to others regarding spiritual well-being. Have I not spoken to you now in asking this of you? It is indeed a great good fortune for anyone to attain freedom to devote oneself wholly toward Self-realization.'

* Swami Muktananda Giri
* Sri Ma's Specal Mission

Swami Muktananda Giri

Swami Muktananda Giri Maharaj was known to the devotees of Ma as Didima. Sri Ma herself referred to her as 'Giriji' sometimes; more often as just 'Ma'. Didima was completely unselfconscious regarding Sri Ma's position in the world. In referring to her, she would say, 'Your mother'. When she had occasion to write to Sri Ma, she would address her by name, as for example, 'Dear Nirmala,' and sign herself, 'with blessings, your mother.'

A little has been written already regarding Didima's early life. She did not change with the passing of years. Her calm acceptance of the many hardships of village life became the serene tolerance of the bewildering changes in the circumstances of city life. She was obliged to share in the limelight which illuminated Sri Ma's activities, but this never disturbed her or made her do or say anything to show that she was even aware of it. She occupied her seat near Sri Ma on rostrums all over the country with quiet dignity. Even during the last years of her life, she could sit for many hours in a *satsang* without any sign of tiredness.

She had all the qualities of a renunciate from her early life; so the assumption of the ochre robes did not indicate the state of an aspirant for dispassion in her case but marked a recognition of what she was already.

The Sangha created in Sri Ma's name had requested Didima to give Initiation to people who came to ask for it at the Ashram. After Bholanath, there was no one who could be considered in the role of a Guru. Didima was an ideal choice. She belonged to a very prestigious monastic order; she herself was a generous-hearted, absolutely undemanding person, overflowing with kindness for those who came to her seeking any kind of redress, spiritual or otherwise. Hundreds of people flocked to her room, to sit with her, listen to her words of solace, or just to receive a touch of her soft fingers on the head.

She never forgot any of her disciples; she kept in touch with them, writing letters herself whenever possible. When they became too numerous for her to handle alone, she accepted the willing services of any one who would help her out. She was very scrupulous regarding her correspondence, as in everything else. My (the author's) most endearing memory of Didima is with a Hindi Primer just a few years before her passing away, when she was perhaps 86 or 87. Surprised, I asked her, 'Didima, what are you studying so intently?' She laughed a little self-consciously and answered, 'You see, many people write in Hindi nowadays. Although they (other Hindi speaking disciples) read out the letters to me, it is never the same as reading them myself. The alphabet is not too dissimilar.' Blessed, indeed are all her disciples, with such a caring Guru.

Didima had that true self-confidence which allows a person to see a joke against himself or herself. Once in a gathering of women Sri Ma was describing the days of her childhood. Didima was also present. In a mood of mischief Sri Ma said, 'My mother had a novel way of pouring oil in the cooking pan. She would put her finger on the top of the bottle and then turn it upside down on the pan. Have you ever seen such a way of pouring oil?' Everyone laughed including Didima. Didima said very calmly and composedly, 'Well, I could not afford to waste even a drop of oil.' She then added with a matching smile of mischievousness 'We were all right as we were; I dare say you could have chosen a family with more means, had such been your will!'

Sri Ma appeared to be embarrassed. She hastened to say, 'No, no, I and my brothers and sisters were very well looked after; we felt no need of anything at all. It is only when we grew up that I heard people say that my parents were not in easy circumstances. We have no recollection of any kind of hardship.'

A glowing tribute to Didima's skill not only in housekeeping but to her abiding sense of sufficiency quite unrelated to actual circumstances.

Didima's behests were obeyed by Sri Ma to the best of her ability, always. In the last years, very uncharacteristically, Sri Ma used to stretch out her hand to touch the heads of people bowing in front of her. Sometimes the visitors not realizing that she would bless them in this way, bowed from a distance then seeing the beautiful gesture of the outstretched hand would hasten forward to get within its reach. On one such occasion, looking at my (the author's) surprised expression, she smiled and said, 'Ma says to me, so many people bow in front of you; you could at least touch their heads in acknowledgement. So I now do her bidding, whenever it comes to my *kheyāla*.'

So thousands should be thankful to Didima for this particular *kṛpā* of the magic touch. It is also quite possible that Sri Ma had been carrying out Didima's wish when she started to 'give' initiations to whoever came forward for it. It had seemed at the time that she had opened the flood-gates of *kṛpā* or grace. No one was refused; even if Sri Ma was busy for the whole day and night she would find time for a few minutes to sit with those who sought to be initiated into a new way of life. We, who always stated with great firmness that 'Sri Ma never gives initiations,' were effectively silenced. She in fact seemed to deputise for Didima by developing a way of carrying out her task, with the help of Bhaskarananda.

Sri Ma said once (to Didi): 'See Didi, I see my mother sitting around, or doing ordinary things. She has drawn such a veil around her, that nobody may know what she is. Such characters, behave in this manner... (not to be noticeable).'

Didi pondered over Sri Ma's words and then wrote in her diary, 'Didima is now 85 years old; her one wish is to be near Sri Ma all the time. She is quite child-like in this matter. Wherever Sri Ma happens to be, Didima is sure to come over and sit near her. If it is her mealtime, she will say 'I am not hungry, I shall eat later.' We used to tease her about this; Didima would laugh with us acknowledging tacitly that she did not wish to leave Ma even for a few minutes.

'Indeed it is difficult to think of another such person as Didima. Hundreds now come to receive initiation from her. It occurs to me that maybe she is not learned or scholarly like other Gurus but by nature she is a true Mahatma. I have been in close contact with her for the last 35 years. Anger, greed, ego, jealousy, enmity are unknown to her. This is not an exaggeration. She is kind and generous toward all. She sees no fault in anyone. If we are referring to somebody's many shortcomings, she is sure to point out at least one good quality in that person. It used to amuse us that for Didima nobody was blameworthy! All who have come in touch with Didima will agree with me.'

Dayanandaji (who used to be Vimaladi in the Ashram) was for many years in the position of attending on Didima. Vimaladi's problem was how to prevent Didima from doing everything herself and not leave anything over for her attendants to do. Even in her very old age, she would wash her own clothes. Vimaladi could be heard very often scolding her charge, 'Now if you catch cold and get a fever, people will take me to task! I shall be answerable to Ma - do you want me to get a scolding?' Didima would soothe her down with soft words and promises of 'better behaviour' in future.

Sometime in early 1963, Didima decided that it was time for her to leave the world. The entire incident is characteristic of her large-hearted concern for every one. In the first week of February, 1963 Didima was in Haradwar. For a few days she seemed to be in a very strange quiet mood, quite unlike her own pleasant outgoing self. One day she was seen to perform her usual ritual of offering flowers and water at the Temple of Śiva and then on her return, she sat in her room as still as a statue. Repeated requests for breaking her fast were unavailing. After some time she went and lay down under the *bel*-tree. Before her attendants could really feel alarm on her account, a telegram had been received from Sri Ma (in Jodhpur at the time) enquiring about Didima and asking her to come to Delhi immediately.

Didima had a vivid vision of a wide river; she was standing at the shore waiting for the boat in which to cross over. The boat came, she climbed aboard, saying to the shadowy figure of the helmsman, 'what about the others who are left standing - I cannot go unless all of them come with me.' The helmsman assured her that everyone would be taken across. After this vision Didima had made up her mind that she had lived long enough and it was time to go. She was always in close rapport with Sri Ma - so Sri Ma in Jodhpur 'saw' Didima saying to her, 'Shall I go away tomorrow?' Sri Ma said very forcefully, 'No, not now, not for a few years as yet!'

After this inner exchange of thoughts, she had asked that a telegram should be sent to Kankhal. The times of Didima lying under the *bel*-tree and Sri Ma's request for the telegram coincided. Someone asked Sri Ma, 'You had already communicated with Didima, what was the need for the telegram? Sri Ma, smiled and said, 'For all of you! Otherwise you would find it difficult to believe that Ma was ready to leave her body at that time and that I made her change her mind.'

Didima left us on August 7, 1970. This time she did not ask for permission. The time and place were suitable for this event which marked the end of an era. Jaipuria House is a *dharmaśālā* for pilgrims in Haradwar. A Bhagavat Saptah was taking place with the usual high standard of arrangements, a hallmark of all functions celebrated near Sri Ma. Didima used to sit next to Sri Ma on the dais everyday listening to the programme. The orater described the birth of Sri Krishna. The age-old story ever-new in the countless re-telling of it, gripped the attention of the audience. Didima got up from her seat on the dais, made her *praṇām* to Sri Kṛṣṇa and returned to her seat. She was very quiet the whole day. Late at night she sat as usual in Sri Ma's room for a while. When it was time for her to go to her rest, she placed her hand on Sri Ma's head in blessing, saying thrice, 'keep well (*bhālo theko*).' Generally Sri Ma always used to reciprocate by joining her palms together and saying, 'You too'. This day the ritual remained incomplete, Sri Ma did not say anything.

Around 1 a.m. Didima felt a little discomfort; Vimaladi enquired anxiously, if she should fetch Sri Ma. Didima said, 'No' quite positively. Vimaladi could see that Didima was wakeful and a little restless. She was in a quandary. Her relief was great to see Sri Ma walking in and taking charge of the situation. Sri Ma tried to give Didima a little honey mixed with ginger-paste, but she hardly took it in. Sri Ma then massaged her chest and held her almost in her arms. She went on calling her, 'Ma, Ma, Ma'. Didima answered in one syllable which sounded like 'Om'.

Didima showed herself fully conscious in the last few minutes, because she raised her joined palms slightly and moved them from side to side around her. It was a farewell gesture of leave taking. She then raised her eyes to Sri Ma's face and so breathed her last breath.

She had been a personification of desireless benevolence toward all; she would no more give succour to the hearts of her disciples by listening to their troubles and tribulations. A veritable Ganga, an all-encompassing confessional for the washing away of sins and sorrows was forever withdrawn, or perhaps not, who knows!

Sri Ma sat in Didima's room clasping her body, for many hours. She herself said later, 'When I saw Paramananda enter the room and roll up his sleeves, I knew he would now take Ma away, so I then put her down.' Sri Ma's radiant smile was overshadowed by her tears falling freely. It has been written again and again that Sri Ma was never seen to grieve over a death; and she did not grieve now, yet this occasion was very unusual. It is difficult to describe the poignancy of the lamentations of Sri Ma over the death of her mother. She went on smiling at people as they flocked to the *dharmaśālā* on hearing the sad news. She would say to them, 'Ma did not even give me a chance to sit with her for a while. So many times she used to say, 'Have you a little time now?' and I would say, 'Right after this appointment I'll have enough time but alas, I never had the time to listen to her or converse with her. Always there were pressing matters which came first. How patiently she waited for me to find a little time for her but I hardly ever could do so!'

So she talked about her mother while Paramananda made all arrangements for the *samādhi* at Kankhal Ashram. The *sādhus* of the monastic order to which Didima had belonged assumed responsibility for the last rites. In due course the solemn internment ceremonies were carried out with the greatest circumspection and honour. Didima's *samādhi-mandir* at Kankhal Ashram became a place for pilgrimage for her inumerable disciples scattered all over the country.

Sri Ma somehow looked a little lost without Didima at her side. The dais also seemed strangely empty. A framed photograph of Swami Muktananda Giriji (Didima) was placed on the rostrum. For many months Sri Ma carried a photograph of Giriji always with her. She would place it by her side or hold it in her lap. Her smile remained undimmed and as glowing as ever, but her eyes looked withdrawn toward memories which she went on sharing with the visitors who came crowding in from far and near.

Among all the opposites she held together so effortlessly, surely the simultaneity of the tears and laughter, on the occasion of Didima's passing away, was unique. It is true that the tragic muse had no role to play near Sri Ma Anandamayi. It can be said that Tragedy touched the lives of the people around Sri Ma at this time because this event definitely marked the beginning of the end of the era of joyousness.

With the withdrawal of the protective aura of the pure selfless love which had enfolded Sri Ma all these years, did she became more and more vulnerable to the endlessly demanding nature of human frailties? To quote one of her own *vāṇīs*, 'Just as the mother-cow licks the entire uncleanliness clinging to the calf and ingests it within herself, so does God His creatures. He draws away all their weaknesses and infirmities and makes them clean and pure. For you (the people), you are just to render service firmly established in the belief that all is His. (Spoken to Mrs. Talyarkhan Mysore, July 1961)

Sri Ma continued to cleanse us all of our impurities. We have read in the scriptures about how the snow-white colour of the lord of Death turned the colour of darkness by ingesting the poison that threatened to destroy the world- We have read about the sufferings of an Incarnation who came to save humanity. Cannot humanity so change itself that God may not suffer for us nor need to come to redress suffering but only to enjoy His creation?

Sri Ma's Special Mission

Dr Prafulla Chandra Datta describes one day's visit to Sri Ma's Ashram; (13.2.59) at Agarpara: He found Sri Ma surrounded by a motley crowd. There were men and women from far off countries as well as the Bengalis from near at hand. The eminent scholar Dr Nalini Kanta Brahma was explaining to a group of foreigners, Sri Ma's message of participation in a joint effort toward the seeking of truth. He was saying, 'Sri Ma says, just as *kirtan* may be kept up for any number of days by relays of singers, similarly God-oriented people may engage in an unbroken (*akhaṇḍa*) *japa*-series, throughout the day and night also. Everyone can participate irrespective of religious orientations, status and occupation in the world, sex, age or country. Those who have a thirst for arriving at Truth, may combine their efforts, irrespective of differences in opinions, divergent paths, variety in Names by which He is remembered - Everyone sensing an identity with others may strive toward achieving the One who alone appears as many.'

Sri Ma herself began to say something and since she was looking at Daya Mata and Swami Kriyananda[2], she spontaneously spoke in English the words 'special mission...' Immediately she stopped and looking at the Indians she said with a smile, 'What is the meaning of Special Mission?' Did I use the words rightly? I always ask for a favour from those who have an affection for me, and alms from those who are indifferent - a gift of 15 minutes every day. Just 15 minutes at the same time every day. No matter in what state or where you are -in your room, outside, whether you are ill or well, whether you are called upon to serve or command - at the appointed time remember Him. There is no question of purity of clothes etc. He is ever the Holy. He is untouched by impurities because it is He who makes everyone pure. Amidst the transient din of the world, to fix a time for remembering daily the Blessed One for achieving the Bliss of Enlightenment. There is no question of country or religion or brotherhoods - a new vista opens up unifying all pilgrims on the path of God-realization.'

Dr Brahma said, 'Sri Ma is making things easy for us. In this modern age, not much time can be given to an austere way of life, but 15 minutes are just possible for everyone!'

Sri Ma said, 'Don't you talk about laying a foundation? If the foundation is not strong then the entire building may collapse. These 15 minutes will be like the corner-stone of total rememberance. The meaning of *akhaṇḍa* (fissureless) *sādhanā* is just this: the daily routine of 15 minutes should be unshakeable.'

Dr Brahma again raised a point: 'Ma there are injunctions regarding fixed timings in all religions. How is this a new dimension?'

Sri Ma: 'Look at it this way. Not all religions are the same. The Hindu observes (if he does at all) the three *sandhyās* (meeting point between night and day, midday and between day and night) the Mussalman says *namāz* five times, the Christians also have their timings and so on. But this little duration of time of 15 minutes cuts through all barriers and diversities. Wherever a *sādhaka* is engaged in *sādhanā*, you also can add your own little effort to that and so create an unity. An individual effort to link up with the totality of human endeavour.[3]'

As a result of Sri Ma's constant reiterations on the theme of dispassion and self-discipline, the function which emerged as the most popular celebration of all was the *samyam saptāha-mahāvrata*. Gradually it acquired an unique characteristic of its own. It had seemed incredible that a man or woman may devote more than three parts of a 24 hour period to the seeking of Truth; God was never that much of a reality to pre-empt all other preoccupations of daily life. But so it happened. Men and women not at all used to any kind of rigourisms, enjoyed keeping fasts, listening to the reading of scriptures, singing *kirtan* and meditating for one hour at a time. Even the kitchen staff were able to join in because, cooking was reduced to a minimal level. The elaborate feasts which marked Sri Ma's presence everywhere did not happen during this week. The *bhaṇḍāra* (feast) took place on the completion of the *samyama-saptāha-mahāvrata*.

Sri Ma's endorsement of all religious functions, rituals and festivals had prevented people from knowing her own preferences, if any, at all. Moreover as her presence enhanced the splendour of all celebrations, each was deemed the most important.

As written earlier, it was Yogibhai, the prince (literally and figuratively) among the devotees, the special disciple in the spirit of Bhaiji, who had first mooted the *samyam saptāha* in 1952. He had suggested, 'Since Sri Ma is always telling us how to practice *sādhanā* while remaining involved in the world, let us work out a schedule for carrying out this *vāṇī* in her presence. She will guide us and we shall know exactly what is expected of us.'

From its simple beginnings it grew into a major undertaking. It found special favour with the Mahatmas because it was congenial to their way of life. They themselves hosted a number of these *samyama-saptāhas*. They were held in places of retreats, remote from the crowded cities, as well as in metropolitan cities like Bombay, Calcutta and New Delhi.

The history of the rediscovery of Naimiṣāraṇya is connected with one such function. Naimiṣāraṇya of epic and legendary fame is situated near the river Gomati in Sitapur district. In October, 1960, Paramananda came to Naimiṣāraṇya to make arrangements for the *samyam-saptāha mahāvrata* as well as a Bhagavat Saptāha.

Unexpected heavy rains raised the level of the Gomati. The entire region was flooded. The rains continued. All the officers from Lucknow and nearby places who were ready to help Paramananda with the arrangements for the camp were discouraged and asked him to choose another site. It seemed to them that Paramananda was being needlessly obstinate and unrealistic. Paramananda, however had implicit trust in Sri Ma's *kheyāla* and stood unshaken in his resolve to pitch the camp where waters had risen to knee-level.

When all this was reported to Sri Ma, she happened to be drinking a glass of water. She said, 'Who knows, but God may miraculously drain away the flood waters!' And so it happened. All persons concerned declared it to be a miracle no less, that the *samyam-saptāha* could be held as scheduled and very successfully too.

At every *samyam-saptāha* one of the 18 Purāṇas are chosen for study and discourses. The Brahma Vaivarta Purāṇa chosen for this occasion was not found in Nimsar[4], in fact nowhere in the North of India.

The blind sage Sri Gangeshwaranandaji appealed to Sri Ma to resurrect Nimsar and establish a Purāṇas Bhavan where all the 18 Purāṇas would be housed for later generations. Financial help came from the family of Singhanias. A beautiful Purāṇa Mandira went up and was consecrated as the Temple of the 18 Purāṇas in 1968. Some of the visitors wondered how an audience of 88 thousand *ṛṣis* could have listened to a discourse without benefit of modern facilities in the age of the Mahabharata. Standing at the site which is traditionally spoken of as the original rostrum for the speaker, they discovered an odd feature of this place. If one spoke loudly the voice carried over to a long distance over empty spaces. So perhaps because of this peculiarity it had been chosen for assemblages of large congregations.

The much revered, erudite speaker Swami Akhandananda Saraswati on seeing the Temple said to Sri Ma, 'A statue of *purāṇa-puruṣa* should also be installed here.' He himself described the Image of the personification of the spirit of the Puraṇas. He had seen a *pat* (icon) of such an Image in the house of the well-known Pandit of Varanasi, Sri Rajeshwar Shastri.

Sri Ma asked if such an icon could be discovered anywhere and a statue modelled on it. So, in this way gradually over the years, the holy site of Naimiṣāraṇya, the place replete with the aura of the austerities, *yajñas*, discourses of countless *ṛṣis*, came alive in our modern age. The temple of Purāṇa Puruṣa was established in 1975.[5] Sri Ma continued to visit Naimiṣāraṇya very often. It was one of the places where she could get some rest from her busy schedule. Swami Naradanandaji of Nimsar was especially pleased with this revival and greater popularity of the once great place of pilgrimage.

Other places of religious significance were rejuvenated by the presence of Sri Ma during these *samyama saptaha mahāvratas*. Every year the number of participants increased. Busy men and women in the world took time off from their various occupations and gathered at some (generally) remote retreat for observing strict rules of minimal diet and sleep. Seven days were spent in almost constant God-remembrance. The highlight of each day was the half hour of conversation with Sri Ma at night. In Sri Ma's presence nothing was difficult, there was no sensation of fatigue or ennui or even hunger or thirst.

Sri Ma's 'special mission' of a corner-stone of the daily 15 minutes toward God-rememberance had truly flowered into a full-fledged *samyama saptāha*. Within thirty years the *mahāvrata* from its simple beginnings had grown into a major undertaking. The heads of the great ascetic orders of the country came in daily contact with a very broad cross-section of our society - there were scholars, teachers, politicians, executives, bankers, civil servants, princes, artists, musicians, doctors, engineers, students, housewives and also those who cannot be put under any category.

The *samyama saptāha mahāvrata* of 1980, that is the penultimate one to take place under Sri Ma's aegis, took place in the prestigious Kailasha Ashram at Rishikesh (Haradwar). One of the regular participants Pratibha Kundu, writes, 'What can be compared with this function? Where there is no concern for food, sleep, rest, recreation, idleness; where there is no time for gossip or useless talk; where the whole day is spent in *japa*, *kirtan*, study, meditation in Sri Ma's presence, audition of scriptures and listening to saints of spiritual greatness. Nowhere else in the world can the ordinary man desirous of spiritual edification come across such congenial atmosphere and such a rewarding experience. Sri Ma calls us all to this dedicated week and gives us fulfilment. Her *vāṇī* for this week is: 'Whatever activity is adopted toward God-remembrance is self-control (*samyama*), that which takes one away from God is indulgence (*bhoga*). The path will not open out unless you live a life of self-discipline.'

The long rostrum was occupied by the great galaxy of renowned Mahatmas dressed in their fire-bright ochre robes. On one side sat Sri Ma resplendant in her pure white clothes.

This Ashram was established in the foothills of the Himalayas, near the holy river Ganga by Swami Dhanaraj Giriji Maharaj, one hundred years ago. The present head of the Ashram Swami Vidyanandaji Maharaj welcomed all the participants (nearly 600) on the first day. It was a magnificent theatre of intercommunication between the ochre-robed renunciates and the laity; the laity comprising of businessmagnates, simple villagers, scholars, professional people, artists, princes and those who served everyone as cooks and servants. Amidst all this variety, Sri Ma sat in her spotless white clothes, holding the attention of the entire community by her beauteous personality. The Mahatmas, in various ways, paid her tribute after tribute. The Mahamandaleshwara Brahmananda Giriji Maharaj of Sanyasa Ashram (Bombay) gave an exegesis of Sri Ma's words regarding the implicit obeying of one's Guru: sacred literature is like the vast ocean; one cannot slake one's thirst at the sea-shore, yet the same waters when they come down as rain through clouds are able to give relief and succour. Sri Ma's *vāṇī* (utterance) is the essence of what all the scriptural teachings are extolling in countless ways.

The Mahamandaleswar 1008 Sri Vidyanandaji said that the way of life which was indicated for renunciates only in the scriptures, Sri Ma had opened out for everyone; irrespective of religious affiliations or country or sex. Sri Ma had shown that the supreme goal of life was attainable by all - this demonstrates her infinite *kṛpā* (grace) for man.

Swami Chidanandaji said, that the termination of the Samyama Saptāha should mean the beginning of another journey of *samyama* in life. Sri Ma is the living Image of God on earth; one has been reborn in her presence, so one should not go back to one's previous way of life.

Swami Swatantranandaji said, Sri Ma wants us to engage in *satsangs* - whether there are more than a thousand people or just two. The Kailash Ashram has been engaged in studying *brahmavidyā*[6] for the last hundred years. It's striving is fulfilled because Brahmavidyā Herself is present here today.

The Mahatmas in looking upon whose saffron-robes, Sri Ma herself always seemed to glow in beauty and splendour, paid her the highest homage as their *Iṣṭa-Brahmavidyā*. In saying this they had said everything that could be said about Sri Ma.

References

1. Vol. 17, pp. 24-25, 23rd February 1961.
2. The President and a member of the Yogada Centre in America.
3. AV Vol. VII, No. 2 pp. 80-82. A list of volunteers was compiled who promised to give '15 minutes' to Sri Ma. Since volunteers enlisted from all over the world, the period of 24 hours was covered many times, an *akhanda-japa* series uniting many religions, many countries and all classes of men, women and even children.
4. Abbreviation of Naimiṣāraṇya.
5. A Research Institute for the study of Paurāṇic Literature has been established in these congenial surroundings.
6. The Supreme Enlightenment envisaged by the Upaniṣads.

CHAPTER SIXTEEN

The Last Flight - Beyond Horizons

I find it impossible to describe Mataji, and have given up trying to do so. She is both a woman and not a woman, for in her bodily form she gives us a living example of what life should be like - and just to see her is to know - and yet after a few minutes in her presence you know that the body is a mere soul, and that Mataji is essentially far beyond its narrow confines ... She has something different for every one of us, each according to his innermost nature and it seems almost wrong to speak or write about such a person as that immediately limits her... it is in the eternal Truth which is so perfectly revealed in Mataji that the world today will find the foundations on which to build a happier future. Mataji has a message for each one who comes to her, but in her very being she is a message for the whole of mankind.

Premananda (Colin Turnbull)[1]

Can I ever abandon that one, who desperately calls 'mother where are you, where are you.' The one who remembers (Me) in his heart and fills his life with the Name, Sees nothing in the universe excepting the form of My Image.

One who does not speak of any other and is pained to see the sorrows of others,

One who remains tranquil in his own sorrow and joy and does not hearken to calumny of others,

When a child cries for his Mother and his tears flow, can I then stay away?

Immediately I give him the shelter of My arms.[2]

The Last Flight - Beyond Horizons

By the Seventies Sri Ma was fully recognised as a uniquely attractive personality of great spiritual power. No one doubted the quiet strength of her impact on all those who came within the orbit of her influence. People waited hours just to get a glimpse of her. They formed long queues to be able to approach her, perhaps to exchange a few words, or make a little offering of flowers. Even at a first meeting she would be recognised at once as the unfailing friend ever at hand to share and lighten the burden of life, or bring greater joy to the living of it.

The pattern of *satsangs* and audiences had been changing so gradually as not to be very noticeable; those who came around at this time knew the formal atmosphere to be normal. They could not imagine that previously Sri Ma was easily available to all and sundry, that there would be unstructured meetings and congregations where one could converse with Sri Ma for long hours. People got used to asking for private audiences and await patiently for their turns to come. There was even a sort of management who took decisions about public *darśans* or private audiences.

Devotees of long standing were easily ousted by hordes of new-comers. Many felt unequal to the situation and stopped flocking to the Ashrams. The days of intimate gatherings, brilliant conversational sessions, interspersed with hilarious laughter convulsing entire groups of people, seemed to be over. Sri Ma hardly ever had time to move around the country at her own *kheyāla*. Her itinerary was drawn up months ahead so that organisers and hosts would have time to prepare suitably for her visit. Functions took on gigantic dimensions. Wherever Sri Ma went, a mammoth crowd would follow even to remote regions like Uttarakashi or Suktal. The sponsors would be expected to invite all the Mahatmas who in general, graced all functions attended by Sri Ma. Sri Ma stopped saying, 'It will so happen if this body has the *kheyāla* toward it' or some such words which made people wait upon her for receiving a guide-line, before they arranged for her travels. Now she would say, 'If you can take this body, you may make arrangements as you see fit.' Alas, for the inevitability of the ascendancy of the human over the divine; the gravitational pull of the earth is too strong, the bird on the wing was sought to be held down and caged!

Sri Ma seemed to have started the process of withdrawal as unobstrusively as the manner of her inconspicuous emergence into the limelight of public acclaim. She had allowed people to get used to her awe-inspiring presence by very slow degrees, she had travelled constantly so that the effect of her charismatic personality would be diffused and the flocks could go back to normal ways of life. So now, like the blazing sun suddenly dimmed by scudding clouds, Sri Ma went into a state of physical unapproachability. She was hardly visible to the press of crowds although whenever she did appear at close quarters, she looked as serene and as beautiful as ever.[3]

In later years, meditating on this aspect of her life it seems reasonable to suppose that it was only an indication of the immeasurable quality of her compassion for her people. If she had suddenly made herself invisible, while all the devotees were as yet used to the glory of her presence, it would have been a devastating experience for the hundreds and thousands who drew their sustenance of life, as it were, from the assurance, Ṃa is here, why worry!

It was given out that Sri Ma was not well and so, many irksome rules of *darśana* had to be imposed. This was not quite grasped as reality by devotees of long standing. They had seen Sri Ma deal with much illness. The ailments had never before disturbed the usual tenor of her ways. Nothing, after all could happen to her, unless it was her *kheyāla* that it would be so. She had succumbed to many 'ailments' for some reason or other and then got rid of them in due time. The desperate prayers for her recovery had never before gone unanswered. No physical causes had engendered the ailments and no medications had been required for their treatments. So no one seriously considered the possibility that this time Sri Ma did not and would not have the *kheyāla* to terminate her indisposition or what looked like it. She was very quiet. She seemed to have contained the joyousness of her usual demeanour. Everyone close to her went about with serious faces - a very unusual state of things.

Apart from the inaccessibility due to overcrowding and the proliferation of functions which seemed to enmesh Sri Ma from all sides, there were other subtle indications that the end was near, but no one interpreted them as such at the time. In September 1980 Didi Gurupriya passed away in Varanasi. Didi had been in Bombay for a long time, to be near her Doctors. Sri Ma herself had seen to these arrangements. In retrospect the dates of various events assume significance. Didi had been suffering for many years. Hari Babaji had always admired her one-pointed dedication to Sri Ma. He had undertaken to perform many religious rites toward Didi's recovery. He was convinced that such scriptural remedial measures could not fail. He would come and sit near Didi's bedside and say, 'Didi, get up! You are not ill anymore!'It remains a fact that while he was alive, Didi also did not quite succumb to her illness.

It did so happen that Didi made a recovery and could go about with Sri Ma for some time. On her part Didi was heard to say very often that she was very grateful to Sri Ma's 'Pitajis' or the eminent Mahatmas, especially Hari Babaji whom she regarded as an insurance against Sri Ma's *kheyāla* of withdrawing herself from the world. It was her conviction that the Mahatmas were worthy anchorages to rivet her *kheyāla*.

Much to Didi's and everyone else's sorrow Hari Babaji, the most constant of Sri Ma's companions from the galaxy of the great sadhus of this time, passed away on January 3, 1970 in Varanasi. He had been ailing for some time and was forever demanding that he should be taken to have *darśana* of Sri Ma. He was in Delhi for medical reasons. Sri Ma paid him frequent visits while she passed through Delhi or even went specially to see him more than once. When his condition deteriorated Sri Ma with the willing consent of all his own devotees brought him to Varanasi to the Ashram. She stayed with him during his last moments. He breathed his last looking steadfastly at her, sitting near the portrait of Lord Gauranga, his *Iṣṭa-devatā*. To him both were one and the same.

It could be a coincidence or not that Didi suffered a relapse within a few years of Haribaba's death. She was increasingly obliged to stay in Bombay to be near her doctors headed by Dr. Surabhai Seth who was in over-all charge of her treatment.

Before her prolonged illness, Didi had been Sri Ma's most constant companion since the days at Shahbagh. She at times had singlehandedly managed Sri Ma's personal service, while helping to lay the foundations of nearly all the main Ashrams and also organize such functions of mammoth proportions as the Savitri Mahayajṇa at Varanasi from 1947-1950. She was instrumental in starting the Kanyapeeth; her painstakingly maintained Diaries are invaluable sources of information regarding Sri Ma's movements from 1926 to 1964.

Once Abhaya had very characteristically raised an unusual question to Didi. He had asked if she had ever seen Sri Ma doze at any time? Didi, not uncharacteristically, had never given this matter a thought, and answered in growing wonderment, 'You know, Abhaya, I never have, for the matter of that, nobody has ever seen Ma overcome by sleep! Even when she was sitting for more than twelve hours at a stretch, as so frequently happened in Dhaka, we never saw her dozing or fatigued. This was the main reason why the fact that Ma was sitting for long hours went unnoticed. People came and went, the newcomers thinking themselves lucky to find Ma still sitting. On the other hand I must say that whenever I happen to doze off while sitting in a *satsang* I wake up with a jerk to find Ma's eyes on me! This happens invariably without exceptions! When I am quite alertly listening to the discourses and hoping that Ma would see what an intelligent interest I am taking in the proceedings, she does not glance at me but no sooner do my eyes begin to close, I find her regarding me steadily!'

Sri Ma joined in the general laughter, but paid the following tribute to Didi, 'You see, her thoughts are always directed here (Sri Ma); no matter what she is doing or with whom she is talking, her thoughts remain one-pointed; but when she dozes off this thread is broken and my *kheyāla* is drawn to her.'

Didi's illness took a serious turn in the month of September 1980. Sri Ma travelled to Bombay from Vrindaban on September 11, arriving on the 12th. It was her *kheyāla* to take Didi to Varanasi the same day, that is, 12th September. She took Bhaiya's permission. Bhaiya[4] made all arrangements efficiently and rapidly. Didi's compartment adjoining Sri Ma's was like a mobile hospital room. Sri Ma arriving at Varanasi the next day, settled Didi in the Ashram but did not stay to see the end. She stayed in Didi's room alone with her for a few moments. The attending girls from the Ashram thereupon saw Sri Ma pass her hand gently from Didi's head to toe, three times. Sri Ma asked permission to leave, 'Shall I go now?' Didi gave her assent, yet Sri Ma repeated her question twice more and elicited her answers accordingly.

Sri Ma left for Vrindaban to attend the Bhagavt Saptah being observed in the Ashram.

Didi was seen to open her eyes at 10 o'clock in the night and look fixedly and serenely at Sri Ma's photograph near her bed. Her eyes remained unblinkingly open for nearly 11 hours, till the moment of her passing away the next morning.[5] Sri Ma sitting in the *satsang* at Vrindaban was heard to exclaim softly, 'Didi has gone away!'

She waited for the news to be conveyed to her and then started back for Varanasi. From Vrindaban to Bombay, Bombay to Varanasi, from Varanasi to Vrindaban and back to Varanasi. Sri Ma spent five consecutive nights on the train. It seemed she could not abide in one place to await the inevitable news of the final parting from a friend of such long standing. Sri Ma on arrival at Varanasi, quietly retired to her room. She gave all necessary instructions to Panu Brahmachari regarding the last rites to be observed. She suggested that the mortal remains should be given such honour and respect as is accorded to the ascetics of our tradition. Didi also had received the *sanyāsa mantra* from Sri Ma like Bhaiji and Bholanath.

So in the time-honoured custom Didi's body was dressed in new ochre-robes of *sanyāsa* and immersed in the holy waters of the Ganges in front of the Ashram which owed its existence, expansion and consolidation almost to her single-handed efforts. The whole Ashram mobilized itself toward observing the ritual ceremonies. Sri Ma remained in her room saying, 'I shall not witness the immersion of this image.'

Sri Ma had never before displayed such an awareness of a final parting although from a worldly point of view many near and dear ones had died in her vicinity. It may be untoward to impute human feelings to Sri Ma but maybe it can be stated that the ballast of her sojourn on earth was shaken a little by the departure of her sister-like companion of more than fifty years. From some words that Sri Ma had spoken about Didi, years before, her audience had concluded that Didi had been born previously to Didima as her first-born child which had not survived infancy. Sri Ma seemed to indicate that the infant girl had come only to herald the coming of Sri Ma; this was the reason why Didi was addressed as such by Sri Ma because Didi means 'elder sister'. If Didi had prepared the way for the birth of Sri Ma, would it be too fanciful to say that by dying she called Sri Ma's attention or *kheyāla* toward the ending of the *līlā* of her life in the world?

That Sri Ma during the year 1981-82 adopted a one-track course toward the final dissolution of ties becomes very clear when we examine the concurrence of events as they unfolded during this time.

Sri Ma's last positive *kheyāla* as far as it can be made out now, was for the celebration of the *atirudra yajña* at Kankhal. This was symbolic in many ways. As with all other manifestation of *śakti* in Sri Ma, the beginning of this *yajña* also originated in a very unobtrusive manner: some of the young women companions of Sri Ma happened to be watching the performance of a *yajña* being performed by one of her devotees. It came to their minds almost simultaneously that how nice it would be if they could arrange for such a function under Sri Ma's aegis. It seemed an impossible dream, because for uncounted centuries such Vedic rituals were the monopoly of the men-folk. But when somebody dared to express this desire in front of Sri Ma, she said lightly, 'Why don't you.' Since Sri Ma seemed agreeable, other people in authority were consulted. Nobody opposed the idea. A small committee was formed consisting of Dr Padma Mishra, Shanta, Nirmala, Parul and Aruna. The second hurdle was money. The young women pooled their resources together, but evidently this would be a drop in the ocean of the total expenses!

The project, however, seemed to snowball drawing together resources and manpower or rather humanpower, to an unprecedented degree. Money came from unexpected sources; an architect of great repute agreed to design the Hall for the *yajña*, in accordance with the Vedic stipulations; skilled engineers and competent overseers appeared of their own free will, eager to be of service. The logistics of the whole undertaking was worked out in detail by Professor Pandit Vamadeva Mishra, a former colleague of Padma Mishra. Sri Ma, quite in her own old style, directed the affairs of the *yajña*. Regarding the choice of the *Ācārya* (main priest), she seemed to approve of Vamadeva Mishra and listened to all his proposals with indulgent understanding, making a few suggestions which were accepted gratefully. Sri Ma, as always, could plug in loopholes with unerring judgement.

The site chosen was Kankhal, a township rich in religious legends, the most famous and widely believed in, being that once Dakṣa Prajapati had started a *yajña* here but which had been destroyed mid-way by the retinue of Śiva because the King had insulted the God. There is an ancient Temple in Kankhal known as the House of Dakṣa near the site chosen for the *atirudra yajña* in Sri Ma's Ashram nearby. All the devout people of Kankhal, all the Heads of Monasteries declared that who else but Sri Ma could have completed the *yajña* of legendary fame at the very site of its first destruction.

It did seem that a magic wand had been waved. The committee of young women felt that everything was being made easy for them. A hidden power flowered into the many-splendoured *atirudra yajña* causing admiration, awe and a bemused feeling of being at once transported to the times of the Satya Yuga when such events were the norm. In answer to Sri Ma's question as to how the general public should participate in this very exclusive ritual, Pandit Vamadevaji said that those who heard the sounds of the Vedic *mantra* and did a circumlocution round the Hall would derive the greatest religious merit from it. Quoting a text, he remarked ruefully that they who performed the *yajña* were like the beasts of burden who carry on their backs a load of supreme value! It is the lay public who were the real beneficiary of such rituals.

Sri Ma had a three-feet wide path made around the Hall. On this path for eleven days and nights, thousands of men, women and children walked slowly in orderly queues with folded hands, listening to the sonorous chorus of more than 135 voices raised in pronouncing the Vedic *mantra* and watching the sacred flames arising from eleven *kuṇḍas* (receptacles) in tongues of yellow, orange, red, saffron, gold, white and grey colours.

Sri Ma took part in all the activities. She seemed to have recovered her normal health and spirits during this interval. She was constantly advising, directing and suggesting improvements towards perfection. Pandit Vamadevaji, although a stranger to begin with quickly came to regard her as the quintessence of the spirit of the *sāstras.* He referred to her in all matters. One Vedic scholar[6] said that she had even at one time corrected the movements of the arm and elbow which is obligatory when singing a particular rhythm, not by saying anything but by doing it herself. This was his moment of revelation as to her complete mastery of scriptural injunctions to the last detail. The Vedic scholars coming from Madras, Gujrat, Uttara Pradesh and Maharashtra formed a congenial group living together for nearly a fortnight in one of the Monasteries (Udāsin Ākharā), following all the rules of an ascetic way of life. Even the local pandits who were participating in the *yajña* lived away from their homes during the fortnight. The entire region became an ancient *ṛṣi-āshram* (forest hermitage) closing the gap between legendary history and modern times.

Responding to Sri Ma's *kheyāla*, the *ācārya* (head priest) allowed the committee of young women to enter the Hall and take their seats among the privileged. This was a departure from the norm. The pandits opined that there were no scriptural injunctions against participation by women; as a matter of fact in ancient times not only did they sit with the audience but also engaged in dialogues with the greatest of scholars.

It was one of Sri Ma's characteristics that she judged every case on its own merits. While the *yajña* was about to begin, one young professional photographer wanted to enter the Hall and use his camera. He was told that no one who had not gone through the process of consecration and initiation could be allowed to enter the Hall. He was very eager and wanted to be told what if anything he could do to qualify himself as he was already a brahmin by birth. Sri Ma sent him to the *ācārya*, who on being told his problem said succinctly '*mātaraṃ pṛccha*' (ask Mother). So the photographer returned to Sri Ma. Very unexpectedly, she made a concession for him, by saying, 'Go to the Ganga, have a bath and change into a new set of washed and unstitched clothes or silken ones.' She also told him to do a certain number of *japa* of the Gayatri Mantra. He was very happy and departed with alacrity to the Ganges.

During the yajña Sri Ma, one day composed a prayer in Bengali which was given out to everyone who was involved in the work as either a participator or spectator. The hymn was:

he atirudrayājñasvarūpa bhagavan:

āmār hṛdaye jyoti prakāśa hau.

[Thou who art manifest as the *atirudrayajña*; pray reveal Thyself in my heart as Enlightenment.

This prayer, no doubt, could lend itself to pages of exegeses; the simplest meaning, however, takes us right from the *karmakāṇḍa* (ritualisms) through the *upāsanākāṇḍa* (devotion) on to the *jñānakāṇḍa* (knowledge) of the Vedic heritage. It is a beautiful aphorism, revealing the harmony which underlies the entire Vedic corpus. Rituals, devotion and knowledge are not exclusive ways but they are simultaneous and so one should understand the message of the Vedas. The Upaniṣads are after all an integral part of the Vedas.

After the *yajña* (April/May, 1981) Sri Ma seemed to retire within herself. Questions remained as if unheard, or given a quiet response, 'whatever happens is how it should be', or 'wait and see'. Her ceaseless wanderings continued but these were not joyous flights from one perch to another; they were carefully programmed ahead so that all eager expectations for a glimpse of the 'Bird' could be fulfilled.

Sri Ma came to Allahabad at the beginning of January (9th and 10th) 1982 to visit the site of the *ardha-kumbha melā.* She stayed in the town for one night in the cottage built for her by Bindu. The Heads of the Akharas (monasteries) came to invite her to join in the procession on the opening day of the Melā. Sri Ma replied, 'See Pitaji, this body is so limp, you will get into difficulties if it sags down further. But if you wish to take it along, do so.'

The Mahatmas answered, 'Thousands are assembled on the shores of the holy rivers. They will derive great merit from your *darśana*. Their and our prayers will support your movements - we shall take the greatest care so that you are not inconvenienced.' Sri Ma smiled and said, 'I am never inconvenienced. Whatever you say Pitaji, is all right with me.'

Sri Ma was taken in the procession, on the back of a caparisoned elephant (so that everyone could have her *darśana*) with all due pomp and ceremony. For the last many such Kumbha Melas at Haradwar and Prayag Sri Ma had been treated not as one of the many dignitaries but as the Personification of the One who is adored and worshipped by the devoted of every religious order.

Sri Ma went to the camp which had been set up on behalf of our Ashram. Unfortunately, heavy rains disrupted and disorganised all arrangements; everything was sopping wet; the huts were near to collapsing. High winds added to everyone's discomfort. Never before had such a thing happened. The Ashram arrangements were always more than adequate at every place where a temporary camp of huts and tents was set up for a festival. All such impromptu get-togethers in Sri Ma's vicinity were always full of the joyous excitement of novelty and adventure but not this time - everything seemed to be getting out of control, so much so that the camp was abandoned before the day of conclusion.

Before leaving Sri Ma invited all the Mahatmas to a meal at Anandamayi Camp. Not only the Mahatmas but all the people who had become known to her at Allahabad over the years. She named each and everyone. She even arranged for a conveyance for a crippled lady who was hesitating to accept the invitation. The hard pressed workers in the Ashram-camp were trying to cope as best as they could - Sri Ma's standard was always perfection in all matters and this they achieved under dire conditions. Nobody realized that this was Sri Ma's farewell gesture to Prayag and the *Triveṇī-sangam* which she had visited very regularly for more than half a century.

At the house[7] where she stayed in the City she praised the family, each member of it by name, and remembered the long years of association with everyone. The family was happy at Sri Ma's words but not a little puzzled because Sri Ma had never before made such an almost valedictory speech. Nobody had the wit to understand that it was truly a farewell that she was taking from a place which had long been associated with her.

1982 had started with the disastrous disarray at the site of the Kumbha-Melā. Perhaps it was an omen. Nothing was as before. Sri Ma continued to be ill and frail looking but ready to acquiesce in all programmes chalked out for her. She was constantly on the move, never getting more than a few days' rest in between the heavy schedules of activities in different towns.

Sri Ma seemed to make another farewell visit to the temple at Nathdwara during this time. Years before she had come to Rajasthan with Bholanath but they could not visit Nathdwara at the time. Now she stood for a long time in front of the Image, in intimate communication with it, as it seemed to the few people who were with her.

People were reminded of her farewell gestures from Shahbagh and other places and Temples from where she took a final departure.

A strenuous journey was undertaken by Sri Ma on March 26th to the distant state of Tripura. The Maharaja of Tripura had invited Sri Ma to pay a visit to the State of her birth and arrangements were being made on an elaborate scale. Tripura was a communist state, the populace expressed some displeasure at this show of according welcome to a 'religious personality'.

It was a tale of misunderstanding and uncalled for panic. According to some onlookers the young communist people themselves could have provided volunteers and taken care of Sri Ma. Although the Chief Minister (of the Communist government) came to pay his respects, a rumour gained ground that some untoward events would take place. The Inspector General of Police did not want to take any risks. The crowd which was increasing by the hour went beyond all calculation. People from far flung villages trooped in to get a sight of the illustrious 'Daughter of Tripura', their own Ma.

Instead of constructing a high rostrum from where Sri Ma would have been visible to all, the management sought to remove her quickly out of the reach of the people. All state functions were hurriedly gone through, before they could be disrupted as feared by the management. The Inspector General whisked her away to the Railway Station under a strict guard. He, evidently felt responsible for her safety while she remained in Tripura. Sri Ma was heard to say *janatā janārdana* (God in the image of crowds) a number of times and that she did not have the opportunity of meeting them. It has been seen countless times that crowds do not inconvenience her and it was just an unfortunate business all round. She was not allowed to respond to the prayers of thousands for a *darśana.* Sri Ma was seen to wilt visibly on her way back from this sojourn. She blamed nobody but herself bore the impact of the peoples' disappointment. She looked tired and unwell.

Sri Ma visited Agarpara Ashram on her return from Tripura - from there she proceeded to Kankhal a very long journey of more than 72 hours. Her travels were not over, she made yet another journey to Kanpur before returning to Kankhal again where preparations were in train for her 86th Birthday Celebration.

Never before had the devotees experienced such a Birthday function. Nothing seemed to go right. Sri Ma was not well enough for anybody to suggest that she should leave her bed. Arrangements for pūjā were made in her room. There was no place for the large congregation to sit because heavy rains washed away the seating arrangements made under a pandal (marquee). People just stood around or had to go elsewhere to get out of the rain. The disorganisation was heart breaking. Sri Ma said later, 'From next year let the pūjā be done to a portrait in the Hall.' Nobody at that time understood this to be the prophecy it was. Everybody thought she was referring to the discomforts experienced by the crowd due to the unexpected rains.

Sri Ma continued to attend the various functions taking place in the Ashram. On June 16 she received the Jagadguru Sri Samkaracarya of Sarada Peetham. Sri Ma had at last found a worthy interlocuter to whom she spoke the revealing words, 'Pitaji, this is not illness. It is a state of tension between the manifest and the recall of the Unmanifest.'

These words need to be interiorised in order to glean a spark of illumination. They hold the clue to the poignancy of divine suffering. To be born is joyous, but then by this very act the Divine Person chooses also to pay the price of mortality, that is death. If nothing else, then this event alone would indicate the quality of mercy and compassion which binds God and creatures together. Perhaps it is because of this truth that Christians give so much importance to the event of Crucifixion which seems so inexplicable to the followers of other religions.

Sri Ma came to Dehra Dun and to Kishenpur Ashram. She attended some of the rites and ceremonies which were taking place almost in an unbroken series of one after the other. The devotees, desperate for changing Sri Ma's *kheyāla* sent up incessant prayers for her recovery. Doctors who were long associated with her - Dr Udupa (Banaras Hindu University) Dr Surabhai Seth (Nanavati Hospital, Bombay) came to Dehra Dun. Sri Ma was gracious to them. They found no disease which could be treated. In answer to Surabhai's question, 'Ma, are you suffering?' she answered, 'Not at all.' She seemed to be apart from the body which was in pain and suffering from some shortness of breath.

Bhaiya (B.K. Shah) came and took up his vigil in Sri Ma's room along with a few others. One day he said forcefully 'Mā, I must see you sitting up before I leave for Bombay!' He said this to nudge her *kheyāla* toward some activity of her limbs which seemed as slack as those of a rag-doll.

After a couple of days Sri Ma indicated to her attendants that she should be propped up to a sitting position. The girls assembled pillows and bolsters and raised her body to a sitting posture. She looked at Bhaiya for a long time, her expression serene and compassionate. Bhaiya understood that she had no *kheyāla* for recovery but that she had made an effort toward fulfilling his words. Bhaiya stood with folded hands and tearful eyes marvelling at the ever-rising effervescence of the fountain of Grace which fulfills in a hundredfold measure even a trifling plea for what is after all one's own ease and comfort!

Ordinarily Sri Ma always gave greatest heed to the requests of Mahatmas. To the Jagadguru Sri Samkaracarya's request for her presence at Sringeri during the Dūrgā Pūjā Festival, she gently made her excuses. To his repeated pleas that she should get well, she reiterated, 'This body has no illness, Pitaji. It is being recalled toward the Unmanifest. Whatever you see happening now is conducive toward that event.' This was his second visit to Sri Ma on his way down from the pilgrimage to the Himalayan Temples. At the moment of bidding him farewell (July 2nd 1982) she again repeated her *kheyāla* of not being able to accede to his wishes saying, 'As the *ātmā* I shall ever abide with you.'

Sri Ma stayed in Kalyanvavan from 5th July to 24th July, where she seemed to withdraw behind an impenetrable wall of unapproachability. *Darśana* was restricted. Sri Ma had no *kheyāla* to listen to letters or messages. Bhaskarananda with some persistence obtained a message for the devotees who were not able to see her at all, 'Strive to become an aspirant toward the fulfilment of the Grace of your Guru.' On July 24th morning around 9 o'clock Patun[8] and Udasji obeying her *kheyāla* of leaving Kalyanvan brought her to Kishenpur Ashram in a car. Sri Ma came to the same Ashram which had witnessed the departure of Bholanath nearly 44 years ago.

Sri Ma had stopped taking food for about 3 months. The attending girls could give her a few drops of water at infrequent intervals. The atmosphere of despair reigned supreme. The desperate question in every heart was 'why should their beloved Mother suffer at all and why could they not do anything to recall her to her usual way of being in the world with them?' Sri Ma perhaps responded to this cry from so many anguished hearts; she spoke once, clearly, apparently to the girls surrounding her bedside:

'Wherever you are, immerse yourself totally in one-pointed *sādhanā*.'

This *vāṇī*, being her last, radiates out to embrace all those who derive (and will derive) their courage and sustenance from her to proceed on the path shown by her to be the most worthwhile goal for all human beings.

Sri Ma was heard to pronounce mantras very softly from time to time. On the night of the 25th she pronounced the sacred *pañcākṣara-mantra* in its reversed form '*Śivāya namaḥ*'. In the Śaiva tradition it is exegeted to mean an indication toward the dissolution of all worldly ties. The *yogin* is ready to dissolve the last worldly tie of the body.[9]

For all of us, the Reality of her presence came to an end on August 27, 1982, around 8 p.m. in the evening.

She Ma had made no farewells or left no instructions with her attendants. The spontaneity with which forces were mobilized and arrangements made for Sri Ma's body to be taken in a procession to Kankhal was truly astonishing. The motorcade had to be halted at the entrance to the holy city of Haradwar; only the vehicle carrying Sri Ma's body advanced slowly so that thousands of people lining the roads could pay their respects.

The foothills of the Himalayas is holy land. All monastic orders have their Head Quarters at Haradwar. By a consensus of opinion the entire body of the Mahatmas came together to assume charge of the physical remains of Sri Ma. No question of sectarian preferences were raised. She who had not worn the ochre robes of any denomination was paid the highest honour of them all. The Mahanirvani Akhada took it upon themselves to arrange for the last rites of samādhi. Sri 108 Mahanta Giridhar Narayana Das Puriji Maharaj had for many years been very close to Sri Ma. Often she had delegated to him some of her own time-honoured acts of blessings toward the crowds, like distributing the *batasas* (sugar puffs) after a *Nāmayajña* or special *kirtan*. Now he came forward to guide the ashram in all matters of ritualistic procedure.

The mourners seemed to comprise of anybody and everybody. The Prime Minister of India, Mrs Indira Gandhi came and mingled with the young women surrounding Sri Ma. The Princes and their families and other dignitaries stood waiting around along with the vast concourse of common people which had assembled from every corner of India. Foreigners and Indians became united in paying their last homages. The Mahatmas who were renunciates already, felt as if they were undergoing the loosening of the most precious tie of all. Swami Brahmanandaji wrote in anguished tones, 'Who will now say so sweetly, 'Baba! Baba!' to us?'

The devotees of Sri Ma were used to the celebrations of her presence amongst them, the much coveted glimpse of the beauteous najestic form, the ineffable joy of encountering the compassionate glance of total acceptance. They were singularly unprepared for bidding farewell to that One Person who had interpenetrated the very texture of their beings. Even if they did not see Ma for a few days, a few weeks or even a few months, they knew she was with them in the very life's breath that they drew, the earth they walked the space which circumscribed them and the time which delimited them. How were they to convince themselves that their earth, their air, their time and their places and they themselves would know her no more. Who could be more privileged than them and who more unfortunate!

A new journey began for all those who were devoted to Sri Ma. Sri Ma after all had said,

'I am ever with you!'

The words of Sri Ma remain as an inexhaustible spring which would sustain everyone for evermore for the journey toward understanding her message to humanity:

To talk of God alone is worthwhile

All else is in vain and pain.

References

1. 'Mother', *Mother as Seen by Her Devotees*, Varanasi, 1956, pp. 71-77.
2. One of the songs, sung very often by Sri Ma's father Bipin Bihari. Sri Ma used to sing it with him in her childhood, also when he spent a few days with her, just before his death. Sometimes she sang it on her own at the request of devotees.
3. A Swiss lady, Odette Baumer recently told me that to her Sri Ma had looked as young and beautiful as a girl of 18 just a few weeks before Sri Ma's final withdrawal from the world.
4. Sri B.K. Shah (Bhaiya) had made himself responsible for Didi's treatment and nursing from the very beginning of her illness. He had said, 'If you call me Bhaiya (brother) then allow me the privilege of taking charge of your affairs from now on. The remarkable spirit of service shown in this matter by Bhaiya, his wife, Lila and his entire family cannot be overestimated. Their home remained an extension to the Ashram for more than thirty years. Sri Ma came to depend upon him as the years went by.
5. From a few words that Sri Ma said about this phenomenon, the knowledgeable people surmised that it was the yogic *kriyā* of *trāṭaka*. After all it was appropriate that Didi's one-pointed undeviating devotion should culminate in a *kriyā* of total absorption or identification.
6. Sri Vyasji Mishra, Professor of Sanskrit, Banaras Hindu University.
7. 31, George Town, the house of late Sri Niraj Nath Mukerji.
8. S.K. Datta of New Delhi.
9. Umapati Sivacarya: *Tiruvarutpayan* verses 84-85.

Glossary of Sanskrit Words

A

abhiṣeka: the ritual cleansing of an image of God

abhyāsa: practice

ābrahmastambaparyantam: from Brahma to a blade to grass

ācārya: teacher

adhivāsa: prelude to the main function; an invocatory session on the eve of the day of worship

āgamanī: (Bengali) invocatory songs

agni: fire

ajñāna: ignorance

ajñātavāsa: hidden retreat; to reside *incognito* in some place.

akhaṇḍa: seamless, unbroken

ambara: sky

ānanda: bliss, joy

anubhava: experience

ārati: cotton wicks soaked in rarefied butter or camphor enkindled to light up images of God as part of ritualistic worship.

artha: wealth, meaning

āsana: yogic posture, seat

āshram: (āshrama) hermitage; a residence for ascetics

aṣṭa-śakhis: eight friends

ātman: self

aṭṭahāsa: ringing peal of laughter

avadhūta: an ascetic who belongs to none of the established orders

B

bādhaka: hindrance

badhu: bride

baandh: (*bāndh* Hindi) barrier, dam

Bhāgavat saptāh: a week-long function when the religious text *śrimadbhagavatam* is recited in the morning and exegeted upon in the evening with appropriate rituals marking the commencement and ending of the celebration.

bhagavān: God

bhajan: devotional songs

bhaṇḍāra: feast

bhāva: state, mystic mood; a condition of the body when all out going senses are turned inwards and contact with the world is in abeyance.

bhikṣā: alms

bhoga: offering of food to the deity.

bīja-mantra: a mystic syllable spoken to the disciple by the Master on the occasion of a spiritual initiation.

brahmacāris: a novitiate, who aspires to become an ascetic in later life; a student in the *ashrama* of his Master for 12 years or so, this is considered the first stage of a man's life.

C

cakras: nucleus; centre; In the yoga philosophy six centres are recognised as important to the nervous system for spiritual exercises.

cit: intellect; consciousness

D

dāhl: pulses

daṇḍā: a staff carried by ascetics

dandee: a carrying chair of canvas and wood borne aloft by four porters. They are used on steep mountain paths by people who are unable to climb on foot.

darśana: audience; seeing

deva-bhāṣā: divine language; Sanskrit

devatā: a particular image of God

dharma: religion

dharmaśālā: a charitable inn for pilgrims

dhoti: the white apparel worn by men

dhvani: resonance

dikṣā: spiritual initiation

duḥkha: sorrow

G

ghāts: bans of a river

gṛhasthāśrama: the second stage of life, that is, marriage and housekeeping. see *brahmactari.*

guṇa: quality

guru: teacher, master

gurukul: a residential school which is run in accordance with scriptural injunctions regarding education of the young.

H

hejagatrāṭa: "O Lord", the first line of a hymn

I

Iṣṭa: pleasing; most desirable

Iṣṭadevatā: the particular image of God which is most dear to the heart of a devotee.

J

jantā: the populace

janatā-janārdana: God manifesting as the populace

japa: silent repitition of the names of God or a *mantra*

japa-sādhanā: the rigorons pratice of *japa*

jaya: victory; cheers at the conclusion or commencement of a function; a refrain added to the names of God when they are sung by assemblies

jayadhvani: the sound of the cheers

jñāna: knowledge

jñānakāṇḍa: The section of the scriptures dealing with knowledge of Brahman namely, the *upaniṣads.*

K

kamaṇḍalu: the water vessel carried by ascetics

karmakāṇḍa: the section of the scriptures dealing with rituals
karma-saṃskāras: predilections; proneness toward a particular course of action
kathā: story
kavirāj: a title of respect; doctor of Indian medicine
kheyala: a whim; a sudden impulse
kirtan: a repetitive form of melody, composed of the Names and words describing the auspicious qualities of the Divine Person; generally there is a leading voice followed by a chorus
kriyās: yogic exercise
kṛpā: grace; benign acceptance
kuṇḍa: a hollow in the ground or a metal receptacle for enkindling fire
kuṇḍalī: a circular formation

L

lakṣaṇas: symptoms, indications
līlā: Divine Play
līlā-kathā: the tales of the ways of an incarnation

M

mahābhāvas: transformation induced by a high spiritual state of awareness of the play of divine power (see *bhava*) these mystic states of the body possible only in that of an incarnation.
mahāpuruṣa: a perfect human being
mahārāṇī: queen
mahatmā: ascetics; a great man
mantra: mystic syllables listed in sacred literature, each symbolizing a Deity; aphorisms from the Vedas or Puranas etc.
mātṛ-satsaṅg: conversation with Sri Ma Anandamayi
maunam: a yogic state of complete silence; temporary vows of silence
melā: congregation of people to celebrate an occasion
mokṣa: liberation, realization of truth.
mṛtyu: death
mudrā: yogic positions of the hands and fingers
murti: image

N

nāma-japa: the silent repitition of the Names of the Lord, keeping count with the help of one's figures or a rosary
nāma-saṃkirtan: see *kirtana*

P

pālki: palanquin
pañcasaṃyoga: a unity comprising of five aspects
paramātmā: Supreme Being
parikramā: circumambulation
pat: icon
pīṭhasthāna: places of pilgrimages sacred to the cult of the Goddess
pradakṣiṇā: see *parikramā*
praṇām: bowdown in front of a deity; obeissance

praśāda: food which has been offered to a deity and hence consecrated
prasanna: pleased; benign
pūjā: worship
puṇya: religious merit
pūrṇāhuti: final offering to an enkindled sacred fire.
purṇakumbha: sacred ewer of water, used on auspicious occasions.

R

rājasic: energetic, active
rāslīlā: the dance of the gopis (maids) with Krishṇa, described in sacred texts is enacted by small children in Vrindaban and other places as part of a religions dance-drama.
ṛṣis: Vedic seers
ṛṣi-āshram: forest hermitage

S

saccidānanda: a term indicating the supreme reality or Brahman, *Sat* (existence) + *cit* (consciousness) + ānanda (bliss, unalloyed joy); sometimes it is used for the personalized form of Brahman, that is, God.
sādhaka: a committed pilgrim; a wayfarer on the religious way of life, a *yogi*
sādhanā: austerities; commitment to the spiritual quest
sādhikā: feminine form of *sādhaka*
sādhu: ascetic
sādhu-samāj: an assembly of renunciates; there are many ascetic orders forming different brotherhoods; every order to authenticated by a recognised founder, whose teachings are transmitted by a chain of master-disciple relationship.
sādhu-samelana: see *sadhu samaj*
Śakti: power; primordial energy at the heart of creation, sometimes personified as the Goddess Durga
samādhi: an experiencing of an inner illumination when all processes of physical or mental activity is stilled; a state of enlightenment not to be compared with trance-like states which can be induced artificially and can not overcome ignorance.
samadhi-mandira: temple errected on burrial place

saṃkalpa: a solemn vow toward a course of action
saṃpradāya: brotherhood; sect
saṃyama: abstention
saṃyama-saptāh: a week-long regimentation of austerities to be practised by ordinary folk as fulfilment of a vow of dispassion for the time being.
sannyāsa: renuciation
sannyāsi: a renunciate
śāstra: scripture
satsanga: an assembly of people

gathered for the purpose of listening to a religions discourse, or to sing *kirtana*

śloka: vedic aphorisms; verse

śri: magnificance; a term of respect for referrng to people

stotra: hymns in Sanskrit

Svabhava: innate nature; the inner self

swāmi: master; a term of respect for addressing renunciates

T

tapasyā: austeritics; spiritual practices

tithi-pujā: the worship of Sri Ma on her Birthday

tyāga: to renounce

U

uḍā pākha: a bird on the wing; a flying bird

upāsanākānḍa: the middle section of the sacred texts leading from rituals to philosophy; contemplative ways of worship.

uṣā-kirtan: early morning hymns

V

vairāgi: wandering minstrels

vairāgya: dispassion

vāṇaprasthis: a couple who have renounced the world together

vāni: utterance, sayings

vāsanā: desire

vedi: platform, altar for installing deities

viśva-kalyāṇa: the well-being of mankind

vyāsāsanā: the exclusive and special seat reserved for the speaker on a sacred text.

Y

yajña: sacrificial ceremony; worship of fire by pouring obtations into if with appropriate rites.

yajña-kunḍa: see *kunda*

yantra: a mystic symbol, signifying a deity

yogi: as ascetic

Index of Names